INNOVATIONS IN
DIGITAL
RESEARCH METHODS

PETER HALFPENNY
ROB PROCTER

Los Angeles | London | New Delhi
Singapore | Washington DC

Los Angeles | London | New Delhi
Singapore | Washington DC

SAGE Publications Ltd
1 Oliver's Yard
55 City Road
London EC1Y 1SP

SAGE Publications Inc.
2455 Teller Road
Thousand Oaks, California 91320

SAGE Publications India Pvt Ltd
B 1/I 1 Mohan Cooperative Industrial Area
Mathura Road
New Delhi 110 044

SAGE Publications Asia-Pacific Pte Ltd
3 Church Street
#10-04 Samsung Hub
Singapore 049483

Editor: Jai Seaman
Assistant editor: Lily Mehrbod
Production editor: Victoria Nicholas
Copyeditor: Catjat Pafort
Proofreader: Rosemary Morlin
Indexer: David Rudeforth
Marketing manager: Sally Ransom
Cover design: Francis Kenney
Typeset by: C&M Digitals (P) Ltd, Chennai, India
Printed and bound by CPI Group (UK) Ltd,
Croydon, CR0 4YY

Chapter 1: © Peter Halfpenny and Rob Proctor 2015
Chapter 2: © Kingsley Purdam and Mark Elliot 2015
Chapter 3: © Kingsley Purdam and Mark Elliot 2015
Chapter 4: © Joe Murphy 2015
Chapter 5: © Paul S. Lambert 2015
Chapter 6: © Mark Birkin and Nick Malleson 2015
Chapter 7: © Paul S. Lambert, William J. Browne and Danius T. Michaelides 2015
Chapter 8: © Lawrence Ampofo, Simon Collister, Ben O'Loughlin and Andrew Chadwick 2015
Chapter 9: © Andy Crabtree, Paul Tennent, Pat Brundell and Dawn Knight 2015
Chapter 10: © Rob Ackland and Jonathan Zhu 2015
Chapter 11: © Michael Batty, Steven Gray, Andrew Hudson-Smith, Richard Milton, Oliver O'Brien and Flora Roumpani 2015
Chapter 12: © R.J. Anderson and Marina Jirotka 2015
Chapter 13: © Mike Savage 2015

Library of Congress Control Number: 2014954811

British Library Cataloguing in Publication data

A catalogue record for this book is available from the British Library

ISBN 978-1-4462-0308-8
ISBN 978-1-4462-0309-5 (pbk)

At SAGE we take sustainability seriously. Most of our products are printed in the UK using FSC papers and boards. When we print overseas we ensure sustainable papers are used as measured by the Egmont grading system. We undertake an annual audit to monitor our sustainability.

INNOVATIONS IN
DIGITAL
RESEARCH METHODS

SAGE was founded in 1965 by Sara Miller McCune to support the dissemination of usable knowledge by publishing innovative and high-quality research and teaching content. Today, we publish more than 750 journals, including those of more than 300 learned societies, more than 800 new books per year, and a growing range of library products including archives, data, case studies, reports, conference highlights, and video. SAGE remains majority-owned by our founder, and after Sara's lifetime will become owned by a charitable trust that secures our continued independence.

Los Angeles | London | New Delhi | Singapore | Washington DC

CONTENTS

List of Figures and Tables   vii

List of Contributors   x

Acknowledgements   xvii

Companion Website   xviii

1   Introduction and Overview   1
Peter Halfpenny and Rob Proctor

2   The Changing Social Science Data Landscape   25
Kingsley Purdam and Mark Elliot

3   Exploiting New Sources of Data   59
Mark Elliot and Kingsley Purdam

4   Survey Methods: Challenges and Opportunities   85
Joe Murphy

5   Advances in Data Management for Social Survey Research   105
Paul S. Lambert

6   Modelling and Simulation   123
Mark Birkin and Nick Malleson

7   Contemporary developments in statistical software
for social scientists   143
Paul S. Lambert, William J. Browne and Danius T. Michaelides

8   Text Mining and Social Media: When Quantitative
Meets Qualitative and Software Meets People   161
Lawrence Ampofo, Simon Collister, Ben O'Loughlin and
Andrew Chadwick

9   Digital Records and the Digital Replay System   193
Andy Crabtree, Paul Tennent, Pat Brundell and Dawn Knight

10 **Social Network Analysis**   221
    Robert Ackland and Jonathan J.H. Zhu

11 **Visualizing Spatial and Social Media**   245
    Michael Batty, Steven Gray, Andrew Hudson-Smith,
    Richard Milton, Oliver O'Brien and Flora Roumpani

12 **Ethical Praxis in Digital Social Research**   271
    R.J. Anderson and Marina Jirotka

13 **Sociology and the Digital Challenge**   297
    Mike Savage

    Index   311

LIST OF FIGURES AND TABLES

FIGURES

3.1	Example of an electoral candidate's website	62
3.2	Rumour spreading graphic	64
3.3	Geographical distribution of immigrant pupils by local authority district types in England, 2003 to 2007	67
3.4	Observation sheet	68
3.5	Probability of postnatal depression across SES by the number of reactive 5-HTT alleles	73
5.1	Illustration of part of a 'variable by case' matrix	107
5.2	Illustration of online resources associated with agencies involved in the storage and distribution of social survey datasets	111
6.1	The research lifecycle	135
6.2	Components of a research infrastructure for social simulation	135
6.3	Elements of a workflow architecture for social simulation	136
6.4	Indicators/externalities a) baseline, b) projection and c) scenario; pollution in the cities of Leeds, Bristol and Southampton	137
7.1	Illustration of using the SPSS package to perform correspondence analysis	144
7.2	An illustration of using a script ('do file') in Stata	150
7.3	Images of Stat-JR in operation	154
7.4	Using Stat-JR from within a DEEP eBook	156
8.1	Volume of tweets about each leader's response to a question in the third debate	176
8.2	Share of positive sentiment for party leaders	177
8.3	Trend in positive sentiment for Cameron	177
8.4	Trend in positive sentiment for Clegg	177
8.5	Volume of tweets expressing positive sentiment about party leaders in the third debate	179

9.1   Example log file   197

9.2   Re-representing logs: a line chart visualizing heart rate over time   200

9.3   Connected and dynamic interactive charts   200

9.4   Synchronizing heterogeneous data   202

9.5   Annotation schema   203

9.6   Annotation sets and coding tracks   203

9.7   Thick description – creating live texts   204

9.8   Fieldwork tracker   206

9.9   Fieldwork tracker log file (an example)   207

9.10   Representing geo-located data   208

9.11   Creating a frequency table of words   209

9.12   Simultaneous concordance   210

9.13   Visualizing crowdsourced data (an example)   213

9.14   Histogram and event series showing dynamic selection
        and interrogation   213

9.15   Spatial distribution of events   214

9.16   Medical emergencies   214

9.17   Emergency medical clinics   215

9.18   Creating and exploring new categories of data   216

10.1   A semantic network of top hashtags from Twitter   221

10.2   A directed and outdegree-weighted network   222

10.3   Articles on top 20 online social networks in Web of Science 2004–13   227

11.1   CASA's MapTube Website showing a) population density in
        2011 and b) changes in density 2001–2011   251

11.2   2011 Population density at the metropolitan scale in Greater London   252

11.3   Moving to 3D visualization and navigating through the models   255

11.4   Augmenting 3D visualization merging the virtual with the real   256

11.5   a) the Dashboard and b) its display in a visualization wall   258

11.6   Real-time tube train locations   259

11.7   Geometry of the tube network and real-time volumes at stations   260

11.8   Impact of closing a mainline station (Liverpool Street) on flow
        of travellers passing through related stations   260

11.9   The spatial density of tweets in London   261

11.10   Geo-located tweets captured from Twitter between 15:00 and 22:00
        BST on Tuesday 9 August 2011   262

11.11   Spatial crowdsourcing: evolving data in real-time   264

11.12   Visualizing model outputs a) in 2D and 3D with b) data at the
        metro-region level and c) at the local level   266

11.13   Using procedural modelling in City Engine to visualize radially
        structured land use activity patterns   268

TABLES

5.1   Summary of selected recent research projects which embody a
       digital social research approach to data management challenges
       linked to social survey research   115

8.1   A summary of some of the more commonly used commercial
       and free text mining tools   184

10.1   Online networks by direction and manifestation of ties   227

10.2   Tools for collection of online network data   231

LIST OF CONTRIBUTORS

Robert Ackland is an Associate Professor in the Research School of Social Sciences at the Australian National University. He gained his PhD in economics at the ANU, focusing on index number theory in the context of cross-country comparisons of income and inequality. Robert has been studying online social and organizational networks since 2002 and he established the Virtual Observatory for the Study of Online Networks (http://voson.anu.edu.au) in 2005. Robert established and teaches the Social Science of the Internet specialization of the ANU's Master of Social Research, and his book *Web Social Science: Concepts, Data and Tools for Social Scientists in the Digital Age* (SAGE) was published in July 2013.

Lawrence Ampofo earned his PhD in social media, security, and online behaviour at the New Political Communication Unit at Royal Holloway, University of London in 2012. He is founder and director of Semantica Research, a company that provides social media analysis for public, voluntary, and private sector organizations. Lawrence tweets as @lampofo.

Professor Bob Anderson is Honorary Research Fellow at the University of Manchester. Having retired as Pro Vice Chancellor and CEO of University Campus Suffolk, Bob joined the Horizon Digital Research Institute in Nottingham. Bob taught for many years at Manchester Polytechnic (later Manchester Metropolitan University). Since 1988, he was taken up mostly with managerial roles, first as Director of the Xerox Research Laboratory in Cambridge, then as Pro Vice Chancellor for Research and Business Development at Sheffield Hallam University, and then at University Campus Suffolk.

When Bob was an active researcher, he, together with Wes Sharrock and John Hughes, undertook a number of what have become classic Ethnomethodological investigations in different settings. These included an entrepreneurial firm, the London Air Traffic Control Centre, and Xerox itself. These investigations were reported in a number of books, reports and papers. Whilst at Xerox, Bob was one of the leading proponents of the use of ethnographic approaches to data collection in the design and development of advanced systems.

Michael Batty is Professor of Spatial Analysis at University College London in the Centre for Advanced Spatial Analysis (CASA). He has worked on computer models of cities and their visualisation since the 1970s and has published several books, such as *Cities and Complexity* (MIT Press, 2005), which won the Alonso Prize of the

Regional Science Association in 2011, and most recently *The New Science of Cities* (MIT Press, 2013). His blogs cover the science underpinning the technology of cities (www.complexcity.info as well as his posts and lectures on big data and smart cities (www.spatialcomplexity.info).

Mark Birkin is Professor of Spatial Analysis and Policy in the School of Geography at the University of Leeds. His major interests are in simulating social and demographic change within cities and regions, and in understanding the impact of these changes on the need for services like housing, roads and hospitals, using techniques of microsimulation, agent-based modelling and GIS. He is currently the project leader for TALISMAN – the spatial data analysis and simulation node of ESRC's National Centre for Research Methods.

William Browne is Professor of Statistics at the University of Bristol where he is director of the Centre for Multilevel Modelling. He is interested in making the statistical analysis of complex structured datasets available and accessible to applied researchers in all disciplines. He took up his chair in Bristol in the Veterinary Sciences department in 2007 but is currently in the process of moving to the Education department (GSOE). He has previously held academic posts in the School of Mathematical Sciences, University of Nottingham and the Institute of Education, London. William's research deals with statistical methodology, in particular Monte Carlo Markov chain methods and multilevel modelling, statistical software development, and the application of statistics to disciplines, including veterinary science, animal behaviour, ecology, education and other social sciences. He is part of the development team of the MLwiN software package and directs the team that is currently developing the Stat-JR package. He has taught statistics to undergraduate and postgraduates in many disciplines and also regularly teaches advanced training workshops.

Pat Brundell is a Research Fellow in the Mixed Reality Laboratory (MRL) at the University of Nottingham. His background is in experimental psychology, with a focus on the evaluation of interactive systems. Since joining the MRL in 2008 he has researched the technologies and methods to support the use of digital records for social science. Pat has also conducted numerous studies of the design process, implementation and use of interactive systems to support entertainment and informal learning in public spaces.

Andrew Chadwick is Professor of Political Science in the Department of Politics and International Relations at Royal Holloway, University of London, where he founded the New Political Communication Unit in 2007. His books include the award-winning *Internet Politics: States, Citizens, and New Communication Technologies* (Oxford University Press) and the *Handbook of Internet Politics* (Routledge), which he co-edited with Philip N. Howard, and *The Hybrid Media System: Politics and Power* (Oxford University Press). Andrew is the founding series editor of Oxford University Press's book series *Studies in Digital Politics*. He tweets as @andrew_chadwick.

Simon Collister is Senior Lecturer in Public Relations and Social Media at London College of Communication, University of the Arts, London. He is currently conducting PhD research at Royal Holloway, University of London's New Political Communication Unit on the mediation of power in networked communication environments. Before entering academia, Simon worked for a number of global communications consultancies, planning and implementing research-led campaigns for a range of public, voluntary, and private sector organizations. Simon tweets as @simoncollister.

Andy Crabtree is Associate Professor and Reader in the School of Computer Science at the University of Nottingham. He is an ethnographer who has conducted a broad range of ethnomethodological studies of work to inform the development of computing systems. Andy was co-director of the NCeSS DReSS Research Node, which developed the Digital Replay System (DRS).

Mark Elliot joined the Centre for Census and Survey Research at the University of Manchester in 1996 and was director from 2005–2008 and was pivotal in the development of the new discipline area of Social Statistics. He is a world leading researcher in the field of Statistical Disclosure, has frequent invitations to speak at international conferences on Confidentiality and Privacy and is consultant to many national statistical agencies including the Office for National Statistics in the UK, US bureau for the Census and the Australian Bureau of Statistics and Statistics Singapore. Mark's work on *Data Intrusion Simulation* and *Special Uniqueness* is regarded as seminal within the disclosure control field. Apart from confidentiality and privacy his main research interests are in data linkage, attitude theory and measurement and impact of attitudes on socio-economic outcomes.

Steven Gray is a Research Associate and spatial software researcher at the Centre for Advanced Spatial Analysis, making the visualization of large complex datasets on maps easier for users and scientists alike. With over 10 years of professional software development under his belt, he has built multiple award winning systems and his work has been featured in various worldwide media outlets (CNN, BBC). In recent years he has specialized on building mobile applications that open up the world of data visualization, mining and analysis to the masses. Steven's current research focuses on distributed high performance computing and analyzing large datasets in real-time (http://bigdatatoolkit.org/).

Peter Halfpenny is Emeritus Professor of Sociology at the University of Manchester. He was Executive Director of the ESRC National Centre for e-Social Science from 2004 to 2010, responsible for the overall strategic management of the Centre's programme of research, outreach and capacity-building. Peter's own research interests are in the integration of computer tools and services into a comprehensive support environment for social science researcher practitioners, and the investigation of the adoption and adaptation of e-Science tools across the social research community.

Andy Hudson-Smith is Reader in Digital Urban Systems at the Centre for Advanced Spatial Analysis (CASA). He is Editor-in-Chief of *Future Internet Journal*, a Fellow of the Royal Society of Arts and a member of the Greater London Authority Smart London Board. His research is focused on location-based digital technologies and has been at the forefront of Web 2.0 technologies for communication, outreach and developing a unique contribution to knowledge. Andy is author of the Digital Urban Blog (www.digitalurban.org). He works on the Internet of Things, smart cities, big data, digital geography, urban planning and the built environment.

Marina Jirotka is Professor of Human Centred Computing in the Department of Computer Science, University of Oxford. Her research interests lie at the interface between the Computer and Social Sciences and focus on methodological innovations. She undertakes research into work practices drawing on ethnographic fieldwork often supplemented by video analysis. Marina has led and collaborated on a number of research projects related to ethical, legal and social issues in ICT. She is a Chartered IT Professional of the BCS and sits on the ICT Ethics Specialist Group committee. She has published widely in international journals and conferences in e-Science, HCI, CSCW and Requirements Engineering.

Dawn Knight is a lecturer in Applied Linguistics at Newcastle University, UK. Her research focuses on corpus linguistics, discourse analysis, lexico-grammar, multimodality and the socio-linguistic contexts of communication. The main contribution of her work has been to pioneer the development of multimodal corpus-based discourse analysis. This has included the shaping a novel methodological approach through the co-development of the Digital Replay System to support the analysis of the relationship between language and gesture-in use based on large-scale real-life records of interaction.

Paul Lambert is Professor in Sociology in the School of Applied Social Science, University of Stirling. He held research posts at the Universities of Cardiff and Lancaster prior to joining Stirling in 2003. His areas of expertise cover social science research methods, social statistics, and the sociological analysis of social stratification and inequality. His most recent research projects have been concerned with the measurement of social stratification and inequality using detailed occupational information; the analysis of social distance and social networks; and methodological research on statistical techniques, data management when using secondary survey data, and Digital Social Research. Paul teaches undergraduate and postgraduate courses on social research methods and social stratification, and had led a number of advanced training workshops on topics including secondary survey data analysis, data management, and statistical modelling.

Nick Malleson is a lecturer in Geographical Information Systems and a member of the Centre for Spatial Analysis and Policy (CSAP) in the School of Geography at the University of Leeds. His primary research interest is in developing spatial computer models of social phenomena with a particular focus on crime simulation. Other main research interests include looking at how the spatial analysis (such as clustering methods, spatial statistics) of new forms of social data can influence research.

Danius Michaelides is a Senior Research Fellow in Electronics and Computer Science at the University of Southampton. His research interests are in distributed computing, distributed information management and web-based tools and technologies, with a particular focus on their application in e-Science and Digital Social Research. Danius has experience working at the interface between Computer Science and Statistics with a PhD in exact tests and distributed computing. More recently, he has been involved in the development of the Stat-JR package.

Richard Milton is a Senior Research Associate at UCL's Centre for Advanced Spatial Analysis (CASA) where he is the key developer of web-based mapping systems, in particular the **MapTube** (www.maptube.org) website. He has worked on the Equator e-Science project in UCL Computer Science where he used GPS tracked sensors to measure environmental factors and display carbon monoxide levels on a 3D model of the city. Previously Richard has worked for a 3D games company writing art tools and plugins for 3DStudio Max and also spent six years working for the UK Meteorological Office, where he developed weather visualization systems.

Joe Murphy is a survey methodologist investigating the causes of and solutions to issues in survey quality and management. His research focuses on the implementation of new data collection processes, new data sources, and analytic techniques to maximize data quality, increase response, and reduce costs. Joe's recent work has been centred on data sources and techniques such as Internet search patterns, social media data analysis (e.g., Twitter), data visualization, crowdsourcing, and social research in virtual worlds.

Oliver O'Brien is a Research Associate and software developer at UCL CASA. He investigates and implements new ways of visualizing spatial data, as part of the Big Open Data Mining and Synthesis (BODMAS) project led by Dr Cheshire, including mapping datasets from the census. His research interests include online web mapping, digital cartography, spatial analysis and data visualization, focusing particularly on transport data and London. Oliver's Bike Share Map, a product of ongoing research into the field, shows a live map of bicycle sharing systems for around a hundred cities (http://bikes.oobrien.com/). He co-authors the Mapping London website (http://mappinglondon.co.uk/), which regularly features good examples of maps created of and for London, from CASA and from the online community in general.

Ben O'Loughlin is Professor of International Relations and Co-Director of the New Political Communication Unit at Royal Holloway, University of London. He is specialist advisor to the UK Parliament's soft power committee. He is co-editor of the Sage journal *Media, War & Conflict*. His last book was *Strategic Narratives: Communication Power and the New World Order* (Routledge, 2013). Ben has recently completed a study with the BBC on international audience responses to the 2012 London Olympics. Ben tweets as @Ben_OLoughlin.

Rob Procter is Professor of Social Informatics in the Department of Computer Science, University of Warwick, where he is deputy head of department and research director of the Warwick Institute for the Science of Cities (WISC), and Exchange Professor, NYU. Previously, he was research director of the ESRC National Centre for e-Social Science, where he contributed to developing innovations in e-Infrastructure, tools and methods in the social sciences.

One focus of his current work is methodologies and tools for big social data analytics. Rob led a multidisciplinary team working with the Guardian/LSE on the 'Reading the Riots' project, analysing tweets sent during the August 2011 riots. This won the Data Visualization and Storytelling category of the 2012 Data Journalism Awards and the 2012 Online Media Award for the 'Best use of Social Media'. He is also a co-founder of the Collaborative Online Social Media Observatory (Cosmos), a multidisciplinary group of UK researchers building a platform for social data analytics. Rob is editor of the *Health Informatics Journal* and advisory board member, *Big Data and Society Journal*.

Kingsley Purdam is a lecturer in Social Statistics at the University of Manchester. His main area of research is in equality issues, citizen engagement and policy making. Specific areas include: governance and human rights as well as research methods in consulting hard-to-reach and vulnerable groups. He is developing an international reputation for his work on helping behaviours and also on what is termed citizen social science. He is presently conducting a scoping study into food rights and food insecurity in the UK with the support of Manchester City Council. He is also using social media data to conduct research on the relation between politicians and the electorate. Kingsley recently completed an ESRC funded review of new data types and methods.

As applicant/co-applicant Kingsley has secured and delivered nearly £1.5 million of research funding across more than 50 challenging research projects, often for government departments. He teaches at postgraduate and undergraduate level on social statistics including using social media data in social research.

Flora Roumpani is a PhD researcher at the Centre for Advanced Spatial Analysis and holds a diploma in Architecture and Engineering from the Department of Architecture in the University of Patras, and an MRes from UCL. During her studies, she worked as a researcher in the Laboratory of Urban and Regional Planning on research projects relating to urban analysis and visualization. For four years, Flora worked as an architect as part of the urban planning team in Doxiadis Associates in several projects in Greece and abroad. Her research interests include issues concerning the future of the city, virtual environments and urban modelling and these are reflected in her blog (http://en-topia.blogspot.co.uk/).

Mike Savage is Martin White Professor of Sociology at the London School of Economics where he is also Head of Department, having previously been a professor at the Universities of Manchester and York. He has longstanding interests in the historical sociology of social class and stratification, where his recent books include *Culture, Class, Distinction* (co-authored) and where he has pioneered 'cultural class analysis'. Mike's concern to reflect on the methodological challenges to the social sciences is longstanding, and his book *Identities and Social Change in Britain since 1940: The Politics of Method* (2010) offers an historical perspective on this point. He is a Fellow of the British Academy, and has been a visiting professor in Paris, Bergen, and North Carolina.

Paul Tennent is a Research Associate in the Mixed Reality Laboratory and Horizon Digital Economy Research Institute at the University of Nottingham. His research focuses on the application and interpretation of sensor-based data in real world settings, and he has worked extensively on creating software frameworks to support the qualitative analysis of complex multimodal data. Paul was the principal developer of the Digital Replay System (DRS).

Jonathan J.H. Zhu (PhD, Indiana University, 1990) is a professor and Founding Director of the Web Mining Lab (http://weblab.com.cityu.edu.hk) in the Department of Media and Communication at City University of Hong Kong, where he teaches new media theory, quantitative research methods, and social network analysis. Jonathan's current research focuses on the structure, content, use, and impact of the Internet, with results published in *Communication Research, Journal of Computer-Mediated Communication, New Media & Society, Cyberpsychology, Behavior and Social Networking, Information, Communication, and Society, Journal of the American Society of Information Science and Technology, Computers in Human Behavior, IEEE Transactions in Visualization and Computer Graphics*, and elsewhere.

ACKNOWLEDGEMENTS

We would like to thank all those who contributed to the achievements of the National Centre for e-Social Science (NCeSS). We would like to express our special thanks to the NCeSS Hub team: Mercedes Arguello, Marzieh Asgari-Targhi, Kenny Baird, Lisa Bell, Laura Bond, Hazel Burke, Keith Cole, Mike Daw, Elaine Edwards, Pascal Ekin, June Finch, Morag Goff, Terry Hewitt, Wei Jie, Farzana Latif, Yuwei Lin, Katy Middlebrough, Frank O'Donnell, Elisa Pieri, Meik Poschen, Tian Qui, Tobias Schiebeck, Gillian Sinclair, Richard Sinnott, Colin Venters and Alex Voss.

COMPANION WEBSITE

This book is supported by a brand new companion website (https://study.sagepub.com/halfpennyprocter). The website offers a wide range of free learning resources, including:

- Chapter summaries
- Links to online sources listed in each chapter
- Links to demos, slides and videos
- Links to current research.

1

INTRODUCTION AND OVERVIEW
PETER HALFPENNY AND ROB PROCTER

1.1 INTRODUCTION

The dramatic increase over the last two decades or so in computing power, in wired and wireless connectivity, and in the availability of data has affected all aspects of our lives. Our aim in this book is to provide an accessible introduction to how social science researchers are harnessing innovations in digital technologies to transform their research methods. In this chapter we provide an overview of how and why e-Research methods have emerged, including an account of the drivers that have motivated their development and the barriers to their successful adoption. The chapters that follow examine how innovations in digital technologies are enabling the emergence of more powerful research infrastructure, services and tools, and how social science researchers are exploiting them.

1.1.1 Digital Data

As everyone exposed to the Internet is aware, the amount of digital data available is expanding very rapidly, both through the digitization of past records and by the accretion of 'born digital' materials that are in machine-readable form from the outset. The digital universe – the data we create and copy annually – is estimated to be doubling in size every two years and projected to reach 44 trillion gigabytes by 2020 (where a trillion is a million million, or 10^{12}) (IDC, 2014). For social scientists, the predictions that more data will be generated in the next five years than in the entire history of human endeavour is both an opportunity and a challenge.

Today, vast amounts of data are generated as people go about their daily activities, both data that is deliberately produced and that which is generated by embedded systems. For example, use of public services is captured in administrative records; in the private sector, patterns of consumption of goods and services are captured in credit and debit card records; patterns of personal communications are captured in telephone records; patterns of movement are logged by sensors, such as traffic cameras, satellites and mobile phones; the movement of goods is increasingly tracked by devices such as radio-frequency identification (RFID) tags; and the advent of the 'Social Web' has led to an explosion of citizen-generated content in blogs and on social networking sites.

Currently, these data sources are barely exploited for social research purposes. The potential benefits to researchers are enormous, offering opportunities to mount multidisciplinary investigations into major social and scientific issues on a hitherto unrealizable scale by marshalling artificially produced and naturally occurring 'big data' of multiple kinds from multiple sources. However, exploiting these digital data sources to their full research potential requires new mechanisms for ensuring secure and confidential access to sensitive data, and new analysis tools for mining, integrating, structuring and visualizing data from multiple sources.

1.1.2 e-Infrastructure

Since the beginning of the new millennium, a world-wide effort has been underway to create the research infrastructure and to develop the research methods that will be needed if the 'data deluge' is to be harnessed effectively for research. A new generation of distributed digital technologies is leading to the development of interoperable, scalable computational tools and services that increasingly make it possible for researchers to locate, access, share, aggregate, manipulate and visualize digital data seamlessly across the Internet on a scale that was unthinkable only a decade or so ago.

e-Infrastructure comprises the information and communication technologies (ICTs) – the networked computing hardware and software – and the digital data that are deployed to support research. A very broad definition has been adopted by Research Councils UK (2014), which spells out more fully the components that are brought together:

> e-Infrastructure refers to a combination and interworking of digitally-based technology (hardware and software), resources (data, services, digital libraries), communications (protocols, access rights and networks), and the people and organisational structures needed to support modern, internationally leading collaborative research be it in the arts and humanities or the sciences.

This definition highlights the complexity of e-Infrastructure and, correspondingly, the enormity of the socio-technical efforts required to efficiently integrate distributed computers, data, people and organizations in order to deliver tools and services that scientists can readily adopt to their advantage in pursuing their research. (In the US, the term cyberinfrastructure is more commonly used than e-Infrastructure.)

e-Research is the generic term that has been coined for the innovations in research methods that are emerging to take advantage of this new and vastly more powerful e-Infrastructure. Similarly, e-Social Science is the research facilitated by the e-Infrastructure. The 'e' in all these terms is short for 'electronic', although it is sometimes rendered as 'enhanced'.

The scope of the book is the application of e-Research methods across the social sciences, including both quantitative and qualitative data collection and analysis. The aim is to introduce the reader to the application of innovative digital research methods throughout the research lifecycle, from resource discovery, through the collection, manipulation and analysis of data, to the presentation and publication of results.

1.2 BACKGROUND

1.2.1 e-Science

Over the period 2001 to 2006, the UK Government invested £213m in an e-Science programme (Hey and Trefethen, 2004). The overall aim of the programme was to invent and apply computer-enabled methods to 'facilitate distributed global collaborations over the Internet, and the sharing of very large data collections, terascale computing resources and high performance visualizations'.[1] The funding was divided between a 'core programme', focused on developing the generic technologies needed to integrate different resources seamlessly across computer networks, and individual Research Council programmes specific to the disciplines they support. The Economic and Social Research Council (ESRC) allocation was £13.6m over the five years, with the major part of this investment devoted to setting up the National Centre for e-Social Science (NCeSS). The Centre had a distributed structure, with a coordinating Hub responsible for designing and managing the programme and eleven large three-year projects devoted to developing innovative tools and services and applying them in substantive fields of inquiry.

The ambition of the overall e-Science programme was to promote the adoption of innovations in digital infrastructure to facilitate bigger and faster science, with collaborators worldwide addressing major research questions in new ways. The initial technical focus was grid computing, driven by a set of 'middleware' standards. These are the shared protocols required for the development of sophisticated software to enable large numbers of distributed and heterogeneous computer systems to be linked and inter-operate, thereby providing researchers with seamless, on-demand access to scalable processing power to handle very large-scale datasets, regardless of the location of the researchers or the data. This model of e-Infrastructure was particularly appropriate to particle physics and such challenges as weather prediction and earthquake modelling. Advances in these areas are dependent on collecting and marshalling data on a vast scale and having huge computing resources to analyse it, accessible by large networks of research teams distributed across the world.

However, the grid computing blueprint for e-Infrastructure proved slow to mature, sometimes difficult to deploy in practice and it did not always offer the most appropriate solutions to scientists' requirements. Meanwhile, other technologies emerged

---

[1]www.epsrc.ac.uk/about/progs/rii/escience/Pages/intro.aspx. (All URLs were accessed on 17 Dec 2014.) Terascale computing achieves speeds of teraflops, where a teraflop is a trillion floating point operations per second.

and alternative solutions to the demand for scalable computing and data storage, such as cloud computing, became available. Alongside this was the flowering of the lightweight systems that are loosely collected together under the title of Web 2.0 (O'Reilly, 2005). While these are technically less powerful than grid-based systems, their relative simplicity – both in terms of implementation effort and ease of use – made them attractive to researchers who did not need sophisticated tools and services, and who were deterred from using grid services by their complexity and the perceived barriers to access. Moreover, many of these Web 2.0 tools and services are freely available on the Internet, and users can find help in adopting them in numerous online forums and support groups. They have been widely taken up because of their ability to deliver easy-to-use services via simple protocols and familiar Web-based user interfaces, and they provide flexible solutions to at least some researchers' needs for advanced computing tools and services. Accordingly, across the sciences the notion of grid computing being at the core of e-science gradually gave way to a wider understanding of e-Infrastructure, embracing a broad range of computing software and services that support the everyday work of scientists.

1.2.2 e-Social Science

From the start of the e-Science programme, the ambitions of grid computing were less matched to those disciplines subsequently encouraged to join the e-Science bandwagon, including the social sciences, where a mixture of numerous quantitative and qualitative methods is used to pursue relatively small-scale issues. These disciplines have very few generic problems requiring complex middleware to coordinate huge distributed computing and data resources. What requirements they do have were already – before the e-Science programme was initiated – well-served by established commercial and open-source packages to, for example, computer-assist personal interviewing, deliver Web-based surveys, manipulate and statistically analyse quantitative data, sort and code qualitative data, and visualize findings in tables, graphs and network diagrams. Moreover, competition between the commercial package vendors seeking sales to the market research industry as well as to the social research community maintained a flow of updates, including integration of different tasks from around the research cycle into single packages. Similarly, much of the open-source software continued to develop through the efforts of often very active and technically adept support groups.

As the NCeSS research programme unfolded within the changing technical environment, instead of focussing on grid computing, e-Social Science broadened out to include a diverse range of initiatives exploring how computer support and networking, as well as new sources of data including that harvested from the Web, could be used in new ways to capture people's views and map their behaviours and their networks. These projects included an exploration of new forms of digital data, such as mobile phone logs and GPS to track people's interactions (see Chapter 9); the creation and exploitation of metadata (that is, data about data, such as its provenance) to facilitate the sharing and reuse of research data (Edwards et al., 2011); linking data about individuals from different sources and the confidentiality and ethical issues that this raises (Duncan et al,. 2011); webometrics, that is, measuring the number, types and patterns of hyperlinks in the Web (Thelwall, 2009); creating maps of geo-referenced data to reveal patterns such as the location of crime hotspots (Hudson-Smith et al., 2009); large-scale social simulations of, for example, the demand for housing in a city and how it changes over time (Birkin et al., 2010); parallelization of statistical routines to make more efficient use of computing time (Das et al., 2010); enabling researchers to collaborate in marking up videos to highlight significant aspects of the social interactions they record (Fraser et al., 2006); mining large bodies of unstructured text for patterns (Ananiadou et al., 2009a; 2009b); and developing software for delivering behavioural interventions over the Internet (Webb et al., 2010). Many of these initiatives will be further described in the chapters that follow.

As these examples reveal, the e-Social Science programme became highly disparate, expanding to include an increasingly wide range of emerging digital technologies, and drawing on many of the new forms of digital data that were becoming increasingly accessible. The various projects demonstrated that a modest input of technical support could ease existing research processes. This proved particularly productive when there was very close engagement between computer scientists and social scientist users in order to track and respond to changing requirements so that research practices and computing tools could co-evolve. However, successful co-production requires that effective local support structures are established and delivered 'at the elbow' of the users (Procter et al., 2013a). This leads on to the wider issue of user adoption, and the barriers to and facilitators for this.

1.2.3 User Adoption

As we noted earlier, the adoption of innovations in research methods and tools has been on a smaller scale to date than the e-Research vision initially anticipated. e-Science's radical ambitions for transforming everyday research have been tempered in the light of growing evidence about the very real barriers slowing widespread adoption of advanced tools and services across the science community. This extends to the social sciences too. We have already noted that computer packages to support most tasks in the social science research cycle were available before the e-science programme was launched. What many social scientists seek are more efficient or user-friendly versions of these existing digital tools rather than a transformation in their approach facilitated by novel e-Infrastructure, and they have often lacked the resources or incentives to take up the new methods that it offers.

Although a small cadre of 'early adopters' – mostly involved in the e-Social Science research programme – have been keen to experiment with innovations and to take risks, adoption of even the broader e-Infrastructure by the wider social science research community has been handicapped by a complex of factors (as has e-Research as a whole: see Voss et al., 2010; Procter et al., 2013a). These include a lack of awareness of the opportunities e-Infrastructure provides; problems in translating innovations in one field into benefits for one's own research; risk aversion; and levels of IT support that are often dictated by institutional policies and priorities rather than individual researcher needs. Late adopters are often resistant to training and require shallow learning curves if they are to invest in new skills and adopt new ways of working. They may feel they can achieve their career goals – publications and promotions – using the tools with which they became familiar as graduate students. This environment is not conducive to the wide uptake of innovative tools and services or the pushing of boundaries.

Another factor hampering uptake is the uncertain path of technological innovation, which affected the whole of the UK e-Science programme from its launch in 2001. During the early stages of any innovation, the existence of competing technical solutions can be a disincentive to adoption. The emergence of alternatives to grid computing middleware, such as Web 2.0 tools as noted above, introduced uncertainty about the future direction of e-Infrastructure technology development. Studies of previous infrastructure innovations suggest that technological uncertainty may deter some potential users from engaging, at least until a clear technical winner has emerged (Edwards et al., 2007). This uncertainty has been amplified over the last decade as publicly funded research services have faced competition from commercial suppliers, for example, in the provision of cloud computing, with infrastructure, platforms and software all offered to users as subscription services. While this relieves users of the cost of support and maintenance, they lose control over the development path, which is driven by commercial priorities.

A further uncertainty in the future trajectory of emergent e-Infrastructure is its sustainability, that is, the resource-intensive path from research, through software development to delivery of services and support to users. To illustrate: even the more tractable new users will adopt new tools and services only when these are 'hardened' to production level, that is, become easy to use, stable, reliable, documented, maintained and fully supported. This requires that software development pathways be created that ensure that e-Infrastructure is able to move beyond the research stage, that is, beyond proofs of concept, demonstrators and prototypes, to production level tools and services. It is ease-of-use and the utility of e-Infrastructure, and its contribution to advancing social scientists' own substantive research that would persuade them to adopt new ways of working.

The achievement of sustainability is adversely affected by several aspects of the current academic reward system. One is the distinction between 'pure' computational research and 'applied' software development, with the former bringing rewards for 'proof of concept' software innovations but the latter – involving re-building the software to make it robust and efficient – being little rewarded within academia, to the extent that there are few developers to be found even in computer science departments, let alone social science departments. Yet without significant development work most 'proof of concept' innovations – such as those emerging from the e-Science programme – are unusable except in the hardware and software context in which the researcher constructed them. Earlier in this chapter, the advantage of software co-production was noted, but this requires collaboration not just between computer scientists and social scientist users, but also the addition of developers to the team, who can re-build innovative tools so that they become project-independent.

There is a similar distinction between both research and development on the one hand and service delivery on the other. The latter requires documentation, online or face-to-face support, FAQs, software maintenance, bug fixes, distribution, porting to new operating systems and so on. Service delivery to support e-Infrastructure is essential for effective and widespread use of e-research resources, but has little place in academia except in a very few specialized units.

Given the co-ordinated efforts of computer scientists, developers and service providers needed to deliver e-Infrastructure that can be readily deployed by users, and the lack of such organizational and human resources in many academic departments, it is not surprising that researchers tend to restrict themselves to the sorts of social science that can be achieved through an unsystematic mix of existing technologies with which they are most familiar.

The next section introduces the materials in the following chapters, which are designed to increase awareness of the opportunities that e-Infrastructure offers to transform social research. We begin with chapters focused on understanding the potential and challenges of new sources of social data for social research, while not forgetting that much can yet be done to enhance the use of more conventional data sources, such as surveys. We then turn to examining innovations where e-Research offers tools that open up new opportunities for social research across a broad range of topics. All of our contributors make clear in their individual chapters that they are aware of the issues around research ethics posed by new sources of social data and more powerful tools for analysis. Such is the importance of this topic that we include a chapter devoted entirely to it. Finally, this book had its genesis, in part, as a response to Savage and Burrow's widely cited paper, 'The Coming Crisis in Empirical Sociology' (2007). We believe that the chapters in this book present plentiful evidence that innovations in digital research methods have the potential to radically transform academic sociology, and we thought it appropriate to let one of the paper's authors have the last word on whether this transformation represents a crisis or an opportunity to be seized.

1.3 THE CHAPTERS

The chapters in this volume have been selected to provide an informative introduction to innovations in social science research methods and tools, along with a review of issues and challenges that remain to be resolved if researchers are to enjoy the full benefits of the innovations.

The chapters reflect the various ways in which social science research has changed under the influence of both new sources of social data and innovations in research infrastructure and tools. The social sciences are known for diversity of methods, and their quite different ideas about how to study and make sense of the social world. One fundamental distinction is what is often referred to as the quantitative-qualitative divide and another is between the use of primary and secondary data. Innovative digital tools have the capacity to blur both distinctions, as several chapters reveal.

Chapter 2: The Changing Social Science Data Landscape

This chapter reviews the new sources of social data being made available by a combination of new data services and changes in government policy on access to administrative records. It also notes the rapid expansion of born digital and big social data – of which social media comprise but one, admittedly high profile, example. In the chapter, Purdam and Elliot examine how access to the new data opens up new opportunities for social researchers and, drawing on an eight-point typology of new kinds of social data, they present a series of real world examples to illustrate how the social sciences can benefit from them. They also discuss some of the potential challenges for social researchers of using these new sources of social data, such as variable data quality, questionable generalizability and representativeness, and restrictions on free access to some kinds of social media data, and they explore the implications of these and other challenges for the practice of social science research.

Purdam and Elliot argue that the almost effortless capacity to collect new kinds of social data poses the risk that researchers will neglect theory in favour of more data-driven methods. They also speculate on how access to social data in real time ('datastreams') might lead to a blurring of the boundaries between research and policy intervention. Finally, in what is a recurring theme throughout this book, they examine some of the ethical issues that accompany the use of new forms of social data in research.

Chapter 3: Exploiting New Sources of Data

In this chapter, Elliot and Purdam take up the methodological challenges, outlined in Chapter 2, that researchers face if they are to make effective use of new sources of digital social data. They employ a series of case studies of research, including election campaigns, civil unrest, migration and mobility, and health and well-being, to illustrate how methodological innovations, such as crowd-sourcing, may be mobilized to meet the challenges.

Opinions on the value of new forms of social data have divided academic social researchers, with some taking the view that the discipline is on the threshold of a renaissance, including opportunities to study the social world in real time. Others dismiss such claims as naïve at best and – at worst – sacrificing methodological robustness and validity for convenience. Regarding the latter, numerous critics have raised concerns that the sheer volume of new forms of social data will make computational methods increasingly attractive to researchers and lead them to ignore the risks of relying on computer power to drive their analyses. One such risk is that posed to the verification and repeatability of results, which arises from using complex, and sometimes proprietary, algorithms that lack transparency; for example, the operationalization of statistical formulae in the packages researchers use are hidden from them. Another risk is that posed to meaningful understanding of social phenomena by the lure of spurious correlations thrown up by over-reliance on inductive methods.

Mindful of these problems, Elliot and Purdam argue that the solution is a middle course, combining new and conventional sources of data in a robust, mixed methods approach that bridges data- and hypothesis-driven traditions. There are, of course, obstacles to be overcome. New sources of data such as social media may increase threats to privacy, and Purdam and Elliot call for more research into ways of countering these threats through improved methods for data anonymization and a new ethical framework. In relation to the latter, they note that it is time that citizens realized the value (economic and social) of their own data and, equally importantly, they argue that commercial interests must not be allowed to constrain researchers' access to new forms of social data.

Chapter 4: Survey Methods: Challenges and Opportunities

In this chapter, Murphy considers the future for data collection and using survey methods in the context of new sources of digital social data and technical innovations in research methods and tools. He sets the scene by discussing current challenges for survey research, such as declining response rates in traditional face-to-face, telephone and mail surveys, alongside the opportunities that technical innovations provide for enhancing the quality and efficiency of survey research methods. Drawing on a selection of major social science surveys, Murphy offers examples that point toward the continuing importance of survey-based methods in the social sciences.

Murphy observes that, despite the proliferation of born digital data, recent years have nevertheless witnessed an explosion in the quantity and diversity of data generated through survey research. This has been facilitated by developments in e-Infrastructure, an example being the unprecedented opportunities for the recruitment and retention of respondents afforded by the public's mass adoption of email and, subsequently, social networking sites. Similarly, survey researchers have benefited from the increasing availability of paradata, that is, data about survey transactions and interactions with respondents, which can be used to gain insights into their motivations and the meaning behind their responses. Such e-Infrastructure affordances have made significant advances in the capture, analysis and dissemination of survey data possible. They lead Murphy to argue that, contrary to predictions that new sources of data will make surveys redundant, they offer ways both to make surveys more effective tools and to meet the challenges that have threatened their value. For example, the availability of administrative data and methods for matching it with survey data hold great promise for minimizing respondent burden and cost. In a different vein, Murphy observes that virtual worlds, such as Second Life, offer new ways of conducting interview-based surveys.

Nevertheless, Murphy reminds us that social media brings new challenges, in particular, the problems of bias through samples of unknown representativeness, and quality assurance. The prospect of using social media as a substitute for traditional surveys – for example, the use of Twitter as a way of measuring public opinion through sentiment analysis – is often heralded as a sign of their imminent demise. Murphy, however, warns of the dangers of relying on such data where there is '... no standardization or check on the validity of the information being shared'. He argues, instead, for more research into the value of Twitter as a means to recruit respondents, citing as an example a recent study where it was used in diary data collection. Finally, Murphy discusses the potential of mobile devices for SMS-based survey delivery, noting its efficacy for administering them at predetermined times or in the context of specific events or – when used in conjunction with GPS – specific places.

Murphy's conclusion is that survey methods are continuing to play a major role in social research, and pessimism about their survival is misplaced. This role, however, is increasingly being shaped by people's use of communication technologies. Given the rapid pace of innovation of these technologies, the future for survey methods remains hard to predict.

Chapter 5: Advances in Data Management for Social Survey Research

As argued in the previous chapter, despite the availability of new sources of social data, making optimal use of more conventional data sources such as surveys remains of critical importance to social research. However, using survey research data can present major challenges for data management. For example, pursuing a particular research question may require linking different datasets, extracting variables, combining them and recoding their values before statistical analysis can start. In this chapter, Lambert argues that data management practices have failed to keep pace with these challenges and explains how e-Research can advance the state of the art, drawing on examples of working with quantitative datasets generated through social surveys taken from the DAMES (Data Management through e-Social Science) project.[2] He argues that enhanced facilities for file storage and linkage, for using metadata to describe data, and for the capture of data preparation routines ('workflows') can raise standards in data management and help researchers share their experience and expertise with one another. (Exercises illustrating each of these facilities can be found at the book's website.)

Lambert concludes by examining the prospects for the adoption of more advanced data management tools and practices. Using an example where 'bottom-up' and 'top down' innovation processes might successfully complement one another, he notes how the push from journals and funding agencies for researchers to publish metadata about their data management is likely to have a decisive influence.

Chapter 6: Modelling and Simulation

Quantitative simulation and modelling are perhaps the most obvious examples of the potential for e-Research methods and tools to revolutionize the study of complex socio-economic problems, and their applications are becoming increasingly widespread. New sources of data and more powerful computational resources have made possible the development of more complex and sophisticated techniques and, of

---

[2]www.dames.org.uk

course, larger-scale models. As Birkin and Malleson point out in this chapter, while modelling and simulation in the social sciences have been around for fifty years, prompted by an earlier wave of innovations in computation, recent advances in both data and computation are now having a profound effect.

This chapter provides an introduction to the state of the art in four model classes that are of particular interest to social scientists – systems dynamic models, statistical and behavioural models, microsimulation models and agent-based models. Examples are presented of each of these classes – a retail or residential location model (spatial interaction model or mathematical/systems dynamic model); a traffic behaviour model (discrete choice or statistical model); a demographic model (microsimulation model); and a crime model (agent-based model). Birkin and Malleson observe that while building ever more sophisticated models of social systems has never been easier, the task of demonstrating that such models faithfully represent an underlying social reality remains the key challenge. They then relate some experiences and lessons from building a prototype social simulation infrastructure capable of providing support for the whole research lifecycle, and they stress, in particular, the importance of model reproducibility, reusability and generalizability. They conclude with a summary of some of the – as yet – unexploited opportunities for social simulation presented by new sources of data (e.g., using mobile phone data to update in real time models of population movements) and the challenges (e.g., data ownership and ethics) that will have to be met if these are to be realized.

Chapter 7: Contemporary Developments in Statistical Software for Social Scientists

In this chapter, Lambert, Browne and Michaelides examine the prospects of the quantitative social sciences being in a position to exploit the power of new social data, computational resources and tools to achieve advances in statistical analysis. They review the range of statistical software packages currently available to social researchers and the factors influencing their patterns of adoption. They illustrate their review with examples of the application of statistical methods in domains such as education, health inequalities and epidemiology. They argue that the profusion of statistical tools, while having the benefit of offering choice to researchers, nevertheless raises significant barriers, both social and technical (and, indeed, socio-technical), that need to be addressed if the power of the tools is to be fully exploited by the social science research community.

Regarding social barriers, the authors note that in the UK there is a lack of capacity in statistical skills within the social research community. Regarding technical barriers, they observe that the proliferation of statistical tools has been at the cost of inter-operability and has created a situation that they describe as 'balkanization'. This can deter researchers from using the tool most appropriate for a particular analysis – rather than the one they are most familiar with – and may also inhibit experimenting with new tools. Echoing the concerns raised by Purdam and Elliot, they also point to problems with transparency, replicability and robustness of statistical analyses using computer packages whose algorithms are not accessible to the user. Drawing on the principles of e-Research for their inspiration, Lambert et al. conclude by presenting some ways of overcoming the social and technical barriers, which they exemplify through their efforts to develop Stat-JR and eBooks, new tools for statistical analysis that promote inter-operability between analysis packages and sharing through better documentation of analysis routines.

Chapter 8: Text Mining and Social Media: When Quantitative Meets Qualitative and Software Meets People

Text mining has developed dramatically in recent years in its power to analyse and extract information from very large bodies of unstructured text. Its applications are motivated by a growing awareness that researchers need more powerful tools in order to benefit from rapidly increasing amounts of textual data being generated through the proliferation and unprecedented levels of take up of Web 2.0 technologies. Chief among these are blogs and social media ('micro-blogs'), the latter exemplified by the rise of platforms such as Facebook and Twitter.

In this chapter, Ampofo, Collister, O'Loughlin and Chadwick explore how text mining using natural language processing (NLP) techniques can provide qualitative social researchers with powerful analytical tools for extracting information from this unstructured data, including harvesting data and analysing it in real time. They survey the range of research tools for text mining, broadly defined, available both in the academic and commercial spheres. People's use of social media is seen by many researchers as providing an ideal source of data through which to monitor rapidly changing situations, hence, it has come to particular prominence during civil unrest (e.g., the so-called 'Arab Spring') and natural disasters (e.g., Hurricane Sandy). Beyond these inherently unpredictable phenomena, one of the most popular emerging applications of social media analysis lies in the tracking of public opinion through the application of NLP-based techniques such as sentiment analysis. These techniques have the capacity to generate results in real time, which offers intriguing possibilities for both commercial and academic research.

To illustrate the potential and challenges of using text mining techniques in social research, Ampofo, Collister, O'Loughlin and Chadwick present overviews of two projects. The first is a study of social media during the televised debates between political party leaders in the 2010 UK general election campaign. The second is also drawn from this election campaign and focuses on the reporting of accusations of bullying against then-Prime Minister Gordon Brown in the British media. The application of NLP-based text analysis tools to social data is still, in many respects, in its infancy. With this thought in mind, the authors conclude by outlining the ontological challenges (echoing the reservations that Elliot and Purdam set out in Chapter 3) and the technical challenges of mining text in social research settings. They note, in the case of social media, increasingly restrictive access policies, and they also consider the ethical implications of text mining used as a social research tool.

Chapter 9: Digital Records and the Digital Replay System

As many of the contributors to this book recognize, the capacity to capture behaviour through the 'digital footprint' that people generate as a by-product of their everyday activities has the potential to transform the practice of empirical social science. In this chapter, Crabtree, Tennent, Brundell and Knight examine how new tools for data collection and analysis make it possible to exploit this data. Their discussion focuses in particular on the development of 'digital records' that enable social science researchers to combine novel and heterogeneous forms of digital data, such as video, text message logs and GPS data, with more traditional and established forms, such as audio recordings and transcriptions of talk.

The authors describe the Digital Replay System (DRS), an open source, extensible suite of interoperable tools for assembling, synchronizing, visualizing, curating and analysing digital records.[3] In Chapter 5, Lambert presents solutions to the data management problems attendant in the use of conventional kinds of social data such as surveys. From this perspective, DRS can be viewed as a prototype for meeting the data management and linking challenges presented by novel sources of social data. Crabtree and his co-authors provide a step-by-step exposition of several different examples; these include capturing rich accounts of people's physiological reactions while on a fairground ride, a corpus linguistics perspective on visitors' interactions in an art gallery, and disaster mapping and management. Collectively, these examples illustrate how the use of a system like DRS can enable the assembly of digital records capturing a wide range of interactions between people that are a by-product of their use of various digital devices, and make them available for subsequent visualization, curation and analysis. Finally, the authors consider future developments, particularly the prospects for making use of mass participation in social science research through the use of mobile devices for the crowd-sourcing of data.

Chapter 10: Social Network Analysis

The distinctive contribution of social network analysis (SNA) to social research is its stress on the importance of studying the structure of relationships between people rather than considering them as unconnected individuals. Like many of the other advances in research methods covered in this book, SNA is a mature methodological tool. Arguably, it owes its rise to greater prominence in recent years to two factors. One is that, as with many other established social research methodologies, e-Infrastructure has extended the scale and complexity of what is achievable, in this case by providing SNA with new and more powerful means to capture social network datasets, analyse them and visualize the results. The second factor is that many of the new types and sources of digital social data – such as hyperlink networks (the structures of links between websites) and social networking sites such as Facebook and Twitter – are inherently relational.

---

[3]http://thedrs.sourceforge.net

In this chapter, Ackland and Zhu review the history and methodological principles of SNA, and survey several of the research tools now available for SNA data collection, analysis and visualization. They draw on examples of studies of Facebook, Twitter, Flickr, online newsgroups and websites to illustrate contemporary and arguably the most prominent uses of SNA – to study people's behaviour in social networking sites. Ackland and Zhu go on to discuss two key ontological questions associated with SNA as a research methodology. The first is its 'construct validity', an issue that has potentially major implications. Simply put, the question is: do the social structures observed in, for example, Facebook, have real-world analogies or are they properties only of the online world, entirely unrelated to its real world counterpart? If the answer is no, then arguably, for all the talk about the opportunities for social research offered by new sources of social data, the impact in terms of increased understanding of social phenomena will be very limited.

Ackland and Zhu's second question relates to debates about the capacity of social research methodologies to distinguish between causality and correlation. Here, they offer a somewhat more optimistic prognosis, observing that data generated through people's activity on, for example, social networking sites, is rich and time-stamped, allowing for more fine-grained analysis, while the sites themselves can be thought of as natural research instruments, ideal for carrying out large scale experiments.[4] Like other contributors to this volume, they conclude with a warning about the pitfalls for researchers of relying on data sources, such as Facebook, that are proprietary and whose access is subject to terms and conditions that may change at any time.

Chapter 11: Visualizing Spatial Data and Social Media

As earlier chapters have emphasized, the social data landscape is changing at an ever-increasing pace. The ways in which data is visualized has always played an important role in its analysis and in the presentation of results, and the ever-increasing volumes of data raise new challenges for visualization methods and tools. In this chapter, following a brief history of geographic information systems (GIS), Batty and his colleagues describe new ways of visualizing social data, with a particular emphasis on mapping. They argue that Web 2.0 mash-ups, layering geographically tagged social data on top of digital maps, enable quick and simple visualization of data, presenting research outcomes in ways that can be easily understood by diverse audiences.

Many of the examples the authors present emphasize how much researchers can achieve using simple, generic technologies and services such as Google Maps and Fusion Tables. Helpfully, Batty and his colleagues at UCL's Centre for Advanced Spatial Analysis (CASA) have packaged these services into useful tools (such as

---

[4]As the recent controversy over the Facebook experiment conducted by researchers at Cornell and the University of California, it is essential to think very carefully about the ethical implications of conducting such studies. See www.theguardian.com/technology/2014/jul/02/facebook-apologizes-psychological-experiments-on-users

MapTube[5]), which not only enable the geo-mapping of datasets with a few button clicks, but also provide ways for researchers to share and re-use each other's efforts.

Another way in which advances in visualization techniques have harnessed the increase in computer power and new sources of data is the creation of fly-through, 3D models and visualizations of, for example, urban environments. More mundanely, but perhaps of greater value to researchers and planners involved in urban science, and the latest of many research areas predicted to be transformed by the advent of big data,[6] are CASA's 'city dashboards', which integrate diverse sources of data to create a real-time visualization of the state of the city and its inhabitants. Example applications include visualizing in real-time the state of mass transit systems. Such tools can provide powerful and intuitive front-ends to the simulations and models presented in Chapter 6, allowing, for example, exploration of the impact of closure of parts of the system.

Batty and his co-authors stress the importance of crowdsourcing and 'citizen science' for creating resources accessible to the public and illustrate this with the example of Open Street Map, a free map of the world.[7] They conclude with some thoughts on the future of visualization as a tool for social scientific investigation and understanding. They predict the emergence of radically different kinds of tools that make use of more abstract forms of visualization, with an increasing emphasis on the use of non-spatial data as the way forward for understanding how social systems function.

Chapter 12: Ethical Praxis in Digital Social Research

Current approaches to ethics no longer seem adequate for twenty-first century social research. We have already noted the concern registered by the authors of preceding chapters about the privacy and confidentiality threats raised by the proliferation of social data. There is an emerging consensus that a new ethical framework for the conduct of social research is necessary in order to protect citizens from harm but, as yet, there is little agreement on what changes it should embody, and how it should be promulgated and enforced.

In this chapter, Jirotka and Anderson examine the ethical issues raised by e-Research methods and what steps the social research community might take to address them. They use three case studies to illustrate the issues. The first describes a flagship UK e-Science project eDiaMoND and the process of gaining ethical approval for its work. The second concerns a recent controversy regarding social science researchers' use of Facebook data called the 'Harvard Meltdown'. The final case study is about developing prototype assistive technology for vulnerable people. Jirotka and Anderson draw several conclusions from these studies: managing ethics in large scale, multi-disciplinary research projects is particularly difficult and some of the founding

---

[5]www.maptube.org

[6]For example, the Center for Urban Science and Progress (CUSP). See cusp.nyu.edu

[7]www.openstreetmap.org

principles of research ethics, such as informed consent, can be burdensome; protecting the identity of sources using conventional techniques for anonymization is becoming progressively less reliable as more and more information about subjects and settings becomes openly available via the Web (identification is always possible given enough correlated data); consenting to take part in research must be done in a principled way and, having consented, participants must have the power in practice – and not just in principle – to withdraw it; and finally, where a project involves interventions in people's lives, researchers must consider what may happen once the project finishes.

They conclude with a discussion of the ethics of big social data. They underline the importance of the well-rehearsed arguments about threats to privacy and confidentiality. They ask what rules should apply to the use of social media in research: does publishing thoughts and opinions in public render informed consent irrelevant? However, their key insight goes further: it questions whether the lure of big social data is persuading researchers to relax their professional judgment about what conclusions are warrantable from the data. Jirotka and Anderson's fundamental argument is that we need to bring ethical considerations into the heart of how we conduct research, from the point where decisions are being made about research goals, through to the collection and analysis of the data and the making sense of the findings.

Chapter 13: Sociology and the Digital Challenge

This final chapter examines the implications of massively increased computational and data resources for social research methods, including the impact on its established practices and future of its disciplines. In it, Savage returns to themes that he and his co-author, Burrows, first raised in their subsequently much-cited paper, 'On the coming crisis of empirical sociology' (Savage and Burrows, 2007). His aim, in part, is to ground expectations of the changes in social research that may follow from digital innovations and, not least, to question their inevitability. As the contributions of the authors of the chapters in this volume convincingly demonstrate, the future of digital sociology is contested: they all agree that the discipline is undergoing a sustained period of innovation, but its future direction is unknown. Together, they make a powerful case for Savage's assertion that the future of digital sociology is not a given, but lies in the hands of current and subsequent generations of practitioners.

1.4 FUTURE DIRECTIONS

1.4.1 Technical Developments

The other chapters in this book, described above, confirm that e-Research has moved on from an early focus on grid computing to encompass a very diverse set of tools, some of which are enhancements of previous software and others that are entirely new. A factor that suggests that this diversity will persist and even grow is the lack of central co-ordination and oversight. In the UK, the national e-Science Centre, which was the hub for the core programme, ceased operating in 2011, as did the

NCeSS Hub in 2010. Other national centres still exist, for example the New Zealand eScience Infrastructure (www.nesi.org.nz), as do several international initiatives, such as the Open Grid Forum (www.ogf.org) and the European Grid Infrastructure (www.egi.eu). The emphases of these centres and programmes, however, are largely high performance computing, providing cloud services and codifying grid standards; areas of limited relevance to the social sciences. Outside these programmes, technical developments are either mostly modest refinements to existing tools, updates to commercial packages driven by competition for market share, or the adoption and adaptation of whatever generic or specialized tools and services researchers find can smooth the path of their own research. The future path of technical developments is therefore impossible to predict, though the drive to harness computing power to enable better research is unlikely to abate.

1.4.2 The Data Deluge

As reiterated in most of the chapters in this volume, we live in an information age characterized by a deluge of digital data (Hey and Trefethen, 2004; Hey, Tansley and Tolle, 2009). The chapters set out many of the potential research benefits to be obtained by collecting and analysing artificially produced and naturally occurring big data of many kinds from numerous sources. However, these benefits will only be realized if the wealth of data is managed in ways that ensure that it is discoverable, accessible, usable and re-usable. Indeed, research data management was a cornerstone of the original e-Research vision.

Accordingly, national e-Research programmes to innovate research methods, tools and infrastructure have devoted significant efforts to raise awareness among stakeholders that research data is a vital resource whose value needs to be preserved for future research by the data originators and by others. Achieving this requires that the data be systematically organized, securely stored, fully described, easily locatable, accessible on appropriate authority, shareable, archived and curated. Fulfilling all of these research data management tasks is a complex socio-technical challenge that stakeholders, whether they are research funders, higher education institutions (HEIs), publishers, researchers or regulators, are currently ill prepared to meet (Procter, Halfpenny and Voss, 2012). There are, as yet, no widely-agreed, mature solutions that can be implemented across all the various platforms that researchers use. Moreover, given the combination of the data deluge and a world recession, the scale of the tasks is increasing while the financial and therefore human resources to undertake the tasks are shrinking.

Ensuring the implementation and sustainability of data preservation will need to take on board the prospect of research becoming more collaborative and research teams being more widely distributed, as signalled in the e-Research vision of researchers world-wide addressing key challenges in new ways. The implications for data management services are summarized in a report from the Department for Business, Innovation and Skills (BIS) in the UK, which concluded, 'A federated infrastructure will be essential to exploit existing and future investments [in data] effectively' (Business, Innovation and Skills, 2010, 9). If such a federated infrastructure is to be achievable, then establishing effective inter-institutional service models will take on increasing importance. HEIs and other research organizations will need to develop strategies and infrastructure solutions that enable the federation of individual data repositories and the virtualization of data services. This will add a further layer of sustainability issues, the opportunities, costs and benefits of such collaborations will need to be carefully examined, and HEIs (both large and small) will need to develop competencies in managing services that span administrative and funding boundaries. In the current competitive environment, with universities locked in a zero-sum struggle for resources, there is little incentive to put effort into the inter-institutional cooperation required.

The term *big* social data serves to draw attention to three salient dimensions that define new forms of social data: volume, variety and velocity, the last reflecting its often real-time and rapidly changing character. Developments linked to the emergence of big social data are happening continually and we cannot be certain what impact such data will have on research processes. It is possible that it will promote the use of new computational social science methods in place of more traditional quantitative and qualitative research methods. It might also influence thinking and re-orientate social research around new objects, populations and techniques; network analysis offers an example here. The analysis of social processes as they actually happen is bound to give researchers insights and interesting avenues to explore that are absent from the often post-hoc reconstructions of events that are available via traditional research instruments and datasets.

Big social data will inevitably force us to rethink the role of academic social scientists. One way forward would be for them to actively seek collaborations with groups, both professional and lay, involved in doing various kinds of 'practical, everyday sociology'. An example of collaboration with professionals might include assisting journalists[8] who increasingly find themselves needing to analyse large datasets in order to report news stories.[9] Examples of collaborating with lay people include 'citizen social science' where members of the public can assist with research through crowd-sourcing data (as illustrated in Chapter 9), by participating in analytical work (Procter et al., 2013b), and even by taking a role in the setting of research agendas (Housley et al., 2014). These examples suggest possibilities for forging a new relationship between academic social science and society at large, a 'public sociology' (Burawoy, 2005), where social scientific knowledge is co-produced by a wide range of stakeholders (Housley et al., 2014) and is subject to greater public oversight and accountability. Initiatives in other discipline areas might provide models for how to proceed in the social sciences: see, for example, the Public Laboratory for Open Technology and Science (http://publiclab.org/), whose 'goal is to increase the ability of

---

[8]See, for example, the 'reading the riots' project, Lewis et al. (2011).

[9]This has given rise to the new specialism of 'data journalism'. News media organizations have also been at the forefront of experiments in citizen journalism and crowdsourcing data analysis. For an example of the latter, see www.theguardian.com/news/datablog/2009/jun/18/mps-expenses-houseofcommons

underserved communities to identify, redress, remediate, and create awareness and accountability around environmental concerns.'

Finally, as is noted in several of the chapters that follow, big social data has given fresh stimulus to debates about research ethics (see e.g., boyd and Crawford, 2012), much of which focuses on the issue of people's right to privacy but which also raises questions about the role and status of academic research. At the same time, we must not lose sight of the broader issue of the ethics of research and innovation (see e.g. Stahl, Eden and Jirotka, 2012, and Chapter 12 in this volume).

1.4.3 Collaboration

e-Research was conceived from the very beginning as a collaborative activity that would combine the abilities of distributed and complementary groups of researchers in order to achieve research goals that individual researchers or local groups could not hope to accomplish. With this in mind, the concept of the 'virtual research environment' (VRE), 'collaboratory' (cf. Olson, Zimmerman and Bos, 2008) or 'gateway' was another widely promoted element of the e-Research vision. VREs were seen as a way to support collaboration and provide integrated, shared access to resources throughout the research lifecycle, starting with literature searches and ending with the publication of results and curated datasets. In one system, accessible by all team members, a shared bibliography would be assembled. A joint laboratory notebook would be kept which would document all the research procedures undertaken. Data would be stored along with metadata recording the operations it had been subject to, and reports would be written collaboratively, with all versions archived, and publications prepared. Once again, experience has shown that the initial vision had to be tempered. VREs exemplify what happens when 'top-down' innovation programmes meet 'bottom up' processes through which individuals and groups of researchers experiment with whatever new technologies are at hand. They often prefer to work out their own – often ad-hoc, bespoke but nevertheless effective – solutions that match their needs and level of technical competence rather better than complex, all-embracing offerings whose adoption might lead to having to abandon favoured tools. A prosaic example is the use of an email list and attachments or freeware such as Dropbox[10] to share documents, rather than struggle to implement a VRE across different institutions' computer systems and seek local support in its use. Similarly, Web 2.0 has provided a host of applications that can be easily adopted to support various stages of the research cycle, such as switching from email attachments to an Internet file hosting and synchronizing service like Dropbox or Google Drive. Those VREs that have survived the turbulence of constant technological innovation and rapidly changing standards tend to be associated with 'big science' projects, such as climate change, and benefit from long-term funding arrangements.[11]

---

[10]www.dropbox.com

[11]See, for example, the Extreme Science and Engineering Discovery Environment (XSEDE) www.xsede.org/web/guest/gateways-listing

1.4.4 Scholarly Communications

Nowhere is this tension between top-down and bottom-up innovation processes in science more clearly evident than in scholarly communications. The past decade has seen the emergence of new ideas about the practice of scholarly communications, with talk of a 'crisis in publishing' and weaknesses in the peer-review system. One outcome is the notion of 'Open Science' (Neylon and Wu, 2009) with its advocacy of more open scientific knowledge production and publishing processes (Berlin Declaration, 2003; Murray-Rust, 2008). This has been inspired by discourses developed in 'Free/Open Source Software' and 'Creative Commons' movements (Lessig, 2004; Benkler and Nissenbaum, 2006; Elliott and Scacchi, 2008). Web 2.0 is widely seen as providing the technical platform to enable these new forms of scholarly communications and bring about a 're-evolution' of science (Waldrop, 2008).

Web 2.0 brings the promise of enabling researchers to create, annotate, review, reuse and represent information in new ways, promoting innovations in scholarly communication practices – e.g. publishing 'work in progress' and openly sharing research resources – that will help realize the e-Research vision of improved productivity and reduced 'time to discovery' (Arms and Larsen 2007; Hey et al., 2009; Hannay, 2009; De Roure et al., 2010). However, despite this increasing interest in Web 2.0 as a platform and enabler for e-Research, understanding of the factors influencing adoption, how it is being used, and its implications for research practices and policy remains limited. Recent studies suggest that there is considerable reluctance – even suspicion – to adopt new forms of scholarly communications among many academics, who fear that this will mean the end of the 'gold standard' of peer-review and the undermining public trust in science (Procter et al., 2010a; Procter et al., 2010b). Equally, it would be a mistake to ignore the capacity of established academic publishers to shape the emerging scholarly communications landscape so as to preserve their role as gatekeepers (Stewart et al., 2012). The future of scholarly communications may, after all, not be so radically different from its recent past.

1.4.5 The Future

The vision that motivated the e-Science programme in the UK and analogous programmes elsewhere was that grid computing-based infrastructure comprising computer power, big data and collaborative teams would transform science. Over the past decade this has morphed into a much more complex e-Infrastructure made up of a plethora of only loosely related tools and services taken up to different degrees and in different combinations and with different levels of enthusiasm even within the same field, allied with rapidly accreting digital data of new types and old. The e-Research facilitated by this maelstrom is transforming social science research, but in unpredictable ways, with many socio-technical barriers to be overcome before its full potential is realized. The aim of this book is to whet the appetite of social researchers to encourage them to explore how innovations in digital research methods might enable their research to advance in ways not possible otherwise.

1.5 ONLINE RESOURCES

Many of the examples of e-Research methods presented in this book already have online resources associated with them. To make these more accessible to readers, we have created a companion website.[12] This provides easy access to this content, including in-depth case studies, datasets, research workflows, tools and services, publications and links to the authors' own websites.

1.6 BIBLIOGRAPHY

Ananiadou, S., Weissenbacher, D., Rea, B., Pieri, E., Vis, F., Lin, Y-W., Procter, R. and Halfpenny, P. (2009a) 'Supporting frame analysis using text mining', *Proceedings of 5th International Conference on e-Social Science, Cologne, June*. Available from http://wrap.warwick.ac.uk/52916 (accessed 12 Dec 2014).

Ananiadou, S., Okazaki, N., Procter, R., Rea, B. and Thomas, J. (2009b) 'Supporting systematic reviews using text mining', in P. Halfpenny and R. Procter (eds) Special Issue on e-Social Science, *Social Science Computing Review Journal*, 27(4): 509–23.

Arms, W.Y. and Larsen, R.L. (2007) *The Future of Scholarly Communication: Building the Infrastructure for Cyberscholarship*. Report of a workshop held in Phoenix, Arizona April 17–19. Sponsored by the National Science Foundation (NSF) and the Joint Information Systems Committee (JISC). DOI: http://dx.doi.org/10.3998/3336451.0011.102.

Benkler, Y. and Nissenbaum, H. (2006) 'Commons-based peer production and virtue', *The Journal of Political Philosophy*, 14(4): 394–419.

Berlin Declaration on Open Access to Knowledge in the Sciences and Humanities (2003) Conference on Open Access to Knowledge in the Sciences and Humanities. Berlin, October. Available from http://openaccess.mpg.de/Berlin-Declaration (accessed 12 Dec 2014).

Birkin, M., Procter, R., Allan, R., Bechhofer, S., Buchan, I., Goble, C., Hudson-Smith, A., Lambert, P., DeRoure, D. and Sinnott, R. (2010) 'Elements of a computational infrastructure for social simulation', *Philosophical Transactions of the Royal Society A: Mathematical, Physical and Engineering Sciences*, 368(1925): 3797–3812.

boyd, D. and Crawford, K. (2012) 'Critical questions for big data: provocations for a cultural, technological, and scholarly phenomenon', *Information, Communication & Society*, 15(5): 662–79.

Burawoy, M. (2005) 'For public sociology', *American Sociological Review*, 70: 4–28.

Crabtree, A., French, A., Greenhalgh, C., Benford, S., Cheverst, K., Fitton, D., Rouncefield, M. and Graham, C. (2006) 'Developing digital records: early experiences of record and replay', *Journal of Computer Supported Cooperative Work*, 15(4): 281–319.

Das, S., Sismanis, Y., Beyer, K.S., Gemulla, R., Haas, P.J. and McPherson, J. (2010) 'Ricardo: integrating R and Hadoop', in *Proceedings of the 2010 ACM SIGMOD International Conference on Management of Data*, New York: ACM. pp. 987–98.

Department for Business, Innovation and Skills (2010) *Delivering the UK's e-Infrastructure for Research*. Available from www.rcuk.ac.uk/RCUK-prod/assets/documents/research/esci/e-Infrastructurereviewreport.pdf (accessed 6 Dec 2014).

---

[12]https://study.sagepub.com/halfpennyprocter

De Roure, D., Goble, C., Aleksejevs, S., Bechhofer, S., Bhagat, J., Cruickshank, D., Procter, R. and Poschen, M. (2010) 'Towards open science: the myExperiment approach', *Concurrency and Computation: Practice and Experience*, 22(17): 2335–53.

Duncan, G, Elliot, M J. and Salazar, J.J. (2011) *Statistical Confidentiality: Principles and Practice*. New York: Springer.

Edwards, P. Jackson, S., Bowker, G. and Knobel, C. (2007) *Understanding Infrastructures: Dynamics, Tensions, and Design*, final report of the workshop History and Theory of Infrastructure: Lessons for New Scientific Cyberinfrastructures, National Science Foundation. Available from http://deepblue.lib.umich.edu/handle/2027.42/49353 (accessed 15 Dec 2014).

Edwards, P., Mayernik, M.S., Batcheller, A., Bowker, G. and Borgman, C. (2011) 'Science friction: data, metadata, and collaboration', *Social Studies of Science*, 41(5): 667–90.

Elliott, M. and Scacchi, W. (2008) 'Mobilization of software developers: the free software movement', *Technology and People*, 21(1): 4–33. Available from www.ics.uci.edu/~wscacchi/Papers/New/Elliott-Scacchi-Free-Software-Movement.pdf (assessed 09 April 2015).

Fraser, M., Hindmarsh, J., Best, K., Heath, C., Biegel, G., Greenhalgh, C. and Reeves, S. (2006) 'Remote collaboration over video data: towards real-time e-social science', *Journal of Computer Supported Cooperative Work*, 15(4): 257–79.

Halfpenny, P., Procter, R., Lin, Y. and Voss, A. (2009). 'Developing the UK e-Social Science Research Programme'. In Jankowski, N. (ed.) *e-Research, Transformation in Scholarly Practice*, Abingdon: Routledge.

Halfpenny, P. and Procter, R. (2010) 'The e-Social Science research agenda', *Philosophical Transactions of the Royal Society A*, special issue on e-Science, 368: 3761–3778, August.

Hannay, T. (2009) 'From Web 2.0 to the global database'. In Hey, T., Tansley, S. and Tolle, K. (eds) *The Fourth Paradigm: Data-Intensive Scientific Research*. Redmond, WA: Microsoft Research. pp. 215–20.

Hey, T. and Trefethen, A. (2004) 'UK e-Science programme: next generation grid applications'. *International Journal of High Performance Computing Applications*, 18(3): 285–91.

Hey, T., Tansley, S. and Tolle, K. (eds) (2009) *The Fourth Paradigm: Data-Intensive Scientific Discovery*. Redmond, WA: Microsoft Research.

Housley, W., Procter, R., Edwards, A., Burnap, P., Williams, M., Sloan, L., Rana, O., Morgan, J., Voss, A. and Greenhill, A. (2014) 'Big and broad social data and the sociological imagination: a collaborative response', *Big Data & Society*, 1(2): pp. 1–15.

Hudson-Smith, A., Batty, M., Crooks, A. and Milton, R. (2009) 'Mapping for the masses: accessing Web 2.0 through crowdsourcing', in P. Halfpenny and R. Procter (eds) Special Issue on e-Social Science, *Social Science Computing Review*, 27(4): 524–38.

IDC (2014) *The Digital Universe of Opportunities*. Executive Summary available at www.emc.com/leadership/digital-universe/2014iview/executive-summary.htm.

Lessig, L. (2004) *Free Culture: How Big Media Uses Technology and the Law to Lock Down Culture and Control Creativity*. New York: Penguin Press.

Lewis, P., Newburn, T., Taylor, M., Mcgillivray, C., Greenhill, A., Frayman, H. and Procter, R. (2011) *Reading the Riots: Investigating England's Summer of Disorder*. Guardian Newspapers/LSE. Available from http://eprints.lse.ac.uk/46297/1/Reading%20the%20riots(published).pdf (accessed 09 April 2015).

Murray-Rust, P. (2008) 'Chemistry for everyone', *Nature*, 451: 648–51.

O'Reilly, T. (2005) 'What is Web 2.0?' September. Available from www.oreilly.com/pub/a/oreilly/tim/news/2005/09/30/what-is-web-20.html (accessed 01 April 2005).

Olson, G.M., Zimmerman, A. and Bos, N. (2008) *Scientific Collaboration on the Internet*. Cambridge, MA: MIT Press.

Neylon, C. and Wu, S. (2009) 'Open Science: tools, approaches, and implications', *Pacific Symposium on Biocomputing*, 14: 540–4. Available from http://psb.stanford.edu/psb -online/proceedings/psb09/abstracts/2009_p540.html (accessed 09 April 2015).

Procter, R., Williams, R., Stewart, J., Poschen, M., Snee, H., Voss, A. and Asgari-Targhi, M. (2010a) 'Adoption and use of Web 2.0 in scholarly communications', *Philosophical Transactions of the Royal Society A: Mathematical, Physical and Engineering Sciences, 368*(1926): 4039–4056.

Procter, R., Williams, R. and Stewart, J. (2010b) *If You Build It, Will They Come?: How Researchers Perceive and Use Web 2.0*. Research Information Network. Available at http://wrap.warwick.ac.uk/56246/1/WRAP_Procter_If%20you%20build%20it%20 will%20they%20come.pdf (accessed 28 Jan 2015).

Procter, R.N., Halfpenny, P. and Voss, A. (2012b) 'Research data management: opportunities and challenges for HEIs', in G. Pryor (ed.) *Research Data Management*. London: Facet Publishing. pp.135–50.

Procter, R., Voss, A. and Asgari-Targhi, M. (2013a) 'Fostering the human infrastructure of e-research', *Information, Communication & Society*, 16(10): 1668–91.

Procter, R., Housley, W., Williams, M., Edwards, A., Burnap, P., Morgan, J., Voss, A. and Greenhill, A. (2013b) 'Enabling social media research through citizen social science'. *ECSCW 2013 Adjunct Proceedings*, 3.

Research Councils UK (2014) *e-Infrastructure*. Available at www.rcuk.ac.uk/research/ xrcprogrammes/otherprogs/einfrastructure (accessed 28 Jan 2015).

Savage, M. and Burrows, R. (2007) 'The coming crisis of empirical sociology', *Sociology*, 41(5): 885–99.

Stahl, B., Eden, G. and Jirotka, M. (2012) 'Responsible research and innovation in Information and Communication Technology: identifying and engaging with the ethical implications of ICTs', in R. Owen, J. Bessant and M. Heintz (eds), *Responsible Innovation*. Chichester: Wiley & Sons. pp.199–218.

Stewart, J., Procter, R., Williams, R. and Poschen, M. (2013) 'The role of academic publishers in shaping the development of Web 2.0 services for scholarly communication', *New Media & Society*, 15(3): 413–32.

Thelwall, M. (2009) 'Introduction to webometrics: quantitative web research for the social sciences', *Synthesis Lectures on Information Concepts, Retrieval, and Services* 1(1): 1–116.

Voss, A., Asgari-Targhi, M., Procter, R. and Fergusson, D. (2010) 'Adoption of e-Infrastructure services: configurations of practice', *Philosophical Transactions of the Royal Society A: Mathematical, Physical and Engineering Sciences, 368*(1926): 4161–76.

Waldrop, M. (2008) 'Science 2.0: great new tool, or great risk?' *Scientific American*. Available from www.sciam.com/article.cfm?id=science-2-point-0-great-new-tool-or-great-risk (accessed 12 Dec 2014).

Webb, T., Joseph, J., Yardley, L. and Michie, S. (2010) 'Using the internet to promote health behavior change: a systematic review and meta-analysis of the impact of theoretical basis, use of behavior change techniques, and mode of delivery on efficacy'. *Journal of Medical Internet Research, 12*(1), e4.

2

THE CHANGING SOCIAL SCIENCE DATA LANDSCAPE

KINGSLEY PURDAM AND MARK ELLIOT

2.1 INTRODUCTION

2.1.1 The Age of Data

More than a century since the ground-breaking social surveys of Booth in London[1] and Rowntree in York in the UK, and the subsequent development of mass observation methods in the 1930s, we are now in an age of almost overwhelming volumes of data about many people's attitudes, circumstances and behaviour. Such data extends from people's views to images of them, their locations and movements, and their communications. The data is very diverse; it includes lifelong health and prescription records, genetic biomarker profiles and family histories, satellite images, digital passports and their use, databases from product warranty forms, consumption transactions, online browsing records, email and web communications, social media, and mobile phone use. As Berners-Lee and Shadbolt (2011:1) highlight, 'data is the new raw material of the 21st Century'.

Social science and the societies that it studies have entered the *age of data,* though not necessarily the *age of data access*. Nevertheless, access to this data is increasing; for example, administrative record data held by public bodies, including government

---

[1]Booth's original work was published in 17 volumes over the turn of the nineteenth century. It has been subsequently summarized, reproduced and interpreted on many occasions. See O'Day and Englander (1993).

>

departments, is being widened.[2, 3] The term 'big data' has been much used to describe the data revolution and whilst a little simplistic as a concept it moves us forward from Sweeney's (2001) discussion of the 'information explosion', insofar as it captures the growth in the collection and availability of information (for discussions see boyd and Crawford, 2012; Mayer-Schönberger and Cukier, 2013; O'Reilly Radar Team, 2011). Big data denotes volumes of data so large that they are kept in so-called data warehouses, which are digital data storage facilities often cutting across different national borders and data regulation regimes. It is the volume of data (when potentially information about all, or nearly all, of a particular population is included, as opposed to a sample), the variety of the variables, and the speed with which it can be discovered and accessed that open up new opportunities for research and methodological innovation (Mayer-Schönberger and Cukier, 2013; IBM, 2013).

The term 'big data' is used differently by different authors, with some including orthodox or well-established forms of social science data, such as survey responses and focus group transcripts (Elliot et al., 2013).[4] The new types of data can have very different origins and structures. Some might be collected primarily for research use, whilst other data might be produced as a secondary outcome to another activity, for example, buying a product online or posting views on a blog. Some of this new data has been around in some form and quantity for some time, but its use in social science research has been limited, perhaps because of access and infrastructural constraints, methodological uncertainties and a lack of interest in, or opportunity for, social research use (Elliot et al., 2013).

In many ways, conceptually the term 'big data' fails to capture the all-encompassing nature of the socio-technical transformation that is upon us. Many people who use the term qualify it by stating that big data is not just about volume but also other features: that data can be captured, updated and analysed in (almost) real-time and that it can be linked through multiple data capture points and processes. However, such characterizations are not sufficient; they still express the notion of data as *something we have,* whereas the reality and scale of the data transformation is that data is now something we are *becoming immersed* and *embedded in.* We are generators of, but are also generated in, the *data environment.* Our behaviour is increasingly documented and collated. Instead of people being researched, they are the research. Hence, we use the term *the age of data to* capture the historical phase that large parts of society have now entered,

---

[2]Within the UK, see www.adls.ac.uk for general information about new access opportunities.

[3]At the time of writing, the UK Administrative Data Taskforce had reported (www.esrc. ac.uk/_images/ADT-Improving-Access-for-Research-and-Policy_tcm8-24462.pdf). If its recommendations are taken up by the UK government, they are likely to lead to a step change in research access to administrative data.

[4]By orthodox social science data, we mean data collected with the specific intent of doing social science. Though, of course, even these data and methods are continually being developed and renewed; we have travelled some distance from the purposive cross-sectional surveys of the early twentieth century in the UK to the online surveys, cohort studies and experimental controlled trials increasingly used today.

and we use the term *data environment* (see Elliot et al. 2008 and 2010 for discussion of the term) to capture the reality of the new relationship between people and what is known about them. This can include a focus not only on explaining why something might have happened, but also on what is currently happening and is going to happen.

If they are going to be used effectively for research, the new data types and large-scale datasets require new approaches to analysis and new skills for social scientists. After all, social science should be capable of producing testable hypotheses using robust research designs and data quality assurance measures even where new types of data are being used. Such data also has its limitations and is not always accessible for social science research use. Moreover, big data does not mean we all have access to the data or that we know everything. There is still a need for purpose-specific data and for approaches based on testing theories.

In this chapter we consider some examples of the new types of social data, including their formats, content, meanings, and the changing relationship between people's digital and non-digital identities. We use real world examples to explore how social science might utilize new types of data to understand social phenomena in new ways and from new perspectives. As well as the data itself, we consider access modalities and processes. It is clear that what is happening in the data environment will change not just how we do social science research but who does it, where it is done and, indeed, what research means. However, as a recent consultation (Elliot et al., 2013: 4) on the use of digital data by social scientists highlighted, some concerns have been raised:

> There is more data for social research but can people use it, under what conditions and do they know how to? (Social scientist, stakeholder interview, 2012)

> There is a growth of under-theorised empiricism in social science...uncritical use of data with limitations in coverage or definitions and the steering of research to things that happened to be measured. (Social scientist, survey, respondent, 2012)

2.1.2 What is Data?

Data is information or knowledge about an individual, object or event. Data can comprise numerical values, quantities of text, sounds or images, memories or perceptions. Often the concept of data suggests information that has a structure and which has been through some kind of processing.

Many examples of new types of data have very different and sometimes unstructured formats, for example, tweets or documents released under a Freedom of Information (FOI) request. In order to develop our understanding of the changing data environment, we outline below a typology of different data types. This typology is based on the idea of data as knowledge but also in terms of each data item carrying with it implicit or explicit metadata, that is, data about the data item, such as its origin, ownership, terms of use and coverage. There are a variety of ways to consider the nature of data but here we combine the key issues into a single framework. We draw on work by Elliot et al. (2010) on behalf of the Office for National Statistics

(ONS) in the UK, which examined the nature of public data, comparing information that is formally in the public domain, such as public administrative records (e.g., the Electoral Register, share holdings and professional occupation lists) and data that is informally in the public domain, such as that posted on the Internet (e.g., via Facebook and blogs). For a related discussion of what they term *datafication,* which refers to the process of recording and quantifying behaviour and events for analysis, see Mayer-Schönberger and Cukier (2013: 73).

We develop our approach here to focus on what can be termed the 'metadata of origin', rather than the actual type of data or whether the data is qualitative or quantitative. The issue of origin is interdependent with issues of data ownership, quality, access and use. A key aspect of this is the law and codes of practice around the recognition of what is 'personal' data. Under the UK *Statistics and Registration Service Act (2007)* (SRSA) personal information is defined as 'information which relates to and identifies a particular person (including a body corporate)'. Information identifies a particular person if the identity of that person – '(a) is specified in the information, (b) can be deduced from the information, or (c) can be deduced from the information taken together with any other published information'.[5] The disclosure of personal information by public bodies, such as the ONS, is a criminal offence. For further information see the UK Anonymization Network[6] and also a recent report by the Information Commissioner (ICO, 2012).

In terms of the metadata of origin approach, we propose an eight-point typology based on the type of generation process involved. Given the complexity and changing nature of the data environment, it can be argued that mapping the data generation process is the only stable way of understanding the variety of data and for developing good practice around the use of different data types.

2.1.3 Data Origin Typology

1. **Orthodox intentional data:** Data collected and used with the respondent's explicit agreement. All so-called orthodox social science data (e.g. survey, focus group or interview data and also data collected via observation) would come into this category. New orthodox methods continue to be developed.
2. **Participative intentional data:** In this category data are collected through some interactive process. This includes some new data forms such as crowdsourced data (e.g. the Everyday Sexism project; see http://everydaysexism.com) and is a potential growth area.
3. **Consequential data:** Information that is collected as a necessary transaction that is secondary to some (other) interaction (e.g. administrative records, electronic health records, commercial transaction data and data from online game playing all come into this category).

---

[5]The definition in the SRSA is very similar to the one contained in the *Data Protection Act (1998).*

[6]See http://ukanon.net

4. **Self-published data:** Data deliberately self-recorded and published that can potentially be used for social science research either with or without explicit permission, given the information has been made public (e.g. long-form blogs, CVs and profiles).
5. **Social media data:** Data generated through some public, social process that can potentially be used for social science research either with or without permission (e.g. micro-blogging platforms such as Twitter and Facebook, and, perhaps, online game data).
6. **Data traces:** Data that is 'left' (possibly unknowingly) through digital encounters, such as online search histories and purchasing, which can be used for social science research either by default use agreements or with explicit permission.
7. **Found data:** Data that is available in the public domain, such as observations of public spaces, which can include covert research methods.
8. **Synthetic data**: Where data has been simulated, imputed or synthesized. This can be derived from, or combined with, other data types.

We utilize this typology further in our discussions below, including the possible overlaps between the data origin types, and how the different types may be used, but we first focus in more detail on the changing nature of the data environment and social science research.

2.2 THE SOCIAL SCIENCE DATA PRESENT

2.2.1 The Data Landscape

It has been clear since the 1980s that the half century either side of the millennium would be characterized by an information revolution (Purdam et al., 2004; Sweeney, 2001). One key aspect of this is the massive increase not just in the amount of data but also in the types of data sources available and in the range of organizations and individuals collecting, storing and using data. For example, it is estimated that in 2014 there are 1.3 billion active Facebook accounts, 0.6 billion active Twitter accounts and 58 million tweets per day (Datablog, 2014).

The growth in different data types, formats and coverage allow new approaches to social science research and evidence-based policy processes. It is perhaps useful to consider an example: the UK government has launched an initiative to measure the nation's happiness and well-being using questions in the Integrated Household Survey.[7] This intentional data gathering sample survey includes questions such as:

How satisfied are you with your life nowadays? How happy did you feel yesterday? How anxious did you feel yesterday? To what extent do you feel the things you do in your life are worthwhile?

---

[7]The Integrated Household Survey combines data collected from the following surveys: General Lifestyle Survey, Living Costs and Food Survey, Opinions Survey, English Housing Survey, Labour Force Survey/Annual Population Survey, Life Opportunities Survey.

The data is collected by professional fieldworkers and the survey takes over a year to complete. The sampling strategy enables inferences to be made to the UK population. At the same time, a university-based project in the UK is measuring happiness by texting a purposive, non-representative sample of volunteers who have signed up to be part of a mobile phone-based study.[8] The participants are asked every few days how they feel on a scale and about who they are with, their location and what they are doing. They are also able to submit a photo should they wish to. From this almost real time and repeated response data, happiness maps can be produced. Other research techniques to measure happiness might be to analyse data from Twitter posts for a sense of happiness or to analyse search engine records for evidence of future planning which can be calibrated as proxies for happiness (again, though, based on non-representative samples). See, for example, Preis et al. (2012) who used Google Trends data in a cross-national study of orientation towards the future and optimism. The self-published, consequential and trace data forms are very different from data gathered as part of random sample surveys. However, all these data and methods for measuring happiness have different explanatory power and value.

The opportunity for social science and policy makers is that citizens are – deliberately or consequentially – creating their own digital archives. This means that data generation with self-published, consequential and trace data is not a distinct (or costly) stage in the research process but is integral to the activity being undertaken. As we discuss below, such data can be collated, visualized and analysed in near real time, and updated continually. Citizens have the tools to document their own lives almost effortlessly and in more detail than ever before through access to monitoring technology and potential access to data about their health, movements and communications. See, for example, the development of so-called life logging and the Quantified Self.[9] Data generation can also take the form of crowdsourced data, where collective intelligence and effort in the form of observations, data preparation tasks, idea generation and individual-level data are deposited and uploaded by volunteers, usually via the internet.[10] Such data can also be collated automatically using software that captures information, including text and images on websites, to build databases. This can include collecting contact information, such as email and postal addresses, to produce samples for more traditional research methods such as surveys.[11]

As social science researchers looking at the wealth of new types of data, we must be mindful of the famous aphorism: 'the medium is the message' (McLuhan, 1964). All data collection instruments, as we consider below, are subjective and performative media (although to differing extents). With the new data sources (and social media sources in particular), this issue is likely to be all the more salient. Social science researchers must be aware that the media and data are mutually embedded in a

---

[8] See www.mappiness.org.uk

[9] See http://quantifiedself.com/about

[10] See, for example, Open Street Map: www.openstreetmap.org

[11] See, for example, https://scraperwiki.com/professional

manner that affects the data we might use. The flip side of this challenge is that the gap between data and subject, between *my-self* and *my-data* or data collected about me, is closing both temporally (data about us is more closely contemporaneous to the activity/behaviour that has generated the data) and ontologically (more and more *the data* and *the activity* are one and the same thing).

So where does this take the social scientist? Is it just more choices about the data to collect, use and link? Or is it more fundamentally a step change in how people's lives are being captured, documented and measured? What challenges are posed, for example, in terms of data access and data quality?

2.2.2 Evolving Traditional Data Types

To understand the changing data environment it is important to begin by reflecting on the expansion and enrichment of so-called orthodox intentional data and, in particular, social surveys. In the UK, longitudinal surveys, including the British Cohort Study,[12] the English Longitudinal Study of Ageing[13] and the Census Longitudinal Study[14] now constitute very rich sources of information for understanding change over decades of people's lives (see also Chapters 4 and 5). International surveys, such as the World Values Survey[15] can provide insights into global opinion. Such surveys and the analyses conducted on them often include contextual data, such as area-level employment rates. The data can be analysed online through tools such as Nesstar.[16] Nesstar allows users to access and analyse archived data, including government survey data such as the Labour Force Survey,[17] the British Social Attitudes Survey[18] and the British Crime Survey.[19] The resource includes information on data origin, sampling and the coding of variables, as well as the original questionnaires. Similar data resources also now exist for qualitative and mixed methods data. Textual data from interviews, focus groups and observational studies can be accessed through, for example, the UK Data Service.[20]

Survey data can be highly detailed and, depending on the sample design, allow inferences to be made to a wider population. However, one of the limitations is the

---

[12]See www.cls.ioe.ac.uk/default.aspx

[13]See www.ifs.org.uk/ELSA

[14]See www.ons.gov.uk/ons/guide-method/user-guidance/longitudinal-study/index.html

[15]See www.worldvaluessurvey.org/wvs.jsp

[16]See nesstar.ukdataservice.ac.uk/webview

[17]See http://ukdataservice.ac.uk/get-data/key-data.aspx

[18]See www.natcen.ac.uk/our-research/research/british-social-attitudes

[19]See www.ons.gov.uk/ons/about-ons/get-involved/taking-part-in-a-survey/information-for-households/a-to-z-of-household-and-individual-surveys/crime-survey-for-england---wales/index.html

[20]See http://ukdataservice.ac.uk

survey process itself in terms of the sample size, usually restricted by cost, which can limit comparisons between areas and groups due to low sample numbers. In addition, response rates can be low, which can introduce bias into the population estimates. The survey questions themselves can also have limitations in terms of constrained responses and self-reporting bias. The latter is where respondents give an answer they feel is expected, rather than what they really think. Moreover, there is also a well-established gap between reported attitudes and what people actually do in practice, and indeed between what people say they do and what they actually do (see De Vaus, 2002; Blasius and Thiessen, 2012).

Secure data that is not regarded as suitable for widespread, unregulated public use can be analysed in so-called 'safe settings' to ensure there are no risks to confidentiality (see, for example, the UK Secure Data Service,[21] the HM Revenue and Custom's (HMRC) Data Lab[22] and the Ministry of Justice (MoJ) Data Lab[23]). The Secure Data Service allows access to individual-level data that is more detailed than that available under standard licensing (such as smaller geographic areas) and so provides potentially richer sources of evidence for social science research. The user analyses the data remotely rather than downloading it. The analytical outputs are then checked by the data provider. The conditions of use are based on licensing agreements with users as well as user accreditation, individual training and trust. HMRC's data lab allows access to individual tax records but requires users to do so at the HMRC's premises under controlled conditions. As part of the MoJ Data Lab, organizations that work with offenders can now apply for their offender data to be linked to the MoJ re-offending data. It is stated that MoJ analysts will prepare a report detailing the re-offending rates against a matched control group of offenders with similar characteristics, together with a conclusion on whether the service provided by the organization is associated with a change in re-offending behaviour. Compared to this, as we discuss below, the infrastructure and guidance for accessing and using new types of data such as Twitter and blogs are not well established but are developing.

The growing access to official administrative records of public service use also includes, for example, patient health records and school performance records through such initiatives as the UK Administrative Data Liaison Service (ADLS).[24] These consequential data sources are, in theory, complete rather than being based on samples and can be of great value given their detail and coverage. However, like all datasets there are likely to be issues of missing data that the social science researcher needs to be aware of, including individuals who have not been traced or recorded. There are also likely to be duplicate records. We discuss an example of this in Chapter 3. Access to specific variables can also be restricted and the coverage, of course, is limited to the variables collected as part of the administration process and the time point of the

---

[21]See http://securedata.data-archive.ac.uk

[22]See www.hmrc.gov.uk/datalab

[23]See www.justice.gov.uk/justice-data-lab

[24]See www.adls.ac.uk

data collection. As a result there are limitations on the number of research questions that can be addressed.

Research access to this kind of administrative data is part of the UK Government's drive towards Open Data, whereby government departments and agencies are being required to provide greater access to service use and performance data for the purposes of transparency and accountability (Open Public Services White Paper, 2011).[25] For an overview see Halford et al. (2013), Wind-Cowie and Lekhi (2012) and Shakespeare (2013). As well as providing an alternative to orthodox intentional data, administrative data also expands the range of available information. The use of such data is likely to be new to many social scientists and its properties, coding frames and terms of use can be very different and may require the acquisition of new skills, alongside new knowledge or greater interdisciplinary working. Nevertheless, it is notable that in a recent survey of over 300 (self-selected) social science researchers, nearly two-thirds had used administrative data in their research (Elliot et al., 2013), although a similar proportion (61 per cent) reported encountering barriers when trying to access such data.

2.2.3 Innovations in Linking Data

Methodologically, there are increasing opportunities to address research questions by data linking using statistical matching and drawing on multiple data sources. Well known examples of this include: the linking of hospital data to the Millennium Cohort Study[26] (see Calderwood, 2007); the Work and Pensions Longitudinal Study (WPLS)[27] which links benefit and programme information held by the Department of Work and Pensions (DWP) with employment, earnings, savings, tax credit and pension records from HMRC; and the Longitudinal Study of Young People in England (LSYPE),[28] which links annual survey data to data from the School Census[29] (as discussed below).

The methodology of data or record linking can be simply one of matching record numbers between multiple sources but can also be probability based. This involves linkages based on similar characteristics as opposed to unique identifiers. Computational statistical techniques are involved in optimizing record matching rules and weighting different variables in the matching process. Data preparation is a key stage of this research design. Account needs to be taken of missing data and data entry errors and quality assurance procedures need to be put in place. For further discussion see Herzog et al. (2007).

---

[25]See http://data.gov.uk/ and also the Open Data Institute www.theodi.org

[26]See www.cls.ioe.ac.uk/default.aspx

[27]See www.adls.ac.uk/dwp

[28]See www.education.gov.uk/ilsype/workspaces/public/wiki/Welcome

[29]See www.gov.uk/government/collections/school-census

It is argued that data linkage can be cost saving and enable analyses to be conducted that would otherwise not be possible or would involve further primary data gathering. Best practices for linking data and the research and ethical issues raised are slowly being developed. A key aspect of this is the terms of use of the different data sources. Some surveys now ask for the respondent's permission for the anonymous use of their responses for the purposes of linking with other datasets. Examples include the National Survey of Wales and the Scottish Longitudinal Study. The UK's Economic and Social Research Council is presently reviewing the area of data access and linkage as part of its Administrative Data Task Force (see Boyle, 2012).[30] The International Health Data Linkage Network is a useful information resource on linked data.[31] For further discussion see Gill (2001), Herzog et al. (2007), Mason and Shihfen (2008) and Chapter 3 in this volume.

2.2.4 Freedom of Information Requests for Social Research

In the UK, legislation has also made public sector information increasingly available for transparency and accountability purposes and potentially for social science research. Under the *Freedom of Information Act 2000* (FOI), requests for detailed records of what we term consequential data held by public bodies can be made. Unless there is good reason not to, the organization holding the data must provide the information within 20 working days.[32] Accepted reasons for refusal include cost, whether the request is vexatious, and if it would prejudice a criminal investigation. The legislation has been widely used to examine transparency in government. Thousands of requests have been made since the introduction of the act, including many in areas that social science research has a track record of examining, such as government decision-making and public spending. Access to this type of data has facilitated research breakthroughs in these areas including, notably: information on MP's expense claims, records of donations to political parties, extent of care home abuse allegations, detention of children in police cells, links between police forces and commercial companies, police work force demographics and gambling spending levels. However, as reported in Lee (2005), the majority of such requests are not for what might be considered standard social science research purposes. Nevertheless, some examples in the UK context include: local authority data on business cases for new schools (Khadaroo, 2008), Ministry of Defence medical data (Seal, 2006), Department of Health data on drug addiction policy (Mold and Berridge, 2007) and police force crime data (Hutchings et al., 2006). It is notable that as of 2013 new regulations relating to open data rights require data released under FOI requests to be prepared in reusable formats, and that the regulations also allow for the data to be used commercially.[33]

---

[30]See www.esrc.ac.uk/_images/ADT-Improving-Access-for-Research-and-Policy_tcm8-24462.pdf

[31] See www.ihdln.org

[32]See www.ico.gov.uk/for_organisations/freedom_of_information/guide/refusing_a_request.aspx

[33]See www.ico.org.uk/news/blog/2013/freedom-of-information-the-next-generation

2.2.5 Commercial Data Sources and Providers

In parallel to these developments, commercial data companies are increasingly providing highly detailed, individual-level information products combining different types of data, including intentional, consequential, trace and synthetic data. The information can include such details as: name, address, full postcode, age, gender, income, occupation, number of children, household income, house type, tenure, education, consumption, length of residence, car ownership, insurance packages, ownership of ICT products, holidays, smoking, leisure activities and social attitudes[34] (Purdam et al., 2004).

Such data is compiled from different sources, including: surveys; warranty forms where citizens agree to the shared use of their details; public records; administrative records such as the Electoral Register and house sale information; and consumption records. Whilst some of this information may be considered personal, it has already been in the public domain in some form or permission for use has been given at origin (see Elliot et al., 2013).

Where information is missing in these commercial data products, it is often imputed or simulated from other data subjects with similar characteristics. Attitude profiling is also used where demographic information is missing. This involves profiling individuals by combining responses to multiple attitudinal questions. These imputation processes can lead to questions of data accuracy. However, there is only limited research in this area. These commercial data sources are available with short lead times and techniques have been developed to combine different types of data often involving large numbers of individuals and variables. Individual record data matched to postcodes and/or individual names can be purchased at relatively low cost.

Commercial data product suppliers are also now providing access to social media data including Twitter posts and analysis of such sources as YouTube, long-form blogs and Facebook, as well as data from online game playing. It is to these types of data we now turn, including what we consider consequential, self-published and trace data.

2.2.6 New Data Types and Approaches

Social media is increasingly seen as an invaluable source of data for social research. Research use of social media data might involve the textual analysis of micro-blogs such as Twitter to code for attitudes (see Chapter 8), explore networks (see Chapter 10) and contextual patterns, and to track movements using user name, time of posting, geography and network links (see Chapter 9). An example of this, which we consider in more detail in Chapter 3, was the collection and coding of 2.6 million Twitter postings during the civil disturbances in England in 2011. The data was used to examine patterns of communication during the riots and content analysis of rumour patterns (see Lewis et al., 2011; Procter et al., 2013a; 2013b). A second example of social media data use involves a study of videos posted on YouTube in response to the release of a film criticizing Islam.

---

[34]See, for example, the Smart Steps service: http://blog.digital.telefonica.com/?press-release= telefonica-dynamic-insights-launches-smart-steps-in-the-uk

The analysis involved examining the nature and content of comments and the links to other uploaded videos and postings to map the scale of the protests and the nature of the dialogue (Van Zoonen et al., 2011). Other studies have examined the nature of political protest by examining online postings and discussions; see, for example, Bowman-Grieve and Conway's (2012) research into dissident Irish Republicanism.

Social media data can also be used in a more exploratory way for social science research. For example, purposive sampling techniques can support the development of research ideas and the testing of concepts. A recent example of such an approach, entitled *The Everyday Sexism Project,* involved the development of a website where the public were invited to report experiences of sexism (Bates, 2014).[35] The data has strengths and weaknesses. It provides an insight into, and examples of, reported sexual harassment. However, the sample is limited. There is no verification and there can be no straightforward extrapolation to provide a measure of prevalence, though the evidence suggests prevalence is significant. A more robust research design might ask respondents to report key demographics, change over time and to describe how their experiences compare with those of people they know in their social networks.

Another functional difference of many of the new data types is that the data is often generated directly by individuals and organizations themselves for their own purposes. A recent example of what we term self-generated data involves a UK police force using Twitter to announce all the emergency calls it received in order to high-light their work over a given period.[36] This constitutes a potentially rich source of data for social science research, produced not via a traditional social science research design but self-reported by an organization. We consider this type of data in more detail below.

The United Nations is embracing the potential of digital evidence in relation to human rights and also examining policy impacts in almost real time.[37] This can take the form of: monitoring food price discussions, money transfer patterns via mobile phone, or tracking health concerns expressed through Twitter or captured in Internet search records. Such techniques can include feedback loops where people's attitudes and behaviour can be followed up. The data can be used to conduct almost real time research. However, data quality assessment practices need to be used and the verification of data still needs to take place. Quality assurance mechanisms are being developed which involve volunteers validating data.

There is a link here to what is termed citizen science and crowdsourcing, whereby people voluntarily allow the collation of their own data, or contribute data that they gather themselves, and also undertake data processing and coding. Data is being generated by citizens not only about themselves but also about issues they might have an interest in. For example, in the Satellite Sentinel Project, citizens are being asked to

---

[35]See www.everydaysexism.com/; www.bbc.co.uk/news/uk-21520385

[36]See http://technorati.com/social-media/article/uk-police-in-twitter-experiment

[37]See www.unglobalpulse.org

volunteer to observe and code images for evidence of human rights abuses (e.g. military activity or signs of explosions) in Sudan sourced from a network of private satellites.

In the changing data environment, there are increasingly detailed records of actual behaviour accumulating alongside survey data on people's reported behaviour, and there is scope for reporting and monitoring behaviour in almost real time to complement more traditional social science research data gathered retrospectively through surveys, interviews and diaries. For example, purchase data collected by supermarkets could be used alongside food diaries; mobile phone movement data could be used alongside self-recorded time use data; and health monitoring data could be used alongside surveys of people's self-reported health.

The step change for social science research lies in the potential, where appropriate, for identifying and bringing together the different data types described in our eight-point typology: orthodox intentional data, participative intentional data, consequential data, self-published data, social media data, trace data, found data and synthetic data. Synthetic data can be used as part of simulation and agent-based studies. For an example, see the recent UK project on the Social Complexity of Diversity, which uses computer-based simulations, and Chapter 6 in this volume.[38]

Moreover, almost real time data opens up opportunities for what may be termed 'real time' or 'live' social science, though this clearly challenges standard practices and timescales in research for data quality assurance and for peer review.

2.3 COMBINING DATA AND MIXED METHODS – KEY RESEARCH AREAS

A useful way to examine and understand the new types of data in context is by comparison with existing forms of social science research data. Through a series of broad social science research policy areas, we will now consider some orthodox intentional data sources and research designs (such as social surveys) and identify other new data sources that might be used in combination with them as part of mixed methods studies. We compare different types of variables in each of the key areas. In doing so, we will use the UK as an example country, whilst acknowledging that data environments vary across countries and that some data sources transcend national boundaries.

2.3.1 Data on Economic Circumstances

Key sources for capturing data on people's economic circumstances in the UK include the Census[39] and the Labour Force Survey (LFS).[40] The Census provides a profile of

---

[38]See http://scid-project.org/about/summary

[39]See www.ons.gov.uk/ons/guide-method/census/2011/index.html

[40]See www.ons.gov.uk/ons/about-ons/get-involved/taking-part-in-a-survey/information-for-households/a-to-z-of-household-and-individual-surveys/labour-force-survey/index.html

the UK population every 10 years. It collects information on people's employment, health and family circumstances. It is a key tool in estimating population change. Data from the Census is available in summary tables as well as in samples of microdata. Specific data tables can also be requested for an administration fee. The questions on economic circumstances are, however, limited. It is notable that it is anticipated that the 2011 Census will be the last full census in the UK and there will be a shift in the future to smaller-scale data gathering and use of administrative records.[41]

The LFS is a quarterly survey of over 60,000 households. The LFS is now linked with the UK Annual Population Survey and includes increased coverage of urban areas down to local authority district level. The data includes a longitudinal component, with respondents being interviewed five times at three-monthly intervals. Questions cover such variables as people's key demographics and occupation, training, health, earnings and benefit claims. Some of the measures are internationally comparable. Access to the data from such surveys as the LFS is often free (although usage is not completely unrestricted).

For many survey datasets, access to particular variables, geographic levels and detailed information is restricted because of concerns about confidentiality and statistical disclosure risks.[42] For example, only samples of UK Census data and certain variable codings are released at particular geographic levels. This can inhibit analysis at lower geographies. For some government surveys and datasets, special licence use versions are available which contain more detailed variable codings and geographic information.

Other sources of data on people's economic circumstances include income data available from commercial data providers. The data is updated from different sources, including surveys and other data gathering tools such as product warranty forms. Such data provides income estimates at the individual level, though these are often imputed. Many of the variables have bounded values, for example, age and income are in bands. Other variables cover people's spending, savings and debts.

Consequential data, such as administrative data, including information on earnings, tax payments and benefits claims, are held by government departments and, if not released directly, can be available for social science research purposes under special agreements. Some commercial information is also available in the public domain. For example, organizations such as estate agents necessarily release data on properties on their books as part of their core business. If made available for research purposes, data from the Citizens Advice Bureau (CAB), and agency and bank consultations concerning debt advice, which includes anonymized client details, type of problem, advice given and outcomes, could also be examined alongside publicly available data from land records and on share ownership.

Open data resources such as OpenStreetMap[43] can be used to map areas of deprivation and can be combined with official data such as the ONS Neighbourhood Statistics.[44] For research into the impact of the economic recession on people's lives,

---

[41]See www.ons.gov.uk/ons/about-ons/what-we-do/programmes---projects/beyond-2011/index.html

[42]See Duncan et al. (2011) for a recent review of this topic.

[43]See www.openstreetmap.org/#map=5/54.910/-3.432

[44]See www.neighbourhood.statistics.gov.uk/dissemination

consequential data from Internet searches for credit advice and locations of cash conversion shops could be of value. Self-published data such as online discussion groups and forums could be used for examining people's attitudes towards the recession and their coping behaviour. For example, the online network and web resource Mumsnet, which is a self-selected online network of parents, has a large number of postings from its members on the recent economic recession. In addition, the organization itself has conducted a survey of its members on the issue of household spending. Example (anonymised) Mumsnet discussion group comments include:

> I have to cook on a very tight budget so when I go shopping I go straight to the reduced selection and always stock up with as much reduced food as possible and either cook it that night and freeze it down, or freeze it straight away. That way my family can eat very healthy for a fraction of the price. ('TAM', 2011)[45]

Here, the social science researcher might code for key information, as they would do in a conventional qualitative textual analysis. This might include coding for: gender, type of food planning, attitude to cooking, healthy eating and family, language use, and comment length. Links to other posts might also yield even richer data. The researcher could also take a direct follow-up approach including posting messages to the online group, collecting information using methods such as purposive surveys, follow-up interviews and online discussions (effectively purposive online focus groups). The key challenge here in terms of social science research lies in the purposive nature of the samples and the limits to what can be claimed about any patterns identified in such self-published data.

Closely linked to data on people's economic circumstances is evidence on people's consumption behaviour and we now consider this.

2.3.2 Data on Consumer Behaviour

In the UK, a key survey of consumer behaviour and household spending is the Family Resources Survey (FRS),[46] which is a continuous survey with an annual target sample size of 24,000 private households. The survey began in 1992. Households interviewed in the survey are asked a wide range of questions about their key demographics and their circumstances (including receipt of welfare benefits, housing costs, assets and savings). An end-user licence version of the data with reduced detail is available via download from the UK Data Service. A special licence version of the FRS is available to approved researchers via the Secure Data Service as described above. The special licence version includes additional variables and increased detail on some variables, particularly geographic location.[47] Access to such data is free or available for a minimal administration fee.

---

[45]See www.netmums.com/family-food/guide-to-cooking-on-a-budget/cooking-on-a-budget

[46]See www.gov.uk/government/collections/family-resources-survey--2

[47]See www.esds.ac.uk/findingData/snDescription.asp?sn=4803

Real time consumption data (a type of consequential data) is also now collated by online companies and supermarkets via loyalty cards. Such data are held on restricted access databases; however, samples have been made available for social science researchers.[48] The data are of considerable commercial value to the companies and organizations that collect and warehouse them. Alongside individual records of behaviour, data mining techniques can be used to identify associations and patterns in the data. For example, the company Dunnhumby works closely with supermarkets and other retailers examining purchasing patterns in order to target marketing and product range, and optimize the personalization of consumer experience.[49] Consumer profiling organizations such as CACI provide data products that contain hundreds of individual-level variables including income, spending, media consumption and types of leisure activities.[50] As outlined above, these data products link multiple sources including: surveys, product warranty forms, public records, administrative records such as the Electoral Register, house sale information and consumption records.

Online search engines such as Google and retailers such Amazon collate search patterns and profile customers by page visits and purchases. Samples of this data (for example, Google Trends and Google Analytics) are made available either freely or for purchase. In terms of administrative records, government departments hold consequential data on benefits claims and payments at the individual level. This could, in principle, be combined with survey data to research patterns in consumer behaviour. Such databases can be so large that the importance of making inferences from a sample to a population is of less concern for certain types of research.

2.3.3 Data on Health and Well-being

The Health Survey of England (HSE)[51] and the English Longitudinal Study of Ageing (ELSA)[52] are two key surveys for examining health outcomes. The HSE is a representative survey of around 15,000 adults and children in England. It combines data on attitudes towards health, eating and exercise with physiological data. Core topics include: general health, smoking, drinking, fruit and vegetable consumption, height, weight, blood and saliva samples. Special topics include: cardiovascular disease, physical activity, accidents, lung function measurement, blood pressure and certain blood components. The data is geo-coded to Government Office Region (GOR) level.

ELSA is a longitudinal survey of around 11,000 people aged 50+ in England, which began in 2002. It includes information on key demographics, income, health

---

[48]Though evidence suggests that this access is reliant on established relationships between commercial organizations and academics (Elliot et al. 2013).

[49]See www.dunnhumby.com

[50]www.caci.co.uk

[51]See data.gov.uk/dataset/health_survey_for_england

[52]See www.ifs.org.uk/ELSA

and cognitive function. Both HSE and ELSA data are freely available and more detailed versions including additional variables and more detailed geographic information are available as restricted access via the Secure Data Service under strict terms of use.

Other sources of health data include consequential data such as General Practitioner (GP) prescribing records. The ADLS is facilitating access to such data by building links with data holders, developing standards and good practice for data sharing and providing training for researchers in safe handling, analysis and publication from such data.[53] Real time prescription data would be a very powerful tool for mapping changes in health and well-being.

The UK Biobank has collated for research purposes genetic and other physiological and behaviour data donated by over half a million citizens for research purposes.[54] Genomic data are a potentially invaluable research tool for the social sciences as well as health sciences. This includes studies where researchers use surveys of twins to try to identify the impacts of both contextual and inherited covariates. For example, research by Sturgis et al. (2010), which involved combining attitude data and physiological information, examined the genetic basis for social trust. In the Millennium Cohort Study,[55] the collection of DNA from data subjects linked to the survey data is becoming more common. This resource has great potential as it allows the possibility of tracking genetic and environmental influences across the life course. As well as these intentional research resources, several commercial DNA profiling organizations have been set up, for example, Britain's DNA, where the public are asked to donate a DNA sample.[56]

Other sources of health data include data traces of online searches recording patterns of health-related queries. Though there is some debate about the accuracy of such methods, the content of tweets and volumes has been shown to be of value in monitoring the spread of flu outbreaks,[57] as have Wikipedia searches (see Ortiz et al., 2011; McIver and Brownstein, 2014).

Similarly, social media postings on health forums can also be collated and analysed. For example, in this anonymized Mumsnet post, a contributor seeks advice about what to do about a potential case of flu:

Not sure if this is just a bad cold or something worse but daughter and I both have it and husband, who's had the flu jab, is fine. Is this risky to the baby? Do I go to the GP in the morning? I thought you weren't supposed to go to the GP with flu symptoms in case you spread it about? Should I look out for reduced movements? argh don't know what I'm supposed to do! Someone please advise as NHS Direct is on a four-hour call back. ('ISS', 2011)

---

[53]See www.adls.ac.uk/safe-researcher-training

[54]www.ukbiobank.ac.uk

[55]See www.cls.ioe.ac.uk/default.aspx

[56]See www.britainsdna.com

[57]See www.google.org/flutrends

Here a social science researcher could code for information including: language, location references, health, flu, use of services, anxiety levels, gender, responsibility for health within the family and health communication issues. The researcher could also look at replies and related posts. Such self-published data are rich in detail and of great potential value in providing examples of individual experiences. Innovation in research design and sampling techniques could aid the development of research that could go beyond qualitative data and individual stories.

It is notable that in health research, crowdsourced data gathering techniques have also been used as part of structured research projects. Examples include researchers using social media to identify people with specific diseases and using online discussion groups to identify examples of side effects of particular drugs. People identified in this way may then be asked to take part in follow-up studies. These developments have been described as akin to an *eBay for health research*, where researchers seek to recruit participants or where people might put themselves forward for participation in studies (Swan, 2012).[58] For health research, a link could also be made to administrative data and FOI requests, such as for data held on government meeting notes in relation to disease monitoring and decisions on vaccination programmes and drug stock piling.

2.3.4 Data on Education, Training and Employment

Key data sources in the UK for examining patterns in education and training include the Census and the Labour Force Survey as discussed above. The cohort studies in the UK also provide access to information on education and training and its role in people's lives in the longer term. There are three large UK cohort studies, which each include over 17,000 people in their samples: the 1958 National Child Development Study (NCDS), the 1970 British Cohort Study (BCS) and the Millennium Cohort Study (MCS).[59] Participants are surveyed usually every 6–8 years, although the MCS is surveying at higher frequency during the early years. Each of these studies includes questions on family background, education, socio-economic circumstances, attitudes, life transitions and health. Both the 1958 cohort and the 1970 cohort are now very rich data sources with detailed information on substantial periods of people's lives. Access to such data is free.

The Longitudinal Study of Young People in England[60] includes questions on key demographics and covers such issues as school course options, extra-curricular classes, parental expectations and aspirations, household responsibilities, resources, absences, truancy, police contact and bullying.

Consequential administrative record data are also available for examining qualification levels of school pupils. The School Census[61] is an annual exercise collated from UK school records. As well as school performance scores, the data includes information

---

[58]Also see www.diygenomics.org/; http://genomera.com

[59]See www.cls.ioe.ac.uk/default.aspx

[60]See www.education.gov.uk/ilsype/workspaces/public/wiki/Welcome

[61]See www.gov.uk/government/collections/school-census

on each pupil's: home postcode, school name, Free School Meal (FSM) entitlement, Special Educational Needs (SEN) status, gender, ethnicity and mother tongue. Access to such data is free, though researcher approval is required and the data have to be used under certain confidentiality conditions.

Other sources of data on education, training and employment might include: online discussion boards of career changes, training feedback, returning to work and individuals searching for work who create their own blogs. One anonymous example reads:

> Hard working 19 year old farm worker looking for work placement on a mixed farm to progress onto an advanced apprenticeship level 3 ideally in the South/SW. (Anonymous, 2011)

Here a social science researcher could code for: type of job, age, gender and geography as well as language use and skills. They could also follow the blogger's Twitter feed to see if the person's circumstances change. Of course, as discussed in Chapter 12 (section 12.6), this does raise ethical issues concerning identification and disclosure. An anonymous example from a discussion forum reads:

> The chances of getting another job with a company that will allow me to work part time and are understanding of the caring issues (so emergency time off when carers don't come) is zero. And I am 45. (Anonymous, 2011)

A social science researcher could code for: age, caring roles, type of employment desired as well as linking with other posts. The data has similarities with 'vox pop' interviews where there is no structured sample frame. But the nature of social media provides the tools for follow-up contact, and linking to other information and sources. However, as has been outlined above, without a sample frame the value of such data is predominantly in terms of the details of individual experiences rather than as a basis for generalizing to a wider population. Moreover, blog posts need to be checked for being accurate representations, as far as that is possible.

2.3.5 Data on Public Attitudes

Many surveys in the public and private sector collect data on the attitudes of the UK population. A key source is the annual British Social Attitudes survey,[62] which began in 1983. It captures the views of a representative sample of around 3,000 people. Alongside key demographics, questions cover a huge range of topics including: public expenditure, welfare benefits, health care, childcare, poverty, the labour market and the workplace, education, charitable giving, the countryside, transport and the environment, the European Union, economic prospects, ethnicity, religion, civil liberties and immigration. Access is free.

Longitudinal surveys are powerful tools for examining people's attitudes over time. The British Household Panel Survey (BHPS) can capture changing attitudes over time. The BHPS began in 1991, initially covering around 10,000 individuals

---

[62]See www.natcen.ac.uk/our-research/research/british-social-attitudes

in over 5,000 households across Great Britain. In 2009, it was absorbed into the Understanding Society panel survey.[63] Alongside the attitudinal data there is information covering: key demographics, employment, socio-economic circumstances, residential mobility, marital and relationship history, and social support. Some of the measures are comparable across equivalent European surveys.

Internationally, the European Social Survey[64] and the World Values Survey[65] provide access to data on public attitudes over 200 countries (see also the European Union Survey on Income and Living Conditions[66]). Again, access is free though a registration fee can be required.

Commercial organizations also conduct on-demand surveys, which include online panels. YouGov[67] is an online opinion-polling organization, which uses signed-up panel members to respond to surveys in return for a small fee. Surveys can be commissioned and completed within 24 hours. There is no limit to the type of issue the survey can cover. Summary findings from previous surveys are sometimes made available via the YouGov website. The data is not available publicly but researchers can commission surveys and have targeted access to particular sample populations in the panels. YouGov have carried out quality assurance of the accuracy of their estimates using their large-scale self-selected panels compared to random sample surveys.[68]

Other sources of attitude data include social media such as Twitter and blog postings. Twitter data, both almost real time and archival, is available free only within certain limits, above which it must be purchased from Twitter or from approved secondary suppliers. However, as well as there being limits on the number of tweets that can be harvested, individual tweeters' demographic information is often incomplete. Techniques are being developed to extract and collate demographic information from social media data and profiles (McCormick et al., 2011). Lots of other metadata can be hugely valuable, such as location, language and numbers and names of people they are following and being followed by. Such data has multiple potential uses beyond just the content of the particular tweet. In terms of attitudes, the coding of tweets and re-tweets and Internet search engine terms for attitudes and meaning can be of considerable value.

Blogging, Twitter accounts and websites can be automatically scraped using software and so-called web bots deployed online for collecting self-published attitudinal data. A recent online discussion in relation to the 2014 vote on Scottish Independence reads:

---

[63]See www.understandingsociety.ac.uk/about

[64]See www.europeansocialsurvey.org

[65]See www.worldvaluessurvey.org/wvs.jsp

[66]See www.cso.ie/en/silc/abouttheeu-silc

[67]See http://yougov.co.uk

[68]It is notable that YouGov is also developing a sample frame of Twitter users linked with panel members.

Personally I cannot see how breaking up the union right now can be a good thing. For example, SNP have said they will join the Euro 'when the time is right' which currently is probably never. In which case they will continue to use the pound and therefore have to accept that interest rates would be set in London. In addition, there's no such automatic right of Scotland joining the EU. Again the SNP have said they are 'confident' that they would start talks from within, but what does that mean? What if they are wrong? Seems like an awfully big risk to me. It seems to me like Salmond is light on the details and the devil as we all know is in the details. (Anonymous, 2011)

In social science research terms the text could be coded for key variables including: gender, values, political knowledge and also linked to other posts. Language use and framing could also be analysed. Again, this data could be combined with traditional social science research tools, by gathering follow-up contact data and inviting authors of posts to participate in a more formal social science research study.

A key data quality concern here is the issue of fake and multiple Twitter accounts and Facebook accounts[69, 70] (including the reported commercial market in creating and managing accounts[71]). In addition, there is the more substantive issue of the differences between people's real life identities (that is, their socio-physical identities) and their online identities. This may be particularly problematic in relation to attitudinal data as attitudinal presentation could well be a key part of constructing an online persona. However, no reliable data exists on the prevalence of this phenomenon or how it impacts on the 'real' attitudinal data. There are some parallels here with the challenges of what is termed performance in existing social research methods, such as where a respondent provides an answer that they think the interviewer wants to hear, and issues around satisficing where a respondent chooses not to express a particular view and/or gives what they see as a socially acceptable response. For further discussion of data quality in survey research see Blasius and Thiessen (2012).

2.3.6 Data on Social Behaviour

Increasingly, social science research is attempting to analyse people's actual behaviour alongside self-reports of their behaviour. In part, this is driven by

---

[69]See Facebook (2012) Annual Report www.sec.gov/Archives/edgar/data/1326801/0001193125 12325997/d371464d10q.htm#tx371464_14

[70]According to the BBC, Facebook has more than 83 million illegitimate accounts. See www.bbc.co.uk/news/technology-19093078

[71]See Ding, J. (2013) 'Twitter underground economy still going strong'. www.net-security.org/article.php?id=1859. Also see 'Twitter Bot Tests Limits of Social Authenticity', Social Media Today. www.socialmediatoday.com/content/twitter-bot-tests-limits-social-authenticity. See also the development of so-called 'click farms'. Aurther, C. (2013) 'How low-paid workers at 'click farms' create appearance of online popularity'. *Guardian*, August 2013 www.theguardian.com/technology/2013/aug/02/click-farms-appearance-online-popularity

evidence that respondents often misreport their behaviour. For example, many more people will state when asked that they voted in an election than actually did (Pattie et al., 2004) and many more report that they recycle household waste than actually do in practice (Whitmarsh, 2009). This might be a result of recall failure, or of social desirability bias reflecting perceptions of the civic duty to vote or be environmentally friendly.

As we have outlined above, there are different types of data sources that capture actual behaviour and data relating to real time activity is of great potential value here. For example, in relation to well-being and health, consequential data such as consumption information and administrative records of gym attendance and mobile tracking data on individual movement and exercise can be used. Mobile application data can also track social network activity. See, for example, Bucicovschi et al. (2013) who used data provided by the communications company Orange to map connections between 1216 cell phone towers. The volume of calls passed from one tower to the next revealed 'communities' and who talks to whom. Not all such data are easily available for social science research, however, and access is often reliant on effective partnerships between researchers and data holders in the private sector.

We consider a hypothetical example of how such a joined-up data approach may be designed. A social science researcher interested in anti-social behaviour has a range of possible data sources to use. They could combine consequential administrative data on anti-social behaviour with intentional data from the British Crime Survey. They might also analyse social media data from police forces and officers. As mentioned above, a police force recently posted tweets of all incidents dealt with in a 24-hour period. Example tweets include:

Call 215 stolen vehicle heading towards Manchester #gmp24 Thursday October 14, 2010 5:03;

Call 216 harassment report in Bolton #gmp24 Thursday October 14, 2010 5:03;

Custody update 101 in police cells at 5 am #gmp24 Thursday October 14, 2010 5:04;

Call 218 neighbour dispute in Wigan #gmp24;

Call 219 nuisance call #gmp24;

Call 220 aggressive shoplifter held at supermarket in Stockport #gmp24.

A social science researcher could code such data for: incident, time, location and language. Follow-up analysis could be conducted in terms of outcome and administrative data on legal prosecution and offender rehabilitation. Qualitative research with people who live in the area and with police officers could also be conducted. Comparisons with other police forces could be made. As outlined above, a multiple data type approach to social science research may create a step change in the explanatory power of research. Other applications for analysing digital data, including social media data, are being developed such as looking at text message and use volumes to anticipate and monitor events and how people are responding to them.

As well as these various forms of data regarding social behaviour, primary intentional type data are increasingly being generated using experimental techniques. These methods involve comparing interventions on test and control groups. The UK Government is pushing forward this approach with its Behavioural Insights initiative (Cabinet Office, 2011). Examples include: the use of information interventions in relation to voting and recycling, public recognition in charitable giving, the use of peer effects in voting and tax payment, and choice framing in relation to organ donation. We consider this kind of data in more detail in Chapter 3.

2.4 RETHINKING DATA – CHALLENGES AND OPPORTUNITIES FOR SOCIAL SCIENCE RESEARCH

New types of data and data gathering are continuing to emerge and will enable new ways of researching social issues, sometimes through links with orthodox intentional data and traditional research designs such as sample surveys. However, these new types of data raise important research design and methodological questions.

Social science should continue to be about testing theories and hypotheses but it needs to embrace the potential value of new sources of evidence and re-evaluate the existing ones. Below we consider some of the emerging opportunities and challenges for social science research.

2.4.1 Researcher/Subject Boundaries

There is a tradition within social science research of involving respondents in the research process and breaking down boundaries between researcher and subject. This tradition has been described as action research and participant research (Bryman, 2013; Emerson et al., 1995; McCall and Simmons, 1969). Here, research is done *with* participants rather than *on* them. Moreover, the research might be led or co-led by a particular interest group, such as service users or organization members.

Extending this, several authors have argued that we are in a time where conventional social science boundaries are being blurred. Elliot (2011) posits that, as the proportion of our lives spent online grows, so the boundary between *data* and *subject* becomes less distinct. In the same sense that a person's real life identity is partially constructed in the memories of others as they interact with him or her, so the person's online self is partially constructed in the data footprints that they leave, intentionally or unintentionally. The activities of others also contribute to constructing these footprints, for example, a photograph of a person might be in the public domain as a result of being posted online by someone else. The photograph might contain identification information and meta-identity information. Given the apparent socio-technical trends, one need not go as far as the Singulatarians (e.g. Kurzweil, 2005) to acknowledge that this transfer of identity is likely to intensify.

Along similar lines, Martin (2012) predicts that the distinction between data and analysis will become less clear. Undoubtedly, as we move from data*sets* to *data streams* and data *arrays,* analytical processes will be less divisible from the data that are analysed. Extending this idea, Perceptual Control Theory (see, for example, Marken, 2010) and its analogues suggest that the data collection-analysis-policy impact workflow could eventually become a closed loop system, even to the extent of policy makers having a 'hands-on' role in its management. So, rather than researchers analysing data and then the results feeding through into policy impact in a lagged and somewhat ad hoc manner, we might envisage researchers-cum-policy analysts directly intervening in social processes using real time data systems as a tool and combining what, in the past, might have been seen as very different data types and different stages of the conventional social research process.

On a more immediate and less speculative note, we observe that as more 'found' data are used in research, the distinction between primary and secondary data itself becomes less consequential. But the use and legal status of any data for social science research needs to be clearly understood by both citizens and researchers alike. There are major data literacy and training issues here that need to be addressed (Elliot et al., 2013). This includes how the new types of data and information may be affecting more traditional data types. For example, how are the ways in which people's attitudes are formulated and expressed changing under the influence of social media?

2.4.2 Data Quality – Reliability, Validity and Generalizability

Data quality is a key issue in any form of social science research. Data quality includes the reliability, validity and completeness of the data. In the rush to use new data there is a risk that the core values of social science, including rigorous research design and hypothesis testing, are put to one side. Orthodox social science research has developed quality control mechanisms over the long term to test the reliability, validity and generalizability of its explanations but at present these mechanisms do not easily extend to many new data types.

Reliability and Validity. A key data quality issue relates to understanding the motivations of the producers of the data and how accurate the data is in relation to its use and the claims that are made from it. For example, a tweet might be generated for fun, to provide information or to persuade or mislead; the motivation obviously affects the meaning of the tweet. With survey data and even, to some extent, administrative data, the impact of respondent motivations is, at least in principle, structured by (or perhaps mediated by) the data collection instrument itself (see Chapter 4). Thus, a well-designed social science research instrument can constrain motivational impact. But this is not so with Twitter data; here people's motivations are given full rein – a tweet might be designed to manipulate or obfuscate, to attract truth or to repel it. It might be designed to fantasize or 'try out an opinion', to provoke a response or simply to create controversy.

As we have outlined above, the issue of the interpretability of tweets is subject to some debate. Verification techniques can be used to check the quality of the data or to profile a person's tweets in order to assess their veridicality and some media are already wise to this.[72] This can involve collating and analysing individual people's tweets over time to look for consistency and changes in attitudes.

Generizability. A common concern for social science researchers is what can be claimed on the basis of the data and, specifically, the question of generalizability. Since the development of sampling theory, more data is not necessarily better in terms of its explanatory power. A good illustration of this is the development of random sample opinion polls, in particular by the Gallup Organization in the USA in the early twentieth century, which led to greater accuracy in estimating. Gallup's market share grew on the basis of better predicting election results on the basis of a random sample survey of several thousand voters compared to a survey of millions of Readers Digest readers in which no particular sampling strategy was in place. In the same way, at present, Twitter data is, at best, only representative of Twitter users (including fake accounts and performative issues) rather than a wider population. As such, depending on the research question, Twitter data can be either very useful or potentially misleading.

A tweet in 2013 by a researcher reads: 'Twitter is of great value to historians as you can analyse and archive public reaction to events'. The question is *which public's reaction?* Estimates suggest that over 7 million adults in the UK (14 per cent) have never used the Internet and this is particularly evident amongst those aged 65 years and over and for those on lower incomes (ONS, 2013; Ofcom, 2010). Only a proportion of Internet users are regular Twitter users (there are 15 million Twitter users in the UK (see Curtis, 2013; Wang, 2013) and hence tweets must be used with great care if bias is to be avoided. Conversely, for a study of young people's attitudes towards drug use, Twitter postings might provide a useful resource for framing a more conventional study involving interviews or a questionnaire survey. Looking forward, it is reported that nearly half of teenagers in the UK have a smart phone and this figure continues to increase (Ofcom, 2011), highlighting that social media usage might become more prevalent in the future.

In this context, orthodox forms of social science data will continue to be important for research questions that rely on statistical inference, for in-depth studies requiring intensive qualitative techniques, and for topics and populations that new types of data and data generation processes do not cover (see Chapter 4). It is important to understand that, even in the age of data, there are still gaps in the evidence base and there is still a need for purpose-specific data and bespoke research design including for hard-to-reach groups. It is also notable that in a recent consultation with over 300 social science researchers in the UK, nearly three quarters thought that methods such as surveys would not be used any less in the future (Elliot et al., 2013).

2.4.3 Data Ownership, Consent and Access

Taking a step back from the core methodological issues, the question of data ownership is another pressing challenge. There is a lack of clarity in the ownership and

---

[72]See, for example, www.mediahelpingmedia.org/training-resources/social-networking/402-trusting-tweets-a-guide-for-journalists

regulation of the use of different types of social media data. Facebook and Twitter postings occur in public but only certain aspects of the resultant data are available to the public.

Twitter claims that tweets are owned by the people who write them, but then treats them collectively as a saleable commodity. There is a process of consent as part of the process of creating a Twitter account. The account holder is prompted that:

> You are responsible for your use of the Services, for any Content you post to the Services, and for any consequences thereof. The Content you submit, post, or display will be able to be viewed by other users of the Services and through third party services and websites (go to the account settings page to control who sees your Content). You should only provide Content that you are comfortable sharing with others under these Terms... You understand that through your use of the Services you consent to the collection and use (as set forth in the Privacy Policy) of this information, including the transfer of this information to the United States and/or other countries for storage, processing and use by Twitter... By submitting, posting or displaying Content on or through the Services, you grant us a worldwide, non-exclusive, royalty-free license (with the right to sublicense) to use, copy, reproduce, process, adapt, modify, publish, transmit, display and distribute such Content in any and all media or distribution methods (now known or later developed). (Twitter, 2013)

Despite these terms of service, it may not be entirely clear to the account holder how their tweets might be used for secondary purposes, including social science research. There is only limited research on how such terms of use compare with other data types and forms of data collection, such as intentional data collected via a survey or the UK Census.

The importance of participant consent and data use protocols are well established in existing social science methods and integral to ethical approval processes (Bryman, 2013). In relation to new types of data, the individuals who, for example, social media data are *about* may not be aware that the data exist or that the data is public and what this means in practice. Even if a person is aware that the data exist, they may not realize that they are being used for secondary purposes (social research or otherwise) and have a commercial value.

Similarly, volunteer and crowdsourced data from observing events may include information on other people taking part in the event. As Gross (2011) argues, the existing frameworks of ethics and particularly informed consent are limited and they need to be overhauled if they are to cope with the scale, intensity and immediacy of the constantly evolving data environment. Such issues are crucial for the ethical development of social science research using new types of data, such as conditional and trace data, and for the effective regulation of uses of the data as the relationships between citizens, state and the commercial sector change (see Chapter 12 for a full discussion). For a discussion of what is termed agile ethics, see Neuhaus and Webmoor (2011) and AOIR (2015) but much more work is needed in this area.

In terms of data access, social media data is held by commercial companies that may choose to sell the data, but are not required to make it freely available for social science research. As Savage and Burrows (2007) have argued, the commercialization of sociology, where the driver is the economic value, could pose a threat to social science research (see also Chapter 13). Specifically, verification, replication and review become much more problematic, as has been found in medical research. To ameliorate these problems, the case needs to be made – probably through government – for regulatory processes guaranteeing researchers' access to new types of data, their provenance, value, validity and reliability, and the analyses and claims made of them. Of course, a key feature is that the data are generated by citizens, and it can be argued that citizens should have some say in their secondary use.

It may well be that we need to move from a milieu of regulated *data protection* to one of policing *data abuse*. Mandatory social science research access by approved researchers would be one mechanism for enacting such a regime. This would not necessarily jeopardize the commercial value of the data to businesses but could be part of a legal and ethical responsibility to the customer and their welfare. In a data abuse framework, one is less concerned about the control of data flows and processes and more with the consequences and specifically harms caused by the actions and choices of individual data processors.

There is an indication of a mobilization in this area, for example, in the work of the Web Science Trust,[73] which is focused on sharing expertise and resources to enable research and understanding of the Web. We consider these developments in more detail in Chapter 3.

2.4.4 Competing Narratives

The new types of data reflect the new reality of the information society and that we are all living interlinked real and virtual lives. The emergence of new data types provides opportunities for new insights and new understandings of what might otherwise be intractable social problems. This can be seen as an opportunity but also a challenge.

Social scientists may face increasing competition to have their findings heard. For example, findings from surveys of public attitudes on particular issues are now competing with the reports of Twitter or blog postings. Each data type has its strengths and weaknesses. However, analysis based on social media data may be produced more rapidly and secure higher profile media coverage than more conventional social science research (with its often lengthy process of design, data collection, preparation, analysis and peer review).

Arguably, social scientists have always been in competition with alternative sources of information about, and explanations of, social phenomena. This

---

[73]See http://wstweb1.ecs.soton.ac.uk

includes journalists, and politicians as well as government department reports. A concern here is the robustness of the evidence base that is being used to inform the claims: it can be based on biased samples, small case studies or personal anecdotes. This might reflect the difference between what a representative survey suggests about what a particular population thinks and 'what a taxi driver thinks' (not an uncommon comment by policy makers) or even what people say to a taxi driver.[74]

The new aspect of this is the scale of the 'what the taxi driver thinks' data now that this can be promulgated through millions of Twitter postings. Where access to social media data is restricted then this denies social science researchers the opportunity to use the data and test the generalizability of findings based on selected posts. Ideally, the data would be available to be used for social science research alongside and in combination with traditional data types. In social sciences, issues of transparency and open data are paramount.

News and media outlets now commonly refer to tweets to exemplify certain opinions or views on an issue. Though this falls a long way short of claiming inference to a population, this is not always made clear. There is a link here to good practices established for journalists when reporting social survey data and the need to include sample size numbers and response rates.[75] As yet, such guidelines are not widely available in relation to the use of social media data.[76] A key principle (which could be at risk in the trend towards data journalism and the pressure for instant analysis and commentary) is that reported results should fairly reflect the data collected.[77] Implementing good practice regarding access and use of new sources of data would imply redesigning data management processes, including the development of reliable methods for coding highly unstructured data.[78] Similarly, new research design and analysis methods will need to be developed and, where the research design requires it, researchers might draw on statistical analysis techniques for non-probability samples, including Bayesian analytical techniques.

Where the data about a population of interest are complete (Mayer-Schönberger and Cukier, 2013), then there is no need for methods based on sampling and inference. However, even in the future this is likely to be limited to certain areas of research. As such, it is important to link our thinking here to well-developed standards in social

---

[74]See www.telegraph.co.uk/news/worldnews/europe/norway/10236246/Norwegian-Prime-Ministers-secret-taxi-shift.html

[75]See, for example, www.britishpollingcouncil.org

[76]Though see the Data Journalism Handbook initiative (Gray et al., 2012).

[77]For further discussion see RCUK Code of Good Practice (2009) and the Research Ethics Guidebook www.ethicsguidebook.ac.uk and www.methods.manchester.ac.uk/resources/ethics/externalguidance/index.shtml

[78]Achieving reliability when coding unstructured data has always been difficult so there is nothing new here, except perhaps that new data sources often generate large quantities of unstructured data.

science research concerning: hypothesis testing, objectivity, metadata, archiving and replication; see Bryman (1998; 2013) for a good overview. To get robust and reliable use out of the new data we need to apply the same principles of rigour as we would to more traditional and established types of data sources: objective research design, data collection, analysis and reporting.

Despite our concerns here, it is clear that the new types of data provide a genuine opportunity for alternative narratives and perspectives to emerge in social science from the changing data environment, as evidence gaps are filled and new evidence is exploited.

2.5 CONCLUSIONS

In this chapter, we have highlighted the wide range of data – both orthodox forms and new data types – that are likely to be used, or considered for use, for social science research in the future. The new data types can track people's daily lives in a more detailed and biographical way than ever before. The potential is that the data retains the strengths of more established forms of quantitative and qualitative data. The risk is that we are distracted by the scale and immediacy of the new data and may lose sight of the carefully constructed and tested rigour of traditional social science research methods.

Within each of the example policy areas we have explored, we note that similar patterns are emerging in the data sources: surveys, cohort studies, administrative data, commercial data, data deriving from new types of media, and trace data. We also note that different data types are now being combined and linked to address particular research questions. The potential of multiple data approaches presents an opportunity for social science research to tackle previously intractable social research questions and to facilitate a closer link to the policy making process by providing results that are grounded in real-world behaviour and delivered in almost real time.

The data identified across the example research areas cuts across all eight data types: orthodox intentional data, participative intentional data, consequential data, self-published data, social media data, trace data, found data and synthetic data. As such data becomes more accessible and the methods for exploiting the data mature, we would expect that selecting and combining data from different parts of the array will increasingly become a routine part of the research process and will transcend traditional divides such as those between qualitative and quantitative methodologies and primary and secondary research and data.[79]

As we have outlined, social science is moving from the idea of *datasets* to *data streams* and *data arrays*. Social science researchers may increasingly use near real time data systems as a tool and combine what, in the past, might have been seen as very different data types. This does not mean it is the end of theory, as has been

---

[79]Tim Berners-Lee has famously predicted that Web 3.0 will be the web of linked data (www.ted.com/talks/tim_berners_lee_on_the_next_web.html). If his prediction is accurate, then we can expect the transformative process we have been describing here – the blurring of traditional social science dichotomies – to intensify further.

debated (Anderson, 2007). Perhaps, more than ever, the testing of theories and hypotheses as a principal of social science research is paramount. Even with inductive techniques such as data mining, theory is still important. Without theory and hypothesis driven research, risks are posed by letting the data lead the research process.

The social and historical evolution of what has been termed the data environment has been, and will continue to be, characterized by a blurring of boundaries between data and subject, between researchers and researched, between research and its impact. In this new challenging context, there is a need to develop a new framework of ethics and good practice for accessing, analysing and archiving such data. This need cuts across society but the social science researchers should be at the forefront of developing and championing this new framework. In the next chapter we examine in more detail the methodological challenges and opportunities of using the new types of data and consider exemplar analyses.

2.6 BIBLIOGRAPHY

Adkins, L. and Lury, C. (2011) 'What is the empirical?', *European Journal of Social Theory*, 12(1): 5–20.

Alasuutari, P., Brannen, J. and Bickman, L. (eds) (2008) *Handbook of Social Research*. London: Sage.

Anderson, C. (2007) 'The end of theory'. *Wired*, Issue 7.

Association of Internet Researchers (AOIR) (2012) 'Ethical Decision-Making and Internet Research: Version 2.0 – Recommendations from the Association of Internet Researchers Working Committee'. Available from http://aoir.org/reports/ethics2.pdf (accessed 06 Dec 2014).

Back, L. and Puwar, N. (2013) *Live Methods*. Oxford: Wiley-Blackwell.

Bates, L. (2014) *Everyday Sexism*. London: Simon and Schuster.

Berners-Lee, T. and Shadbolt, N. (2011) *There's Gold to be Mined from All our Data*. University of Southampton. Available at http://eprints.soton.ac.uk/273090/1/Times%20OpEd%20TBL-NRS%20Final.pdf (accessed 6 Dec 2014).

Blasius, J. and Thiessen, V. (2012) *Assessing the Quality of Survey Data*. London: Sage.

Bowman-Grieve, L. and Conway, M. (2012) 'Exploring the form and function of dissident Irish Republican online discourses', *Media, War and Conflict*, 5(1): 71–85.

boyd, D. and Crawford, K. (2012) 'Critical questions for big data', *Information, Communication and Society,* 15(5): 662–79.

Boyle, P. (2012) *Improving Access for Research and Policy, ESRC*. Available from www.esrc.ac.uk/_images/ADT-Improving-Access-for-Research-and-Policy_tcm8-24462.pdf (accessed 6 Dec 2014).

Bryman, A. (1998) *Quantity and Quality in Social Research*. London: Routledge.

Bryman, A. (2013) *Social Research Methods*. Oxford: Oxford University Press.

Bucicovschi, O., Douglass, R.W., Meyer, D.A., Ram, M., Rideout, D. and Song, D. (2013) *Analysing Social Divisions Using Cell Phone Data*, in Proceedings of the 3rd International Conference on the Analysis of Mobile Phone Datasets (NetMob'13). Boston, MA. Abstract available from www.orange.com/en/about/Group/our-features/2013/D4D/Folder/best-scientific (accessed 02 Feb 14).

Cabinet Office [Behavioural Insights Team] (2011) *Behavioural Insights Team Annual Update 2010–11*. London: Cabinet Office. Available from www.gov.uk/government/

uploads/system/uploads/attachment_data/file/60537/Behaviour-Change-Insight-Team-Annual-Update_acc.pdf (accessed 07 Dec 2014)

Calderwood (2007) 'Methodological challenges in enhancing the MCS through linkage with data from birth registration and centrally collected hospital records', paper presented at *Exploiting Existing Data for Health Research' Conference,* St Andrews, 18–20 September.

Curtis, S. (2013) 'Twitter claims 15m active users in the UK'. Daily Telegraph September 6th 2013 Available from www.telegraph.co.uk/technology/twitter/10291360/Twitter-claims-15m-active-users-in-the-UK.html (01 Dec 2014).

Datablog (2014) Facebook: 10 years of social networking, in numbers. Guardian Datablog February 2014. Available from www.theguardian.com/news/datablog/2014/feb/04/facebook-in-numbers-statistics (01 Dec 2014).

De Vaus, D. (2002) *Surveys in Social Research.* London: Routledge.

Duncan, G., Elliot, M.J. and Salazar-Gonzalez, J.J. (2011) *Statistical Confidentiality.* New York: Springer.

Elliot, M.J. (2011) 'Privacy, identity and disclosure', Keynote talk at The International Conference on Communication, Computing and Security. Rourkela, February 2011.

Elliot, M.J., Purdam, K. and Smith, D. (2008) 'Statistical disclosure control architectures for patient records in biomedical information systems', *The Journal of Biomedical Informatics,* 41: 58–64.

Elliot, M., Mackey, E. and Purdam, K. (2010) *Data Environment Analysis – Annual Report.* London: Office for National Statistics.

Elliot, M.J., Purdam, K. and Mackay, E. (2013) *Linked Data and New Forms of Data For Social Research.* Oxford: OERC Research Report.

Emerson, R.M., Fretz, R.I. and Shaw, L.I. (1995) *Writing Ethnographic Fieldnotes.* Chicago: Chicago University Press.

Gill, L. (2001) *Methods for Automatic Record Matching and Linkage and Their Use in National Statistics,* The National Statistics Methodology Series, ONS. Available from www.ons.gov.uk/ons/guide-method/method-quality/specific/gss-methodology-series/index.html (accessed 08 Dec 2014).

Gray, J., Chambers, L. and Bounegru, L. (2012) *The Data Journalism Handbook. How Journalists Can Use Data to Improve the News.* O'Reilly Media. Available from http://datajournalismhandbook.org (accessed 08 Dec 2014).

Gross, A. (2011) 'The economy of social data: exploring research ethics as device', *The Sociological Review,* 59(2): 113–29.

Halford, S., Pope, C. and Weal, M. (2013) 'Semantic web digital futures? Sociological challenges and opportunities in the emergent semantic web', *Sociology,* 47(1): 173–89.

Herzog, T.N., Scheuren, F.J. and Winkler, W.E. (2007) *Data Quality and Record Linkage Techniques.* New York: Springer.

Hutchings, J., Bywater, T., Davies, C. and Whitaker, C. (2006) 'Do crime rates predict the outcome of parenting programmes for parents of 'high-risk' preschool children?' *Educational and Child Psychology,* 23(2): 15–25.

IBM (2013) *The Four Big Vs of Big Data.* Available from www.ibmbigdatahub.com/infographic/four-vs-big-data (accessed 08 Dec 2014).

ICO [Information Commissioner's Office] (2012) *Anonymisation: Managing Data Protection Risk. Code of Practice.* Available from http://ico.org.uk/for_organisations/data_protection/topic_guides/anonymisation (accessed 12 Dec 2014).

Khadaroo, I. (2008) 'The actual evaluation of school PFI bids for value for money in the UK public sector', *Critical Perspectives on Accountancy* 19(8): 1321–45.

Kurzweil, R. (2005) *The Singularity is Near.* London: Penguin.

Lee, R.M. (2005) 'The UK Freedom of Information Act and social research', *International Journal of Social Research Methodology: Theory and Practice*, 8(1): 1–18.

Lewis, P., Newburn, T., Taylor, M., Mcgillivray, C., Greenhill, A., Frayman, H. and Procter, R. (2011) *Reading the Riots: Investigating England's Summer of Disorder.* London: Guardian Books.

Marken, R.S. (2010) 'Perceptual control theory', *Corsini Encyclopedia of Psychology*: 1–2.

Martin, D. (2012) *Data Technology and Infrastructure.* Data Horizons Worksession, University of Manchester. Unpublished.

Mayer-Schönberger, V. and Cukier, K. (2013) *Big Data: A Revolution That Will Transform How We Live, Work, and Think.* London: Murray.

Mason, C.A. and Shihfen, T. (2008) 'Data linkage using probabilistic decision rules: a primer, birth defects research (Part A)', *Clinical and Molecular Teratology*, 82: 812–21.

McCall, G.J. and Simmons, J.L. (eds) (1969) *Issues in Participant Observation. A Text and Reader.* Reading, MS: Addison-Wesley Publishing.

McIver, D.J. and Brownstein, J.S. (2014) Wikipedia Usage Estimates Prevalence of Influenza-Like Illness in the United States in Near Real-Time, *PLOS Computational Biology*.

McLuhan, M. (1964) *Understanding Media: The Extensions of Man,* 1st Ed. New York: McGraw Hill; reissued by MIT Press, 1994.

McCormick, T., Hedwig, L., Cesare, N. and Shojaie, A. (2011) Using Twitter for Demographic and Social Science Research: Tools for Data Collection. Available from http://paa2013.princeton.edu/papers/130624 (accessed 08 Dec 2014).

Mold, A. and Berridge, V. (2007) 'Crisis and opportunity in drug policy: changing the direction of british drug services in the 1980s', *Journal of Policy History*, 19(1): 29–48.

Neuhaus, F. and Webmoor, T. (2011) 'Agile ethics for massified research and visualization', *Information, Communication & Society,* 1: 1–23.

O'Day, R. and Englander, D. (1993) *Mr Charles Booth's Inquiry: Life and Labour of the People in London Reconsidered.* London: Hambledon.

Ofcom (2010) The Demographics of Internet Access – The Communications Market 2010: UK. Available from www.ofcom.org.uk/static/cmr-10/UKCM-4.16.html (accessed 08 Dec 2014).

Ofcom (2011) A Nation Addicted to Smartphones. Available from http://media.ofcom.org.uk/2011/08/04/a-nation-addicted-to-smartphones/ (accessed 08 Dec 2014).

ONS (2013) *Internet Access Update.* London: Office for National Statistics. Available from www.ons.gov.uk/ons/rel/rdit2/internet-access-quarterly-update/index.html (accessed 06 Dec 2014).

O'Reilly Radar Team (2011) *Big Data Now: Current Perspectives from O'Reilly Radar.* Beijing: O'Reilly.

Ortiz, J.R., Zhou, H., Shay, D.K., Neuzil, K.M. and Fowlkes, A.L. (2011) 'Monitoring influenza activity in the United States: a comparison of traditional surveillance systems with Google flu trends', *PLoS ONE*, 6(4). DOI: 10.1371/journal.pone.0018687

Pattie, C., Seyd, P. and Whitely, P. (2004*) Citizenship in Britain, Values, Participation and Democracy.* Cambridge: Cambridge University Press.

Preis, T., Moat, H.S., Stanley, H.E., and Bishop, S.R. (2012) 'Quantifying the advantage of looking forward', *Scientific Reports*, 2. Article number: 350. DOI: 10.1038/srep00350

Procter, R., Vis, F. and Voss, A. (2013a) 'Reading the riots on Twitter: methodological innovation for the analysis of big data', *International Journal of Social Research Methodology,* 16(3): 197–214.

Procter, R., Crump, J., Karstedt, S., Voss, A., and Cantijoch, M. (2013b) 'Reading the riots: what were the police doing on Twitter?' *Policing and Society,* 23(4): 413–36.

Purdam, K., Mackey, E. and Elliot, M. (2004) 'The regulation of the personal', *Policy Studies,* 25(4): 267–82.

RCUK (2009) Policy and Code of Conduct on the Governance of Good Research Conduct. Available from www.rcuk.ac.uk/RCUK-prod/assets/documents/reviews/grc/RCUKPolicyandGuidelinesonGovernanceofGoodResearchPracticeFebruary2013.pdf (accessed 08 Dec 2014).

Rowntree, S. (1902) *Poverty: A Study of Town Life*. London: Macmillan.

Savage, M. (2009) 'Contemporary sociology and the challenge of descriptive assemblage', *European Journal of Social Theory*, 12(1): 155–174.

Savage, M. and Burrows, R. (2007) 'The coming crisis of empirical sociology', *Sociology*, 41(5): 885–99.

Seal, A. (2006) Correspondence: UK statistical indifference to military casualties in Iraq. *The Lancet* 367 (9520), 29 April 2006–5 May 2006. pp. 1393–4.

Shakespeare, S. (2013) *Shakespeare Review. An Independent Review of Public Sector Information*. London: HM Government. Available from www.gov.uk/government/uploads/system/uploads/attachment_data/file/198752/13-744-shakespeare-review-of-public-sector-information.pdf (accessed 08 Dec 2014).

Stanley, L. (2008) 'It has always known and we have always been "other": knowing capitalism and the "coming crisis" of sociology confront the concentration system and Mass Observation', *Sociological Review*, 56(4): 535–51.

Sturgis, P., Read, S., Hatemi, P.K., Zhu, G., Wright, M.J., Martin, N.G. and Trull, T. (2010) 'A genetic basis for social trust?' *Political Behaviour*, 32: 205–30.

Swan, M. (2012) 'crowdsourced health research studies: an important emerging complement to clinical trials in the public health research ecosystem', *Journal of Medical Internet Research* 14(2): e46. DOI: 10.2196/jmir.1988 (accessed 08 Dec 2014).

Sweeney, L. (2001) 'Information explosion', in P. Doyle, J.I. Lane, J.M. Theeuwes, and L.V. Zayatz (eds), *Confidentiality, Disclosure and Data Access: Theory and Practical Applications for Statistical Agencies*. New York: Elsevier Science. pp.43–74.

Twitter (2013) Terms of Service: https://twitter.com/tos. Accessed 2013.

Van Zoonen, L., Vis, F. and Mihelj, S. (2011) 'YouTube interactions between agonism, antagonism and dialogue: video responses to the anti-Islam film Fitna', *New Media and Society*, 13(8): 1284–1300.

Wang, T. (2013) https://twitter.com/TonyW/status/375889809153462272 (accessed 08 Dec 2014).

Whitmarsh, L. (2009) 'Behavioural responses to climate change: asymmetry of intentions and impacts', *Journal of Environmental Psychology*, 29: 13–23.

Wind-Cowie, M. and Lekhi, R. (2012) *The Data Dividend*. Demos: London.

2.7 ONLINE RESOURCES[80]

Big Data Debate British Academy – www.britac.ac.uk/events/2012/The_Big_Data_Debate.cfm
Google Trends – www.google.com/trends
Methods@Manchester – www.methods.manchester.ac.uk
Nesstar – http://nesstar.esds.ac.uk
Oxford e Research Centre – www.oerc.ox.ac.uk
Oxford Internet Institute – www.oii.ox.ac.uk
Radical Statistics – www.radstats.org.uk
Research Methods Centre – www.ncrm.ac.uk

---

[80]All URLs accessed 17 Dec 2014.

Researching Social Media – http://researchingsocialmedia.org
Social Research Methods – www.socialresearchmethods.net
Survey Network – www.surveynet.ac.uk
Text Mining Centre – www.nactem.ac.uk
UK Data Service – http://ukdataservice.ac.uk

3

EXPLOITING NEW SOURCES OF DATA

MARK ELLIOT AND KINGSLEY PURDAM

3.1 INTRODUCTION

In this chapter we explore a series of case study examples of innovative research design, uses of new types of data, data combination and analysis, and the opportunities and challenges they present for social science research. We are not primarily concerned here with data generation processes such as synthetic data production or simulation. Our focus is on methods and approaches for analysing and combining data rather than methods for creating data, although we acknowledge that such a boundary can be artificial.

As discussed in Chapter 2, data for researching human activity, decisions, preferences and behaviour are being collected and collated as people go about their daily lives. Increasingly, the default setting for a citizen in the information society is to provide, generate and archive data about themselves and others, often by automated processes, such as in the tracking of online behaviour through the storing of digital communications and the location and movement data recorded by mobile phones. As a consequence, for some social science research, the data collection process might no longer be a distinct phase of the research design but an integral part of the activity as it happens. The observer, the observation and the observed continue to merge, but this is not without tensions.

What might traditionally have been labelled social science is now widely practised, with data being collected and social issues being researched by a diverse range of organizations and individuals across different sectors: within academia more disciplines beyond the social sciences are investigating the social; social science research is increasingly being conducted by the private sector; and citizens themselves are also engaging. As a result, the boundary of social science has itself become the subject of debate. As Marres (2012: 143) observes, there has been a 'radical expansion in the range of actors, devices and settings caught up in the recording, reporting and analysis of social life'.

Social science research methods need to be responsive to the immediacy of people's digital lives, the data they produce and the challenges of multiple and sometimes competing vantage points (Savage and Burrows, 2007; Back and Puwar, 2013). For Marres (2012), this heralds the prospect of a 'renaissance' for social science research and a 'redistribution' of social science research methods. New data, new forms of collection and new types of research can test and challenge existing social science research hierarchies, preconceptions, orthodoxies and explanatory frameworks. (See also Boyd and Crawford, 2012; Mayer-Schönberger and Cukier, 2013; United Nations, 2012 for further discussion concerning the possibilities of research using so-called big data.)

At the same time, challenges are presented with respect to data access and validation, and confidentiality and privacy. Whilst there has been a growth in the types and availability of data it does not necessarily mean that more robust research or more evidence-based policy-making will result. The standards and ethics that apply to existing social science research data collection and analysis need to be adapted to new types of data but this poses new challenges. Specifically, there are numerous pressing methodological, ethical, and theoretical questions including: How are research studies being designed around new types of data? What data handling, management and storage good practices are required? Who owns the data and who can have access for social science research purposes? How representative is the data? Can analysis using new data be replicated and findings validated?

In this chapter we examine these questions through a series of illustrative case studies that highlight innovative use of data, methods and techniques, and which demonstrate the opportunities and challenges for social science research presented by new sources of data. The case studies include: attitudinal, behavioural, administrative, communication, movement, crowdsourced and genetic data. We aim to highlight through these case studies examples of the analytical approaches and skills that social science researchers may need in order to make the most of new data sources and types.

3.2 RESEARCH DESIGN, DATA USE AND ANALYSIS – ILLUSTRATIVE CASE STUDIES

The illustrative case studies in this section were selected following a review of social science research methods and on the basis that they provide useful exemplars of using new types of data or new analytical approaches that reflect innovations that go beyond existing methods. We begin by examining a mixed method study of electoral candidate communication during an election.

3.2.1 Case Study 1: Elections, Communication and Campaigning

Responsiveness is a key prerequisite for effective democratic representation. More-over, research by Johnston et al. (2012) has highlighted that the more ways in which people are contacted by a political party the more likely they are to vote for it. In this mixed method study the aim was to examine communication and, in particular, the use of the Internet and social media by electoral candidates during an election. The study focused on the 2010 UK General Election. The research conducted by South-ern (2014) innovatively combined: an online audit of web presence, website use and interactivity, an email response study, and qualitative interviews with electoral can-didates. The study linked data on website interactivity (such as use of blogs and com-ments tools), search engine page rank data, personalized email communication from individual candidates, and administrative data on campaign spending. The research needed to be completed within the four-week time period of the election, which posed considerable data gathering challenges.

As a first step, the websites of all electoral candidates in the sample were identi-fied through a combination of techniques that involved looking at national party home pages and searches using key terms that included the candidate's name, party and constituency. In total, the websites of 2,250 candidates were examined during the first week of the election campaign. A sub-sample of 775 candidates' websites in 172 marginal constituencies was examined in more detail in order to measure the use of Web 2.0 technologies such as blogs, Twitter and YouTube. The websites were coded both in terms of whether they were a standard political party website or if they were a more personalized candidate website, and in terms of interactivity (the extent to which the website facilitated communication and interaction between candidates and the electorate). In addition, Internet search engine rankings were collected to provide an indicator of the public profile, popularity and potential importance of each of the websites. This information was combined with data on gender, age, electoral competiveness, electoral spending, type of constituency and its population, as well as some attitude survey data (for example, candidates' attitudes towards communica-tion with constituents). These other data sources included the Electoral Commission's candidate returns data (Electoral Commission, 2011), the Comparative Candidate Survey (CCS)[1] and the UK Census.[2]

In order to examine the nature of email communications by candidates, a covert research design was implemented to replicate real world conditions. This method enabled the measurement of an electoral candidate's responsiveness to emails and was more robust than simply asking the candidate whether they respond.

Each electoral candidate in the sample of marginal constituencies was sent an email by a hypothetical student voter. The email requested information on the candidate's and their party's policies on employment opportunities for graduates

---

[1]See www.comparativecandidates.org

[2]See www.ons.gov.uk/ons/index.html

and how much personal debt students were facing. The email was drafted in a colloquial style. The candidates' email addresses were gathered from four sources: central party web sites, the candidates' personal websites, social media profiles and address lists online. If all of these sources had been checked and an address still had not been found this was recorded as 'no address'.[3] Of course, it was imperative that the candidates viewed the email as genuine. Candidates' replies were analysed and responses were compared in terms of party, characteristics of candidate, electoral context and response time. Email responses were coded according to a four category scheme: (i) The candidate acknowledged and answered the specific question asked in the email by the hypothetical elector; (ii) They responded with information on a related issue; (iii) A generic, more campaigning style election reply was sent; or (iv) The candidate merely requested the elector's constituency address. The type of email account used by the candidates to respond was also recorded (i.e. whether the email address was a named personal email address or a general party email address).

John Leech MP, Working Hard for South Manchester

Welcome to my website. Here you can find the latest news of my work both in south Manchester and in Parliament. It has details of how to contact me; updates on my latest campaigns and surveys so you can tell me about the important issues locally and nationally.

You can now also read my thoughts on local and national issues on my blog: www.john-leech.co.uk/blog

Kindest regards,

John Leech MP

Local Choice, Local Champion for Manchester, Withington

Liberal Democrat Transport Spokesman

Email Me

John's Blog is here!

YES! TO FAIRER VOTES

Figure 3.1   Example of an electoral candidate's website

---

[3]No email address was found for 20 per cent of candidates in the sample; the searching was very detailed and thorough, going beyond what might be expected of a member of the electorate to undertake if looking for a candidate's email address.

Figure 3.1 shows an example of a candidate's website and the communication tools supported. All the electoral candidates' websites were coded for communication and interactivity, including use of such tools as blogs, Twitter and Facebook, and how often these were updated. The different data were combined into a single dataset to enable the statistical modelling of the key factors associated with the likelihood of an electoral candidate having an interactive and responsive election campaign.

The research findings highlighted the variation in use of Web 2.0 communication tools by political parties and also in terms of the competiveness of the election. Most candidates had an identifiable email address. Of those contactable by email, responses were received from 60 per cent. There were considerable differences in the response rate and content relevance of responses by the candidates' individual characteristics, political party and constituency context. In some cases there was only limited use of email and autoreply emails.

Using an integrated, mixed method approach, the research captured different dimensions of the use of the Internet for communication and campaigning by electoral candidates. Such data provided insights into the use of the Internet, which might not have been fully captured in a traditional survey or via qualitative interviews alone.

3.2.2 Case Study 2: Researching Civil Unrest in the UK

The aim of this case study was to capture the nature of, and communication around, civil protests in the UK. The research (Lewis et al., 2011; Procter et al., 2013a; 2013b) used a combination of novel computational and more conventional social science research methods.[4] Large volumes of tweets were collated and the language use analysed, and metadata such as geographic location mapped and visualized. The primary focus was on the analysis of Twitter postings during the riots in England in the summer of 2011 as a way of monitoring both events and people's attitudes and behaviour. Social science researchers worked alongside the *Guardian's* journalists and digital media team in conducting the analysis and in reporting the findings.

A sample of 2.6 million tweets from around 700,000 Twitter users were accessed from Twitter as part of a research partnership between the research team and Twitter. This volume of data required techniques that are not conventional in social science research, although the skills underpinning the techniques include, for example, thematic analysis, conventional data coding and reliability checks. The tweets were manually coded in terms of function (whether they were supporting a rumour or challenging it). Re-tweeting was used as an indicator of whether a tweet had been read and so provided evidence of information diffusion. Aggregate analysis was also conducted on the type of Twitter account (for example, whether it was individual or organizational), number of tweets per account, number of followers and number of friends.

---

[4]See www.theguardian.com/uk/2011/dec/05/reading-the-riots-methodology-explained

Part of the analysis focused on the most active users and a typology of users was produced which took account of how people present and define themselves via public platforms such as Twitter, including the use of fake accounts. Manual coding was then used to code the information content of the tweets to capture the ways in which people engage with rumours in social media.

Interactive data visualization techniques were used as part of this study, as Figure 3.2 illustrates.

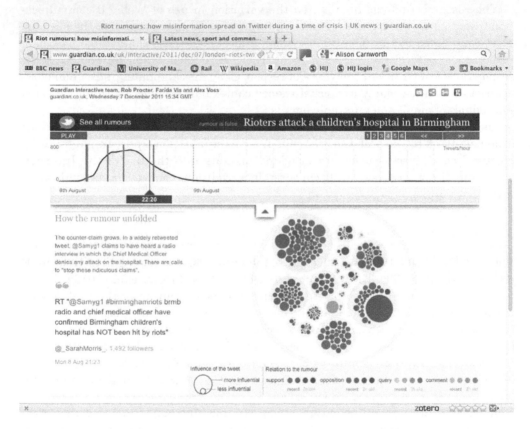

Figure 3.2   Rumour spreading graphic

Extract from visualization of the time line of a rumour showing information flows (large circles) supporting the rumour (green) and flows challenging it (red). Each individual circle represents a tweet and its size reflects the influence (i.e. number of followers) of the account that tweeted it. For the interactive visualizations, see www.guardian.co.uk/uk/interactive/2011/dec/07/london-riots-twitter

This study provided insight into communication patterns, and how people engage with and react to rumours that would not have been captured through more traditional social science methods alone, such as observation-based studies or post hoc interviews.

With the right combination of tools for data collection and analysis, studies using social media data can be conducted in a very short timeframe. This presents its own challenges, however, especially when the research is driven by opportunity and the news agenda. Whilst such research has its place, it is important that such factors do not lead to the neglect of clear research questions and hypothesis-driven research. This is not to be dismissive, but to recognize that this kind of rapid data collection and analysis comprises a different type of social research, sometimes more akin to commentary.

Free software tools now exist that allow the collection of Twitter data by certain self-specified topics and key words during a fixed time period, and for producing visualizations of the data.[5] There are also commercial software tools such as DiscoverText,[6] which can provide access to samples of Twitter data for a fee. Other tools enable searches for recent tweets by key words and by particular users.[7] These tools allow social science researchers to collate individual tweets or provide summaries of postings by date and time, key word, type, source, language, country and also by image and links to published commentary such as newspaper articles. The tools provide opportunities for powerful and comparatively rapid data gathering when compared with more traditional kinds of social science research. For example, rather than conducting a survey to ask people about their attitudes and their changes over time, a social science researcher could examine their tweets and code for particular values, following them as they may change. However, as we outlined in Chapter 2, issues of sampling bias, limits on generalizability and performance need to be considered.

The use of any social science research method needs to take into account the population of interest and the sample being accessed. In relation to analysing tweets this might include demographics of the sample. The particular population of Twitter users or YouTube videos that are being accessed and whether they are complete or partial would need to be clearly defined. The limitations of the generalizability of the data need to be mapped out and a further challenge relates to matching the data to well-specified hypotheses and research questions.

Social media platforms can change the data they collect and also change the details of the data they release or make available publicly, and the conditions of access attached to it. A consequence is that information available at one time might not be available at a later date. This may hinder comparability over time and prevent replication of research. One possible way to counter this is for researchers to create their own archives to ensure there is a lasting record of the data used in their research that can be later used for follow-up studies and quality assurance (Elliot et al., 2013). Unfortunately, terms and conditions imposed by some social media platforms may prohibit the sharing of such archives with other researchers.[8]

3.2.3 Case Study 3: Researching Migration and Mobility in England

The aim of this study was to examine recent migration patterns of hard-to-reach groups in England. The research, conducted by Jivraj et al. (2012), used School

---

[5]See, for example, Webometric Analyst http://lexiurl.wlv.ac.uk

[6]https://discovertext.com

[7]See, for example, Snapbird http://snapbird.org and Tweetarchivist www.tweetarchivist.com

[8]Twitter is one example. See https://twitter.com/tos

Census data alongside survey data to map the migration of people to England from the A8 countries (the Czech Republic, Estonia, Hungary, Latvia, Lithuania, Poland, Slovakia and Slovenia).

The School Census contains information on each child attending state schools in England. The dataset is a statutory record that is collected annually and provides the opportunity to track pupils over time in terms of their academic development and mobility. It is a key source for monitoring educational performance. The variables include pupils' names, addresses, age, ethnicity, first language, exam and assessment scores, Free School Meal benefit entitlement, attendance and special educational needs, alongside three group variables: local authority, school and school class. The dataset contains around eight million pupils in 25,000 schools. It does not include children below school age or those who are in private education or who are being home educated (see Department for Education (2011) for more details on the dataset).

The data can be used to examine internal migration flows and in this study data was combined with National Insurance number data and compared with data from other sources. The analysis centred on identifying the spatial distribution of A8 country migrants at the national level and down to local authority level, and their movements both within England and between England and other countries. The School Census data cannot be used to measure migration directly, but only as a proxy. A8 migrants in the School Census were identified using ethnicity as a proxy indicator. This is not an exact identification but the authors cross-validated their categorization with aggregate estimates from the National Insurance number data.

The research highlighted the concentration of A8 migrants in London and in Boston, Lincolnshire (an area that has not recently encountered large-scale immigration). Figure 3.3 shows the location quotient (LQ) values for A8 and all other pupil immigrants in each local authority type in England, relative to the total pupil population. A LQ indicates where a group is underrepresented or overrepresented in an area relative to its prevalence in the total population. The A8 pupil immigrants were concentrated in London local authorities. A8 immigrants were also overrepresented in small cities (for example, Oxford) and large cities (for example, Southampton). However, they were under-represented in the principal metropolitan cities, including Birmingham, Sheffield, Newcastle-upon-Tyne, Leeds, and Liverpool. The local authority with the highest LQ for A8 pupil immigrants was Boston, Lincolnshire.

Evidence from other data sources such as the International Passenger Survey (IPS) was also analysed.[9] The IPS is a sample survey, which collects information about passengers entering and leaving the UK. It involves around 800,000 interviews a year. Interviews are carried out at all major ports and entry points. The survey results are used by various UK government departments, including the Department for Transport, the Home Office, HM Revenue and Customs and Tourist Boards. The analysis of the IPS highlighted the reason for migration and how A8 migrants were much more likely than other migrants to be coming to the UK to take up a specific job.

---

[9]See www.ons.gov.uk/ons/guide-method/surveys/respondents/household/international-passenger-survey/index.html

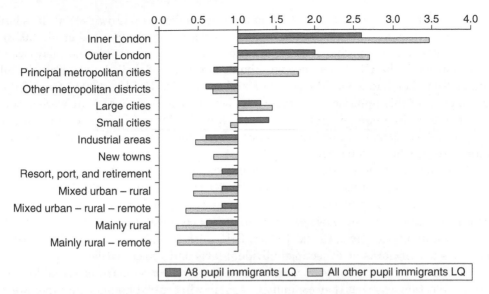

Figure 3.3 Geographical distribution of immigrant pupils by local authority district types in England, 2003 to 2007 (measured by location quotients (LQs))

Source: Jivraj et al., Environment and Planning A 2012, Volume 44. Pion Ltd.

There were some limitations to the study. One was that the School Census data do not capture those children who migrate to England when they are younger than five years old. The analysis also had to make the assumption that those who left the dataset before the start of the school year in which they reached the age of 15 had left England, given that schooling is compulsory up to age 16. However, despite its limitations, the administrative data from the School Census provides unique insights into the migration and mobility of smaller populations at the local level, beyond that available from other surveys and data sources.

The findings from analyses of the School Census have informed policy responses in relation to population movement, service demand and resource allocation at the local authority level.

3.2.4 Case Study 4: Researching Street Begging – Crowdsourced, Citizen Science Observer Data

The aim of this study was to examine the nature of street begging in central London in the UK, and to pilot a citizen social science methodology based on the idea of the monitorial citizen (Schudson, 1998). The monitorial citizen is a conception of citizenship where, even though citizens are not civically active, they are still watchful and will mobilize when they feel their input is required.

In this study, conducted by Purdam (2014), a group of volunteers were recruited to be observers of a particular social issue as a pilot study of what has been termed 'citizen social science' (Procter et al., 2013c: 51). Volunteers have been engaged in research in many ways in the past. Most recently the high profile, purposive survey of social class in the UK conducted by the University of Manchester and the BBC has highlighted not only the interest of sections of the public in their own social class but also their willingness to participate in social research online (Savage et al., 2013). More directly related, perhaps, is the Mass Observation movement in the early twentieth century in the UK, where people submitted reports of their daily activities and events that they had seen (Madge and Harrisson, 1938; Hubble, 2006). One of the key aspects of this approach was reporting issues such as poverty that were otherwise going undocumented. However, the work of the Mass Observation movement was the subject of some considerable debate about how robust and generalizable the data were (Kushner, 2004; Sheridan, 1993).

The specific focus of this study was counting the number of people seen begging. The volunteer observer method for social science research piloted here is linked to observer and ethnographic methodologies, including what are termed spot, instantaneous and experience sampling methodologies used in anthropological research (Altman, 1974; Borgerhoff and Caro, 1985; Chick, 1994; O'Brian, 1998; Ozdemir, 2008). These methodologies usually focus on collecting individual-level and subjective data.

A group of thirteen volunteers were recruited to be observers. The criterion for volunteer selection was that they commuted regularly in central London, and they were recruited by snowball sampling. The volunteers were not directed to go to specific areas but to conduct their observations during their daily commute in and around central London, though these were known to be busy, high-density routes. They were instructed to note down if they saw anyone begging over a two-day period, noting their estimate of the beggar's age, their appearance, and the time and location of the observation. It was suggested that the volunteers keep a notebook as they went about their travels and complete the data table provided at the end of each day. The volunteers were asked not to have any direct contact with the people they saw begging during the observation period and were asked to be as discreet as possible when recording their observations.[10] Figure 3.4 shows the recording sheet for the observations.

Day no [ ] Date [ ]							
Total number of people seen begging that day [ ]							
Journey/ place	Location: e.g., on street, near tube entrance, in tube	Time	Male or Female	Age approx: (adult, young person or child)	General description of appearance	Baby/child present	Any other comments

Figure 3.4 Observation sheet

---

[10]The volunteers were advised to report any problems to the lead social researcher and to report any issues of immediate concern to the police.

The volunteers identified 24 people begging during a total of 66 journeys in central London by tube, bus and on foot. Most people were seen begging on their own (or at least standing alone) though some were in groups. Of those people who were observed begging, 18 were male and six were female. Five of the women begging had babies with them.

The findings from this pilot study were used to provide a preliminary understanding of the nature and type of street begging in likely hotspot areas. The findings were then used to inform the decision on the undertaking of a larger study of forced labour and its links to street begging, in particular, the scope, form and geographical focus that the study would take.

A number of ethical issues are raised in relation to the role of the observer, the potential political role of reporting and the use of covert methods (Spicker, 2011). It is notable that these methods were justifiable and are not precluded by the codes of ethics of research councils such as the Economic and Social Research Council (ESRC, 2010) or professional bodies such as the British Sociological Association (BSA, 2002). The observer role for citizens does raise concerns about issues of surveillance (Lyon, 2001). One can look to debates around state informers and collaborators and, for example, anti-communism campaigns in the McCarthyism period in the USA in the 1950s. However, in this study the volunteers were not acting as 'spies' and did not have a direct role in the research but were just motivated observers/data collectors in the nature of the study, though they may have had their own personal motivations. If there is a comparison, perhaps it is more in relation to a citizen being an eyewitness to a crime or a witness in a court trial or citizens participating in neighbourhood watch schemes. The focus here was on involving citizens in social science research data gathering as part of a formal social science research process that was subject to the usual ethical approval standards and good practices. The data gathered would be used as part of published research and part of an open and transparent process, subject to the same ethical standards as any other social science research project. The volunteer observers were trained in line with the highest standards of social science research practice.

It is notable that related techniques have been used in research on language and sound, where electronically activated ear recorders are fitted to volunteers and recordings are made of sounds at particular times of the day. It is argued that such tools gather data that would otherwise go unnoticed or unreported using more conventional data gathering techniques. (See Mehl and Robbins, 2012 for discussion of the use of the recording technology.)

Observations were only captured at a limited number of locations for a limited time period so the findings cannot be generalized. However, the method has the scope to be extended to provide more general quantitative coverage using transect sampling, specific and multiple sampling points and using multiple observers. Such approaches are being used to map journey routes by combining GPS and survey data through mobile phone technology (see, for example, Raento et al., 2009).

The innovation in this case study is in recruiting volunteers to record observations whilst they go about their daily activities. Such an approach has potential for different applications and for gathering data and conducting research that might otherwise not be possible, either due to issues of resources or due to the scale of information gathering possible. There are also links here to wider debates regarding responsible citizenship (Ilcan, 2009), action research methods and what can be termed emancipatory social science (Purdam, 2014). Co-led and collaborative citizen social science research, when linked to a theory of justice, could produce evidence and research that not only serves to monitor but challenge oppression and inequality in a coordinated way. Not only would citizens be involved as observers but also be enabled to report on their own lives in a structured way. Such a democratizing approach has the potential to be transformative and lead to new forms of continuous social science through collaborative knowledge production within a robust and ethical social science framework.

In many ways, commercial organizations are already using similar types of participatory and opportunistic data generation approaches (Elliot et al., 2013), for example, from mobile devices and online behaviour tracking, but it is primarily data that citizens have generated about themselves as they go about their usual activities. As such, there is a connection with debates about ownership of data and the role of the citizen in the data process.

3.2.5 Case Study 5: Researching Attitudes, Behaviour and Learning Using Eye Tracking Data

This small-scale, lab-based study (Beattie, 2010) aimed to examine the recognition and impact of product labelling and advertising with a specific focus on environmentally friendly products. Eye movement tracking techniques are now being used to study attitudes and behaviour more directly than traditional survey instruments allow. Uses include capturing aspects of social interaction to identify differences between reported views and actual views. Eye movement technology using specialized contact lenses or multiple digital cameras can record the amount of time the eye fixes on particular objects in the field of vision and the point of vision. Initial points of focus can be compared with how the eye then moves focus onto other information in the field of view and how the focus may return to different points of information.[11]

Eye tracking techniques allow the measurement of gaze and focus. As Boraston and Blakemore (2007: 896) state, 'eye-tracking allows the direct, objective and quantitative observation of behaviour, and through the analysis of fixation patterns can indicate which information from a scene is available to the brain.'

Often used for in-vitro studies, measures of eye movement and visual attention can be used to provide insights into cognitive processing and aid understanding of attitudes and behaviour. Such approaches sit within the wider field of body language research and the developing area of the digital mapping of body language and expressions including facial movements. For example, experimental research has explored computer recognition of facial expressions, including happiness (see BBC, 2013b). Eye tracking methods have been used as part of child development

---

[11]Such data gathering techniques can also be combined with brain activation data from MRI scans (see Gramatikov et al., 2007 for example) with the potential to add depth to the interpretation of the eye movements.

studies, language acquisition and reading research, and in mental health diagnosis. They have also been used in marketing to optimize visual advertising and web page design (see, for example, Boraston and Blakemore, 2007; Evans and Saint-Aubin, 2005; Kruger, 2013; Rayner, 1986).

In his study of attitudes towards climate change, Beattie (2010) used eye-tracking methods to capture consumers' recognition of carbon footprint labelling alongside all the other information on the packaging of products such as light bulbs, orange juice and washing machine liquid detergents, focusing on so-called 'green choices'. Beattie examined the association between the observational data gathered using eye tracking technology with evidence about attitudes towards tackling climate change collected via traditional methods such as surveys and interviews. The study was limited in size in that only small groups of people were tested and Beattie reports data from just ten participants, although he made multiple observations of their eye movements. He did not extend his study to actual consumer purchases, just eye tracking observations and attitudinal data.

Beattie concludes that carbon footprint information is important and does capture people's attention when they are looking at product labels but eye focus varies by product and is, in part, linked to prior knowledge of the product's association with climate change impact.

Despite the innovative methodology, some caution needs to be attached to the findings, given the limited number of cases and measurements. However, the study does highlight the use of technology in gathering data, which has the potential to go beyond evidence available from more traditional qualitative and quantitative research methods often based on self-reporting or purchasing records. Of course, there is a link here to more established observation and participant observation based techniques which are used in a wider range of research contexts. Large-scale observational datasets will undoubtedly come to the fore as data from digital sensors becomes more commonplace and these too will generate new challenges.

3.2.6 Case Study 6: Researching Social Policy Interventions using Experimental Approaches

The aim of this set of case studies was to try to identify the causal processes behind specific attitudes and behaviour change. Social scientists and public policy evaluators are increasingly using experimental designs in randomized controlled trials (RCTs) involving control groups (Torgerson and Torgerson, 2008). These are in the tradition of experimental design in medical and psychological research, where people are allocated to one of two (or more) groups, either through random assignment or through matched profiles (for example, on relevant demographics), and one (or more) of the groups is subject to an intervention in order to test its impact compared with the control group in the attempt to identify causal effects. Multiple groups can be compared and interventions varied in order to capture their impact in detail. Such research designs aim to overcome some of the limitations of surveys, which are reliant on self-reported attitudes and behaviour and which are limited in what they enable to be claimed as causal effects.

Such trials and intervention-based approaches can be challenging due to the ethical issues raised by experimenting with people's lives. These can be more problematic in medical and drug trails where a control group is not given the intervention or where an experimental group is given a trial drug. However, in social science where the interventions are not usually medical or likely to involve denying a particular group access to a service for any extended period, then the ethical issues, though still important, can be less of a barrier (see Torgerson and Torgerson, 2008).

Policy makers have shown an increasing interest in experimental approaches and the UK government set up a behaviour research initiative that primarily uses experimental methods (Cabinet Office, 2011). Numerous experiments examining the mechanisms of behaviour change have been conducted in this framework. Examples include: controlled trials of parenting and caring, service take up, healthy lifestyles, signing petitions, recycling, energy conservation, charitable donating, organ donation, payment of taxes, voting, attendance at medical appointments and smoking cessation. Interventions that have been investigated include: information provision using different media (e.g. text message), letter and form design, financial rewards, raising norm awareness (that is, using information about what other people, such as what a person's neighbour, are doing) and changing choice architectures (e.g. changing defaults) (see, for example, Thaler and Sunstein, 2009; John et al., 2011; Cotterill et al., 2012. See House of Lords (2011) for a review of developments and limitations in the UK).

We look here at one study in detail: research into environmental awareness and attitude change amongst young people. Goodwin et al. (2010) conducted a randomized control trial of the effects of a school-based intervention on the environmental attitudes and knowledge of young people. Over 700 pupils from 27 schools were included in the study. These schools were separated into three groups: a control group, a group subject to a single intervention, and a group for which the intervention lasted over a month. The interventions involved: additional lessons on environmental change, DVDs to watch, quizzes and computer games to play.

The study included before and after attitude surveys conducted in class and also a survey that the children took home to complete with their parents/guardians. Two challenges were: establishing the partnership with the schools in order to secure their participation; and the issue of pupils completing the second phase of the tasks.

The headline finding was that the study revealed no impact from the short or long term interventions on attitudes and behaviour towards the environment amongst either the young people or their parents compared to the control group. The authors concluded that environmental education programmes used in the schools studied did not have an impact on environmental attitudes and that the key drivers of attitudes remain family, peer group and media influences, rather than interventions delivered in the classroom.

The innovative aspect of these kinds of research design is that they have the potential to go beyond survey research evidence in terms of identifying causal processes. However, they can often be limited in terms of generalizability due to the scale of the studies that can be feasibly undertaken and the resultant high standard errors on any estimates. Moreover, whilst such techniques are well established in medical and psychology research, their use in social and public policy contexts is relatively new in the UK and there are limitations in terms of what interventions can be tested and the ethical implications of conducting RCTs in vivo.

3.2.7 Case Study 7: Researching Health and Well-being Outcomes using Genetic Data

The aim of this study was to test two competing models for the genetic component of postnatal depression. The research, conducted by Mitchell et al. (2011), combined genetic and social demographic data and was focused on examining an alternative model to the orthodox biological diathesis stress model for genetically mediated health and well-being outcomes. The orthodox model states that both environment and genetics can be risky or protective and that the effects are additive, or if interactive, then are still anchored on an intercept which corresponds with what might be termed 'normal functioning'. The alternative, the genetic susceptibility model, suggests that some individuals (with given genetic predispositions) are sensitive to environmental covariates in both negative and positive directions.

The study used the USA Fragile Families and Child Well-being Study (which combines socio-demographic, health and genetic data). The survey used a stratified, multistage, probability sample of children born in large US cities between February 1998 and September 2000 and their parents. The researchers used years in education as their environmental indicator equating shorter education with poor environment and longer education with good environment. Social scientists might want to question this somewhat simplistic classification but the findings are compelling nonetheless. They replicate existing work showing that, after controlling for known covariates, a relatively short education in combination with a reactive genetic component increases the probability of depression. However, they also found that the genetic effect changes direction when number of years in education increases. In other words, 'whereas the S or 12 homozygotes are positively associated with [post natal depression] in unfavourable

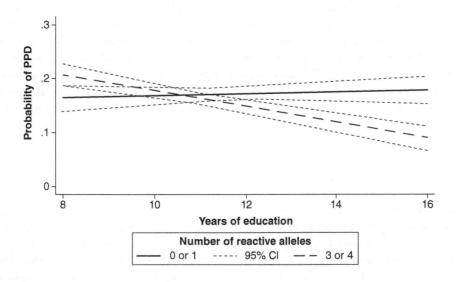

Figure 3.5 Probability of postnatal depression across SES by the number of reactive 5-HTT alleles

environments, they are negatively associated with [post natal depression] in favourable environments' (Mitchell et al., 2011: 190). This result can be seen clearly in Figure 3.5.

Without such a large-scale dataset combining socio-demographic and genetic data, the identification of this sort of relationship would not be possible. Using genetic data alongside social survey data is likely to be new for many social science researchers and requires a new understanding of different types of variables and their properties, including their terms of use and their limitations.

3.3 DISCUSSION AND CONCLUSIONS

In this chapter we have examined examples of social science research that have used new types of data and innovations in methods. Some of the examples are developments or extensions of existing methods, used in new ways to explore different types of data. Nevertheless, they highlight how the types of data available for, and used in, social science research are continuing to grow.

Across the examples we have highlighted issues such as: the need for rigorous research design, the ethics of using these new types of data, data ownership, access, data format and standardization, combining, analysing and visualizing different types of data, data limitations, including sampling and generalizability, quality assurance, replication and archiving. Many questions – methodological, ethical, and theoretical – are raised in relation to social science research use of new types of data and methods. A convention in orthodox social science is that research should primarily be hypothesis-driven, even if pilot and scoping studies are used to develop and refine research questions. As such, it is the research questions that should come first rather than the data. Letting the data lead the analysis carries the risk of the availability and the properties of the data driving the research agenda rather than the reasoned development of hypotheses based on prior investigations and theories. Of course this is not a new problem – secondary data analysts have wrestled with it since the first survey – but there are additional risks with the new types of data given their immediacy and volume. For example, what does it mean that thousands of people post tweets about a government policy or social issue? Without knowing the relationship of those tweeting to the population and/or a sample frame, such a question is difficult to answer. These are not just academic concerns; there is a real risk of ill-informed reporting and decision and policy making.

However, it is important to explore how the new data types can best be utilized and such methodological exploration will necessarily be, in part, driven by the data. Inductive, data-driven approaches may also be helpful for some substantive questions providing that there is a theoretical framework for the research. The new types of data provide the potential to both explore existing research questions in new ways and to address new questions. There is scope to identify and use individual-level data that is more detailed, for example, in terms of geographical coverage, than that which might be available from nationally representative surveys. As social science researchers increasingly work with *data streams* and *data arrays* rather than datasets, it is plausible that, as with many other classical distinctions, the boundary between deductive and inductive processes will become fuzzier. So, whilst it is important that best practice is followed in terms of testing research hypotheses in a robust way with reference to existing methods and taking account of the existing knowledge, we should not be closed to the possibility that the new data open up a completely different way of thinking about the relationship between data, research, the researchers and the researched. This could include exploring questions that may not have been previously thought amenable to empirical testing. However, theory is, in our view, still the key to credible and meaningful social science research.

Elliot et al.'s (2013) purposive survey of UK academics highlights the potential of many of the new data types. This survey also captured reports of considerable current or anticipated use of such data types as: electronic health records, trace data from Internet use, consumption data, movement tracking data, and Twitter and blog data. At the same time, the authors also found that the academics consulted believed that orthodox and purpose-specific social science research processes such as surveys would maintain their importance in the future.

A possible way forward is not to think of the new types of data and approaches as replacing the orthodox, but rather to think in terms of the added value that they bring. So, for example, whilst Twitter data can enable the instant tracking of the attitudes and networks of a certain part of the population, a representative survey can provide information on the attitudes of the whole population and a longitudinal survey can help examine how people's attitudes have changed during their lives. Similarly, data gathered in almost real time could be used alongside traditional survey and administrative data; for example, reports of police call-outs alongside contextual data could be used to map reported incidents and model the likelihood of future crimes (see Brunsdon et al., 2009). Each approach has a purpose and value but serves different functions and each data source has its strengths and weaknesses in terms of its explanatory power. Just as qualitative interview and survey response data can be criticized for their performative and partial aspects, including social desirability bias, so can people's tweets. Such limitations need to be clearly acknowledged in the research design and analytical process.

There are certainly new opportunities for understanding and measuring social change but the enormous data volumes also highlight the importance of robust and open computational analytical methods and research underpinned by good practice in terms of design, analysis and ethics. In short, the data and methods still have to be fit for purpose. (See Woodfield et al., 2013; Rogers, 2013.) Different data and methods can be used to cross-validate one another and also as part of calibration tests. Mixed methods approaches can add considerable value and explanatory power; the more different data and methods that can be used to tackle a research question the more powerful they become as cross-validators for one another. Conversely, data from different sources can conflict. But such differences can enhance the research process and be useful in driving further research questions to explain the differences. A key component of mixed methodology research is to develop ways in which various sources of evidence might be combined and weighted. There is a genuine opportunity for alternative narratives and perspectives to emerge from the changing data environment as evidence gaps are filled and new evidence is exploited using highly detailed data.

It is notable that whilst we have considered methods for analysing new types of data it can also be the case that existing social science research methods can be adapted to utilize social media platforms and data, for example, using virtual ethnography to draw on the growing self-generated archives of everyday life, as highlighted by Beer and Burrows (2007), and running focus groups online and interviews via the Internet (see, for example, Salmons, 2010).

3.3.1 Ethical Issues for Social Science Research

New ethical challenges are posed by the use of new types of data, including social media and administrative data (see Chapter 12 for a full discussion). Such challenges include: ownership, access and disclosure risks. New questions concerning what is public data and data protection need addressing. For example, to what extent is someone who is described in a tweet posted by another person having their privacy breached? Under what circumstances can data linking techniques be used to combine data that have different terms and conditions of use?

More data clearly means more collection and so closer scrutiny of people's lives. The potential risks to privacy were well anticipated by debates regarding the so-called surveillance society (Lyon, 2001). It is notable that the UK Information Commissioner (ICO, 2012) has conducted a review and produced new guidance on data handling, anonymization and privacy in datasets, with specific consideration of new types of data, within the framework of the UK *Data Protection Act (1998)*. Qualitative research by Mancini et al. (2011) has explored the impacts and privacy issues raised by tracking data specifically in relation to individual behaviour in a family context, where family members could track each other's movements (see also Tun et al., 2012).

Data anonymization remains an under-developed area in relation to social media data. For example, to what extent are tweets anonymous if they refer to other named individuals or organizations or if supposedly anonymous accounts are linked with named accounts? A key area of both legal and good practice clarification is in relation to privacy and consent for use, and which attributes of social media datasets, such as tweets, user profile information, linked data, etc. are accessible for research and publication. As Gross (2011) argues, the existing frameworks of ethics and particularly consent are limited and they need to be overhauled if they are to cope with the scale, intensity and immediacy of the constantly evolving data environment. As one respondent to Elliot et al.'s (2013: 23) survey of UK academics stated, there is a 'lack of clarity on how to handle new types of data with regard to data protection and copyright'. In this context, the development of new ethical and data handling frameworks are crucial for research in order to ensure effective regulation of data use. Without this, there is a danger of increased restrictions on data use, for example, if data owners respond to uncertainties over privacy protocols by denying access to their holdings. (See Neuhaus and Webmoor, 2011 for a discussion of what they term agile ethics and also AOIR, 2012.)

More broadly, it is clear the relationship between citizens, the state and the commercial sector is changing. As Elliot et al. (2013) argue, it may well be that we need to move from a milieu of regulating *data protection* to one of policing *data abuse*. In a data abuse framework one is less concerned about the control of data flows and processes and more with the consequences and, specifically, harms caused by the actions and choices of data processors. At the same time, it is increasingly being argued that citizens themselves need to realize the value (economic, existential and social) in their own data (see, for example, Bambauer, 2011; Mayer-Schönberger and Cukier, 2013; Purdam, 2006).

3.3.2 Data Access Issues for Social Science Research

It is of undoubted benefit to society that social scientists are continually learning, building the evidence base and developing new methods in a cumulative and critical way. Engaging with the new types of data is an important aspect of this. Society will be failing to make best use of the new data unless it is made available for wider research use. As was outlined in Chapter 2, this includes data held by commercial organizations. Social science research will become increasingly partial if commercial companies hold and restrict access to rich sources of data that can help explain social science questions. Some commercial social media companies have research initiatives working in partnership with social science researchers, for example, Microsoft's Social Media Research Lab,[12] although it is not clear there is a willingness on their part to pursue this in a more systematic way. See also the Data For Development initiative by Orange.[13]

Without such data access, we will experience a repeat of the early twentieth century situation in the UK where successive governments provided very little access to census data or other official statistical data. As we have discussed in Chapter 2, the public sector in the UK (and elsewhere), through its Open Data agenda, is now at the forefront of facilitating open data analysis/programming events.[14] It is important that publicly held data are accessible within short time frames at limited costs and are available in non-disclosive, high-quality formats. This could be through licensing or through some data commons or virtual safe setting where the data is analysed remotely. This could follow the model of social science researchers using public sector data as part of the UK Secure Data Service.[15] There are already some developments in this area, including what is termed data philanthropy (see, for example, Kirkpatrick (2011) and ongoing data partnerships set up by the United Nations Global Pulse initiative). Here the focus is on data holders sharing data for informing policy. In terms of benefits for the organization sharing their data, this could include creative partnerships, research and innovation, as well as providing interesting research projects and applications for staff.

Social scientists should be championing the access to new data types, including administration and social media data, other data held commercially and the setting

---

[12]See http://socialmediacollective.org/about

[13]See www.d4d.orange.com/home

[14]See also similar developments in the USA and www.data.gov which has over 100,000 government datasets available for public access.

[15]See http://securedata.data-archive.ac.uk

up of partnerships where appropriate. A radical extension to Freedom of Information legislation could legally require anonymized forms of commercial data to be made available for research purposes at marginal cost. Public resource mechanisms could be set up to enable this to work (see also United Nations (2012) and, as outlined in Chapter 2, see the new guidelines for public bodies providing data under the UK *Freedom of Information Act 2000* requests). For further discussion, see Bambauer (2011) on the data commons, civic duty and privacy rights.

Mandatory social science research access by approved researchers would be a major step forward. This would not necessarily jeopardize the commercial value of the data to businesses but, as with the work of the UN Global Pulse, could be part of a legal and ethical responsibility to the 'customer' and their welfare. Moreover, many governments and state agencies themselves are legally allowed to record electronic communications such as email and web browsing, sometimes in real-time. Yet, access to such data for social science research purposes is restricted, including for some government departments.

As we have outlined, citizens and researchers could create their own archives to ensure there is a lasting record of the data used in research that can be later used for follow-up studies and quality assurance (Elliot et al., 2013). There are some innovative examples of these. The Internet Archive[16] has over 240 billion web pages dating back to 1996. This service can also be used by researchers to create their own archives. The initiative recently launched by the British Library to archive online materials, including web pages and blogs, is to be welcomed (see BBC, 2013a). The Web Science Trust is leading on the development of resources and tools for analysing and understanding the Internet and e-Research. An aspect of this is the idea of Web Observatories and so-called Personal Data Stores, which allow individuals to manage and maintain their digital data and also to potentially realize some of the economic and social value of it (Tiropanis et al., 2013; Van Kleek et al., 2014).

3.3.3 New Ways of Working for Social Scientists?

Now and in the future, social scientists are likely to find themselves working with very different types of data including: physiological information and measurements, genetic and biomarker data, behavioural data from automatic sensors and trace data. This may require, far more than is currently the case, working in partnership with data holder organizations across different sectors and in mixed interdisciplinary research teams and projects.

For large volumes of digital data, skills in computation and software engineering will be of value. This would include skills in harvesting data online, producing software to mine and code large volumes of textual data (for a discussion see Elliot et al. (2013); Woodfield et al. (2013)). The ESRC/JISC funded COSMOS[17] initiative is proposing to

---

[16]See http://archive.org

[17]See www.cosmosproject.net

support access to new types of data and analytical tools through the development of an interdisciplinary virtual research environment (Housley et al., 2014).

A key challenge with the new data types is an understanding of their form and content. Where there is scope for linking different types of data, including administration data, skills in probability and statistical matching would be important. Where data has geographical coding, skills in digital mapping and visualization would be of value. The tool kit of the social scientist will need to evolve but, nevertheless, the fundamental skill set of social scientists highlighted in the training focus of the research councils will remain important. These include: theoretically-informed hypothesis testing, research design, literature reviews, an understanding of quantitative and qualitative data types, sampling, data gathering, research ethics and peer review. The evaluation of data quality and fitness for purpose will remain a high priority.

In summary, it is clear that the new data types and analytical approaches open up new opportunities to research previously intractable social problems from different angles and perspectives and in more detail than ever before. In short, there are lots of new ways of doing social science. However, there are still limits to what we know; there are still gaps in the evidence base and there will still be a need for purpose-specific research, including investigations of vulnerable and hard-to-reach groups. There is a risk in assuming that all lives and issues are being documented in the age of data.

Given the present rate of innovation, it seems certain new types of data will continue to emerge, and in response, new ways of doing social science will be developed. Existing research, methods and data will become increasingly subject to challenge and competition from new approaches. This is likely to include new forms and time frames of dissemination and, in certain cases, the shortening of conventional social science research processes. However, an understanding of the data, its structure, and an awareness of its limitations should remain at the heart of empirical social science. We hope our selection of illustrative case studies and signposting have provided some indication of the opportunities but also the challenges ahead.

3.4 BIBLIOGRAPHY

Altmann, J. (1974) 'Observational study of behavior: sampling methods', *Behavior*, 49: 227–67.

Association of Internet Researchers (AOIR) (2012) Ethical Decision-Making and Internet Research: Version 2.0 – Recommendations from the Association of Internet Researchers Working Committee. Available from http://aoir.org/reports/ethics2.pdf (accessed 09 Dec 2014).

Back, L. and Puwar, N. (eds.) (2013) *Live Methods*. Oxford: Wiley-Blackwell.

Bambauer, J. (2011) 'Tragedy of the data commons', *Harvard Journal of Law and Technology*, 25: 1–66.

BBC (2013a) *UK Libraries Archive Web Pages and Celebrity Tweets*. Available from www.bbc.co.uk/news/entertainment-arts-22037199 (accessed 09 Dec 2014).

BBC (2013b) *The Face Machine that Knows if You're Happy or Bored*. Available from www.bbc.co.uk/news/technology-23633394 (accessed 09 Dec 2014).

Beattie, G. (2010) *Why Aren't We Saving the Planet? A Psychologist's Perspective*, London: Routledge.

Beer, D. and Burrows, R. (2007) 'Sociology and, of and in Web 2.0: some initial considerations', *Sociological Research Online,* 12(5): 17.

Boraston, Z. and Blakemore, S.J. (2007) 'The application of eye-tracking technology in the study of autism', *The Journal of Physiology*, 581(3): 893–8.

Borgerhoff, M.M. and Caro, T. (1985) 'The use of quantitative observation techniques in anthropology', *Current Anthropology*, 26: 232–62.

boyd, D. and Crawford, K. (2012) 'Critical questions for big data', *Information, Communication and Society*, 15(5): 662–79.

British Sociological Association (BSA) (2002) 'Statement of ethical practice', *British Sociological Association*. London: BSA.

Brown, J. (2013) 'Dumbing down, minister? Michael Gove gets his educational facts from marketing surveys for Premier Inn and UKTV Gold', *The Independent,* 13 May 2013.

Brunsdon, C.F., Corcoran, J., Higgs, G. and Ware, A. (2009) 'The influence of weather on local geographical patterns of police calls for service', *Environment and Planning B: Planning and Design*, 36(5): 906–26.

Cabinet Office [Behavioural Insights Team] (2011) *Behavioural Insights Team Annual 2010–11*. London: Cabinet Office.

Chick, G. (1994) 'Experience sampling in anthropological research', *Cultural Anthropology Methods Journal*, 6(2): 4–6.

Cotterill, S, Richardson, L. and Moseley, A. (2012) 'Can nudging create the Big Society? Experiments in civic behaviour and implications for the voluntary and public sectors', *Voluntary Sector Review*, 3(2): 265–74.

Department for Education (2011) *School Census*. London: Department for Education. Available from www.education.gov.uk/schools/adminandfinance/schooladmin/ims/datacollections/schoolcensus (accessed 09 Dec 2014).

The Economist (2010) 'The Data Deluge', *The Economist*, February 25 2010.

Electoral Commission (2011) *Party and Election Finance (PEF) Online Registers*. London: Electoral Commission.

Elliot, M., Purdam, K. and Mackey, E. (2013) *Data Horizons – New Forms of Data for Social Research*, Economic and Social Research Council.

ESRC (2010) *Framework for Research Ethics*, Economic and Social Research Council.

Evans M.A. and Saint-Aubin, J. (2005) 'What children are looking at during shared storybook reading', *Psychology Science,* 16(11): 913–20.

Goodwin, M.J., Greasley, S., John, P. and Richardson, L. (2010) 'Can we make environmental citizens? A randomized control trial of the effect of a school-based intervention on the attitudes of young people', *Environmental Politics*, 19(3): 392–412.

Gramatikov, B.I., Zalloum, O.H., Wu, Y.K., Hunter, D.G. and Guyton, D.L. (2007) 'Directional eye fixation sensor using birefringence-based foveal detection', *Appl Optics*, 46(10): 1809–1818.

Gray, J., Chambers, L. and Bounegru, L. (eds.) (2012) *The Data Journalism Handbook: How Journalists Can Use Data to Improve the News*, O'Reilly Media. Available from http://datajournalismhandbook.org (accessed 08 Dec 2014).

Gross, A. (2011) 'The economy of social data: exploring research ethics as device', *The Sociological Review,* 59(2): 113–129.

Hey, T. and Trefethen, A. (2003) *The Data Deluge: An e-Science Perspective,* UK e-Science Core Programme, University of Southampton.

House of Lords (2011) *Behaviour Change, Science and Technology Select Committee 2nd Report of Session Report 179 2010–12*, London: The Stationery Office.

Housley, W., Procter, R., Edwards, A., Burnap, P., Williams, M., Sloan, L., Voss, A. and Greenhill, A. (2014) 'Big and broad social data and the sociological imagination: a collaborative response', *Big Data & Society*, 1(2): 1–15.

Hubble, N. (2006) *Mass-Observation and Everyday Life*. London: Palgrave.

Ilcan, S. (2009) 'Privatizing responsibility: public sector reform under neoliberal government', *Canadian Review of Sociology*, 46 (3): 207–34.

Information Commissioner's Office (ICO) (2012) Anonymisation: Managing Data Protection Risk Code of Practice. Available from https://ico.org.uk/media/1061/anonymisation-code.pdf (accessed 08 Dec 2014).

Jivraj, S., Simpson, L., and Marquis, N. (2012) 'Local distribution and subsequent mobility of immigrants measured from the school census in England', *Environment and Planning A*, 44(2): 491– 505.

John, P., Cotterill, S., Richardson, L., Moseley, A., Smith, G., Stoker, G. and Wales, C. (2011) *Nudge, Nudge, Think, Think: Experimenting with Ways to Change Civic Behaviour*. London: Bloomsbury.

Johnston. R., Pattie C., Cutts D., and Fisher, J. (2012) 'Spending, contacting, and voting: the 2010 British general election in the constituencies', *Environment and Planning A*, 44(5): 1165–84.

Kirkpatrick, R. (2011) *Data Philanthropy: Public and Private Data Sharing for Global Resilience*. Available from www.unglobalpulse.org/blog/data-philanthropy-public-private-sector-data-sharing-global-resilience (accessed 09 Dec 2014).

Kruger, H. (2013) 'Child and adult readers' processing of foreignised elements in translated south african picturebooks: an eye-tracking study', *Target*, 25(2): 180–227.

Kushner, A. (2004) *We Europeans? Mass-Observation, Race and British Identity in the Twentieth Century*. Farnham: Ashgate.

Lee, R.M., Fielding, N. and Blank, G. (2008) 'The internet as a research medium: an editorial introduction to the Sage handbook of online research methods', in Fielding, N., Lee, R.M. and Blank, G. (eds) *The Sage Handbook of Online Research Methods*, London: Sage.

Lewis, P., Newburn, T., Taylor, M., Mcgillivray, C., Greenhill, A., Frayman, H. and Procter, R. (2011) *Reading the Riots: Investigating England's Summer of Disorder*. London: Guardian Books.

Lyon, D. (2001) *Surveillance Society: Monitoring Everyday Life*. Buckingham: Open University Press.

Madge, C. and Harrisson, T. (1938) *Britain by Mass-observation*. London: Penguin.

Mancini, C., Rogers, Y., Thomas, K., Joinson, A., Price, B., Arosha, B., Jedrzejczyk, L. and Nuseibeh, B. (2011) 'In the best families: tracking and relationships', *29th International ACM Conference on Human Factors in Computing Systems*, ACM CHI 2011, 07–12 May 2011, Vancouver.

Marres, N. (2012) 'The redistribution of methods: on intervention in digital social research, broadly conceived', *The Sociological Review*, 60 (S1): 139–65.

Mayer-Schönberger, V. and Cukier, K. (2013) *Big Data: a Revolution that will Transform How we Live, Work and Think*. London: John Murray.

Mehl, M.R. and Robbins, M.L. (2012) 'Naturalistic observation sampling: the electronically activated recorder (EAR)', in Mehl, M.R. and Conner, T.S. (eds) *Handbook of Research Methods for Studying Daily Life*. New York: Guilford Press: 176–192.

Mitchell, C., Notterman, M.D., Brooks-Gunn, J., Hobcraft, J., Garfinkel, I., Jaeger, K., Kotenko, I. and McLanahana, S. (2011) 'Role of mother's genes and environment in postpartum depression', *Proceedings of National Academy of Sciences of the United States of America*. May 17; 108(20): 8189–93.

Neuhaus, F. and Webmoor, T. (2011) 'Agile ethics for massified research and visualization', *Information, Communication and Society*, 15(1): 43–65.

O'Brian, R. (1998) 'Stationary spot behavior checks and extended observation: adapting time allocation to marketplaces', *Field Methods*, 10(3): 57–60.

Ozdemir, A. (2008) 'Shopping malls: measuring interpersonal distance under changing conditions and across cultures', *Field Methods*, 20(3): 226–48.

Procter, R., Vis, F., and Voss, A. (2013a) 'Reading the riots on Twitter: methodological innovation for the analysis of big data', *International Journal of Social Research Methodology*, 16(3): 197–214.

Procter, R., Crump, J., Karstedt, S., Voss, A. and Cantijoch, M. (2013b) 'Reading the riots: what were the police doing on Twitter?' *Policing and Society*, 23(4): 413–36.

Procter, R., Housley, W., Williams, M., Edwards, A., Burnap, P., Morgan, J., Voss, A., Rana, O., Sloan, L. and Greenhill, A. (2013c) 'Enabling social media research through citizen social science', *ECSCW 2013 Adjunct Proceedings*: 51–56.

Purdam, K. (2006) 'The nations data', *Evidence and Social Policy*, 2(2): 227–48.

Purdam, K. (2014) 'Citizen social science and citizen data? Methodological and ethical challenges for social research', *Current Sociology*, 62(3): 374–92.

Raento, M., Oulasvirta, A. and Eagle, N. (2009) 'Smartphones: an emerging tool for social scientists', *Sociological Methods and Research*, 37(2): 426–54.

Rayner, K. (1986) 'Eye movements and the perceptual span in beginning and skilled readers', *Journal of Experimental Child Psychology*, 41(2): 211–36.

Rogers, S. (2013) *Facts Are Sacred*. London: Faber and Faber.

Salmons, J. (2010) *Online Interviews in Real Time*. London: Sage.

Savage, M. (2009) 'Contemporary sociology and the challenge of descriptive assemblage', *European Journal of Social Theory*, 12(1): 155–74.

Savage, M. and Burrows, R. (2007) 'The coming crisis of empirical sociology', *Sociology*, 41(5): 885–99.

Savage, M., Devine, F., Cunningham, N., Taylor, M., Li, Y., Hjellbrekke, J., Le Roux, B., Friedman, S. and Miles, A. (2013) 'A new model of social class? Findings from the BBC's great british class survey experiment', *Sociology*, 47(2): 219–50.

Schudson, M. (1998) *The Good Citizen*. New York: The Free Press.

Sheridan, D. (1993) 'Writing to the Archive: Mass-Observation as autobiography?' *Sociology*, 27(1): 27–40.

Social Research Association (SRA) (2003) *Ethical Guidelines*, London: Social Research Association.

Southern, R. (2014) 'A mixed-methods approach to capturing online local-level campaigns data at the 2010 UK general election', in Gibson, R., Cantijoch Cunill R.M. and Ward S. (eds), *Analyzing Social Media Data and Web Networks*. London: Palgrave-Macmillan.

Spicker, P. (2011) 'Ethical covert research', *Sociology*, 45(1): 118–33.

Thaler, R.H. and Sunstein, C.R. (2009) *Nudge: Improving Decisions about Health, Wealth, and Happiness*, London: Penguin.

Tiropanis, T., Hall, W., Shadbolt, N., De Roure, D., Contractor, N. and Hendler, J. (2013) 'The web science observatory', *IEEE Intelligent Systems*, 28(2): 100–4.

Torgerson, D.J., and Torgerson, C. (2008) *Designing Randomised Trials in Health, Education, and the Social Sciences: An Introduction*, New York: Palgrave Macmillan.

Tun, T.T., Bandara, A.K., Price, B., Yu, Y., Haley, C., Omoronyia, I. and Bashar, N. (2012) 'Privacy arguments: analysing selective disclosure requirements for mobile applications', *20th IEEE International Requirements Engineering Conference*, 24–28 September 2012, Chicago, Illinois.

United Nations (2012) *Big Data for Development: Opportunities and Challenges: A Global Pulse White Paper*. Available from www.unglobalpulse.org/BigDataforDevWhitePaper (accessed 08 Dec 2014).

Van Kleek, M., Smith, D.A., Tinati, R., O'Hara, K., Hall, W. and Shadbolt, N. (2014) *7 Billion Home Telescopes: Observing Social Machines through Personal Data Stores*, in SOCM2014 Workshop on the Theory and Practice of Social Machines, WWW2014.

Weller, M. (2011) *The Digital Scholar: How Technology Is Transforming Scholarly Practice*. London: Bloomsbury.

Woodfield, K., Morrell, G., Metzler, K., Blank, G., Salmons, J., Finnegan, J. and Lucraft, M. (2013) Blurring the Boundaries? New Social Media, New Social Research: Developing A Network to Explore the Issues Faced by Researchers Negotiating the New Research Landscape of Online Social Media Platforms. National Centre for Research Methods Methodological Review paper.

3.5 ONLINE RESOURCES

Archive (2013) – http://archive.org

Cosmos Project – www.cosmosproject.net

Office for National Statistics – www.ons.gov.uk/ons/index.html

Office for National Statistics, *International Passenger Survey* – www.ons.gov.uk ons/guide-method/surveys/respondents/household/international-passenger-survey/index. html

Sentistrength – http://sentistrength.wlv.ac.uk

Snapbird, *Search Beyond Twitter's History* – http://snapbird.org

Social Media Collective *About* – http://socialmediacollective.org/about

Statistical Cybermetrics Research Group, *Webometric Analyst 2.0* – http://lexiurl. wlv.ac.uk

Tweet Archivist, *Powerful, Affordable Twitter Analytics* – www.tweetarchivist. com

UK Data Service (2012) *Secure Access* – http://securedata.data-archive.ac.uk

Webometrics – http://webometrics.wlv.ac.uk

4

SURVEY METHODS: CHALLENGES AND OPPORTUNITIES

JOE MURPHY

4.1 INTRODUCTION

Survey research has traditionally been a process beginning with the formulation of research hypotheses, followed by the construction and testing of a valid question-naire, sampling of survey respondents from the eligible population, administration of the survey for data collection, and processing, analysis, and dissemination of the results. This deliberate process has been carried out and refined over the years to provide data to answer many specific research questions. The result of traditional survey research is what Groves (2011) termed 'designed data' – data with a pre-specified purpose and use in mind. Typically, these data are analysed in and of themselves, without being supplemented or augmented with data from other sources. However, recent years have witnessed an explosion in the quantity and diversity of data associated with surveys. With the advent of computer-assisted interviewing (CAI) in the 1990s, paradata, or 'data about data' allowed researchers to harness information about survey transactions and interactions with respondents to make meaningful insights into the motivation and meaning behind respondents and responses. The availability of external administrative data sources and methods for matching them with survey data has provided additional insights with a minimum of respondent burden and cost. Similarly, developments in e-Infrastructure discussed in this book have made possible advances in the capture, analysis and dissemination of survey data.

As Groves (2011) explains in the 75th Anniversary issue of *Public Opinion Quarterly*, 'We're entering a world where data will be the cheapest commodity around, simply because society has created systems that automatically track transactions of all sorts.' Sometimes referred to as 'big data' or, as Groves describes it, 'organic data,' information is available on an exponentially increasing basis from our everyday lives. Search engines and social media track and can provide data on our information seeking and sharing content, while smartphones, cameras, scanners, meters and sensors of all varieties can track our purchases, movements, and patterns of behaviour.

With the rise of Facebook, Twitter, and the like, social media, in particular, represents a potential goldmine when it comes to supplementing survey methods and data (see Chapter 8 for an example). Compared to the expense of traditional in-person, mail, telephone, and web survey modes, the shift towards communication via online social networks may allow the researcher access to previously unimaginable resources about people's characteristics, opinions, behaviours, and networks. Today's methods of communication, involving smartphones, video chat, instant messages, blogs and podcasts, to name a few, is enormously different from how people communicated with each other just ten years ago, and the pace of change is only increasing as society adapts to newer communication forms (Conrad and Schober, 2008). But survey researchers are just beginning to investigate the possibilities these resources have for supplementing, or in some cases supplanting, traditional survey methods. The shift towards communication via social networks and social media present brand new challenges in the identification of methods to determine representativeness and are forcing us to rethink how we ask questions and engage respondents. These challenges require careful consideration of survey designs to minimize total survey error (Biemer, 2010) and produce accurate estimates.

The advances in technology and e-Infrastructure over the last two decades have come amidst new challenges for the survey discipline. The extent to which surveys can provide a cost-efficient and reliable source of information hinges on the participation of research subjects and survey response rates have been in serious decline (Baruch and Holtom, 2008; Curtin et al., 2005). It seems the general public has become less willing to complete surveys, citing reasons for refusal such as lack of time, feelings that surveys can be an invasion of privacy, and that surveys offer nothing of value to the respondent. After years of being inundated by junk mail, telemarketers, and spam, respondents may simply be fed up with the traditional survey approach and not willing to distinguish it from other solicitations for their time. Technologies that are now commonplace, such as caller ID, have made it easy for respondents to screen their calls and avoid interaction with survey interviewers altogether. The effect of declining response rates has been an issue for the traditional modes of in-person, telephone, and mail surveys alike, resulting in higher costs to conduct research and a greater threat of reduced quality in resulting estimates.

Another threat to the efficiency and quality of survey research specific to telephone surveys has been the declining rates of telephone coverage as more households eschew landline service in favour of mobile (cellular) phones and become 'wireless only' (Blumberg and Luke, 2009). In fact, nearly a decade ago, Holbrook, Green and Krosnick (2003) suggested that telephone numbers can no longer be relied upon for survey sampling. Coverage compares the target population in a survey to the list available for sampling, also known as a sampling frame. The sampling frame defines a set of elements from which a survey researcher can select a sample of the target population (Currivan, 2004). Telephone surveys, conducted using traditional methods, run the risk of missing entire segments of the population if not supplemented with a mobile phone frame. With the inability to rely on a landline telephone sampling frame in which telephone exchanges could be matched to geographic areas, dual-frame (landline and mobile) approaches have arisen. Innovative sampling techniques such as Address-Based Sampling (Iannacchione, 2011) have also been developed to select respondents from lists of mailing addresses where methods like Random Digit Dialling may have sufficed in the past. However, with the rapidly shifting nature of mobile communications, methods innovations will need to keep pace to assure survey researchers are able to access their target populations.

This chapter highlights the challenges facing survey research today and in the future, as well as the opportunities for enhancing and improving the quality and efficiency of survey research methods with the advent of technical innovations. Examples from major social science surveys are included to describe the state of the art as well as point toward the future role and importance of e-Research in survey methods and the social sciences more broadly.

Three components of e-Infrastructure are especially relevant here – administrative data and paradata, online and social media resources, and mobile and emerging computing and communication technologies. As opposed to simply focusing on the potential these components of e-Infrastructure have for survey data, this chapter takes a more holistic view, touching on benefits for all stages of survey development and deployment, including sample building, questionnaire design and pretesting, data collection, and analysis and dissemination. By no means does this chapter represent an exhaustive catalogue of the impact and potential of e-Infrastructure on survey methods, but instead it gives a glimpse into how survey researchers are utilizing previously unavailable resources, and how they may in the future, achieve the persistent goals of surveys – accuracy, precision, timeliness, efficiency and relevance.

4.2 APPLICATION EXAMPLES

4.2.1 External Data Sources

Paradata

The advent of computer-assisted interviewing (CAI) in the 1990s allowed survey researchers to harness, for the first time, automatically generated, detailed, and standardized data on the survey process itself. In 1998, Mick Couper, a leading survey methodologist at the University of Michigan, coined the term 'paradata' to refer to the data that are automatic by-products of computer-assisted interviewing (Couper, 1998). Paradata is similar to metadata (or 'data about data') but refers specifically to information central to the collection of data. Paradata comes in many varieties and from many sources. CAI software makes available keystroke and audit trail files that allows the analyst to trace the entire path through a survey instrument taken by a survey interviewer or respondent, including the act of backing up to prior items, time spent on a particular question or section, and time and date-stamp information associated with the survey.

Nicholaas (2011) discusses several other major categories of paradata that can be useful in gaining insights or making adjustments for surveys. Survey call attempt records are routinely collected by CAI systems, allowing the analyst to use these data in modelling or imputing missing values. Interviewer observations about an area or dwelling can supplement directly collected data from a respondent. Interaction with a survey respondent at the doorstep can provide some indication of the types of information that may be missing if reasons for refusal or non-participation are correlated with the survey outcomes of interest. These interactions can also be valuable in assessing approaches to gaining cooperation with respondents and interviewers' success in their tactics. Audio recordings of interviews or respondent interactions are another source of paradata and have been used on several studies to verify the legitimacy of the survey interview or allow for quality control of interviewers' work (Biemer et al., 2001). Speizer et al. (2009) describe a comprehensive system for processing computer audio-recorded interviews (CARI) to enable research staff to review and manage the audio files recorded during the interview, rate them for quality, and provide feedback to the interviewers.

Paradata has the potential to improve survey data collection management and data quality by allowing the researcher to identify problems with an instrument or interviewer performance quickly, to generate quality control measures, and to produce accurate and timely cost information. CAI surveys like the US National Survey on Drug Use and Health (NSDUH) now routinely make use of paradata in the survey process. The NSDUH is the primary source of statistical information on the use of illegal drugs, alcohol, and tobacco by the US civilian, non-institutionalized population aged 12 or older. The survey collects data through face-to-face interviews with a representative sample of the population at the respondent's place of residence (SAMHSA, 2011). The NSDUH makes use of paradata for interview monitoring in several ways. For example, the survey calculates the amount of time spent on a question compared to a 'Gold Standard' (GS) timing deemed appropriate for a respondent to fully comprehend the information of that particular screen. The survey compares the percentages of interviewers falling below the GS to get a sense of the magnitude of 'shortcutting' – a common concern for data quality in interviewer-administered surveys (Penne, Snodgrass and Barker, 2002).

Wang et al. (2005) used paradata on the NSDUH to examine how the calling strategies of interviewers can affect contact and cooperation rates. They analysed records from the NSDUH's 'record of calls' (ROC). Upon each visit to a sampled dwelling unit, interviewers enter case status information into the ROC using a handheld device. The paradata elements include the outcome of the call (non-contact, refusal, completed screening, completed interview, etc.) and an open-ended notes field for recording information to inform case management and scheduling. Other elements, including the time and day of the call, are automatically recorded in the handheld computer. The results are transmitted back to a central database daily and can be reviewed by an interviewer's supervisors in a web accessible case management system (CMS). The paradata revealed that calling times – defined by the time of the call (before or after 4:00 pm) and the day of the week (weekday vs. weekend) – were related to the probability of contact on the first attempt for the screener. Evidence was also found that using less intensive follow-up efforts to obtain responses from initially non-responding sample members would not necessarily lead to appreciably different survey estimates than those obtained with greater effort. Further, reduction of interviewing effort on a per case basis, at least on the surface, could lead to reductions in data collection costs, resulting in a more efficient data collection effort.

Another application for paradata on the NSDUH is for the early detection and remediation of potential interviewer falsification. Falsification of survey responses introduces bias when falsified responses do not match values that would have been provided by eligible respondents (Schräpler and Wagner, 2003). Item falsification occurs when an interviewer completes individual items on the survey without input from the respondents. Unit falsification, or curbstoning, occurs when an interviewer falsifies the entire survey. Interviews that are excessively short or long compared to expectation are subject to increased verification efforts to determine whether any protocol violations were committed by the interviewer. This technique can be useful in the detection of potential falsification when the falsifying interviewer spends less time (shortcutting) or more time completing the interview than the typical respondent. Analyses in Murphy et al. (2004) show how falsification detection can be improved through the systematic review of response data and metadata such as module and item timings. Through early detection and remediation, the threat of falsification to survey bias and increased costs can be reduced.

Despite the insights that have been gained through incorporating the monitoring of paradata into the survey process, the use of paradata is still nascent and much research is needed to identify the elements that must be collected and analysed in order to improve data quality, efficiency, and analytic capacity. As we begin to fully understand the potential of paradata sources like eye tracking (Graesser et al., 2005) and biofeedback – 'real time information from psychophysiological recordings about the levels at which physiological systems are functioning' (Horowitz, 2006; AAPB 2015) we will have the ability to further improve the accuracy and add to the insights gained through survey data collection.

Administrative Data

Another source of data available through e-Infrastructure that can supplement those collected from surveys is administrative databases. Large-scale social surveys often link survey responses with administrative data at the area or household level using unique individual identifiers or respondent characteristics.

Administrative data matching, or record linkage, can be used to create survey frames, remove duplicate cases from files, or combine different files to study relationships on two or more data elements (Winkler, 2006). Record linkage methods compare data elements such as name and address across multiple files to find matches on the same entity. Winkler describes several examples of administrative data matching in survey research. For example, the 1990 US Decennial Census Post Enumeration Survey (PES) matched individuals to the Census so that a capture-recapture methodology could be employed for estimating undercoverage and overcoverage. This method is similar to estimating the number of fish in a pond – you capture a set of fish, tag them in some way to identify them later, put them back in the pond, give the fish some time to swim around, capture a second set (' recapture'), count the number recaptured and tagged, and finally use this information to estimate the total number of fish in the pond (Groves, 2012; Murphy, 2009). Computerized matching procedures were used in the 1992 US Census of Agriculture to reduce the need for manual clerical review. Administrative lists were used to match farms, individuals, partnerships, and corporations. A validation study following the matching confirmed that the matching procedures identified more duplicates automatically than the clerks were able to identify in the previous Census of Agriculture.

Jenkins et al. (2004) provide an example of a study linking survey responses to UK government records on benefits and tax credits using five different methods. One method used respondent-supplied National Insurance Numbers to link with administrative data and the others used combinations of demographic information such as sex, name, address, and date of birth. The authors found that the administrative data were relatively accurate when assessed in terms of false positive and false negative rates with self-reported data. The matching exercises pointed to the potential benefits of supplementing household survey responses with administrative data.

For the World Trade Center Health Registry, a study following more than 70,000 enrollees who were exposed to dust and debris and the psychological trauma from the September 11, 2001 World Trade Center disaster, Murphy, Pulliam and Lucas (2004) describe the process by which administrative lists were systematically deduplicated using an algorithm to identify likely duplicates and assess the resulting increase in quality and reduction in cost and respondent burden. These methods are important for environmental exposure registries which face the challenge of compiling a cohort that may be exposed to some substance or contaminant across years or decades. Because these cohorts disperse across time, multiple data sources are often used to identify potential registrants, including administrative databases.

4.2.2 Social Networks and Online Communities

Facebook

With the relatively recently boom in popularity of online social networks , a new source of data to supplement, or perhaps in some cases supplant, survey data is available that was barely imaginable a decade ago. Launched in February 2004, Facebook boasts over 1.28 billion active monthly users as of March 2014 (Facebook, 2014). Users can sign up for free, complete a profile, and share information about themselves, such as hometown, current city, education, employment, interests, and favourites. Users post photos, videos, notes, and status updates with the intention that their personal contacts (referred to as 'friends' on Facebook) will view and comment on these communications. Facebook is also used to make new contacts and follow, or 'like,' different groups, organizations, or products. The Pew Research Center conducted a survey of 1,802 Internet users in the United States and found that Facebook is used by 67 per cent of US adults, but coverage is highest among young adults and women (Duggan and Brenner, 2013).

Facebook is a potentially valuable resource for survey researchers in several ways. First, it represents a population from which study participants may be recruited.

While there are currently no existing validated methods for drawing a representative sample from the general population on Facebook, let alone among Facebook users, targeted advertisements can be placed to recruit participants for a convenience sample or for smaller-scale pretesting, such as cognitive interviewing, which is generally less reliant on samples from which results will be generalized.

Facebook is especially well-suited for conducting convenience sample surveys of hard-to-reach populations (Bhutta, 2012). For example, Bhutta was able to conduct a survey of thousands of Catholics using Facebook independently in a matter of weeks and for very little cost. Her survey replicated key correlations found in standard surveys, although her sample skewed toward females, younger people, the better educated, and the religiously active. Bhutta began her search for Catholic respondents on Facebook by creating a group called 'Please Help Me Find Baptized Catholics!' She also contacted the administrators of several Facebook groups to solicit their help in recruiting volunteers for the study. In total, nearly 7,500 people joined the group within a month and were sent the link to the survey.

Rhodes and Marks (2011) utilized Facebook for locating and retaining sample members – a chronic challenge for longitudinal surveys. Retention of survey participants in a longitudinal study is important to address the potential for non-response bias, and the Internet has offered additional options, like Facebook, for aiding this process. Rhodes and Marks searched for and contacted participants in the Saving for Education, Entrepreneurship, and Downpayment for Oklahoma Kids study (SEED) and encouraged them to contact the study to complete a telephone interview. They identified two categories of interviews associated with Facebook – those who completed the interview as a direct result of the Facebook contact, and those who took the Facebook contact as a prompt and subsequently completed the interview. While finding some demographic differences in the types of respondents who completed the interview as a result of the Facebook locating and tracing methods, the authors concluded that Facebook can be an effective tool for locating and contacting sample members not responding to more traditional contact methods.

The real potential for Facebook in survey research may lie in the ability of researchers to access the 'social graph' – the network of entities and individuals linked on the site (Sage, 2013). The Graph API is where information on users' characteristics, connections, 'likes' and sharing behaviours can be retrieved. Facebook Applications or 'apps' can be built for the direct administration of surveys, the building of population registries, and for the tracing of participants in longitudinal studies. Apps, with the user's permission, can allow the researcher to link information collected in the application with the user's characteristics, social networks, and usage data to supplement the breadth of the data, much in the way administrative records are used to enhance survey data collection.

Twitter, Google, and Infoveillance

Social networks like Twitter allow for mass-scale sharing of thoughts, opinions, and behaviours worldwide and provide an opportunity to draw insights from data where survey data have traditionally been employed. In recent years, researchers have begun analysing massive volumes of Twitter posts ('tweets') and search queries from Google to demonstrate that people's information-seeking and information-sharing behaviours online are correlated with phenomena such as flu outbreaks, introduction of new nicotine delivery products, tobacco tax avoidance, and even weekend box office sales for movies (e.g., Ginsberg et al., 2009; Ayers et al, 2011a; 2011b; Goel et al., 2010). Murphy et al. (2011b) explore the surveillance of an emerging drug trend for *Salvia Divinorum*, using Twitter feeds and Google search trends, and compare tweets and Google search volume to reports from publicly available survey data. These studies exemplify the emerging fields of infoveillance and sentiment analysis. Infoveillance is the automated and continuous analysis of unstructured, free text information available on the Internet (Eysenbach, 2009). Sentiment analysis is the automated computational coding of text to determine if expressed opinions are positive, neutral, or negative (see the following section for more information on sentiment analysis). Applied to sources like Twitter tweets and Google searches, these approaches have been shown, in some circumstances, to produce results that correlate with and even predict those collected through traditional data collection methods. For example, Eysenbach (2009) found a high correlation between clicks on sponsored search results for flu-related keywords and actual flu cases using epidemiological data from 2004 to 2005. Polgreen et al. (2008) showed that search volume for influenza-related queries was correlated with actual reported flu from 2004 to 2008.

As a supplement or alternative to traditional survey research, infoveillance has some attractive qualities. The sheer volume of Google search queries and posts on Twitter provide a glimpse into the thoughts of at least some subset of the general population. As evidenced by prior studies, these streams have the potential to replicate health trends, often providing an earlier indication of trends than can reasonably be supplied via surveys. With data available on the Web, no burden is placed on survey respondents because there are no respondents, as traditionally defined. The speed at which one can investigate a topic of interest using infoveillance greatly exceeds that of a traditional survey approach. Whereas a survey requires sample identification, question construction, contact attempts, and data collection prior to analysis, infoveillance requires only access to the stream of Google queries and tweets and a method for analysing the content. Infoveillance suffers, however, from a high degree of obscurity around several of the most important tenets of survey methodology. The degree to which queries and tweets represent the general population, let alone a specific target population for any given study, is practically unknown. The lack of information on the coverage of these data makes it impossible to construct accurate population-based estimates. Those who search or post are not guided in any way that is related to the information sought. In essence, the respondent is making up his or her own questions to a survey, and thus, there is no standardization or check on the validity of the information being shared. How do the results of these studies compare to estimates obtained though traditional survey methods? What does it mean if these new methods can produce results that correlate with, or even appear to predict, those collected through traditional survey methods, but the representativeness and other error properties of tweets and search queries are unknown? These are questions with which survey analysts will need to contend with as they consider the role of Twitter and other online social network data sources in survey research.

Another application for Twitter in survey research is as a means for diary data collection. Diaries are used as a data collection method in which the respondent is asked to record events as they occur, as opposed to retrospectively responding in a standard survey format (Butcher and Eldrige, 1990). Cook et al. (2012) conducted an exploratory study to test the feasibility of asking diary style questions on Twitter and to determine how participants would respond. Their motivation was based on the fact that when Twitter first emerged in 2006, it prompted users to respond to the question, 'What are you doing?' as would a diary instrument.[1] One idea is that Twitter respondents may be more likely to complete their diary because of Twitter's availability on desktop computers as well as mobile phones and tablets. The constant access respondents have to Twitter can reduce non-response, as well as measurement error caused by retrospective responding. Twitter diaries, compared to traditional diary interfaces, can result in decreased respondent burden if respondents are familiar and fluent with the Twitter client user interface. The motivation for sharing may also translate to increased likelihood of reporting on Twitter. Of course, this raises the concern of the effects of social desirability bias and runs counter to the conventional thinking about respondent confidentiality in survey administration – however, it is likely that some respondents will prefer Twitter as an interface precisely because they can share their behaviours and opinions with friends or the entire world. The authors conducted Twitter diary studies with three distinct non-probability samples of Twitter users: Hispanics, young adults, and diabetics. Participants were asked to tweet responses to questions asked via a study Twitter account in a variety of question formats. Each participant was assigned to a diary on one of three topics: diet, activity, or mood. The authors compared responses by public Tweet versus private direct messages (DMs – a private message only visible to the recipient). They found that participants utilized the DM option when they did not want to tweet publicly. Across all diaries, 30 per cent of participants DM'd one or more responses. This suggests that participants did not necessarily view the Twitter survey as a requirement to publicize their responses. The Twitter platform made participants highly accessible, but their privacy concern was not necessarily a limitation given that they could DM their responses.

Opinion Mining and Sentiment Analysis

The explosion of data afforded by the Internet calls for more sophisticated and automated research methods. One such method for making sense of the oceans of data available to supplement survey research is web mining, and more specifically, opinion mining (Liu, 2012). Web mining draws meaningful content from hyperlinks, page content and usage logs. Data mining and machine learning methods use algorithms to pull, organize, and analyse content by topic. Methods from this toolbox include web crawling, social network analysis, structured data extraction, opinion mining and sentiment analysis, among others. Opinion mining, specifically, is the computational

---

[1]Twitter updated the prompt to 'What's Happening?' in 2009.

study of opinions, sentiments, subjectivity, evaluations, attitudes, appraisal, affects, views, emotions, etc., expressed in text. These methods can be applied to free form data from large surveys themselves, or from other sources such as online social networks to draw meaningful insights to supplement survey data.

Sentiment analysis makes use of natural language processing algorithms to code data into, for example, positive, neutral, or negative statements about a topic. Davies and Ghahramani (2011) applied sentiment analysis to Twitter statuses, modelling happy versus sad sentiment, and showed that language-independent models can predict sentiment with high accuracy in specific settings. The authors also show how sentiment distributions can be modelled by geographic regions, while incorporating information from neighbouring regions. Importantly, the authors outline the considerations when creating a system to analyse Twitter data and present a scalable system of data acquisition and prediction for monitoring Tweet sentiment in real time.

Opinion mining can be utilized directly with survey data themselves. Because the time and expense involved in traditional qualitative coding, methods are increasingly prohibitive, Tesfaye (2011) discusses text mining techniques as an increasingly attractive alternative to traditional qualitative coding for open-ended survey data. She compared traditional coding with text analytical and natural language processing strategies based on open ended responses from the 2008 Nationwide Survey of High School Physics Teachers. Tesfaye argues that by integrating these automated processes and knowledge from the fields of linguistics and natural language processing, survey methodologists better understand the patterns inherent in their data and analyse answers from open ended survey questions more efficiently. As Tesfaye concludes, 'If data is indeed the new oil, natural language processing could be the new rig' (p.19).

Virtual Worlds

One of the more futuristic possibilities for conducting surveys made possible by e-Infrastructure is conducting interviews with embodied conversational agents (ECAs) in online virtual worlds. ECAs are graphical depictions of humans (a.k.a. 'avatars') that interact in human-like ways.

One realm in which avatars are already being employed for survey research is Second Life (SL) – an online three-dimensional world in which users ('residents') create avatars and interact with their environment and each other. Residents in SL can communicate through instant messages and voice chat. As opposed to Facebook and Twitter, which typically augment the real-life persona and relationships, SL residents represent themselves in ways that depart from real-life appearances and personalities (which introduces challenges for survey research, to be sure).

Residents in Second Life come from more than 100 countries. Usage is measured in terms of user-hours; 481 million user hours were logged in 2009 (Linden Lab, 2011). As of November 2008, the most active users were 25–44 years old (64 percent of hours logged) and male (59 percent of hours logged) (Linden Lab, 2009). Unfortunately, Second Life no longer publishes user statistics but anecdotally, popularity of the site has plateaued since 2008. Second Life provides a context-rich environment for conducting cognitive interviews and other survey pretesting activities (Dean et al., 2009; Murphy et al., 2010). The system allows the researcher to target and recruit specific types of residents through classified-type advertisements, online bulletin boards, and word-of-mouth in the virtual world, which can be more efficient and cost-effective when compared with traditional newspaper ads or flyers that are typically used to recruit in-person cognitive interview subjects (Dean et al., 2011). Text-based chat and voice chat can be collected for analysis, offering full transcripts of cognitive interviews. The only elements of in-person cognitive interviews missing from the paradata are facial and physical expressions, although SL residents can manipulate these for their avatars to a certain extent.

Richards and Dean (2013) used Second Life to evaluate the Randomized Response Technique (RRT) – a survey method designed to elicit accurate responses to sensitive questions. The RRT provides two questions (one sensitive and the other not sensitive) with a known response distribution and randomizes the question a respondent receives via an action with a known probability, such as a coin toss. Only the respondent sees the outcome of the random action. Since the researcher is not aware which question the respondent is answering, the idea is that the respondent will feel less stigma in answering the sensitive item, if the coin toss determines this is the item selected for response. The researcher can calculate proportions for each response to the sensitive question since the probability of receiving that item is known. Since the randomizer is concealed from the researcher in a typical administration, the method is difficult to evaluate. Richards and Dean replicated an evaluation in Second Life in which they controlled the randomizer via a 3-dimensional virtual coin flip. They evaluated eight RRT in a non-probability survey of 75 participants in Second Life, randomly assigning participants to face-to-face (or 'avatar-to-avatar'), voice chat and web survey modes. The authors were able to conclude that RRT compliance was low and that respondents were sceptical of the utility of the approach. Conversely, respondents found the interactive and unique features of the interview technique engaging, suggesting that a 'gamified' approach to surveying in Second Life may be fruitful for future research.

4.3.3 Mobile Computing

One of the most radical shifts in recent years with which the survey world is beginning to contend is the shift towards mobile and handheld multi-mode communication devices. These devices typically fall under the names 'smartphones' and 'tablets.' Smartphones in particular have enjoyed a boom in popularity in recent years. As of 2014, a majority of US mobile subscribers of all age groups own smartphones (Nielsen, 2014). The label 'phone' really belies the capabilities of these devices. Not only can they serve as mobile telephones, but allow the user to access email, the Internet, global positioning systems (GPS), cameras, and accelerometers among ever increasing features. Keating (2012) offers a multitude of potential applications for mobile devices in survey research including questionnaire administration, respondent diaries, short messaging service (SMS or texting), and Bluetooth capabilities. Examples of consumer smartphone applications to record data, diaries, and geolocation include diary data collection, dietary trackers, air quality and environmental exposure assessments, fitness trackers, biomarker collection, and location trackers. Keating points out potential challenges to using smartphones for survey tasks as well, including human subjects concerns, potential sample biases, and deployment logistics.

SMS Text Messages

The pervasiveness, low cost and convenience of mobile phones make short-message-service (SMS) texting an ideal application for disseminating as well as gathering health information from consumers (Fjeldsoe, 2009). SMS allows for the administration of health surveys immediately following some event at a predetermined periodicity. SMS can also supplement data collection and health communications and is currently being used by researchers to address health knowledge, risk reduction, social support, and patient involvement (Coomes et al., 2012; Uhrig, 2012).

Texting is currently being employed in several studies to remind sample members to complete survey tasks according to a pre-determined schedule, since prior literature shows that it can be a cost-effective, low-burden way to re-contact sample members. In a series of experiments in Finland, Virtanen et al. (2007) randomly assigned respondents to receive a mail survey reminder through a conventional letter or as a text message to their mobile telephones. The response rate was significantly higher for the group that received the SMS reminders. A few other experiments suggest that SMS systems can effectively increase medication and appointment adherence as well as sustain health promotion behaviours such as smoking cessation, diabetes, asthma management, and depression (Cole-Lewis and Kershaw, 2010). Furberg (2012) describes work employing SMS to integrate daily health diary reminders, compliance prompts following incomplete or missed entries, and a suite of health promotion messaging content. In this way, SMS and text messages have the potential to impact participant satisfaction, retention, and data quality, among other future implementations. Despite early promises much work needs to be done to provide rigorous evaluations of SMS in survey research applications.

Smartphones and Mobile Devices

It is worth noting that the social network sites described above are increasingly being accessed on mobile devices. Technological advances in mobile devices and programming will continue to make these devices an increasingly useful tool for survey researchers. Smartphones and tablets, with high-resolution screens, high-speed data connections, text messaging, and many other features are now the devices of choice for consumers. Advances in network and communications infrastructure have allowed for making fast, mobile access available to large proportions of the population, and increasingly worldwide (Fuchs and Busse, 2008; UN News Centre, 2010).

The full-featured and programmable nature of these devices, along with their popularity, make the smartphone an attractive tool for survey researchers (Raento, Oulasvirta and Eagle, 2009). Survey researchers have been experimenting with handheld devices since they came on the scene (Shermach, 2005; Townsend, 2005). Peytchev and Hill (2009), however, note that the systematic research typically required for use of new 'modes' of data collection has not yet been extensively conducted for mobile devices. Issues such as limited screen size and the location of a respondent completing a smartphone survey require investigation. Nonetheless, there are already numerous choices for survey researchers who want to conduct surveys using mobile devices, including companies such as SurveySwipe, Techneos, Vovici, and Zoomerang,[2] among many others. A recent search of Apple's 'App Store' for 'mobile survey research' resulted in nearly 50 applications available, including several free apps.

4.3.4 Crowds and Clouds

Another recent development of interest to survey researchers is the advent of online crowdsourcing. Crowdsourcing is 'the act of a company or institution taking a function once performed by employees and outsourcing it to an undefined and generally large network of people in the form of an open call' (Howe, 2006). As described by Duan et al. (2011), crowdsourcing has been applied in the survey research area as an innovative recruitment tool and data collection method. Crowdsourcing can be used as a recruitment method to build a panel, similar to online recruitment methods. It can also be used to administer questions and collect responses from a large sample of respondents when surveys are posted on crowdsourcing websites or in smartphone applications. Crowdsourcing can be used to construct more diverse samples than traditionally recruited samples, such as in web surveys. Duan et al. conducted a pilot study in Africa to measure differences between crowdsourcing and in-person interviews collecting establishment information through a mobile app. They found the crowdsourcing approach led to increased compliance with the survey tasks, ability to reach a younger population, and efficiency in data collection as compared to in-person administration. Unfortunately, they also found that the resulting sample was not representative of their target population and overall had a lower rate of response compared to the in-person administration.

Cloud computing is a component of e-Infrastructure that allows for ubiquitous, convenient, on-demand network access to a shared pool of configurable computing resources such as networks, servers, storage, applications, and services (Mell and Grance, 2011). The cloud can be provisioned and released quickly with little management effort or service provider interaction. Survey researchers have just begun to take advantage of cloud-based solutions to improve data collection efficiency. Harris (2012) describes the process by which the US Energy Information Administration (EIA) has employed cloud technology for electronic data collection. For the EIA,

---

[2]www.surveyswipe.com; www.techneos.com; www.vovici.com; www.zoomerang.com

cloud computing has effectively reduced IT and lifecycle sustainment costs and has increased flexibility and speed in IT implementations. An internal assessment found that the EIA was previously using 116 disparate applications and systems to support energy statistics programs and that data was being effectively compiled but not effectively managed.

In terms of survey data collection, one can envision that cloud resources can be utilized to store, maintain, and organize the ever-increasing volume of data associated with the survey process, from field management to data collection, to analysis, to dissemination. Reallocation of resources saved by implementing cloud-based solutions could be used to address the many questions posed in the following section concerning the future of survey research methods and data collection strategies.

4.3 EXTENSION FOR FUTURE RESEARCH

Social science surveys are designed to produce estimates that are accurate, precise, timely, efficient, and relevant. While traditional methods still comprise the majority of survey research conducted today, new technologies, social media and e-Infrastructure bring with them new opportunities to supplement survey methods and the estimates obtained from surveys.

Researchers looking to incorporate these new resources into survey methods must be aware that information and communications and technologies are undergoing rapid changes at the moment and that caution should be taken when evaluating and incorporating these new methods. At present, the new methods are heavy on promise and light on theory. The challenge to researchers is to assure that new methods are being evaluated and held to the same standards as traditional ones. New methods must be evaluated from multiple perspectives. The total survey error framework offers a paradigm under which we may objectively consider the roles and appropriate use of e-Infrastructure resources in survey research. This framework considers the impact of methods on both sampling error (sampling scheme, sample size, estimator choice) and nonsampling error (specification, non-response, frame, measurement, data processing) (Biemer, 2011). But there are additional considerations such as cost and timeliness that may prompt one to considering the use of newer technologies even if they may not be able to match established methods in terms of known quality.

As discussed in Chapter 12 of this volume, ethical issues must also be considered when a new mode or technology is being evaluated. In the zeal to adopt and use new communications technologies and platforms, prudence is advocated in thinking about research ethics as they may apply in this new world of e-Research. Importantly, informed consent of survey participants is a basic tenet of scientific research on human populations. We must be continually cognizant of the need to offer both privacy and confidentiality with regard to the data collected during the process. Web sites and social media platforms include privacy statements and policies, many of which note that posted data may be collected and analysed in aggregate. The privacy statement of Facebook, in particular, has been scrutinized for its length, changing rules over time, and obscurity where user privacy is concerned. Social networking sites profit heavily from the use of information produced by users and by selling aggregate data to advertisers for their use in targeting narrow slices of the buying population.

Utilizing these new resources as things stand assumes that researchers can ethically obtain and analyse data via web scraping or collecting data from social media platforms without obtaining a priori informed consent. To obtain informed consent when using passive research methods may be virtually impossible and the act of obtaining this consent may have an effect on the behaviour of the people providing the data, potentially introducing bias and reduced availability of such data in the future if individuals become less likely to share as a result.

While this chapter shows the strong need for additional survey methods benefiting from new sources of social data, the future remains wide open with more questions than answers. These questions are currently being considered and debated by survey researchers and have been the topic of several recent thought pieces. For example, Murphy et al. (2011a) offer several questions warranting investigation when it comes to evaluating the potential for innovations in survey research:

4.3 1 Quality Issues

When we evaluate new technologies that may benefit survey research, what data quality issues from the total survey error framework must we examine? Is it sufficient to find a consistent link between, say, tweets on a topic and a time series of data produced by traditional survey methods and assume the properties of the latter apply to the former? How reliable and valid are data collected through the Internet and social media platforms and how can we objectively evaluate the validity of data resulting from the actions of thousands or millions of people across the globe? What tools and techniques are needed to be able to assess reliability and validity in these new modes?

4.3.2 Lessons from Adjacent Disciplines

What research, including that presented in this volume, is being done in social science fields adjacent to survey research to utilize the internet and social media for increased quality, efficiency and timeliness? These fields include, among others, marketing, media studies, health communications, and human-computer interaction. How can survey research, as a discipline, best link into these adjacencies and benefit from this research in a rapidly changing world of data and e-Research tools?

4.3.3 Communication Preferences

What can we expect from research subjects in the new world of communications? Will survey respondents actively share information with survey researchers via social media and new technologies such as smartphones? Will they provide their permission for researchers to access their existing data for research purposes? Will they fully understand the potential ramifications of giving this permission? How can we best tailor requests for such information? Will the two-way nature of social media communication create the expectations that survey researchers will share information back with respondents, letting them know how they compare to their peers and the general population on the measures of interest?

What information can or should we share back with respondents and does the promise of this type of transparency motivate respondents and reduce survey error? If we are to make use of the two-way and interactive nature of social media, how can we do so without sacrificing confidentiality or raising other respondent concerns?

What modes of communication do different types of survey respondents prefer when being contacted for or when completing a survey? Can a lengthy survey be conducted appropriately from a smartphone interface? What risks are there when a respondent may be completing a survey on such a device when not appropriate (e.g., while driving or in public places that risk a breach of confidentiality)? Is there a difference between what respondents say they prefer and what methods they use to respond?

Is it ethical to use publicly available social media data for research purposes without the user's consent? Is there an expectation that even though these data are public that they should not be downloaded and combined with other similar data for analysis? What guarantees do researchers have that those using social networking sites are indeed of the age required by that platform and should age validation be required before any data are used for research purposes?

4.3.4 Representativeness

What are the demographic profiles of users of different systems or technologies and how do they differ from the general population or specific populations of interest for survey researchers? Will we be able to compile accurate frame data to draw representative samples from e-Infrastructure sources?

As evidenced by this multitude of outstanding questions and ethical considerations, the future holds promise for improving survey research, but a great deal of uncertainty regarding exactly how and when new methods will be appropriate to supplement the traditional ones. New technologies could be used to supplement traditional survey approaches and encourage participation from those respondents who have access to and are comfortable with new technologies. With the proliferation of possible survey modes brought on by new technologies, there is the potential to increase participation if people appreciate the ability to choose their preferred response mode (Dillman, 2000; Schaefer and Dillman, 1998). Although mode preference can lead to increased participation in that mode, it may not always result in higher overall response rates, and the effect of appealing to mode preference on non-response bias is still an open question (Olson, Smyth and Wood, 2012).

While new digital technologies may not ultimately replace traditional approaches, it is important to continue evaluating the potential of new technologies and social media tools and their role in survey research to stay current during a time of fast-paced evolution in communications.

4.5 BIBLIOGRAPHY

Association of Applied Psychophysiology and Biofeedback (AAPB) (2015) Psychophysiology | Biofeedback. Available from http://biofeedback.org/about/psycophys (accessed 18 Jan 2015).

Ayers, J.W., Ribisl, K. and Brownstein, J.S. (2011a) 'Using search query surveillance to monitor tax avoidance and smoking cessation following the United States' 2009 "SCHIP" cigarette tax increase', *PLoS One*, 6(3), e16777.

Ayers, J.W., Ribisl, K.M. and Brownstein, J.S. (2011b) 'Tracking the rise in popularity of electronic nicotine delivery systems (electronic cigarettes) using search query surveillance', *American Journal and Preventive Medicine*, 40(4): 448–53.

Baruch, Y. and Holtom, B.C. (2008) 'Survey response rate levels and trends in organizational research', *Human Relations*, 61(8): 1139–60.

Bhutta, C.B. (2012) 'Not by the book: Facebook as a sampling frame', *Sociological Research and Methods*. March 21. doi: 10.1177/0049124112440795

Biemer, P.P. (2010) 'Total survey error: design, implementation, and evaluation', *Public Opinion Quarterly*, 74(5): 817–48.

Biemer, P.P., Herget, D., Morton, J. and Willis, G. (2001) 'The feasibility of monitoring field interviewer performance using computer audio recorded interviewing (CARI)', *Proceedings of the American Statistical Association, Survey Research Methods Section*. Available from www.amstat.org/sections/srms/proceedings/papers/2000_183.pdf (accessed 10 Dec 2014).

Blumberg, S.J. and Luke, J.V. (2009) 'Reevaluating the need for concern regarding noncoverage bias in landline surveys', *American Journal of Public Health*, 99(10): 1806–10.

Butcher, R. and Eldrige, J. (1990) 'The use of diaries in data collection', *The Statistician*, 39: 25–41.

Cole-Lewis, H. and Kershaw, T. (2010) 'Text messaging as a tool for behavior change in disease prevention and management', *Epidemiologic Reviews*, 32(1): 56–69.

Conrad, F.G. and Schober, M. (2008) *Envisioning the Survey Interview of the Future*. Hoboken, NJ : John Wiley and Sons.

Cook, S., Richards, A., Dean, E. and Haque, S. (2012) '"What's happening?" Twitter for diary studies', paper presented at the 67th Annual Meeting of the American Association for Public Opinion Research, Orlando, Florida.

Coomes, C.M., Lewis, M.A., Uhrig, J.D., Furberg, R.D., Harris, J.L. and Bann, C. (2012) 'Beyond reminders: a conceptual framework for using short message service to promote prevention and improve healthcare quality and clinical outcomes for people living with HIV', *AIDS Care*, 24(3): 348–57.

Couper, M. (1998) 'Measuring survey quality in a CASIC environment', *Proceedings of the Section on Survey Research Methods of the American Statistical Association*.

Currivan, D.B. (2004). 'Sampling frame', in M. Lewis-Beck, A. Bryman and T.F. Liao, (eds), *Encyclopedia of Social Science Research Methods*. Thousand Oaks, CA: Sage.

Curtin, R., Presser, S. and Singer, E. (2005) 'Changes in telephone survey nonresponse over the past quarter century', *Public Opinion Quarterly*, 69: 87–98.

Davies, A. and Ghahramani, Z. (2011) 'Language-independent Bayesian sentiment mining of Twitter', paper presented at the 5th SNA-KDD Workshop '11 (SNA-KDD'11). San Diego, CA.

Dean, E.F., Cook, S.L., Keating, M.D., and Murphy, J.J. (2009). Does this avatar make me look fat? Obesity and interviewing in second life, *Journal of Virtual Worlds Research*, 2(2). http://jvwresearch.org (accessed 10 Dec 2014).

Dillman, D.A. (2000) *Mail and Internet Surveys: The Tailored Design Method*. New York, NY: Wiley.

Duan, S., Bailey, J.T. and Link, M.W. (2011) 'Data collection method innovation: utilizing a crowdsourcing application to collect factual information in Africa', paper presented at the 36th Annual Conference of the Midwest Association for Public Opinion Research, Chicago,

IL. Available from www.mapor.org/confdocs/absandpaps/2011/2011_slides/3d2Duan.pdf. (accessed 09 April 2015).

Duggan, M. and Brenner, J. (2013) 'The demographics of social media users – 2012'. Available from http://pewinternet.org/~/media//Files/Reports/2013/PIP_SocialMedia Users.pdf (accessed 09 Dec 2014).

Eysenbach, G. (2009) 'Infodemiology and infoveillance: framework for an emerging set of public health informatics methods to analyze search, communication and publication behavior on the Internet', *Journal of Medical Internet Research*, 11(1), e11.

Facebook (2014) Key Facts. Available from http://newsroom.fb.com/Key-Facts (accessed 10 Dec 2014).

Fjeldsoe, B.S., Marshall, A.L. and Miller, Y.D. (2009) 'Behavior change interventions delivered by mobile telephone short-message service', *American Journal of Preventive Medicine*, Feb;36(2): 165–73. doi: 10.1016/j.amepre.2008.09.040 (accessed 10 Dec 2014).

Fuchs, M. and Busse, B. (2008) 'The coverage bias of mobile web surveys across European countries', *International Journal of Internet Science*, 4 (1): 21–3.

Furberg, R. (2012) 'SMS-adjunct to support data quality and compliance in health survey research', paper presented at the 67th Annual Conference of the American Association for Public Opinion Research, Orlando, FL.

Ginsberg, J., Mohebbi, M.H., Patel, R.S., Brammer, L., Smolinski, M.S. and Brilliant, L. (2009) 'Detecting influenza epidemics using search engine query data', *Nature* 457(7232): 1012–14.

Goel, S., Hofman, J.M., Lanaie, S., Pennock, D.M. and Watts, D.J. (2010) 'Predicting consumer behavior with Web search', Proceedings of the National Academy of Sciences, 107(41): 17486–90.

Graesser, A.C., Lu, S., Olde, B., Cooper-Pye E. and Whitten S. (2005) 'Question asking and eye tracking during cognitive disequilibrium: comprehending illustrated texts on devices when the devices break down', *Memory and Cognition*, 33(7): 1235–47.

Groves, R.M. (2011) 'Three eras of survey research', *Public Opinion Quarterly,* 75(5): 861–71. doi: 10.1093/poq/nfr057

Groves, R. (2012) 'How do we conduct a post-enumeration survey?' Available from http://directorsblog.blogs.census.gov/2012/05/17/how-do-we-conduct-a-post-enumeration-survey/ (accessed 09 Dec 2014).

Harris, S. (2012) 'It is in the clouds: electronic data collection', Federal CASIC Workshops, Washington, DC. Available from https://fedcasic.dsd.census.gov/fc2012/ppt/09_harris.ppt (accessed 09 Dec 2014).

Holbrook, A.L., Green, M.C., & Krosnick, J.A. (2003). 'Telephone vs. face-to-face interviewing of national probability samples with long questionnaires: comparisons of respondent satisficing and social desirability response bias' *Public Opinion Quarterly*, 67, 79–125.

Horowitz, S. (2006) 'Biofeedback applications: a survey of clinical research', *Alternative and Complementary Therapies*, December.

Howe, J. (2006) 'The rise of crowdsourcing', *Wired Magazine*, 14(6). Available from www.wired.com/wired/archive/14.06/crowds.html (accessed 10 Dec 2014).

Iannacchione, V.G. (2011) 'The changing role of address-based sampling in survey research', *Public Opinion Quarterly*, 75(3): 556–75.

Jenkins, S.P., Lynn, P., Jäckle, A. and Sala, E. (2004) 'Linking household survey and administrative record data: what should the matching variables be?', ISER Working Paper 2004–23. Colchester: University of Essex.

Keating, M. D. (2012, May). 'Smartphones as a research tool'. Presented at 67th Annual Conference of the American Association for Public Opinion Research, Orlando, FL.

Linden Lab (2009) *The Second Life Economy – First Quarter 2009 in detail*. Available from http://community.secondlife.com/t5/Features/The-Second-Life-Economy-First-Quarter-2009-in-Detail/ba-p/642113 (accessed 10 Dec 2014).

Linden Lab. (2011) *The Second Life Economy in Q2 2011*. Available from http://community. secondlife.com/t5/Featured-News/The-Second-Life-Economy-in-Q2-2011/ba-p/1035321 (accessed 09 Dec 2014).

Liu, B. (2012) *Sentiment Analysis and Opinion Mining*. San Rafael, CA: Morgan and Claypool Publishers.

Mell, P. and Grance, T. (2011) The NIST Definition of Cloud Computing: Recommendations of the National Institute of Standards and Technology. NIST Special Publication 800–145. Available from http://csrc.nist.gov/publications/nistpubs/800-145/SP800-145.pdf (accessed 09 Dec 2014).

Morales, L. (2011) 'Google and Facebook users skew young, affluent, and educated'. Available from www.gallup.com/poll/146159/facebook-google-users-skew-young-affluent-educated.aspx

Murphy, J. (2009) 'Estimating the World Trade Center tower population on September 11, 2001: a capture-recapture approach', *American Journal of Public Health*, 99(1): 65–7.

Murphy, J., Baxter, R., Eyerman, J., Cunningham, D. and Kennet, J. (2004) 'A system for detecting interviewer falsification', *Proceedings of the American Statistical Association, Survey Research Methods Section*. Available from www.amstat.org/sections/srms/ proceedings/y2004/files/Jsm2004-000517.pdf (accessed 10 Dec 2014).

Murphy, J., Pulliam, P. and Lucas, R. (2004) 'Sample frame de-duplication in the World Trade Center health registry', *Proceedings of the American Statistical Association, Survey Research Methods Section*. Available from www.amstat.org/sections/srms/ proceedings/y2004/files/Jsm2004-000514.pdf (accessed 09 Dec 2014).

Murphy, J.J., Dean, E.F., Cook, S.L., and Keating, M.D. (2010). *The Effect of Interviewer Image in A Virtual-world Survey*. Research Triangle Park, NC: RTI Press.

Murphy, J., Dean, E., Hill, C.A. and Richards, R. (2011a) 'Social media, new technologies, and the future of health survey research', paper presented at the 10th Conference on Health Survey Research Methods. Peachtree City, GA.

Murphy, J.J., Kim, A., Hansen, H.M., Richards, A.K., Augustine, C.B., Kroutil, L.A. and Sage, A.J. (2011b) 'Twitter feeds and Google search query surveillance: can they supplement survey data collection?', *Proceedings of at Association for Survey Computing Sixth International Conference*. Available from www.rti.org/pubs/twitter_ google_search_surveillance.pdf (accessed 09 Dec 2014).

Nicolaas, G. (2011) 'Survey paradata: A review'. ESRC National Centre for Research Methods Review paper 107Available from http://eprints.ncrm.ac.uk/1719/1/Nicolaas_ review_paper_jan11.pdf (accessed 08 Dec 2014).

Nielsen (2014) 'Smartphone milestone: half of mobile subscribers ages 55+ own smartphones.' Available from http://www.nielsen.com/us/en/insights/news/2014/smartphone-milestone-half-of-americans-ages-55-own-smartphones.html (accessed 18 Jan 2015).

Olson, K., Smyth, J. and Wood, H. (2012) 'Does giving people their preferred survey mode actually increase survey participation rates? An experimental comparison', *Public Opinion Quarterly*, 76(4): 611–635.

Penne, M.A., Snodgrass, J. and Barker, P. (2002) 'Analyzing audit trails in the National Survey on Drug Use and Health (NSDUH): means for maintaining and improving data quality', *Proceedings of the International Conference on Questionnaire Development, Evaluation, and Testing Methods (QDET)*. Charleston, South Carolina. Available from www.blaiseusers.org/2003/papers/Analyzing_audit_trails.pdf (accessed 08 Dec 2014).

Peytchev, A. and Hill, C.A. (2010) 'Experiments in mobile web survey design: similarities to other modes and unique considerations', *Social Science Computer Review*, 28(3): 319–35.

Polgreen, P.M., Chen, Y., Pennock, D.M. and Nelson, F.D. (2008) 'Using Internet searches for influenza surveillance'. *Clinical Infectious Diseases*, 47: 1443–8.

Raento, M., Oulasvirta, A. and Eagle, N. (2009) 'Smartphones: an emerging tool for social scientists', *Sociological Methods and Research*, 37(2): 426–54.

Rhodes, B.B. and Marks, E.L. (2011) 'Using Facebook to locate sample members', *Survey Practice*, October. Available from http://surveypractice.wordpress.com/2011/10/24/using-facebook-to-locate-sample-members/ (accessed 09 Dec 2014).

Richards, A.K., and Dean, E.F. (2013). 'Second life as a survey lab: exploring the randomized response technique in a virtual setting', in *Social Media, Sociality, and Survey Research*. Hoboken, NJ: John Wiley & Sons, Inc. pp. 133–147.

Sage, A. (2013) 'The Facebook platform and the future of social research', in *Social, Media, Sociality and Survey Research*. Hoboken, NJ: John Wiley & Sons, Inc. pp. 87–106.

SAMHSA. (2011) *Results from the 2010 National Survey on Drug Use and Health: Summary of National Findings*, NSDUH Series H-41, HHS Publication No. (SMA) 11–4658. Rockville, MD: Substance Abuse and Mental Health Services Administration, 2011.

Schaefer, D.R. and Dillman, D.A. (1998) 'Development of a standard e-mail methodology', *Public Opinion Quarterly*, 62: 378–97.

Schräpler, J.P. and Wagner, G.G. (2004) 'Identification, characteristics and impact of faked interviews in surveys an analysis by means of genuine fakes in the raw data of SOEP', IZA Discussion Paper Series. Available from http://ftp.iza.org/dp969.pdf (accessed 18 Jan 2015).

Shermach, K. (2005) 'On-the-go polls', *Sales & Marketing Management*, 157(6): 20.

Speizer, H., Kinsey, S.H., Heman-Ackah, R.K. and Thissen, M.R. (2009) 'Developing a common, mode-independent approach for evaluating interview quality and interviewer performance'. *Federal Committee on Statistical Methodology*, Washington, DC. Available from www.rti.org/pubs/kinsey_iii-c.pdf (accessed 08 Dec 2014).

Tesfaye, C.L. (2011) 'Is there a greater analytic potential for open-ended survey questions? A comparison of analytic strategies', paper presented at the 36th Annual Conference of the Midwest Association for Public Opinion Research, Chicago, IL. Available from https://blogs.commons.georgetown.edu/mlc-resources/files/2011/12/MAPOR-final-paper.pdf (accessed 09 Dec 2014).

Townsend, L. (2005) 'The status of wireless survey solutions: the emerging "power of the thumb"', *Journal of Interactive Advertising*, 6(1): 52–8.

Uhrig, J.D., Lewis, M.A., Bann, C., Harris, J.L., Furberg, R., Coomes, C.M. and Kuhns, L. (2012) 'Addressing HIV knowledge, risk reduction, social support, and patient involvement using SMS: a proof-of-concept study', *Journal of Health Communication*, 17(Supplement 1): 128–45.

UN News Centre (2010) 'Communications prices falling worldwide, UN reports'. Available from www.un.org/apps/news/story.asp?NewsID=33867&Cr=telecom (accessed 09 Dec 2014).

Virtanen, V., Sirkiä, T. and Jokiranta, V. (2007). 'Reducing nonresponse by SMS reminders in mail surveys', *Social Science Computer Review*, 25 (3) 384–395.

Wang, K., Murphy, J., Baxter, R. and Aldworth, J. (2005) 'Are two feet in the door better than one? Using process data to examine interviewer effort and nonresponse bias', Proceedings of the 2005 Federal Committee on Statistical Methodology (FCSM) Research Conference. Available from http://fcsm.sites.usa.go/05papers/Wang_Aldworth_etal_VIB.pdf (accessed 09 Dec 2014).

Winkler, W.E. (1995) 'Matching and record linkage', in B.G. Cox et al. (eds) *Business Survey Methods*. New York: Wiley. pp. 355–384. Available from www.census.gov/srd/papers/pdf/rr93-8.pdf (accessed 10 Dec 2014).

Winkler, W.E. (2006) 'Overview of record linkage and current research directions'. U.S. Census Bureau Research Report Series (Statistics #2006–2). Available from www.census.gov/srd/papers/pdf/rrs2006-02.pdf (accessed 09 Dec 2014).

5

ADVANCES IN DATA MANAGEMENT FOR SOCIAL SURVEY RESEARCH

PAUL S. LAMBERT

5.1 INTRODUCTION

Despite the proliferation of new sources of social data, to many commentators these are exciting times for social survey research, characterized by increases in the scale, quality and accessibility of survey data resources. Whilst this chapter concentrates upon recent innovations linked to e-Research, such as new facilities for data organization, many recent developments derive from the continuation of other long-run trends in the provision of social survey datasets. These include improvements in data collection methods (see Chapter 4); developments in data analysis methods (see Chapter 7); and initiatives to aid the comparability of survey data, for example, the harmonization and standardization of datasets across countries or time periods, facilitating cross-national and longitudinal comparative analysis (Harkness, 2008). Perhaps most noticeable of all, however, has been the accumulation of steadily more large-scale social survey datasets, which record increasingly rich data about the survey participants. For instance, the UK's Understanding Society longitudinal survey is a vast undertaking by social science standards, involving repeated extended interviews with more than a hundred thousand respondents, collecting detailed and extensive information about them covering fine-grained measures of socio-economic, attitudinal, health and bio-social data (Laurie, 2010). The Understanding Society survey, moreover, is just one of several major government sponsored surveys of a similar scale in the United Kingdom, and is accompanied by various comparable studies across other nations. Overall, the exciting product of the various long-run trends in the quality of social survey research has been the steady accumulation in volume, and improvement in quality, of data resources for survey data analysis. Indeed, reflecting these developments, it has been commonplace to describe the social sciences as increasingly 'data rich' with regard to survey data sources.

Nevertheless, some of the long-run trends in survey research might be regarded less positively (see also Chapters 3 and 4). The actual exploitation of data resources has often been observed to be lower than would be desirable given the scale and quality of information available (Williams et al., 2004). Moreover, response rates to voluntary questionnaires have declined through time, with non-response having implications for analytical quality (de Leeuw and de Heer, 2002), and doubts have been raised about the quality of information obtained through new forms of internet survey for various reasons (Batinic et al., 2002). Indeed, some authors have suggested that survey evidence may increasingly be superseded by analysis of other large-scale data, such as governmental administrative records, which were not collected deliberately for the purpose of social investigation (Savage and Burrows, 2007). However, the combination of depth and breadth of information recorded on deliberate social surveys tends to far outstrip the possibilities for informed multivariate statistical analysis that may be possible using other administrative data, whilst ongoing developments in statistical analysis can help mitigate problems of missing or biased data (Davidov et al., 2011). On balance, these factors suggest that large-scale social surveys offer particularly promising and high quality tools for social investigation (Goldthorpe, 2005).

In this chapter, after a brief summary of the features of social survey research itself, the focus turns to 'data management' for social survey research, highlighting its importance and relevance, and describing how e-Research methods can be used to assist in the process of data management in applied social research. e-Research approaches offer facilities for storing and linking data files, and for the description of data preparation and analysis, and such provisions can help address many of the day-to-day challenges that researchers experience in this domain.

5.2 FEATURES OF SOCIAL SURVEY RESEARCH DATA

Social survey research is commonly defined as the deliberate and systematic collection and analysis of the same pieces of information from different units, producing data that can be stored in the characteristic 'variable-by-case matrix' (Marsh, 1982). The variables, usually represented in columns, refer to the distinctive elements of information, such as the responses from different questions, whilst the cases (or rows) refer to the units of analysis, such as the individual respondents or other response units. Figure 5.1 illustrates a typical example of a section of a variable-by-case matrix from a real life social survey.

Figure 5.1 reveals several other characteristic features of social survey research data. First, the data shown is a small extract from the UK's British Household Panel Survey (BHPS; University of Essex and Institute for Social and Economic Research, 2010), which has been accessed in this instance from the UK Data Service.[1] In survey research there is a distinction between 'primary' survey research (involving the collection of new data using a survey design) and 'secondary' research (accessing and analysing data which was originally collected by another party). Figure 5.1 therefore

---

[1]http://ukdataservice.ac.uk

illustrates an example of secondary data; arguably, most of the social scientists who are involved in the day to day work of social survey research are undertaking secondary analysis, as it has many attractions such as efficiency, scale, transparency and replicability (Kiecolt and Nathan, 1985; Cole et al., 2008). Indeed, there are many data provider organizations that make access to secondary data, over a range of time periods and national settings, relatively easy (UK Data Archive, 2012; CESSDA, 2012; Cole et al., 2008).

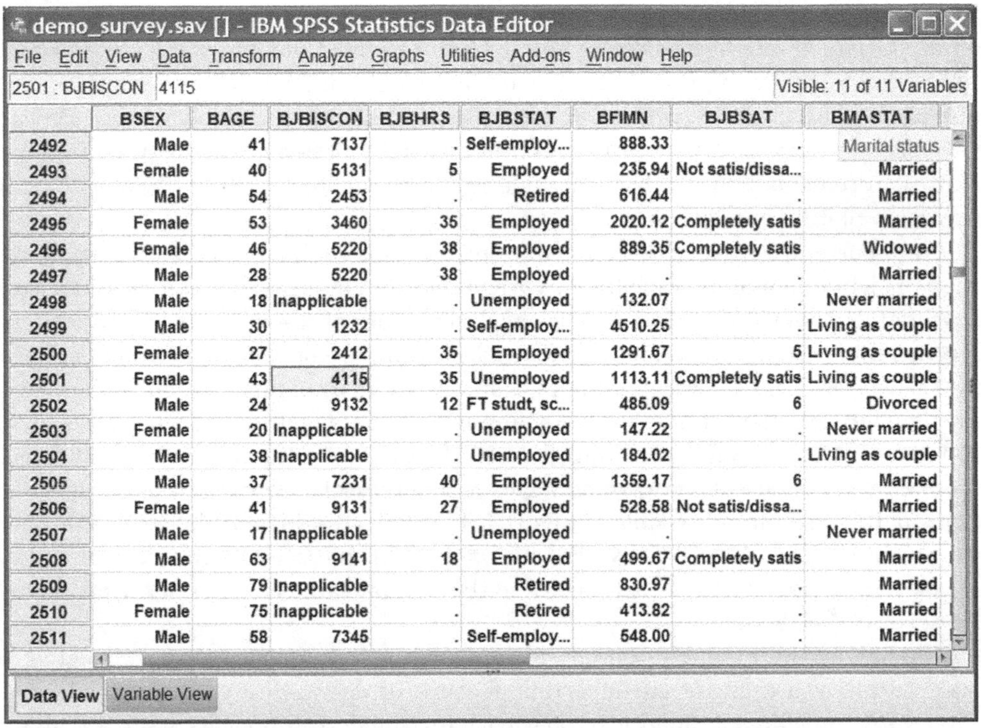

	BSEX	BAGE	BJBISCON	BJBHRS	BJBSTAT	BFIMN	BJBSAT	BMASTAT
2492	Male	41	7137	.	Self-employ...	888.33	.	Marital status
2493	Female	40	5131	5	Employed	235.94	Not satis/dissa...	Married
2494	Male	54	2453	.	Retired	616.44		Married
2495	Female	53	3460	35	Employed	2020.12	Completely satis	Married
2496	Female	46	5220	38	Employed	889.35	Completely satis	Widowed
2497	Male	28	5220	38	Employed	.	.	Married
2498	Male	18	Inapplicable	.	Unemployed	132.07	.	Never married
2499	Male	30	1232	.	Self-employ...	4510.25	.	Living as couple
2500	Female	27	2412	35	Employed	1291.67	5	Living as couple
2501	Female	43	4115	35	Unemployed	1113.11	Completely satis	Living as couple
2502	Male	24	9132	12	FT studt, sc...	485.09	6	Divorced
2503	Female	20	Inapplicable	.	Unemployed	147.22	.	Never married
2504	Male	38	Inapplicable	.	Unemployed	184.02	.	Living as couple
2505	Male	37	7231	40	Employed	1359.17	6	Married
2506	Female	41	9131	27	Employed	528.58	Not satis/dissa...	Married
2507	Male	17	Inapplicable	.	Unemployed	.	.	Never married
2508	Male	63	9141	18	Employed	499.67	Completely satis	Married
2509	Male	79	Inapplicable	.	Retired	830.97	.	Married
2510	Female	75	Inapplicable	.	Retired	413.82	.	Married
2511	Male	58	7345	.	Self-employ...	548.00	.	Married

demo_survey.sav [] - IBM SPSS Statistics Data Editor

File Edit View Data Transform Analyze Graphs Utilities Add-ons Window Help

2501 : BJBISCON 4115 — Visible: 11 of 11 Variables

Data View Variable View

Figure 5.1 Illustration of part of a 'variable by case' matrix

Reprint Courtesy of International Business Machines Corporation, © International Business Machines Corporation.

Notes: Data is part of the UK's BHPS. Columns represent 'variables' and rows represent 'cases' (survey respondents). All data is stored numerically, but many of the variables have 'value labels' added to the appropriate numeric codes, such as 1='Male', 2='Female' in the BSEX column.

Next, we note that the cases in Figure 5.1 represent a small selection from a larger volume of records: the sample shows an arbitrary selection of 20 cases and 11 variables from a dataset that features 9,845 cases, and 859 different variables. Contemporary social survey research is generally characterized by access to quite large numbers of cases and of variables. The selection of variables for a survey is, of course, driven by the interests of the data collectors. In terms of the selection of cases, survey datasets occasionally comprise complete coverage of all cases from a population of interest (i.e. a 'census') or more commonly they form a sample of cases, often designed to be representative of the population from which they were drawn (Kalton, 1983).

Summarizing and analysing a large variable-by-case matrix is only likely to be feasible using appropriate software. Chapter 7 discusses the analytical contributions of software packages that are used for the analysis of social surveys. Figure 5.1 uses a screenshot of the software IBM SPSS Statistics (SPSS),[2] which is a proprietary package that supports operations of data organization and statistical analysis on both small and large datasets. SPSS is a popular choice of package for academic researchers in many countries, and is also widely used by public and private sector research agencies. It is generally regarded as a relatively accessible package, particularly for those without extended previous statistical training. However, there are a great many other statistical software packages suitable for handling and analysing survey data. For example, Stata[3] supports slightly more advanced functions of data management and analysis than SPSS, whilst retaining a comparatively accessible format; R (The R Project for Statistical Computing)[4] is freeware with more demanding programming skill requirements but which has a wide range of capabilities (see Chapter 7 for a summary of different options).

An important feature of these software packages is their capacity to store not just the numeric values of the variable-by-case matrix, but also important supplementary 'metadata' about the survey data, such as descriptions of the contents of any particular variable through a 'variable label', and information on the coding scheme used for the values of a categorical measure. Usually, this sort of information is also made available in documentation files. For example, metadata on the BHPS records shown in Figure 5.1 is also published online (see ISER, 2012), but the storage and display of metadata in statistical software packages is a very useful aspect of such programs. Some of this metadata is visible in Figure 5.1, such as the variable labels visible over the column called BMASTAT (which tells us that this particular variable records the measured marital status of each case) and the textual value labels that are displayed for several variables.

The balance of textual and numeric data within social surveys and the software used to analyse them is an important feature of day-to-day work with surveys. Firstly, the labelling of numerical codes with textual descriptions as described above is a routine requirement within survey analysis. Secondly, survey exercises themselves commonly include some questions that are recorded as a free-text answer (for example, a respondent might be asked to describe their current occupation, or they might be asked to indicate their ethnic group from a short list of suggestions that includes an opportunity to write in their own description). Whilst survey analysis packages primarily deal with numeric data (in Figure 5.1, all of the information behind the cell entries is numeric in format, even though some of it is presented through textual value labels), most packages also have the capacity to store textual records if required. In practice, it is relatively unusual for survey researchers to

---

[2]SPSS Inc. was acquired by IBM in October, 2009.

[3]www.stata.com

[4]www.r-project.org

include the original verbatim textual responses in the dataset that they work with, since coding large numbers of textual descriptions can be burdensome and text is of limited benefit for statistical analysis. However, there is a significant discipline within social research that uses specialist software packages to analyse large-scale collections of free-text responses (di Gregorio and Davidson, 2008) or to selectively search data resources for textual records.

In most instances, survey researchers code any free-text responses that they collect into a more restricted range of categories. Sometimes, coding decisions are made on an ad hoc basis. As an indicative example, after reviewing the response received, a research team might decide to code self-descriptions of ethnic group into three further categories: 'Mixed ethnicity', 'Regional identity' and 'Any other'. In other instances, where the topic area is well established, a researcher may be able to take advantage of existing resources, such as publications or supplementary software, in order to assign standardized numeric codes to textual descriptions. This is how the data on the variable BJBISCON within Figure 5.1 is obtained, since this data gives a numeric code that indicates an occupational title, and was obtained by collecting free-text occupational descriptions and using the CASCOT software (a routine for linking occupational descriptions to standardized codes; see IER (2011)) to code them to standardized units.

Lastly, Figure 5.1 illustrates some important complexities in working with survey data. Textbooks that introduce the statistical techniques of analysis that can be applied to social survey data tend to use examples of 'clean' datasets, where every case has a valid value for every variable, and all the variables have a simple and easily analysed set of numeric values. In reality, most survey data start life in a more 'messy' state, of which Figure 5.1 illustrates certain examples. For instance, it shows cases with missing data, indicated here by the 'inapplicable' labels in column 3, and the 'system missing' indicator in columns 4, 6 and 7 (represented as a single dot in the SPSS software). The figure also shows examples of variables with a complex categorical form. For example, column 3, 'BJBISCON' shows the numeric codes of the International Standard Classification of Occupations 1988, a coding frame for around 350 occupational titles where each numeric value represents a different occupation (see ILO 1990, 2012). This sort of detailed record of categorical positions provides the analyst with rich descriptive information but, for the purposes of statistical analysis, some summary measure, such as scaling the ISCO units according to a measure of social stratification with far fewer categories, is likely to be desirable.[5]

---

[5]This example is one where the 'functional form' of a variable can be adapted. Functional form refers to the way a variable's information is used in statistical analysis. A metric and linear functional form arises when the numeric values for a measure have a direct arithmetic meaning that develops in a linear relationship with other measures. In social science applications most measures are not metric but 'categorical' (i.e. their numeric values indicate membership of one category rather than another, such as 'male' compared to 'female') and steps must ordinarily be taken to adapt the data to sustain appropriate analysis. Moreover, even those measures that can be treated as metric may nevertheless have a non-linear relationship to other variables, which can be accommodated by adjustments to the data. For a discussion focusing on the treatment of measures of occupations see Lambert and Bihagen (2014).

The figure also shows some examples of data that are probably erroneous – in case 2501, for instance, we see a record for an individual who is noted as having a job (ISCO=4115, the code for 'Secretaries'), and reports working 35 hours a week (information from the column headed WJBHRS), yet for whom their 'employment status' (the column headed BJBSTAT) is recorded as being 'Unemployed'.

5.3 EFFECTIVE DATA MANAGEMENT FOR SOCIAL SURVEY RESEARCH

After it has been collected, there are several opportunities for the enhancement and adaptation of social survey data. For example, the variables within datasets could be subject to further adjustments, such as recoding categories, or performing standardization or harmonization operations. There are also commonly several different datasets that could be productively linked together to enhance an analysis. These two examples, of recoding and adapting variables within datasets and of data linkage, are particularly prominent elements of the 'data management' process, a phrase that we use here to refer to the handling and preparation of data for the purposes of research analysis (that is, after it is collected, and prior to statistical analysis).

Social survey methodologists have traditionally concentrated upon either the data collection stage of the process, such as in guidelines for questionnaire design, administration and sampling (de Vaus, 2002; Fink, 2002), or the statistical analysis of survey data, such as in efforts to develop statistical models that adequately account for complex survey data structures (Chambers and Skinner, 2003; Davidov et al., 2011). However, the data management phase is an equally important and consequential stage within survey research. Indeed, for many researchers, it represents an extended and challenging activity, which is contestable and debatable, and which may well have a substantial impact upon the subsequent results of data analysis. Three themes in data management concerned with the handling and organization of data resources are discussed below.

5.3.1 Data Management as Controlling, Monitoring and Supporting Access to Data

A common use of the term 'data management' is concerned with the hosting and control of data resources, for example, by data archivists and survey managers (Corti et al., 2014). In all of the sciences, data archive organizations have made a major contribution over the last decades in setting standards for storing, and controlling access to, data resources (Research Information Network, 2011). The social sciences have been particularly well served, benefiting from sustained infrastructural support for data storage and distribution on national and cross-national scales over many decades (UK Data Archive, 2012; CESSDA, 2012; Cole et al., 2008). Four important features of good practice in this respect are illustrated in Figure 5.2. Panel 1 depicts guidelines on the provision and storage of information and documentation of new data. Such instructions help researchers to record and supply suitable metadata associated with their data, which can be organized into accessible and robust formats that data archives may then record, store, catalogue and distribute to others. Panel 2 of Figure 5.2 illustrates how data distributors provide clear specification of conditions over dissemination and use of resources: it summarizes a standard information file featuring citation requirements linked to the data. Panel 3 of Figure 5.2 depicts the existence of systems for distributing data: it shows the NESSTAR tool, a popular online means of exploring the basic contents of datasets that are also available for subsequent download. Lastly, panel 4 shows how data distributors have mechanisms in place to both monitor and support users in their exploitation of data resources: it summarizes information provided about the provenance and features of the survey data.

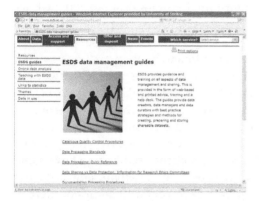

Panel 1: From www.esds.ac.uk/support/dataman-guides.asp

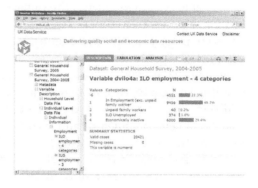

Panel 3: Available from 'explore online' links at http://ukdataservice.ac.uk/get-data.aspx

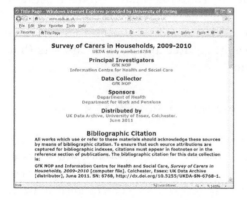

Panel 2: From doc.ukdataservice.ac.uk/doc/6768/mrdoc/UKDA/UKDA_Study_6768_Information.htm

Panel 4: From doc.ukdataservice.ac.uk/doc/6768/read6768.htm

Figure 5.2   Illustration of online resources associated with agencies involved in the storage and distribution of social survey datasets

Notes: Images taken from websites linked to the UK Data Service (retrieved 3 Feb 2015)

The images shown in Figure 5.2 emphasize the positive features of access to data, in terms of the ways in which researchers are supported in working with datasets. Behind the scenes of such facilities, however, there are sustained debates concerning legal issues over the storage and provision of what is often personal, sensitive and/ or confidential individual level survey data (see Chapters 3 and 4), since data providers are ordinarily required to take steps to prevent disclosure of data which could identify specific individuals or which could have a detrimental effect upon study participants or the survey project itself (see Corti et al., 2014). In several instances, data suppliers make decisions to substantially restrict access to data resources in order to minimize such risks. Several social survey studies are only made available in highly secure labs or secure online environments. In the UK, for example, government-run secure access labs are the only points of access to certain potentially disclosive survey studies such as the Census Longitudinal Studies (Young, 2009) whilst the UK Data Service Secure Access facility (UK Data Service, 2013) offers remote access to potentially disclosive data from selected large-scale research services. Elsewhere, the international LIS project uses a semi-automated job monitoring system to achieve comparable provisions (LIS, 2012), and various other uses of software to monitor and control access to data are discussed by Bender and Heining (2011). In addition, data suppliers often choose to provide direct access only to data resources that have been modified to minimize disclosure risk. Attenuating data, such as by reducing the detail of measures of geography or economic activity, is a common strategy in this regard (Purdam and Elliot, 2007). Such practices are likely to have some deleterious consequences for analytical work. It is easy to anticipate how reducing measurement detail on survey variables compromises the data. In addition, there is evidence to suggest that restrictive data environments can deter researchers from using datasets at all, since complex access arrangements can make even routine data manipulations and analyses difficult to perform. Those secondary survey resources that avoid imposing constraints on their use, such as the international survey projects at IPUMS-I (Minnesota Population Center, 2011) and the European Social Survey (Fitzgerald and Jowell, 2011), experience far greater uptake than datasets that are available under more restrictive conditions.

5.3.2 Data Management as Processing Data for the Benefit of Research

Most of this chapter discusses aspects of data management that involve the direct handling and processing of data, rather than more wide ranging overview activities. It has already been indicated, as in Figure 5.1, that there are many complex aspects to the organization of social survey data that is stored in a 'variable by case' matrix. Data is often partial or missing for some cases, which requires decisions about the processing of those cases as 'missing data', and there may be other measures in the dataset, such as sampling weights, that can be applied to the data to enable generalizing to the whole population. Commonly, several datasets can be productively linked together for analysis; for example, survey records from the same respondents in different years. In almost all survey datasets, some degree of transformation of the variables is required to adjust the functional form of a measure. For example, a complex categorical measure might be recoded into a smaller range of different categories to facilitate statistical analysis, or a linear scale might be transformed in order to allow for a different distributional relationship to be analysed. Moreover, in applied research projects, the appropriate strategies are unlikely to be virgin territory. A good scientific approach should involve retrieving information on how such issues were dealt with in previous relevant studies, and replicating them when possible, perhaps including an explicit sensitivity analysis within the work to compare and contrast alternative routes. Taking advantage of previous efforts might require links to be made between the current dataset and some other externally published information resource, a task of information retrieval and matching, which is often non-trivial.

All of these challenges of data management have been recognized for some time, but not necessarily made any easier to address. We would argue that two major activities in data management for social survey research can be identified. The second, discussed further below, involves dealing with the profusion of online information resources and their effective exploitation. The first was partially addressed some years ago but continues to raise challenges for applied researchers; it concerns the provision and use of statistical software to support data management tasks. The importance of this activity has been noted by several writers and was well summarized by Procter:

> A program like SPSS ... has two main components: the statistical routines, which do the numerical calculations that produce tabulations and summary measures of various kinds, and the data management facilities. Perhaps surprisingly, it was the latter that really revolutionized quantitative social research. (2001: 253)

The contribution of statistical software to data management is very substantial, since many statistical software packages feature facilities to perform the tasks alluded to above in a relatively fast and efficient way. The authors of software, indeed, are well aware of the importance of this aspect of their packages, and it is increasingly common to see textbooks and software manuals dedicated to data management functionality in specific software packages (e.g., Levesque, 2010; Mitchell, 2010; Long, 2009; Boslaugh, 2005). However, statistical software is, for most social scientists, quite difficult to use for all but the most basic data management tasks. This arises for two reasons. First, there are many different operations that may be applied to data, often encompassing software-specific extension routines that require considerable study to fully understand. The popular statistical analysis package Stata, for example, includes a whole suite of specialist commands for the organization and preparation of longitudinal survey datasets with repeated records from the same subjects. Second, methodologists often argue that in order to use statistical software effectively for data management tasks, it is necessary for a user to undertake the tasks by programming within the command language of the relevant package, so that the steps taken can be readily recorded and stored for future use (Boslaugh, 2005; Long, 2009; Kohler and Kreuter, 2012). This is often referred to as 'syntax programming' or 'scripting' (also discussed in Chapter 7), a challenging and abstract task for many social science data users that is not a routinely taught in introductory research methods courses. 'Good' users of statistical software are urged to construct clearly documented and well-organized workflows of scripts in appropriate languages (Long, 2009), but these are quite challenging to construct and require meticulous preparation.

The book's website[6] provides sets of exercises intended to familiarize the reader with important data management tasks. The first exercise, which draws on materials prepared for extended training workshops organized by the DAMES project (Data Management through e-Social Science),[7] highlights means of opening datasets, adjusting variables, and matching data from external sources. Fluency in scripting for these software packages is not something that can be achieved overnight, but the reader is nevertheless encouraged to open each package and perform these basic data management tasks by way of illustration of what can (and should) be done to process data effectively in this manner.

Two important features of the first set of exercises are worth emphasizing. One concerns the relevance of metadata within the work. Some metadata are stored in the script files, in the form of annotations with information on the provenance of the data and on data management activity. Much of the important metadata, however, is stored in the data file itself, in terms of records such as value labels and variable labels for each column in the dataset. Typically, such metadata is invaluable for undertaking statistical analysis, and so its careful processing and recording is especially important to using survey datasets effectively with such software packages (Long, 2009). The second feature concerns the organization of the tasks, which in these examples flow sequentially from opening the original dataset to saving the updated and revised dataset. The sequence of processes is usually important, and is one reason why great attention is often paid to organizing analysis in a coordinated set of steps comprising a workflow (Long, 2009).

5.3.3 Using Online Resources to Support Data Management

Many of the activities involved in the preparation of data for analysis benefit from online information resources providing, for example, data coding instructions and routes to access secondary data and its documentation (see also Figure 5.2). Moreover, since the wider themes of digital social science embrace the sharing and organization of digital data and the effective exploitation of complex and distributed information resources, there are obvious points of connection between e-Research and the requirements of data management in survey research.

e-Research opportunities have already been explored in several extended projects in the social science domain. Selected examples are noted in Table 5.1, which gives

---

[6]https://study.sagepub.com/halfpennyprocter

[7]See www.dames.org.uk/workshops

a short summary of the contribution of each and links to the projects' websites. In different ways, Internet services and software packages have been developed that facilitate information retrieval and data storage. Examples cover the curation and retrieval of metadata and supplementary external resources that can support data processing, and storage arrangements that can better facilitate the hosting and exploitation of data, potentially with high standards of federated security, as well as the capacity to deal with data and/or its analysis on a very large scale.

Table 5.1 Summary of selected recent research projects which embody a digital social research approach to data management challenges linked to social survey research

DAMES (Data Management through e-Social Science), www.dames.org.uk	
	The DAMES project involves developing new online provisions in a series of case studies and application areas in data management. One concerns the GESDE online resources for data in themed areas described in the text. Other themes cover data on health and on social care, and a programme of capacity building activities. Most of the DAMES resources are accessible through portal systems built in the LifeRay software, and feature remote file store systems that allow users to store and (potentially) distribute data to others.
Methodbox, www.methodbox.org/www.methodbox.org	
	Methodbox is a project with a focus on health data resources. Using a similar idea to the GESDE services, it serves as a dynamic depository for research users of health datasets who can supply information files relevant to the analysis of these data to other users. It also integrates its search facilities with routines for searching the contents of data resources that are generated by the UK data service ESDS.
NeISS (National e-Infrastructure for Social Simulation), www.geog.leeds.ac.uk/projects/neiss/index.php	
NeISS	The idea behind the NeISS project is to support in a coordinated environment the storage and analysis of data for simulation models on a large scale, and to facilitate their analysis and the visualization of results. Various elements of data processing feature within key stages of the NeISS model, such as selection and processing of measures and recoding of relevant variables.
PolicyGrid, www.policygrid.org	
	The focus of PolicyGrid of relevance to data management is their attention to metadata on social research data objects – the project built information retrieval systems that search metadata and extract relevant data. Whilst this project has limited use of social survey datasets, its attention to metadata systems is of importance to all social science data management interests.
CESSDA (Council of European Social Science Data Archives), www.cessda.org	
	CESSDA, which acts as an umbrella organization for national data archives and their support services, has pioneered the use of online systems for distributing data and metadata concerning social surveys on a very large scale. By building software for data searching and the visualization of results, it has made a direct contribution to digital social science.

Many of the initiatives described in Table 5.1 have focused specifically upon particular application areas or analytical requirements, and have generated new tools that combine the organization and analysis of complex data resources. As an illustrative example, we will next elaborate upon the construction and implementation of two closely related resources for social science data that have been generated during our own DAMES project on 'Data management through e-Social Science'.

The Grid Enabled Specialist Data Environments (GESDE) and the Data Fusion Tool

The GESDE services represent a group of three specialist data depositories through which supplementary data resources concerned with the measurement of occupations, educational qualifications and ethnicity are shared between, and made readily accessible to, other researchers via online portals. The three portals are known as GEODE (focusing upon occupational data, see www.geode.stir.ac.uk); GEEDE (focusing upon data on educational qualifications, see www.dames.org.uk/geede); and GEMDE (focusing upon data on ethnicity and migration, see www.dames.org. uk/gemde). In each case, the resources are motivated by an understanding that social science researchers often either themselves produce, or would benefit from access to, metadata and information resources on survey measures in each subject area. Such information resources often come in the form of excerpts of software command syntax illustrating the coding of variables, or data or documentation files which explain a particular mapping of records. Particularly prominent examples are often referred to as 'translation matrices' and 'coding frames' which help to recode an original variable (for example, denoting occupations) into an alternative measure (for instance, denoting occupation-based social class) which might be more suited to statistical analysis and/or represents a harmonization or standardization that supports wider comparisons.

In the three subject areas covered by GESDE, there are extensive information resources already existing across the social sciences. These are sometimes distributed online through voluntarily maintained webpages (Ganzeboom, 2011) or, alternatively, by government agencies or research support projects (ONS, 2012). Often, however, such resources remain hidden from the social science research community. As Treiman has noted (2009: 404), they are often pledged by researchers as being 'available from the author on request' but, in practice, can be very difficult to track down and are often misplaced. Such resources, whenever they are produced, would benefit from being securely documented and, when possible, made available to others by accessible means, and it is these two contributions that the GESDE services attempt to make.

To achieve these aims, three separate portals were built by the DAMES project, each comprising a website where a visitor could log in as a registered user and deposit (or update information on) relevant resources. They could also search and retrieve resources from the portal, either as a registered user or as an unregistered guest. The portals ran on two different servers and used slightly different architecture (see also Warner et al., 2010). The portals and their operating procedures are described further at the DAMES website and in technical papers published there. To give a taste of their contribution, a second set of exercises on the book's website are available which outline instructions for locating, reviewing and experimenting with the DAMES portals.

Typical uses of the GESDE services included retrieving information resources from the portals and linking them to a survey dataset, and depositing new information resources which might then be made available to other researchers. A relatively intuitive interface was designed in each service to allow users to retrieve data deposited by others (the more common requirement); or to submit and disseminate data resources directly themselves (a relatively less common requirement). Behind the scenes, the portals systematically stored and organized metadata records and connected them to submitted datasets but, in general, they kept these more complex features out of sight of users. The potential contributions of the GESDE services are quite substantial, since they have the capacity to provide users with easy access to identify and to exploit large volumes of advanced information resources in their specialist domains.

Several other projects also represent comparable approaches to developing repositories of information, largely on the basis of user contributions by social science researchers. In the UK, the MethodBox project has a similar approach to data resources linked to the analysis of health services (see Table 5.1), and the P-ADLS resource provides access to data linked to UK Administrative Data resources (ADLS, 2012).

One unique feature of the GESDE services is a connection between the information resources on these services and another facility from the DAMES project, a resource known as the Data Fusion Tool (Warner et al., 2010).[8] This tool provides a mechanism to allow the linking together of data files using either 'deterministic' or 'probabilistic' criteria. The former is the more common requirement when working with survey data, whereby a user may need to link together two different information sources on the basis of a shared variable or variables (for example, connecting together a microdata file with occupations, such as is illustrated in Figure 5.1, with a separate data matrix that links occupations to social class categories).[9] This can be done with appropriate scripting in software packages (as illustrated in the first set of exercises on the book's website) but file matching proves to be a particularly challenging and off-putting aspect of programming for many social scientists. The data fusion tool automates the file matching process, and can be invoked through two alternative routes, either by following links to a 'job preconfiguration tool' within the GESDE portals (for instructions see the DAMES project webpages) or, alternatively, by downloading an open-source

---

[8] At the time of writing, this applies only to the 'GEODE' and 'GEEDE' facilities.

[9] The latter matching process, 'probabilistic' matching, is typically associated with imputing survey information on the basis of incomplete records and was a topic that was developed in a separate project theme from the wider DAMES project – see www.dames.org.uk/themes. html#theme1_2.

package for 'workflow modelling' and opening and running a file matching workflow in that package on their own data resources (see Turner, 2012).

5.4 CONCLUSIONS

5.4.1 Uptake and Prospects of Digital Research Innovations in Social Survey Research

Data management activities have much to gain from e-Research innovations. We have described how the GESDE tools offer the opportunity to improve research quality through better processing of the measures within survey datasets. Attention in e-Research has also been paid to achieving access to data that is subject to complex security requirements, demonstrating that more effective arrangements can be put in place that would avoid restrictions to data access and quality (Sinnott, 2009). In addition, researchers have examined workflows composed of a series of data management processes that link and enhance datasets, developed generic workflow modelling tools for social science data management and demonstrated how they could improve research quality (e.g., Turner and Tan, 2012; Turner, 2012). However, arguably, none of these initiatives has yet had a major impact upon social survey research activity.

A significant challenge for many emergent e-Research tools concerns uptake by established research communities. In the domain of social survey data management, facilities are already available for processing data through well-known statistical software packages and many users make do with these. Similarly, for data requiring secure access, researchers make do with solutions such as safe settings labs or online access to data in restricted conditions. These ways of working are attractive to researchers because they are familiar, but they raise challenges to the progressive diffusion of digital innovations. For example, researchers tend to invest heavily in software-specific skills (such as programming) or institutional-specific arrangements (such as means of accessing secure labs), but restricting themselves to these is to the detriment of openness to, or compatibility with, other projects.

Many proficient software users might struggle to see the payoff from exploiting new tools over-and-above those they are currently using. There are, nevertheless, major benefits to be obtained from emergent e-Research tools in the area of data management. Opportunities for information retrieval are enhanced; documentation and storage of metadata is facilitated; more satisfactory federated security facilities are available. In general terms, improved research practice is made more feasible, such as in sensitivity analysis of alternative measures, improved exploitation of strategies for harmonization and standardization, and accurate documentation. Yet, whilst it is possible to make a strong scientific argument that facilities such as GESDE should make a major contribution to research in areas using measures related to their thematic topics, it may not be so easy to persuade researchers in the field to exploit their resources. At the time of writing, for example, logged usage of the GESDE systems is low, involving only a few hundred users, which is far fewer than regularly access other online sources of support in survey data analysis, such as UK Data Service websites.

If simply claiming that e-Research tools have a contribution to make is not sufficient to entice people to use them, what steps might be taken? In the case of data management, the answer would seem to lie in steps now being taken by journals and research funding agencies to mandate publishing (alongside other outputs) of metadata about data management in appropriate digital formats as a condition of publication or funding (see Procter, Halfpenny and Voss, 2012).

5.4.2 Data Management for Social Survey Research

Social survey datasets are widely used as the basis of applied research analysis across all social science disciplines. Surveys come in many different forms, but they can be particularly attractive in being able to facilitate the analysis of large volumes of data and, if records are collected through a suitable sampling design, to reveal empirical patterns that are representative of the wider population. Nevertheless, it is commonplace to hear doubts expressed about evidence on social processes that is based upon survey data, or that it is easy to show anything with statistics (see Huff, 1954). Many such doubts are founded upon scepticism about the quality of measurement of social concepts that can be achieved through surveys: do we really believe, for example, survey evidence which suggests that Danes are 15 percentage points happier than Swedes, who, in turn, are almost 30 points happier than Germans (see Christensen et al., 2006)? Whilst the measures behind some survey evidence could be genuinely questioned, researchers have a robust scientific defence in highlighting that sustained methodological research offers the opportunity to collect survey records of genuinely high reliability and validity. Many such questions therefore boil down to issues of what we have described as data management: how data, once collected, is processed and organized prior to statistical summary.

The quality or otherwise of survey measures hinges on how they are processed and this is particularly critical for measures of concepts or 'key variables' (Burgess, 1986) that are central to social science data enquiry. In many respects, e-Research offers the next step forward in improving survey research evidence, having the capacity to significantly improve the quality of statistical measures within survey datasets through facilitating improved data management, particularly on key variables. In combination, innovations in e-Research also have the capacity to support improved data analysis (see Chapter 7) and, indeed, in the integration of data analysis and data management (for example, there are templates combining data management and analysis within the 'Stat-JR' system, which is described in Chapter 7).

5.5 BIBLIOGRAPHY

ADLS (2012) *P-ADLS: Portal of the Administrative Data Liaison Service.* Available from www.adls.ac.uk/padls/ (accessed 10 Dec 2014).

Batinic, B., Reips, U.-D. and Bosnjak, M. (eds) (2002) *Online Social Sciences.* Seattle, WA: Hogrefe and Huber.

Bender, S. and Heining, J. (2011) *The Research-Data-Centre in Research-Data-Centre Approach: A First Step Towards Decentralised International Data Sharing*. Nürnberg: Working paper 07/2011 of FDZ-Methodenreport: Methodological Aspects of Labour Market Data, Research Data Centre, Institute for Employment Research.

Bibby, J. (1983) *Quotes, Damned Quotes, and –: An Anthology of Sayings, Epithets, and Witticisms – Several of Them Something to do with Statistics*. Halifax: Demast Books.

Boslaugh, S. (2005) *An Intermediate Guide to SPSS Programming: Using Syntax for Data Management*. London: Sage.

Burgess, R.G. (ed) (1986) *Key Variables in Social Investigation*. London: Routledge.

CESSDA (2012) *Council of European Social Science Data Archives*. Available from www.cessda.net (accessed 09 Dec 2014).

Chambers, R.L. and Skinner, C.J. (eds) (2003) *Analysis of Survey Data*. New York: Wiley.

Christensen, K., Herskind, A.M. and Vaupel, J.W. (2006) 'Why Danes are smug: comparative study of life satisfaction in the European Union', *British Medical Journal*, 333: 1289–91.

Cole, K., Watham, J. and Corti, L. (2008) 'The provision of access to quantitative data for secondary analysis', in N. Fielding, R.M. Lee and G. Blank (eds), *The SAGE Handbook of Online Research Methods*. London: Sage. pp. 229–54.

Corti, L., Van den Eynden, V., Bishop, L. and Woollard, M. (2014) *Managing and Sharing Research Data: A Guide to Good Practice*. London: Sage.

Davidov, E., Schmidt, P. and Billiet, J. (eds) (2011) *Cross-Cultural Analysis: Methods and Applications*. Hove: Psychology Press.

de Leeuw, E. and de Heer, W. (2002) 'Trends in household survey non-response: an longitudinal and international comparison', in R.M. Groves, D.A. Dillman, J.L. Eltinge and R.J.A. Little (eds), *Survey Nonresponse*, New York: Wiley. pp. 41–54.

de Vaus, D. (2002) *Surveys in Social Research,* 5th Edition. London: Routledge.

di Gregorio, S. and Davidson, J. (2008) *Qualitative Research Design for Software Users*. Maidenhead: Open University Press.

Fink, A. (ed.) (2002) *The Survey Kit, Second Edition*. Thousand Oaks, CA: Sage.

Fitzgerald, R. and Jowell, R. (2011) *Measurement Equivalence in Comparative Surveys: The European Social Survey (ESS) – From Design to Implementation and Beyond*. London: City University, Centre for Comparative Social Surveys, Working paper series, paper no. 3.

Ganzeboom, H.B.G. (2011) *Harry Ganzeboom's Tools for Deriving Status Measures from ISCO-08*. Available from www.harryganzeboom.nl/isco08/index.htm (accessed 10 Dec 2014).

Goldthorpe, J.H. (2005) 'Progress in sociology: the case of social mobility research', in S. Svallfors (ed.), *Analyzing Inequality: Life Chances and Social Mobility in Comparative Perspective*. Stanford, CA: Stanford University Press. pp. 56–82.

Harkness, J. (2008) 'Comparative survey research: goals and challenges', in E. De Leeuw, J. Hox and D.A. Dillman (eds), *International Handbook of Survey Methodology*. London: Psychology Press. pp. 56–77.

Huff, D. (1954) *How to Lie with Statistics*. London: Gollancz.

IER (2011) CASCOT: Computer Assisted Structured Coding Tool. Warwick: Institute for Employment Research, University of Warwick. Available from www2.warwick.ac.uk/fac/soc/ier/software/cascot (accessed 10 Dec 2014).

ILO (1990) *ISCO-88: International Standard Classification of Occupations*. New York: International Labour Office.

ILO (2012) *ISCO: International Standard Classification of Occupations*. New York: International Labour Office. Available from www.ilo.org/public/english/bureau/stat/isco/

ISER (2012) *BHPS Documentation*. Colchester: Institute for Social and Economic Research, University of Essex. Available from www.iser.essex.ac.uk/bhps/documentation/volb/allrecs.html (accessed 01 April 2015).

Kalton, G. (1983) *Introduction to Survey Sampling*. Beverley Hills, CA: Sage.

Kiecolt, K.J. and Nathan, L.E. (1985) *Secondary Analysis of Survey Data*. Thousand Oaks, CA: Sage.

Kohler, H.P. and Kreuter, F. (2012) *Data Analysis Using Stata,* 3rd Edition. College Station, Texas: Stata Press.

Lambert, P.S. and Bihagen, E. (2014) 'Using occupation-based social classifications', *Work, Employment and Society, DOI: 10.1177/0950017013519845.*

Laurie, H. (2010) *Continuity and Innovation in the Design of Understanding Society: the UK Household Longitudinal Study*. Colchester: Understanding Society Working Paper Series (2010–2), University of Essex. Available from www.understandingsociety.ac.uk/research/publications/working-paper/understanding-society/2010-02.pdf (accessed 09 Dec 2014).

Levesque, R. and SPSS Inc. (2010) *Programming and Data Management for IBM SPSS Statistics 18: A Guide for PASW Statistics and SAS users*. Chicago: SPSS Inc.

LIS (2012) *LIS: Cross-national Data Center in Luxembourg*. Available from www.lisdatacenter.org (accessed 10 Dec 2014).

Long, J.S. (2009) *The Workflow of Data Analysis Using Stata*. Boca Raton, FL: CRC Press.

Marsh, C. (1982) *The Survey Method: The Contribution of Surveys to Sociological Explanation*. London: Allen and Unwin.

Minnesota Population Center (2011) *Integrated Public Use Microdata Series, International: Version 6.1 [Machine readable database]*. Minneapolis: University of Minnesota. Available from https://international.ipums.org (accessed 10 Dec 2014).

Mitchell, M.N. (2010) *Data Management Using Stata: A Practical Handbook*. College Station, TX: Stata Press.

ONS (2012) *Office for National Statistics, Guidance and Methodology: Harmonisation Programme*. Available from www.ons.gov.uk/ons/guide-method/harmonisation/harmonisation-programme/ (accessed 10 Dec 2014).

Procter, M. (2001) 'Analysing survey data', in G.N. Gilbert (ed.), *Researching Social Life,* 2nd Edition. London: Sage. pp. 252–68.

Procter, R.N., Halfpenny, P. and Voss, A. (2012) 'Research data management: opportunities and challenges for HEIs'. In G. Pryor (ed.) *Research Data Management*. Facet Publishing. pp.135–50.

Purdam, K. and Elliot, M. (2007) 'A case study of the impact of statistical disclosure control on data quality in the individual UK Samples of Anonymised Records', *Environment and Planning A,* 39(5): 1101–18.

R Core Team (2013) *R: A Language and Environment for Statistical Computing*. Vienna: R Foundation for Statistical Computing.

Research Information Network. (2011) *Data Centres: Their Use, Value and Impact*. London: The Research Information Network. Available from www.rin.ac.uk (accessed 10 Dec 2014).

Savage, M. and Burrows, R. (2007) 'The coming crisis of empirical sociology', *Sociology,* 41(5): 885–99.

Sinnott, R.O. (2009) 'Grid security', in L. Wang, W. Jie and J. Chen (eds), *Grid Computing: Infrastructure, Service and Applications*. London: CRC Press. pp.307–33.

StataCorp (2013) *Stata Statistical Software, Release 13*. College Station, TX: StataCorp LP.

Sturgis, P. (2008) Designing samples', in G.N. Gilbert (ed.), *Researching Social Life,* 4th edition. London: Sage.

Treiman, D.J. (2009) *Quantitative Data Analysis: Doing Social Research to Test Ideas*. New York: Jossey Bass.

Turner, K.J. (2012) *Social Science Workflows with CRESS*. Stirling: University of Stirling, Department of Computing Science and Mathematics.

Turner, K.J. and Tan, K.L.L. (2012) 'Rigorous development of composite Grid services', *Network and Computer Applications,* 35(4): 1304–16.

UK Data Archive (2012) *UK Data Archive*. Colchester: University of Essex. Available from www.data-archive.ac.uk (accessed 09 Dec 2014).

UK Data Service (2013) UK Data Service – Secure Access. Available from http://ukdataservice.ac.uk/get-data/how-to-access/accesssecurelab.aspx (accessed 02 Feb 2015).

University of Essex and Institute for Social and Economic Research (2010) *British Household Panel Survey: Waves 1–18, 1991–2009 [computer file],* 7th edition. Colchester, Essex: UK Data Archive [distributor], July 2010, SN: 5151.

Warner, G.C., Blum, J.M., Jones, S.B., Lambert, P.S., Turner, K.J., Tan, K.L.L., Dawson, A. and Bell, D. (2010) 'A social science data fusion tool and the DAMES infrastructure', *Philosophical Transactions of the Royal Society, Series A, 368*(1925): 3859–73.

Williams, M., Collett, T. and Rice, R. (2004) *Baseline Study of Quantitative Methods in British Sociology*. University of Plymouth: C-SAP Project report to the British Sociological Association.

Young, H. (2009) *Technical Working Paper: Guide to Parallel and Combined Analysis of the ONS LS, SLS and NILS*. London: Centre for Longitudinal Study Information and User Support. Available from http://calls.ac.uk/wp-content/uploads/Guide-to-parallel-and-combined-LS-analysis.pdf (accessed 10 Dec 2014).

6

MODELLING AND SIMULATION
MARK BIRKIN AND NICK MALLESON

6.1 INTRODUCTION

The application of simulation models has been a major growth area for social sciences over the last 15 years, probably dating back most crucially to the appearance of Growing Artificial Societies (Epstein and Axtell, 1996) in which, according to the cover notes, the authors attempt to 'grow a proto-history of civilisation' which embraces demographics, culture, conflict, economic production and trade. An appreciation of concepts such as agent-based modelling, social simulation, or artificial society itself is now widespread in research and social science literature.

Notwithstanding this recent, and welcome, upsurge of interest, it is important not to overlook the fact that social scientists have used models extensively for many decades. For example, and perhaps most famously, the ideas of systems dynamics (Forrester, 1969; 1971) have been used to formalize the characterization of stocks, flows, interactions and feedback for social organizations at scales ranging from individual firms (e.g. Beer, 1972) to cities (Wilson, 1974) and, most controversially of all, to the global economy (Meadows et al., 1972). Given that all of these are essentially mathematical models – in which the stocks and flows are regulated through the interdependencies between one another and other key system parameters – then this legacy could be traced back much further, for example to Ravenstein's (1885) 'Laws of Migration', which are themselves widely seen as a precursor to later applications of gravity or spatial interaction models in economics and geography (Tobler, 1995).

The sociology of the Chicago School of the 1920s and 1930s provides another pillar of social science research history with profound modelling implications. In particular, the celebrated characterization of the urban social landscape as an ecosystem transforming itself through successive waves of 'invasion and succession' (Park and

>

Burgess, 1925) gave rise to notable attempts in the post-war period to develop a factorial ecology of cities (Shevky and Bell, 1955; Rees, 1970) based on a much more empirical or statistical modelling approach. In this instance too, the desire to characterize the tapestry of urban neighbourhoods through models of the statistical regularity in key indicators (such as social class, family status, ethnicity and so on) could also be traced back much further, for example, to Charles Booth and his poverty maps of London in the Victorian era (e.g. Harris et al., 2005; see also the Charles Booth archive at booth.lse.ac.uk).

Furthermore, it is by no means fair to suggest that agent-based simulation is unique or groundbreaking in the use of discrete decision-making units as the object of analysis. Right back in the 1950s the economist Guy Orcutt was already suggesting that the distributional consequences of financial and social policies should be understood not as an aggregate proposition but in relation to its cumulative impact across a population of distinct individual or household units (Orcutt, 1957). Thus, the field of microsimulation has been actively pursued by an international and multidisciplinary community for more than 50 years (see Zaidi et al., 2009; Tanton and Edwards, 2013, for an outline of contemporary activities).

A complete review and classification of modelling approaches in the social sciences is beyond the scope of this chapter. However, these examples do serve to emphasize that there is considerable diversity in model-based approaches to social science. In the next part of this chapter, case studies will be presented of each of the four model classes introduced above – a spatial interaction model (mathematical model); a traffic behaviour model (statistical model); a demographic model (microsimulation model); and a crime model (agent-based model).

These examples also serve to make the point that modelling and simulation are not new activities in the social sciences. They are not even dependent on the advent of modern computational techniques in the post-war period. Nevertheless, the transformative effect of sustained computational advances on social modelling and simulation has been profound. The nature of this transformation will be explored further in this chapter, with primary reference to the most recent wave of computational developments, which can be conveniently bundled under the label of 'e-Research'. The main themes to be covered will be disaggregation and model sophistication; new sources of data and approaches to model validation and verification; the calibration and optimization of model parameters; visualization of model outputs; and collaboration between model developers, users and other interested parties.

A framework and architecture for a social simulation e-Infrastructure will then be presented, including an introduction to an architecture that has been developed by a multi-disciplinary team, and a description of its key features. Model functionality will be discussed and examples of workflows that connect infrastructure components will be introduced. Examples and applications of this social simulation infrastructure will be outlined in relation to academic, governmental, public and commercial organizations.

The chapter will conclude with a discussion of the future for social simulation modelling and e-Research, including remaining obstacles and barriers. The issues to be addressed will include real-time social simulation; self-organization and model learning; crowdsourced simulation models; and social, cultural, political and ethical issues associated with the e-simulation process.

6.2 DIFFERENT TYPES OF MODEL

According to circumstance, the purpose of modelling in social science could be to formalize the understanding of how a social system operates, to predict a future state of the system, or to examine the effect of perturbations, whether natural or induced by human intervention. In all cases, however, it may be reasonable to suggest that a number of complementary activities are necessary if the activity is to be successful:

1. A model of the individuals themselves, which recognizes the heterogeneity in a population of social actors;
2. A model of the interactions between the individuals (as 'consumers') and those institutions and organizations who act as 'providers' of jobs, education, health care, goods and the other substantive elements of everyday social life;
3. A model of the interactions between individuals, their networks and distinctive behavioural patterns;
4. A model capable of recognizing trends of diversity between different groups, and variations in both space and time.

A combination of different models of these four types would provide a fairly comprehensive approach to social modelling. In this section of the chapter, examples of each of these model types will be presented, before the influences of e-Research are considered in the subsequent section and following this, the contribution of these models to a framework for social simulation modelling will be articulated.

6.2.1 Models of a Population of Actors

It is, of course, entirely possible and consistent, for example, with a 'systems' approach, to describe demographic groups as stocks, represented as $X(a, b, c)$, the number of people who share characteristics a, b and c, let's say age, gender and ethnicity respectively.

The central idea behind microsimulation is simply to replace this stocks-based view of the world with a representation of the characteristics of each individual in the population, which can be described as $P(i, n)$ – for each of i individuals, a score or category for attribute n.

The key features and advantages of this microsimulation approach include the following:

- It is an efficient way to represent the population and its diversity. van Imhoff and Post (1998) give an example in which the objective is to model variations in fertility according to the socio-economic and demographic characteristics and child-bearing history of individual parents. The authors demonstrate that relatively moderate combinations of attributes lead to an explosion of possible states, many of them permanently unoccupied. When some level of spatial disaggregation is introduced, then this issue is instantly magnified, hence the great interest of geographers and regional scientists in spatial microsimulation (Birkin and Clarke, 2012).

- The use of lists of individuals rather than grouped counts allows rules to be easily applied regarding the behaviours, activities or transitions of each population member. In core economic applications of microsimulation, these rules frequently relate to taxation or benefits, which can be easily parsed at a molecular level – for example, an individual is only eligible for housing benefit with an income less than £12,000, or for a pension at age 65. In demographic applications such as the previous illustration, then transition rules may be equally robust but also powerful, for example, in a model step of one year then the age of an individual will progress from (a) to (a+1).

- Flexible aggregation is possible. Thus to present the model outputs as a count of individuals of age a, gender b and ethnicity c, then the individuals can simply be summed across the relevant categories. Therefore, the microsimulation model (MSM) is also fully compatible with a systems view of the world.

Although this discussion has been couched in terms of individuals, there is no reason why a MSM could not be specified as a population of other types of discrete unit. In practice, households have been used at least as often as individual people as the building blocks of a microsimulation, but other components such as houses, hospital beds, firms or telephone cells might equally well be used.

6.2.2 Interaction Models

The most important class of models, which link together consumers and producers for a specific service activity are spatial interaction models (SIM). The model represents the flow of people or commodities between pairs of locations, usually referred to as 'origins' and 'destinations'. For example, in a retail market the origin locations would typically be residential neighbourhoods and the destination locations would be shopping centres. The locations are physically separated, and the accessibility between each origin-destination pair can be represented as a straight-line distance or as the composite trip cost of getting from one place to another.

The important feature of all SIMs is that they embody an element of *theory* about the operation of the underlying system. Essentially this theory is simply that entities interact most strongly when they are close together; and that the interactions between large entities are more significant than the interactions between small entities. In view of parallels to the behaviour of objects in the natural world, this is also referred to as a 'gravity model'; however, the robustness of the foundations of the SIM, for example, in information theory and mathematical optimization (Wilson, 1970) should not be overlooked. Thus the SIMs are themselves special cases of a broader class of entropy-maximizing model (EMM).

Although a fuller discussion is beyond the scope of this chapter, it is also worth noting that the EMM approach can be applied to many other kinds of social and economic model in which the linkages are not necessarily spatial. For example, if one were to define the origin and destination terms as sectors of the economy, with the distances between them as some measure of connectivity (e.g. steel and cars are more closely connected than hairdressing and fisheries) then the SIM might easily represent a version of the well-known 'RAS' or input-output model of economic activity (Leontief, 1986; Hewings, 1985).

One of the most appealing features of the SIM approach is its flexibility. For example, different model formulations are possible according to the specification of the origin and destination weights – what Wilson (1971) refers to as the *family* of spatial interaction models.[1] If the origin weights are defined analytically so that the flows from each location sums to a known origin mass (for example, the expenditure of each neighbourhood in a retail market), then the model is origin- or *production-constrained*. Again, the retail model is typically given as an example on the assumption that each resident has a need to shop. A *destination-constrained* model is the inverse, where it is the trip ends that are known – perhaps a residential location model with fixed housing stocks. Where both trip origins and destinations are fixed, then a *doubly-constrained* model results. The journey-to-work model is a good example where allocation of flows is the primary concern. With no trip-end totals, then the models are *unconstrained*, which could be the case when looking at something like migration. Clearly, many hybrids are also possible, for example, if quotas were used to introduce a migration threshold.

6.2.3 Behavioural Models

It has been argued – with some justification – that neither of the model-types introduced so far makes sufficient allowance for behavioural variations that distinguish human decision-making in the social sciences from the actions of entities in the natural world. Thus, two planets have no 'choice' about the gravitational attraction that connects them, whereas individual consumers have a very real choice about which retail destinations they might patronize. In order to fully recognize the diversity of individual decision-making, procedures are needed which recognize the subtlety of the interactions between individual agents (e.g., sharing information and experience) and between individuals and their environment (e.g., prior knowledge and experience of a place). In recent years, agent-based simulation has been championed as a modelling approach with many more suitable features.

---

[1]The spatial interaction model can be expressed in a general form as follows:

$$T_{ij} = a_i b_j O_i D_j \exp(-\beta d_{ij})$$

where T_{ij} is a flow (of goods, people, money, etc.) between locations i and j; O_i and D_i are respectively the mass terms associated with the origin and destination; a_i and b_j are weights associated with these locations; d_{ij} is the distance between each pair of locations; and β is a distance impedance term. For example, in a model of retail trade O_i would typically be the population in a residential area i and D_i a measure of the floor space at a shopping centre j, and now T_{ij} shows the 'catchment areas' for each retail centre.

At one level – in terms of the way that the entities are represented – MSM and agent-based models are not all that dissimilar, as has been argued elsewhere (e.g., Wu et al., 2008). Thus, both rely on a molecular resolution of individual people or agents in the system. Both approaches also rely heavily on the notion of 'rules'. However, whereas for MSM these rules are generally quite deterministic in their character ('if an individual is unemployed, then benefits are payable'), in the ABM these rules are much more flexible and adaptive.

Thomas Schelling's classic model of ethnic segregation (Schelling, 1971) remains an instructive exemplar of this distinction. A simple grid of residents is proposed, and in addition to location these residents have a single attribute – call this colour A or colour B. A number of spaces in the grid are left vacant and residents are selected at random to move to a vacant space. In a SIM, the key criterion in selecting a vacancy would be distance travelled, and a similar rule could equally well be embedded in a MSM. In Schelling's 'agent' version, however, the decision relates to the mix of resident characteristics (or 'colours') in the target neighbourhood. Agents will typically prefer to move to neighbourhoods where there is some representation amongst other agents of a similar kind/colour. In this way, the model becomes *adaptive* because as the agents move, the composition of neighbourhoods will change, and along with it the movement preferences of the agents themselves. Through this mechanism Schelling is able to demonstrate that segregation can occur as the different agent types become concentrated in distinct neighbourhoods, and interestingly, that this can happen even when the preferences of the agents are quite weak. Numerous interactive demonstrations of the model are available online – see, for example http://ncase.me/polygons.

In addition to their adaptive nature, a second property of agent-based models that has attracted much comment is *emergence*. Systems become emergent when complex and unexpected structures arise from simple agent rules, as in the previous example when segregation occurs – in many cases unexpectedly – from simple neighbourhood preferences. For some commentators this makes ABM well-suited to the study of social systems, in which complex structures are the norm rather than the exception.

6.2.4 Statistical Models

Models capable of measuring changes in the distribution of social phenomena over time, or for identifying significant patterns within social data, are a crucial adjunct to the approaches already described. For example, using a spatial interaction model one might use a regression model to compare the flows generated by the SIM to an observed set of flows from a census or survey. Perhaps one might even search for the best-fitting regression model as a means of calibrating critical parameter values in the model, that is, beta in the previous examples. Alternatively, segregation in an ABM could be demonstrated using a statistical measure such as the Index of Dissimilarity.

These models can be characterized as 'statistical' because they are empirically-grounded, rather than embodying any prior notion or 'theory' about the system of interest. However, more complicated instances can arise in a number of ways. For example, suppose that when residents are moving house, then they don't only think about the 'colour' of their neighbours, but also whether there are children of a similar age, shared educational backgrounds, appropriate transport links and local services. Here, one might require some kind of multivariate analysis to make sense of the patterns and interdependencies that can be observed (in practice, clustering has been a favoured approach e.g., Vickers and Rees, 2007).

Now let us suppose further that neighbourhoods are indeed stratified on multivariate grounds, and that in some of the more affluent or high status neighbourhoods the children show more success in their school careers than some of the lower status neighbourhoods. To what extent is this determined by the leafy nature of the place itself, or is it moderated by the educational background and social characteristics of individual parents; or by the quality of the local schools? Is the contribution of individual teachers or classes a significant factor, now or in the past? In order to tease out the strength and structure of such relationships, an enormous variety of *multi-level models* could be specified and evaluated (Jones, 1991). Such models have proved popular not just for the assessment of pupil performance, but also health status, voting behaviour, labour market success and many others.

Finally, let us imagine instead a more naïve (or at least neutral) perspective, in which we would simply like to determine whether there are areas in which the concentration of high-performing pupils is particularly high and where these areas might be. We can worry later about the link to specific schools, demographic groups and so on. Approaches to the problem of pattern recognition, using methods such as spatial autocorrelation and kernel density estimation, have been especially important for researchers seeking an understanding of social variations in the incidence of crime (e.g., Ratcliffe and McCullagh, 1999) and health (e.g., Openshaw et al., 1988).

In short, statistical models, which are typically data intensive and empirically-driven, have an important role both in the validation of other models and theories, and as analytical instruments in their own right.

6.3 IMPACT OF E-RESEARCH ON SOCIAL MODELLING AND SIMULATION

In the discipline of geography, the period following the Second World War is commonly seen as a period of rapid and profound transformation, in which an earlier focus on the uniqueness of individual places and regions is supplanted in a more nomothetic and analytical approach, underpinned by tangible theories about the nature of spatial relationships. Although the reasons for this evocatively styled *quantitative revolution* are multi-faceted (see, for example, Barnes (2008) for a considered review) there is no doubt that easy access to both data and computation was a considerable factor. From the evidence already considered, it is unlikely that the experience of geographers was atypical for the social sciences in general, and it was at this time that most of the modelling approaches discussed above came into prominence. For example, we have already seen the advent of microsimulation in the 1950s (Orcutt, 1957), and the advent of factorial ecologies using North American census data to test empirically the pre-war theories of the Chicago sociologists (Shevky and Bell, 1955). Gravity models themselves first appeared in the 1950s, on a wave of enthusiasm for 'social physics', in which scientific analogues for social processes were explored widely (e.g. Schaefer, 1953).

Since the 1960s, the experience of individual disciplines seems to be more mixed. For economists and psychologists, quantitative and mathematical approaches remain fundamentally important; for sociologists, much less so. In geography, perhaps something of a middle-ground has been adopted, in which the growth of Geographical Information Systems (GIS; see Chapter 11) has continued to provide a vein of spatial data and basic analytical capabilities in a discipline in which the matrix of theories has increasingly veered towards the qualitative, behavioural and humanistic. For the substantial minority who have continued in the quantitative tradition, the last decade of developments in e-Research has provided exciting and productive opportunities. In this section, the nature of these opportunities will be considered under a variety of headings: model disaggregation, new data sources, calibration, visualization and collaboration.

6.3.1 Model Disaggregation

Looking back at early examples of modelling in both academic and policy research, the lack of detail in these models can seem alarming. For example, the well-known Haydock shopping model of the late 1960s was used to assess the impact of a major new out-of-town retail development using a study area divided into just 244 residential zones and 47 retail destinations for a single retail commodity and assuming an homogeneous customer base (Foot, 1981). The real sadness is that, because such models were dismissed so robustly at that time (see, for example, the particularly damning and influential critique of Lee (1973)), the credibility of the approach in some circles has never been fully restored. However, it is clear that tremendous advances in computation permit the construction of enormously more detailed models, as well as the invention of radically new styles of modelling work. For example, Khawaldah et al. (2012) describe an updated version of the Haydock problem, but in which customer behaviours can be disaggregated across demographic characteristics such as age and gender, car ownership, ethnicity and social class, all of which is possible in a simple spreadsheet (in contrast to the resource-hungry mainframe applications of the past). Elsewhere, applications have been described in which supermarket locations have been repeatedly tested across hundreds of thousands of potential sites in order to assess the possibilities for new development that are at once lucrative, not anti-competitive, and address gaps in market provision (Birkin and Culf, 2001). Parallel processing applications have been described in which the computationally intractable problem of network optimization can be tackled[2] – again from a large array of potential

---

[2]The combinatorial problem of selecting a relatively small number of actual locations from a relatively large number of potential sites becomes explosively large, even for problems which are unrealistically limited in practical terms e.g. selecting ten locations from 100 sites is a problem with more than 10^{12} possible solutions.

destinations (George et al., 1997). Even the models themselves have been subjected to revision and reformulation using genetic programming approaches to explore a wide universe of alternative specifications (Diplock, 1998).

In other related work on the simulation of complex dynamics, agent-based models are now proposed which incorporate the behaviour of billions of agents (Epstein, 2009). Whilst one might challenge the need for model constructions that represent the population of the whole planet at an individual scale, the fact that a solution to this problem can even be contemplated suggests the extent to which computational restrictions are no longer paramount in the modelling process.

6.3.2 New Data Sources

More recently, computational muscle has been complemented by the increasing power of data, which may be even more significant. In the physical sciences, discussions about 'big data' have perhaps been crystallized most effectively in the notion of the 'fourth paradigm' of empirically rich and data driven research (Hey et al., 2009). However, even within the social sciences an appreciation of related issues can be traced back at least as far as 2007, and the identification of a 'crisis in empirical sociology' (Savage and Burrows, 2007), in which the availability of data from volunteered sources alongside massive public reserves, commercial resources and numerous others provide a critical threat to the legitimacy of established samples and surveys (see Chapters 2, 3 and 4 for a review). It is also interesting to note that arguments about data-driven approaches to model design, testing and calibration were anticipated in the hugely interesting and important research into the 'Geographical Analysis Machine' in the late 1980s (Openshaw et al., 1988).

Geographers, in particular, have relied in the past on survey data sources, including the Census of Population and Households, which, although sporadic in its coverage both topically and temporally, can at least boast enormous breadth of coverage. Here again, however, new sources promise access to continuously updateable resources with unforeseen richness of behaviour and lifestyle preferences, movement and activity patterns, opinions and attitudes (Goodchild, 2007; Malleson and Birkin, 2012). Indeed, so effective are these novel replacement sources that even the census may now be considered as unnecessary (Office for National Statistics, 2013).

6.3.3 Calibration

It is not clear that the fundamental aim of models in social science is to reproduce the machinations of the real world in all its intricate detail or that the fundamental aim of a simulation is to mimic the response of a system to external shocks with great accuracy. The traditions of 'Occam's Razor' – in essence, the principle that any model should be stripped down to its bare essentials – are deeply ingrained in many places. In particular, this seems to be true amongst the agent-based social simulation community, amongst whom the role of model as a pedagogic device or thought experiment is highly cherished (see, for example, Edmonds and Moss (2005)).

Nevertheless, for other members of the community, the problem of calibration, or matching models to reality, is a crucial one. To an extent, this reflects the observation that building sophisticated models is actually not all that hard – the difficult part is in doing it well, in demonstrating that the model represents an underlying social system, and not some unrecognizable abstraction. In Andrew Sayer's words, the problem is one of 'Understanding Models versus Understanding Cities' (Sayer, 1976: 853). The principle of equifinality, which recognizes that the same solution may be reached by many models or approaches, is also of particular significance to complexity scientists. If this is the case, then surely it is necessary to demonstrate not just that a model exhibits behaviour that has some identifiable resonance with a real system, but that it can be calibrated (or validated) as a robust representation of its essential components.

The combination of e-Research trends – in particular, greater data availability and computational power – provides significant impetus to the process of model calibration. As we have seen above, more detailed and disaggregated representations are feasible than ever before, with the possibility of detailed calibration to reliable and fine-grained data, or even to cross-validation between datasets. In recent work on housing and regeneration in the city of Leeds, these possibilities were articulated with moderate success. Starting with a model in the style of Schelling (see above), it was argued that the drivers of the relocation process needed to be extended substantially beyond the single factor of ethnic segregation. From a combination of literature and previous empirical studies, seven major factors were identified and embedded in the decision-making process of each individual agent. This model was calibrated against 2001 census data and the household movement was then simulated over a twenty year period. The model outputs were validated using commercially generated research data for the first seven years of the simulation window, that is, up to 2008. Finally, the usefulness of the simulation was demonstrated in relation to relevant policy scenarios, including a new mixed tenure housing development and a proposal to accelerate regeneration through the provision of a new rapid access transport corridor (for more details see Jordan et al., 2012).

6.3.4 Visualization

The ability to represent data, experimental results, models and simulations in an appealing graphical format (and to switch between various domains with easy-to-use interfaces) seems to have become an important feature in promoting computational applications for the natural sciences and engineering. For example, the AstroGrid project (2001–10) – funded by the UK e-science programme, but also with a strong international dimension (www.astrogrid.org) – not only incorporated the ability to capture massive volumes of astronomical data, and to hypothesize or search for significant features and patterns, but also the ability to display images in a spectacular and engaging way. More broadly, magnificent examples of digitally generated, remote imagery are now being produced regularly by the space probes. In other fields, such as bioinformatics, high resolution images are providing an aid to scientific understanding as well as pedagogic and wider social engagement

(Roberts et al., 2012). Visualization can provide practical value in a variety of other applications, for example, as an aid to reconstructive surgery, or manufacturing design and maintenance (Jackson et al., 2005).

In the social sciences, particularly those with a strong spatial emphasis such as geography, planning and transport studies, the advent of GIS has provided a visual stimulus to data analysis and interpretation running right back to the earliest applications of the technology in the 1960s. Later developments have taken this activity on to a new scale of ambition, and in some cases applied value (see Chapter 11). An excellent example would be Luc Anselin's GEODA software, which combines GIS with statistical modelling and spatial data analysis. Moving beyond the traditional domain of mapping spatial data, the software incorporates econometric estimation and autocorrelation metrics (in simple terms, the search for pattern) and, crucially links the two together so that it is possible to see immediately, for instance, not just that there might be statistical outliers within some dataset but *where* those outliers are located, and hence permit users to engage immediately with questions such as correlation or even causation (Anselin et al., 2006).

The latest research seeks to augment these applications with a modelling and simulation capability, which will be discussed later in this chapter. Most recently, the CASA team at UCL have created a number of web-based tools for spatial mapping and visualization, through the GeoVUE, Genesis and latterly TALISMAN projects[3] (see Chapter 11).

6.3.5 Collaboration

In situations where mathematical models, simulations or other forms of analysis become particularly robust, then it may be appropriate to supplement human decision-making with recommendations and insights generated by computer software. Such programmatic applications are typically referred to as Expert Systems (ES) or Decision Support Systems (DSS) and have been prevalent in the social sciences as well as in engineering and physical sciences. For example, in health care, DSS may lead practitioners through a set of practical decisions to prescribe medication or some other form of treatment. For geographers, the use of GIS has provided appropriate platforms for Spatial Decision Support Systems (SDSS) or Planning Support Systems (PSS), for example, in the context of land-use planning (Geertman and Stillwell, 2003) or impact analysis and optimization of commercial networks (Birkin et al., 2003). In these cases, a support system is typically conceived as a group of tightly coupled modules, which may integrate data, provide analytic capabilities, models and simulations, together with visual representation of (scenario) outputs and, hopefully, a user-friendly external interface.

If the technologies listed above can be made freely available, perhaps also with an emphasis on the relevant semantic methods for finding and selecting these resources, then the size of the community with the ability to contribute can be increased by several orders of magnitude. The work of organizations promoting interoperability

---

[3]www.geotalisman.org

and open standards, such as the Open Grid Software Initiative (OGSI), is therefore significant in this regard (especially in providing an impetus to changing practices of reproducible research), as are the contributions of the Open Data strategy (see Chapters 2 and 3) and various Open Publishing initiatives in relaxing the social and legal barriers to shared ownership and utilization.

6.4 SOCIAL SIMULATION INFRASTRUCTURE

From our review of social simulation modelling and its applications, we can conclude that such approaches are often rich in both data and theory. The essence of the modelling approach is to articulate theories of social behaviour and interaction, which can be refined and tested in the real world through processes of calibration and validation. Suitably robust models may be exploited to address problems in planning or policy evaluation. There are many parallels between this view of social simulation modelling and approaches within other data-intensive scientific disciplines. In this section, we report on the first attempt to design a simulation infrastructure for the social sciences – the (National) e-Infrastructure for Social Simulation (NeISS) project (Birkin et al., 2010), which began in 2009 with funding from the Joint Information Systems Council (JISC).[4] The overall framework and some key components of this infrastructure are described below.

At a high level, e-infrastructure can be seen as an attempt to bring together elements of the research lifecycle that are relevant to a specific application domain. One possible conceptualization of this research lifecycle framework is illustrated in Figure 6.1. This view is intrinsically user-focused: it considers the range of tools and services that might be required by a researcher in order to conduct a complete investigation. As the label implies, the various components are linked in a cycle rather than a linear sequence, although for the purposes of discussion the assembly stage at the top of Figure 6.1 can be regarded as a reasonable point of entry. This conceptualization of the research lifecycle underpins many scientific applications of e-Infrastructure – a particularly notable example is the MyGrid Bioinformatics workbench,[5] which aims to blend together key elements of the bioinformatics research lifecycle within an integrated data and service infrastructure.

The principles are similar in many other applications in the physical sciences, engineering, environmental studies and elsewhere, such as medicine and earth sciences (for example, Astrogrid, DigitalSky, Geon).

In order to construct an infrastructure capable of providing a range of component services that are relevant to the social simulation research lifecycle, a rather more linear or hierarchical view of the requirements is required. The design agreed by the NeISS team is illustrated in Figure 6.2. Each of the layers in the figure formed a major Work Package in the production phase of the NeISS.

---

[4]see www.geog.leeds.ac.uk/projects/neiss/index.php

[5]www.mygrid.org.uk

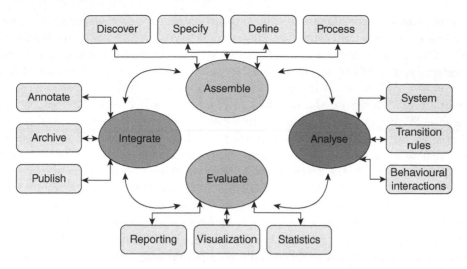

Figure 6.1   The research lifecycle

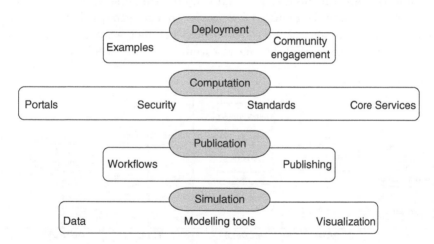

Figure 6.2   Components of a research infrastructure for social simulation

A workflow oriented version of the NeISS platform is shown in Figure 6.3. The major components in the workflow are data integration, simulation, visualization, and interactions with a repository of outputs. Individual elements of the workflow can be construed as an implementation of the key stages of the research lifecycle in a social simulation context. The enactment of multiple workflows under alternative configurations can therefore produce the effect of cycling through the stages of this lifecycle.

An important feature of NeISS workflows is that storing and enacting the same workflow on multiple occasions should provide the same outputs – it is *reproducible*. This could be particularly useful in the process of model calibration, in which an analyst wants to execute a similar sequence of model steps in order to find a configuration which is closely matched to real life. It is also straightforward to reproduce the same sorts of experiments for different urban areas, or for larger regions, or in principle even for whole countries. However, it is also *updateable*, for example, if new information becomes available about the behaviour of commuters; and more importantly, it is robust to permutation, so that a variety of 'what if' scenarios could be explored, such as what happens if a new congestion charge is introduced, or a new bus route. Moreover, the workflow is *generalizable* across sectors with reasonable ease. Within the NeISS project, similar examples have been considered relating to housing, crime and policing, and provision of health care as well as transportation. Although some of the detail of the simulation models needs to be extended for multiple applications, the architecture of the workflows is broadly unchanged. The workflows are also *extensible*: so, for example, if it were necessary to introduce a new range of functions – perhaps an optimization capability which seeks to find a solution to a specified problem (e.g. reduce congestion by 50 per cent, or get 5,000 passengers on the trains) – then new modules could be defined and embedded within the same framework. Finally, the workflow should be *differentiable* – it should be possible to reconfigure the workflow quite easily to meet different constituencies of users. In practice, this is most likely to turn on the way that results are published from the process, and perhaps on the way that data inputs are generated, that is, different interfaces might perhaps be required for a variety of user groups. This has been quite an important consideration for the NeISS project in which a variety of levels of users have been identified from relatively naïve through to rather sophisticated.

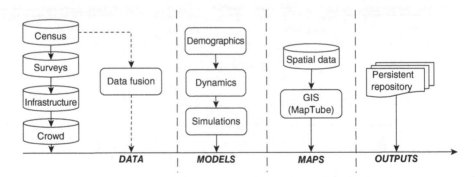

Figure 6.3 Elements of a workflow architecture for social simulation

The utilization of the infrastructure at an operational level can be understood using the examples of Figure 6.4. The first objective of the simulations shown here has been to estimate vehicle pollution using a simulation model of traffic flows, and in practice this means combining census data about population types and movements with traffic survey data about choice of transport mode and route selection. When coupled with appropriate assumptions about vehicle emission properties, this leads to estimates of pollution for a *baseline*, i.e., the situation as it is now. The simulation can then be flexed by the incorporation of a demographic forecasting model into the workflow, providing a straightforward means to project the impact of population changes on air quality. Thirdly, a scenario capability is introduced which, in this case, emulates the impact of road pricing strategies in an urban area. The reproducibility of the simulations is demonstrated through its application to three different cities – Leeds, Bristol and Southampton – and, in addition to air quality, the effects of reduced vehicular traffic on congestion, trip costs and road accidents are also considered.

This illustration demonstrates some of the value that can be provided through simulation, not just to planners and policy-makers but also to the general public. Showing the public how their individual decisions have an impact on the wider community is one way of providing value to the general public through NeISS simulation projects. Another way could be to illustrate to people what the impact would be if 'everyone made the same decisions I did'.

For example, crowd-sourced survey tools could be used to collect data about preferences under various scenarios based on lifestyle and demographic data (for example transport preferences) to create different models of people's usage/preferences for public/private transport and their journeys. The survey data could then be recalibrated with existing models to show the results, and if public transport could be proven to be cheaper, and/or more efficient, then people might be persuaded to switch from private to public transport.

The tool could also be used to investigate other scenarios when different factors are changed (for example, more bus routes being created, trains running more frequently, etc.).

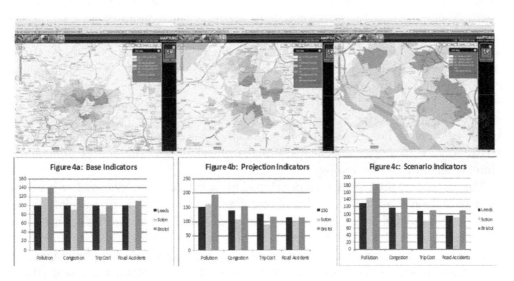

Figure 6.4 Indicators/externalities a) baseline, b) projection and c) scenario; pollution in the cities of Leeds, Bristol and Southampton

6.5 CURRENT TRENDS, ISSUES AND PRIORITIES

In spite of the progress that has been made over a long period of time, which increased in the second half of the Twentieth Century, and which accelerates more quickly with the advent of new methods and infrastructures (some key features of this progression have been highlighted in previous sections of this chapter), it can nevertheless be argued that social scientists have as yet only begun to scratch the surface in exploiting the potential of models and simulation approaches.

Consider, for example, a problem that has some qualitative similarities with the e-Infrastructure use cases presented earlier. From an outbreak of an infectious disease in the centre of a major metropolis, it is now possible to generate elegant simulations of the progression of cases through space and time (e.g., Ferguson et al., 2005; Epstein, 2009). From these simulations, it is possible to explore various policy ramifications, such as the effectiveness of immunisation programmes, or social distance measures including the closure of schools or even workplaces. What remains difficult is to embed these simulations with any appreciable degree of confidence in the real behaviour patterns of the (infective) individuals in this epidemiological system. One of the main reasons for this is that even now researchers still lack a detailed knowledge of how these individuals move around, the frequencies with which they meet one another and the social circumstances in which these contacts take place.

For the first time, the kinds of data needed to unlock problems of this type are now becoming available. For example, analysis of tweets can trace behaviour patterns, movements and networks of interaction (e.g., Malleson and Birkin, 2012). Telecommunications providers may be capable of leveraging even more powerful datasets – for example, Telefónica's recent launch of the SmartSteps product.[6] appears to signal its confidence in tracing customer movements in and out of retail destinations with unprecedented detail and accuracy. Such datasets are massive and require significant processing capacity, and yet there is no fundamental reason why such patterns might not be inferred at something approximating real time. Other devices such as traffic sensors, and even retail loyalty cards, are equally capable of capturing behavioural events in real time (see Chapter 2).

Given that data itself will become progressively more voluminous, it can be expected that increasing attention will need to be devoted to the technologies for their exploitation. For instance, despite the advances described earlier in this chapter, relatively little progress has been made towards the holistic understanding and simulation of the urban system.

The obstacles to progress are not merely technological, however. Even as data becomes ever more ubiquitous, the ownership of that data and the rights to its exploitation, for both commercial and social value, can be expected to become increasingly contentious (see Chapters 3 and 12). While there is nothing new in much of this (see, for example, Goss (1995) for a polemic which remains powerful and still feels contemporary), the increasing scale of the problem and a persistent failure to establish accepted ethical standards for the use of data – including pronounced international disparities – points to the politics of data as a potential battlefield for the future.

Of equal significance, perhaps, is that no amount of model sophistication, simulation accuracy or data intensity can determine the comparative desirability of social outcomes from investigations of the type that have been discussed here. Is it acceptable

---

[6]http://dynamicinsights.telefonica.com/488/smart-steps

to restrict the movement capabilities of individuals in order to reduce the transmission risk for an infection? To what extent? Can a congestion charge be justified to reduce the impacts of pollution on child health in a city? Are the social barriers introduced by a gated community justifiable to reduce the exposure of its beneficiaries to crime? The kinds of questions with which social scientists need to occupy themselves can be substantially enriched by simulations supported by e-Infrastructure. Although its methods may continue to evolve at a rapid pace, only the most naïve of observers would conclude that social science itself will become any the less challenging or fruitful for the researchers of the future.

6.5 BIBLIOGRAPHY

Anselin, L., Syabri, I. and Kho, Y. (2006) 'GeoDa: an introduction to spatial data analysis', *Geographical Analysis*, 38: 5–22.

Barnes, T. (2008) 'Geography's underworld: the military–industrial complex, mathematical modelling and the quantitative revolution', *GeoForum*, 39(1): 3–16.

Beer, S. (1972) *Brain of the Firm: The Managerial Cybernetics of Organisations.*: London: Penguin.

Birkin, M. and Culf, R. (2001) 'Optimal distribution strategies: one company's experience in the application of regional science techniques to business planning problems', in G. Clarke and M. Madden (eds), *Regional Science in Business*, Springer, 223–242.

Birkin, M., Clarke, G., Clarke, M. and Culf R. (2003) 'Using spatial models to solve difficult retail location problems', in G. Clarke and J. Stillwell (eds), *Applied GIS and Spatial Modelling*, John Wiley & Sons, 35–54.

Birkin, M. and Clarke, G.P. (2012) 'The enhancement of spatial microsimulation models using geodemographics', *The Annals of Regional Science*, 49: 513–32.

Birkin, M., Procter, R., Allan, R., Bechhofer, S., Buchan, I., Goble, C., Hudson-Smith, A., Lambert, P., DeRoure, D. and Sinnott, R. (2010) 'Elements of a Computational Infrastructure for Social Simulation', *Philosophical Transactions of the Royal Society A: Mathematical, Physical and Engineering Sciences*, 368(1925): 3797–3812.

Diplock, G. (1998) 'Building new spatial interaction models by using genetic programming and a supercomputer', *Environment and Planning A*, 30, 1893–1904.

Edmonds, B. and Moss, S. (1985) 'From KISS to KIDS: an 'anti-simplistic' modelling approach', *Multi-agent and multi-agent-based simulation, Lecture Notes in Computer Science*, 3415: 130–44.

Epstein, J. (2009) 'Modelling to contain pandemics', *Nature* 460(7256): 687.

Epstein, J. and Axtell, R. (1996) *Growing Artificial Societies: Social Science from the Bottom Up*. Washington, DC: Brookings Institution Press.

Ferguson, N., Cummings, A., Cauchemez, S., Fraser, C., Riley, S., Meeyai, A., Iamsirithaworn, S. and Burke, D. (2005) 'Strategies for containing an emerging influenza pandemic in Southeast Asia', *Nature* 437: 209–14.

Foot, D. (1981) *Operational Urban Models*. London: Methuen.

Forrester, J. (1969) *Urban Dynamics*. Cambridge, MA: MIT Press.

Forrester, J. (1971) *World Dynamics*. Cambridge, MA: MIT Press.

Geertman, S. and Stillwell, J. (2003) *Planning Support Systems in Practice*. Berlin: Springer.

George F., Radcliffe N., Smith, M., Birkin, M. and Clarke, M. (1997) 'Spatial interaction model optimisation on parallel computers', *Concurrency: Practice and Experience*, 9(8): 753–780.

Goodchild, M. (2007) 'Citizens as sensors: the world of volunteered geography', *GeoJournal*, 211–221.

Goss, J. (1995) 'We know who you are and we know where you live: the instrumental rationality of geodemographics systems', *Economic Geography*, 71: 171–98.

Harris, R., Sleight, P. and Webber, R. (2005) *Geodemographics, GIS and Neighbourhood Targeting*. Chichester: John Wiley.

Hewings, G. (1985) *Regional Input-Output Analysis*. Beverley Hills, CA: Sage.

Hey, T., Tansley, S. and Tolle, K. (2009) *The Fourth Paradigm: Data-Intensive Scientific Discovery*. WA: Microsoft Research.

Jackson, T., Austin, J., Fletcher, M., Jessop, M., Liang, B., Pasley, A., Ong, M., Ren, X., Allan, G., Kadirkamanathan, V., Thompson, H. and Fleming, P. (2005) 'Distributed health monitoring for aero-engines on the grid: DAME', *IEEE Aerospace Conference*, Montana. Available from www.cs.york.ac.uk/arch/publications/byyear/2005/distributed-health-monitoring-for-aero-engines-on-the-grid-dame.pdf (accessed 11 Dec 2014).

Jones, K. (1991) *Multi-level Models for Geographical Research*. Norwich: Environmental Publications.

Jordan, R., Birkin, M. and Evans, A. (2012) 'Agent-based modelling of residential mobility, housing choice and regeneration', in A. Heppenstall, A. Crooks, L. See and M. Batty (eds), *Agent-Based Models of Geographical Systems*. Springer: Berlin. pp. 511–24.

Khawaldah, H., Birkin, M. and Clarke, G. (2012) 'A review of two alternative retail impact assessment techniques: the case of Silverburn in Scotland', *Town Planning Review*, 82(2): 233–60, doi 10.3828/tpr.2012.13

Lee, D.B. (1973) 'Requiem for large scale urban models', *Journal of the American Institute of Planners*, 39(3): 163–178.

Leontief, W. (1986) *Input-Output Economics*. New York: Oxford University Press.

Malleson, N. and Birkin, M. (2012) 'Estimating individual behaviour from massive social data for an urban agent-Based Model', *8th Conference of the European Social Simulation Association*, Salzburg.

Meadows, D.H., Meadows, D.L., Randers, J. and Behrens, W. (1972) *The Limits to Growth*. New York: Universe Books.

Office for National Statistics (2013) *The Census and Future Provision of Population Statistics in England and Wales*. London: ONS.

Openshaw, S., Charlton, M., Craft, A. and Birch, J. (1988) 'Investigation of leukaemia clusters by use of a Geographical Analysis Machine', *The Lancet*, 331: 272–3.

Orcutt, G. (1957) 'A new type of socio-economic system', *The Review of Economics and Statistics* 39(2): 116–23.

Park, R. and Burgess, E. (1925) *The City*. Chicago: University of Chicago Press.

Ratcliffe, J.H. and McCullagh, M. (1999) 'Hotbeds of crime and the search for spatial accuracy', *Journal of Geographical Systems*, 1: 385–98.

Ravenstein, E. (1885) 'The laws of migration', *Journal of the Statistical Society of London*, 48(2): 167–235.

Rees, P. (1968) *The Factorial Ecology of Metropolitan Chicago*. Chicago: University of Chicago Press.

Roberts, N., Magee, D., Song, Y., Brabazon, K., Shires, M., Crellin, D., Orsi. N., Quirke, R., Quirke, P. and Treanor, D. (2012) 'Toward routine use of 3D histopathology as a research tool', *The American Journal of Pathology*, 180: 1835–42.

Savage, M. and Burrows, R. (2007) 'The coming crisis of empirical sociology', *Sociology*, 41(5): 885–99.

Sayer, R. (1976) 'Understanding models versus understanding cities', *Environment and Planning A* 11(8): 853–62.

Schaefer, F. (1953) 'Exceptionalism in geography, a methodological examination', *Annals of the Association of American Geographers,* 43(3): 226–49.

Schelling, T. (1971) 'Dynamic models of segregation', *The Journal of Mathematical Sociology* 1(2): 143–86.

Shevky, E. and Bell, W. (1955) *Social Area Analysis.* Stanford, CA: Stanford University Press.

Tanton, R. and Edwards, K. (eds) (2013) *Handbook of Spatial Microsimulation.* Berlin: Springer.

Tobler, W. (1995) 'Migration: ravenstein, thornthwaite, and beyond', *Urban Geography,* 16: 327–43.

van Imhoff, E. and Post, W. (1998) 'Microsimulation methods for population projection', *Population: An English Selection, New Methodological Approaches in the Social Sciences,* 10(1): 97–138.

Vickers, D. and Rees, P. (2006) 'Introducing the area classification of output areas', *Population Trends-London,* 125(2006): 15–29.

Wilson, A. (1970) *Entropy in Urban and Regional Modelling.* London: Pion Ltd.

Wilson, A. (1974) *Urban and Regional Models in Geography and Planning.* New York: John Wiley.

Wilson, A. (1971) 'A family of spatial interaction models and associated developments', *Environment and Planning,* 3(1): 1–32.

Wu, B., Birkin, M. and Rees, P. (2008) 'A spatial microsimulation model with student agents', *Computers Environment and Urban Systems,* 32: 440–53.

Zaidi, A., Harding, A. and Williamson, P. (eds) (2009) *New Frontiers in Microsimulation Modelling.* London: Ashgate.

7

CONTEMPORARY DEVELOPMENTS IN STATISTICAL SOFTWARE FOR SOCIAL SCIENTISTS

PAUL S. LAMBERT, WILLIAM J. BROWNE AND DANIUS T. MICHAELIDES

7.1 INTRODUCTION

This chapter provides a brief review of statistical software applications in social science research, before describing and illustrating some exciting new developments in interoperability and documentation that have emerged from recent technologically oriented projects.

7.1.1 Background on Statistical Software in Social Research

In broad terms, statistical software, as it is used for social science applications, tends to feature three elements. It supports mechanisms for accessing, storing and (if required) modifying social science datasets (both with regard to the data itself, and metadata about the data, such as informative names and coding labels for variables); it features facilities such as mathematical algorithms which allow operations and statistical analyses to be applied to the data, and which can be called upon by the user through a textual programming language or pre-set menus; and it features a means for displaying summaries of the results of the operations and analyses that the user invokes, in graphical or tabular forms.

Whilst the analyses undertaken in the social sciences are sometimes highly advanced in statistical terms, most software is developed with the expectation that the user does not need advanced statistical or programming expertise in order to

>

implement the techniques. Usually, the expectation is simply that the user learns how to invoke specific techniques in the terms of the package, through some form of proxy specification, such as naming the type of model or analysis to be run. Figure 7.1 provides an illustrative example of a researcher using the popular general purpose package IBM SPSS Statistics software (SPSS)[1] to analyse statistical relations between two categorical variables as recorded on a survey dataset. In this package, three windows are typically visible to the user: the 'Viewer' which shows the outputs from processes; the 'data editor', which shows the dataset being analysed; and the 'syntax' window, which shows the commands that the user has written to be executed. In this example, the technique being used is known as correspondence analysis and it is being invoked by the 'correspondence...' command shown on the syntax window. Notably, as is typical of social science examples, the commands shown are not restricted to statistical analyses – some of the earlier lines in the SPSS syntax include actions to restrict the data analysis to cases without missing values on any of the relevant measures, and an action to apply sampling weights to the correspondence analysis results. These precursor operations are often labelled as 'data management' and are discussed in Chapter 5 in this collection.

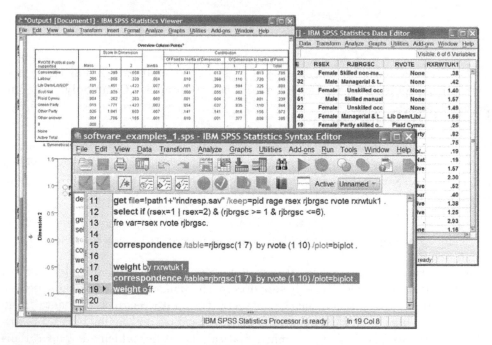

Figure 7.1   Illustration of using the SPSS package to perform correspondence analysis

The figure shows selected outputs from the analysis (the 'Viewer' window); part of the underlying data (the 'data editor' window), which features examples of categorical and partially observed variables; the commands run in SPSS are recorded in the 'syntax' window and include applying sampling weights (the variable 'rxrwtuk1') to the analysis. (Reprint Courtesy of International Business Machines Corporation, © International Business Machines Corporation.)

---

[1]SPSS Inc. was acquired by IBM in October, 2009.

SPSS (illustrated in Figure 7.1) is a relatively well-known proprietary package with functionality that covers both statistical analysis and data management. In terms of statistical analysis, SPSS features a wide range of statistical models and other descriptive techniques. However, SPSS is not the only general purpose package in contemporary use in the social sciences. It is arguably rivalled in popularity by Stata (StataCorp, 2013), another general purpose package which supports a somewhat wider range of advanced statistical techniques, whilst other general purpose packages such as SAS (SAS, 2012) and Minitab (Minitab, 2010), and the freeware R (R Core Team, 2013), also have substantial communities of users in the social sciences. These general purpose packages support many data analysis and data processing functions, although they could be described as 'expensive' to researchers, both in a metaphorical sense, insofar as investment in training and skills in these packages is a long term process, and in a literal sense, since some of the packages require considerable financial investment. Some general purpose packages have achieved fairly dominant positions in certain user communities: for example, arguably through its successful promotion of institutional licensing arrangements to universities, SPSS achieved dominance in the discipline of sociology and its related subject areas in the approximate period 1990–2005, to the extent that it came to shape the very methods and interpretations of statistical analysis in this field (Uprichard et al., 2008).

In addition, a great many specialist software packages are also regularly used in social science research. Specialist packages can be characterized as those that focus upon provision of particular analytical techniques. Commonly, different specialist packages are adapted unevenly by different social science disciplines: prominent examples include Limdep's influence in economics (Greene, 2000); the influence of lEM (Vermunt, 1997) and TDA (Röhwer and Pötter, 1999) for categorical and event history data analysis in sociology; and the influence of HLM (Raudenbush et al., 2011) and MLwiN (Rasbash et al., 2011) for multilevel modelling in educational research. For many researchers, however, the use of specialist packages is supplementary to their use of a general purpose package, undertaken because the specialist package provides an extension analysis or facility which is either not available, or is less efficiently performed, in the general purpose package. Indeed, in several instances, the general purpose packages have, through their upgrades over time, come to incorporate new techniques of analysis that were previously only available through specialist software, in some instances leaving the relevant specialist packages increasingly obsolete.

Ultimately, in combination, a vast array of statistical software tools is used by social science researchers. In a voluntarily maintained listing, Cologne University Statistical Resources enumerates, and provides links to, 163 statistical software packages (CUSR, 2010); Uprichard et al. (2008: 606) estimate that over 50 packages have been used for social science teaching and research in recent decades; and the Centre for Multilevel Modelling reviews 14 software packages on the theme of multilevel modelling in the social sciences alone (CMM, 2012a). Varied uptake of packages is evident, for example, from the range of software support that is provided by social science research methods training resources (e.g. UCLA,

2014; CMM, 2012b) or textbooks (see for instance the dozens of different software resources that are described across the influential Sage series *Quantitative Applications in the Social Sciences*).

Various factors might explain the proliferation of statistical software tools in the social sciences. The nature and variety of quantitative datasets and their measures represent one reason. The measures within social science datasets come in complex functional forms – that is, rather than each variable representing an arithmetic scale which can be summarized adequately through the linear relations between them, social science variables are often categorical, and/or are subject to censoring or partial observation (i.e., the absence of values for selected cases for known or unknown reasons), or non-linear interdependencies. These features of functional form have prompted a steady expansion of techniques of analysis and the ongoing development of software packages to support them. For instance, social science examples have been central to developments in tools for the analysis of categorical variables and of analytical methods that recognize complex latent and/or multiprocess relations between measured variables (Greenacre and Blasius, 1994; Greene, 2000). Additionally, some social science datasets have large numbers of cases, and/or very large numbers of variables, which require special capacities for data storage and organization. Many social science datasets also have non-standard designs – such as a complex sampling scheme with accompanying sampling weights, or a longitudinal design (e.g. featuring repeated contacts with the same subjects), or a hierarchical clustering structure of interest (whereby individual cases are clustered into numerous wider groups, such as workplaces, schools or families). These complexities benefit from specific treatments that have traditionally been achieved through routines within (different) social science software packages (see CMM, 2012a).

Further reasons behind the wide range of statistical software in applied research include push factors such as disciplinary traditions in training (and in canonical research texts) which lead to different expectations about analytical methods and software in different subject areas (Gelman and Cortina, 2009). Regional and sectoral variations in institutional licensing arrangements also represent a significant push factor in many contexts. Additionally, pull factors may include the diffusion of new statistical and analytical ideas through time, leading to innovative new analytical and software approaches (this is perhaps compounded by the individualized nature of the many software developments which originate in the academic sector, where researchers have often personally pursued and developed new tools to address particular analytic problems). Selective recent examples of software developments emergent from the innovation of academic methodologists include the techniques and software of Social Network Analysis (de Nooy et al., 2011; Ackland and Zhu, Chapter 10 of this volume); methods of social simulation (Gilbert, 2008; Birkin and Malleson, Chapter 6 of this volume); and interest in adopting a Bayesian perspective on statistical analysis leading to the development of new packages with that capacity (e.g., Lunn et al., 2000), and to Bayesian extension routines being written for existing packages (Gelman and Hill, 2007; Browne et al., 2002). Lastly, the development of new digital resources, which have improved processing capacities and have facilitated the preparation of new software routines, have in the last decade given increased momentum to recent software developments (Crouchley and Fligelstone, 2004; Crouchley et al., 2008).

Some aspects of the use of statistical software in the social sciences have, of course, changed dramatically over recent decades. Though something of an oversimplification, the period 1960–1985 can be portrayed as one of few software alternatives, where social science researchers used one of a small set of general purpose packages or, for more complex analytical tasks, wrote, or used, extension routines in a standard programming language such as Fortran. Early examples were often subject to significant computer memory constraints that precluded the easy storage or analysis of particularly large datasets. Arrangements often required researchers to submit jobs to mainframe computers making a full pre-specification of the job in advance, and to wait several hours for results to be returned, often in the form of voluminous paper printouts in rather crude numerical or graphical formats (though some writers have highlighted how these early arrangements paradoxically forced upon researchers better practice in the organization and documentation of their work than is commonplace nowadays – e.g. Treiman (2009), Chapter 4).

Contemporary software packages may be barely recognizable in their functionality compared to their precursors. Most packages support the rapid invocation of datasets with few limits on the form, structure or scale of the data that can be supported. A very wide range of statistical and graphical outputs is typically available in response to a few short commands. Speed of processing, facilities for reviewing data and re-running analysis, and output quality in terms of graphs and tables of results have all improved markedly, and the cumbersome nature of extended pre-submission requirements has, in large part, been addressed.[2] Nevertheless, other software challenges have arguably emerged. The term 'Balkanisation', which is more usually used to describe political transformations, refers to the breaking up of a structure into discreet, and competing, factions. Since around 1985 – perhaps linked to growing access to personal computers – software use in the social science research sector could be described as increasingly Balkanised, with a wider range of (non-compatible) general purpose packages in use, and the development of distinct, and often programmatically opaque, specialist packages. At the time of writing, the great many alternative software options often have strong boundaries between them, whereby licence issues, direct commercial competition between packages and training and programming incompatibilities prevent easy interoperability. On the face of it, having so many variations in software packages may not seem an efficient approach to scientific investigation: a pressing question for those interested in software

---

[2] It is worth noting that some contemporary trends are resulting in a return to requirements for pre-specification. The process of bureaucratization, for instance, might have led to a growth through time in requirements being made that data may not be transferred directly to users, but need be analysed by transferring pre-specified jobs to be run at a secure location, then results returned to the user. Separately, growing interest in emergent techniques of analysis that have vast computational requirements, such as large scale social simulations or approaches to 'data mining', also lead to arrangements for analysis which involve submitting whole jobs to a queue and waiting for results to be returned.

development, therefore, is whether better coordination, harmonization or standardization could ever supplant the current Balkanisation of software approaches.

7.2 CHALLENGES FOR THE EFFECTIVE USE OF STATISTICAL SOFTWARE IN THE SOCIAL SCIENCES

Since there are well-recognized problems with the uptake and impact of advanced statistical analysis in many social science disciplines, we would argue that some of the major challenges for statistical software applications are less to do with the direct capacity for undertaking analysis, than about achieving effective exploitation of existing resources. Despite having a wealth of quantitative data resources and statistical tools available to analyse them, in many countries there is a perceived dearth of sufficiently numerate and/or software-skilled social scientists to take full advantage. Two negative consequences of these shortages seem to have been low levels of exploitation of many relevant data resources and the narrowing of focus of those who do apply advanced statistical techniques to increasingly specialist areas (a process which is argued to have led to increasing distance between statistical and mainstream social science literature – e.g. Payne (2007)). In the UK, in response, the Economic and Social Research Council (ESRC) has supported a series of initiatives designed to increase social researchers' fluency in statistical analysis (e.g. MacInnes, 2009; ESRC, 2012).

A wider problem with statistical applications in social science research may emerge from the contrasting motivations of the three expert communities involved in the process, namely social scientists, statisticians and computer programmers. Priorities differ, and communication or mutual understanding between these groups can be limited (Browne et al. 2012a). At the current time, for instance, many statisticians would argue that there are important limitations to the 'frequentist' statistical techniques taught as standard and widely used by the majority of social scientists, and that alternative statistical approaches are available and should be more widely adopted (Gelman and Hill, 2007); equally, many software designers would see flaws and inefficiencies in the disproportionate reliance on proprietary packages that tend to be invoked largely in isolation from other research communities.

7.2.1 Interoperability and Transparency

Two particularly important issues concern 'interoperability' and 'transparency'. The former refers to the capacity to translate comparable tasks between software applications, and the latter the extent to which tasks applied to social science datasets are clearly documented and, ultimately, support replication by others (Freese, 2007). As noted above, current practices can be characterized as featuring low interoperability and low levels of replication.

Interoperability is important because it could be expected to lead to increased consistency of research between projects, aiding harmonization or standardization. Significantly, it could also improve the chances of the most suitable statistical techniques being identified and applied to a research problem, since it could allow, in principle, the researcher to 'cherry pick' the best statistical tools from different software packages for the task in hand (Mitchell 2005). Many social science researchers do already use more than one statistical package but most, perhaps understandably, focus on a small range, such as one general purpose package and one or two specialist packages.

Levels of interoperability in the social sciences are not high at present: the format of the data stored, the means of implementing analyses, and the display of results (i.e. the three elements of packages as noted above), all tend to be different from package to package and, at least for the case of proprietary software, the authors and distributors of the software may have a direct motivation to keep things this way. Nevertheless, a few activities that may promote greater interoperability can be highlighted, such as training texts and Internet resources that show how to perform similar tasks in multiple packages (e.g., CMM 2012b; Allison 2009). Additionally, a limited contribution to interoperability can be found within some software packages, which occasionally feature facilities to help analysts to move between software applications, such as by reading in datasets in formats produced by other packages and, in some instances, featuring 'plug-ins' that allow one package to call upon another within the environment of the first package. For example, SPSS supports plug-ins for the programming languages Python and R and their libraries (e.g. Levesque, 2010); Stata supports plug-ins for specialist software packages (e.g. Crouchley et al., 2008; Leckie and Charlton, 2012); in 2001, an interface from MLwiN to WinBUGS was developed to enable comparison between results in those two packages (see Browne, 2009) and this application acted as a precursor to the work which will be discussed in the next section. Such developments in making links between software facilities offer exciting opportunities for greater fluency in methods, but tend to be limited to a small range of specific packages and versions. On the contrary, as noted above, different packages are often in direct competition with each other and their producers have little motivation to promote interoperability. Indeed, the extreme model of proprietary software may even reject interoperability with earlier versions of the same software – some packages have weak backwards compatibility and, instead, make the presumption that users must upgrade to the latest version, perhaps even changing their programming habits, to continue exploiting the software.

Transparency can also be promoted within the languages of particular software packages, through advocacy of and training in the effective documentation of the tasks performed. Several publications have recently demonstrated mechanisms to achieve high quality documentation through well-organized software invocations (Long, 2009; Kohler and Kreuter, 2012; Treiman, 2009). A common theme of these studies is that analysts are urged to record the full process of their analysis from start to finish in the manner of a scientific log book. Ordinarily, this might be achieved through constructing a sequence of interrelated command files specific to a software package; these command files may be extensively annotated with explanatory information, and can be readily stored and transferred to others (see also Chapter 5 in this volume). Such documentation means, in turn, that other researchers will be able to use the relevant command files to exactly re-trace the steps originally taken. Methodologists generally are in widespread agreement that such transparent documentation, which supports replication and re-use, has substantial scientific benefits, since it allows criticisms of work to be accurately informed, and encourages the cumulative development of knowledge through analyses built upon the foundations of previous studies (Freese, 2007).

In social science research communities, the strategy of invoking software packages through carefully prepared, annotated and organized textual commands is popularly known as using 'syntax files' in SPSS (Collier, 2009), or 'do files' in Stata (Kohler and Kreuter, 2012), or more generally as recording analysis 'scripts' or 'log files'. Figure 7.2 illustrates an example, here showing a 'do file' in Stata that runs a brief sequence of related statistical models on a dataset and summarizes the results.

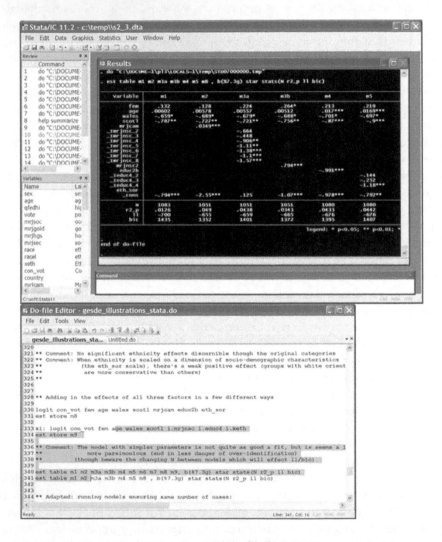

Figure 7.2 An illustration of using a script ('do file') in Stata

The image shows a user running a sequence of related statistical models, then storing and comparing their results. The 'do file' illustrates annotated comments on the work that facilitate documentation. The analysis features a model of voting preference as explained by socio-economic characteristics. The example shown is from an illustrative workshop exercise and is also available from www.dames.org.uk/workshops.

In the short or medium term, the pattern of social science data analysis is such that it is hard for any researcher to undertake complex applied work effectively without performing detailed script programming in one or more specific packages. This, in itself, is a major challenge for the research sector, not least since the majority of software packages offer alternative, and seemingly easier to use, non-textual invocation methods, and it is these which are widely taught in introductory level courses. Many excellent training resources are available covering textual programming in leading packages, whether in textbooks (Levesque, 2010; Rabe-Hesketh and Skrondal, 2008; Kohler and Kreuter, 2012; Gelman and Hill, 2007) or free online resources (UCLA, 2012; CMM, 2012b), and many researchers choose to enrol on residential courses that provide short intensive introductions to relevant software skills (University of Essex, 2015).

The capacity to use scripting effectively to invoke statistical software is such a useful research skill that we would urge readers to expose themselves to the first steps in using textual commands to undertake operations in important software languages. On the book's website,[3] we provide a short exercise that takes the reader through the process of opening a data file which is available online, and running a short statistical analysis through the programming languages of five important packages: SPSS, Stata, R, MLwiN, and lEM.[4] Linear regression models are very important tools of statistical analysis, so the example features opening an anonymized extract from a large-scale social survey containing data suitable for a regression analysis (data preparation for the same files is featured in Chapter 5 on data management), then running a regression model in the three general purpose packages (SPSS, Stata and R). The two specialist packages MLwiN and lEM are designed to provide functionality for specific statistical models, so the illustrative command files prepared for these packages use the same data to run slightly different statistical analyses, namely a two-level random intercept multilevel model for MLwiN (see also Rasbash et al., 2011) and an 'RCII' association model in lEM (see also Vermunt, 1997).

Learning to use statistical software in the manner highlighted in the exercise is demanding, but from most perspectives marks a clear requirement for effective processing of complex data resources and methods of analysis (Treiman, 2009; Long, 2009). In many respects, the fluent script programmer is well equipped to perform further statistical analyses and take advantage of whatever new statistical facilities evolve through time (in this respect, the support for user-contributed extension routines, which is a major feature of the general purpose packages Stata and R, is especially worth noting, since these are increasingly the source of exciting innovations in statistical analysis that sometimes have a considerable impact upon social science user communities – e.g., Turner and Firth (2007); Rabe-Hesketh and Skrondal (2008)). Nevertheless, the 'script programmer' model of statistical software exploitation is application specific. Moreover, learning to use textual commands in any language can be both burdensome

---

[3]https://study.sagepub.com/halfpennyprocter

[4]A more extended document introducing the use of syntax commands for each of these packages was prepared by the DAMES research node and is available online from www.dames.org.uk/workshops

and offputting, and the levels of specialist knowledge involved probably serve to promote, rather than reduce, divisions between statistical software traditions. One example can be seen in the thriving user communities of programmers using the languages of influential statistical software packages, as is evident in software specific mailing lists and publication outlets such as *The Stata Journal* and *The R Journal*. In many ways, these communities provide excellent scientific models of progress towards effective exploitation of complex software and data resources, but they also have the potential to become rather closed or conservative environments, at risk of limited engagement with emergent statistical resources or requirements from other communities. Indeed, whilst advanced levels of programming skills are clearly helpful to progress with statistical software, the corollary might be that the challenges of effective exploitation in the social sciences might best be solved if social science researchers were made to take supplementary degree level training in statistics and in computer programming (and perhaps also, for good measure, in Information Science). Though a trite observation, this is surprisingly close to the truth: in many cases, influential social statisticians are often originally trained in a statistical or natural science discipline. However, such levels of requirements would seem an imperfect solution, and again might help to explain the low levels of exploitation of many statistical data resources in the social sciences.

Alternatively, it seems preferable to ask what other contributions statisticians or programmers could make to facilitating more effective contributions in the use of statistical software. In this regard, the themes of e-Research, which cover collaboration, coordination and enhanced analytical capacity, engage neatly with the requirements of statistical analysis in the social sciences. Below we introduce two recent developments from the ESRC funded 'e-Stat' project, known as 'Stat-JR' and 'eBooks', which aim to make significant inroads into confronting the challenges described above. The software Stat-JR (Browne et al., 2012a; 2012b) focuses upon solving the problem of lack of interoperability between packages, whilst its eBook facilities (Michaelides et al., 2012) offer opportunities for accessible documentation and support of complex and extended analytical exercises.

7.3 STAT-JR: A TOOL FOR STATISTICAL ANALYSIS

Stat-JR was originally conceived by the late Jon Rasbash, after whom the package is named, as an easy-to-use tool supporting interoperability in the implementation of advanced statistical applications across software packages in a coordinated, generic and computationally efficient environment. The package was subsequently developed over the period 2009–13 by a team at the Universities of Bristol and Southampton. Written using Python, it first became widely available with a beta release of Spring 2012 (Browne et al., 2012a; 2012b). The package has been developed in the first instance to be installed on a user's PC. It exploits a range of statistical routines, drawing upon existing statistical software, including both freeware and proprietary packages, and also including its own statistical analysis facilities. Ordinarily, to exploit Stat-JR, a user would need to install the Stat-JR program and explicitly notify it of the location of other software already on the PC as relevant. Typically, this is done by providing information on the directory in which the relevant software is stored (for example, to exploit the interoperability of the package, a user would normally need to edit a settings or 'configuration' file to indicate where other packages, such as Stata or SPSS, are installed on their machine).

Stat-JR provides a user interface, ordinarily accessed through a web-browser, to a series of options which enable a user to link a nominated *dataset* with a statistical analysis *template*. The linkage between these two components, the dataset and template, lies at the heart of Stat-JR's contribution. The templates represent a series of operations that may be applied to nominated variables within the dataset. Templates can support a variety of data oriented tasks, including data management operations such as recoding or standardizing variables. In most circumstances, however, a user would exploit a template in order to run a particular form of statistical model on their dataset, since Stat-JR provides many templates that support relatively advanced and difficult to implement statistical models. The Stat-JR system allows the user to specify features of the particular template being used, such as linking variable names from the dataset with model parameters from the template, then Stat-JR allows the user to invoke the analysis as it has been specified, whereupon they will be given access to, amongst others, software specific implementation information (such as a log file) on the model; an algebraic representation of the statistical analysis; and graphical and tabular results from the analysis as appropriate.

The team who have developed Stat-JR are keen to promote its use across research sectors. The software is currently free to download for academic users in the UK, but a charge is levied for other users. A second exercise available on the book's website provides commentary on a series of suggested actions that cover downloading, installing and exploiting Stat-JR for data analysis. They include operating the package through the use of menu options, which is likely to be a more accessible means of using the package in the first instance, and the alternative means of operating the package using scripts. Readers should note that the software does have some quite challenging elements, such as dependencies on some other computational software being installed over and above the relevant statistical software packages (e.g., a C++ compiler and .NET files may need to be installed, see Browne et al. (2012b)).

The implementation of Stat-JR examples may prove quite a challenging exercise for the new user. However, whether through implementing the package directly or by reading through the relevant user guides (Browne et al., 2012a; 2012b), it should be obvious that the work offers some significant responses to the challenges in statistical software provision. For one, it allows users a relatively easy way to set up and run complex statistical models, including providing access to highly computationally efficient estimation algorithms compared to those included in many analytical packages. Second, it provides documentation and information on analyses, through making available relevant software code and algebraic representations of the models involved. Lastly, its generic nature supports easy invocation of interoperability functionality by supporting rapid changes between different relevant approaches, including support for relatively difficult to access statistical derivations such as MCMC algorithms for Bayesian modelling. Figure 7.3, panels 1–3, seek to illustrate these features, showing images of Stat-JR (beta version) after various specifications have been set within the processing of a model.

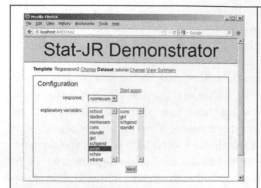

Panel 1: Selecting variables from a dataset (called 'tutorial', a dataset about student educational attainment) to link them with an analysis template (here 'Regression 2', a template for linear outcome regression models).

Panel 2: Choosing how the statistical model will be estimated, including the software package on which to apply it.

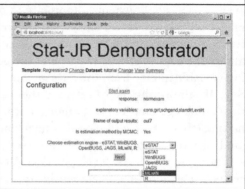

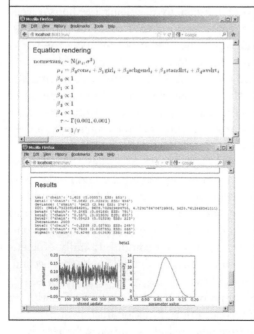

Panel 3: Selected results after running the statistical model (representation of the statistical model equation, and presentation of the parameter estimates and diagnostic information about them).

Figure 7.3   Images of Stat-JR in operation

These images show a more simplified display format than is commonly used; see Browne et al. (2012a; 2012b) for extended commentary upon the operation of Stat-JR, including further images, with explanatory annotations, of its implementation.

7.3.1 DEEP eBooks for Stat-JR: Tools for Documentation and Training

One aspect of the Stat-JR package offers a particularly exciting opportunity for supporting interoperability and transparency in performing relatively advanced statistical analysis. The development of the DEEP eBooks system for Stat-JR (see Michaelides et al., 2012) provides a system for the documentation and invocation of a complex set of statistical analytical tasks, including model specification and estimation through appropriate software.

A Stat-JR DEEP eBook involves a user writing and maintaining a digital, machine readable version of an account of their work. Such a record should include outputs, but also feature sufficiently well-integrated and detailed information on the preparation of the work, which another user could replicate and reproduce the results of the analysis in full. The user would also typically be able to jump effectively between different subsections, covering different elements of the process undertaken at earlier and later stages. Importantly, a feature which can distinguish a DEEP eBook produced by Stat-JR from a more conventional log book is the capacity of the former to support dynamic content, for instance, whereby a user of the DEEP eBook could edit a component of it, resulting in a change being made to the data or analysis, and subsequently to the dynamically generated results of the analysis, whilst all of this is undertaken without disrupting the underlying integrity of the record.

Figure 7.4 shows one image that is illustrative of the way in which DEEP eBooks for Stat-JR can be exploited. The scenario here involves an analyst applying a statistical model to a social science dataset. The page of the DEEP eBook that is open, visible on the main right-hand pane of the figure, shows the model specification and results generated: the user has set this model up to run through the Stat-JR software and the user has the capacity to alter the specification of the model through the DEEP eBook as they choose. Behind the scenes, however, are extended electronic records of the process of data construction, analysis specification and model results. The outputs from these are visible on the different pages of the DEEP eBook (which would be accessed through the left-hand navigation column), and the details of them are saved in the longer record of the complete eBook.

In a final exercise, we suggest two activities to help the reader to further understand the basic concept of DEEP eBooks in the context of Stat-JR, highlighting a documentary note (Michaelides et al., 2012) and implementing a simple example of a DEEP eBook. The implementation opens up an example of a statistical model specification. Once the model activity is opened (known as an 'eBook reading event'), the user has the opportunity to modify content at any of the relevant stages of the DEEP eBook. The particular example highlighted is designed as a learning aid, since it allows a student to read through materials and then make small changes to the analysis under discussion in order to explore and enhance their understanding interactively. The same resource could equally be used by a researcher during the course of her analysis, particularly as a device to store and share emergent results across a team. There are significant overheads to the latter use, however, since the research user would ordinarily have to spend time learning how to generate DEEP eBooks themselves, rather than simply taking an existing template. In the language of the Stat-JR eBooks, this would entail them becoming an effective 'eBook author', rather than a 'eBook reader' (Michaelides et al., 2012).

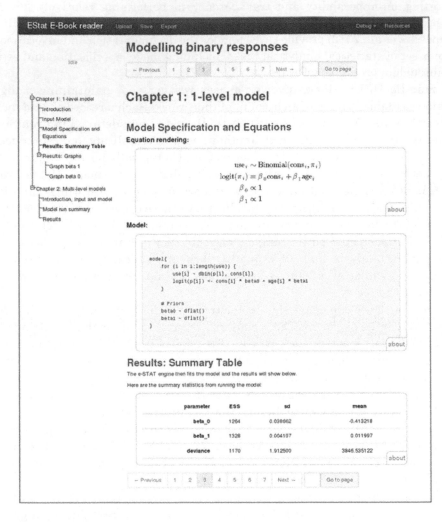

Figure 7.4 Using Stat-JR from within a DEEP eBook

This page of the DEEP eBook shows the specification of and results from a statistical model. The user is able to navigate backwards and forwards within the DEEP eBook (left hand area), potentially changing settings on the model, leading to a dynamic update to the results shown on this page.

The exciting contribution of Stat-JR eBooks as regards statistical software is their capacity to host a wide variety of advanced software estimation options, spanning different software implementations, in a coherent and transparent format. The wider vision of Stat-JR eBooks includes facilitating the use of much more advanced methods of statistical analysis, since the user will have a wide range of sophisticated estimation resources at their fingertips and will be able to understand their contributions (by looking up, when relevant, algebraic or textual model descriptions, and to access software logs and syntax commands as they arise). Simultaneously, DEEP eBooks might also facilitate greater use of existing quantitative data resources in the social sciences, partly because they aid the process of conducting statistical analysis generally, but mainly because they offer facilities for sharing replicable records of both data preparation and data analysis activities (for example, we could imagine that novice users could access the DEEP eBook from a previous research project that used a complex survey dataset, and use it either to replicate the earlier analysis, or adapt the application to suit a slightly different set of variables and models as desired). Therefore, although the Stat-JR eBooks are at an early stage in their dissemination and adoption, we are optimistic that they may be able to make a major contribution to the effective exploitation of statistical software in the social sciences.

7.4 CONCLUSIONS

'You can't teach an old dog new tricks'

Ultimately, the statistical software usage patterns of social scientists are shaped by individual researchers making choices over which package or packages to work with. In this regard, researchers have tended to be highly stable in their usage patterns: in the spirit of the adage quoted above, the dominant model may seem to involve researchers sticking to the package (or narrow range of packages) that they received training in during the early stages of their career (and/or which is available in their institutions). Perhaps as a consequence of the perceived high investment in existing skills, and the apparently daunting costs of learning to use new software, changes in practice seem to be very hard to induce. This might apply generally to choices about which software is used in itself, but is also relevant to the means by which the software is implemented (such as by using scripts or menus) and to the particular methods of statistical analysis that are performed (such as which modelling or analytical paradigm is applied).

Nevertheless, new statistical and computational capabilities, and reviews of the work process itself (Long, 2009) often make a compelling case for a change in practice. We have, for example, described new innovations in interoperability, and in documentation and training, that have exciting potential and really ought (under a scientific model which prioritizes the cumulative development of knowledge – see Steuer (2003)) to result in considerable uptake. We have also noted ongoing developments in popular statistical software approaches, such as the enduring success of certain general purpose packages and innovations in specialized applications. A particularly interesting question concerns how such developments will contribute to the future map of statistical software use. Inferring from past patterns, it is hard to imagine a time when well managed commercial packages will not form a major part of the statistical software landscape. At the current time, Stata stands out as a popular commercial package with a wide community of users who exploit it in a manner that accommodates the great majority of effective practices in social science research, as we have highlighted above (such as supporting easy documentation, a wide range of analytical capabilities, and a successful developmental community). Equally, well designed and maintained freeware and open source software can be expected to meet the needs of many researchers, whilst offering greater opportunities for collaborative and innovate applications. R, in particular, seems likely to be a growing force in statistical software, at least for the short and medium term, since it is now widely used by statisticians generally, has a successful developmental community which generates robust extension libraries, and has made significant inroads into many applied disciplines, often displacing other statistical analysis packages in the process. Regrettably, however, the advanced programming and statistical skills which are necessary to exploit R effectively seem unlikely to allow for its universal adaptation amongst the wide ranging user-communities within the social sciences.

Projecting forward from previous experiences, we can fully anticipate the continued development of multiple packages with a mixture of features and licence arrangements. Accordingly, as illustrated by Stat-JR and the DEEP eBooks facilities within Stat-JR, there is likely to be great value in the construction of tools that support easy to implement documentation, alongside interoperability covering advanced methods of statistical analysis.

7.5 BIBLIOGRAPHY

Allison, P.D. (2009) *Fixed Effects Regression Models*. Thousand Oaks, CA: Sage.

Browne, W.J. (2009) *MCMC Estimation in MLwiN (Version 2.10)* Bristol: Centre for Multilevel Modelling, University of Bristol.

Browne, W.J., Draper, D., Goldstein, H. and Rasbash, J. (2002) 'Bayesian and likelihood methods for fitting multilevel models with complex level-1 variation', *Computational Statistics & Data Analysis,* 39(2): 203–25.

Browne, W.J., Cameron, B., Charlton, C.M.L., Michaelides, D., Parker, R.M.A., Szmaragd, C., et al. (2012a) *An Advanced User's Guide to Stat-JR (Beta release)*. Bristol: Centre for Multilevel Modelling, University of Bristol.

Browne, W.J., Cameron, B., Charlton, C.M.J., Michaelides, D.T., Parker, R.M.A., Szmaragd, C., et al. (2012b) *A Beginner's Guide to Stat-JR (Beta release)*. Bristol: Centre for Mutlilevel Modelling, University of Bristol.

Centre for Multilevel Modelling (2012a) *Multilevel Modelling Software Reviews*. Available from www.bristol.ac.uk/cmm/learning/mmsoftware (accessed 10 Dec 2014).

Centre for Multilevel Modelling. (2012b) *Multilevel modelling Online Course*. Available from www.bristol.ac.uk/cmm/learning/online-course (accessed 10 Dec 2014).

Collier, J. (2009) *Using SPSS Syntax: A Beginner's Guide*. London: Sage.

Cologne University Statistical Resources (CUSR) (2010) *Statistical Software*. Available from www.uni-koeln.de/themen/statistik/software/liste.e.html (accessed 10 Dec 2014).

Crouchley, R. and Fligelstone, R. (2004) *The Potential for High End Computing in the Social Sciences*. Lancaster: Centre for Applied Statistics, Lancaster University.

Crouchley, R., Stott, D. and Pritchard, J. (2008) *Multivariate Generalised Linear Mixed Models via sabreStata (Sabre in Stata), Version 1*. Lancaster: Lancaster University. Available from http://sabre.lancs.ac.uk (accessed 10 Dec 2014).

de Nooy, W., Mrvar, A. and Batagelj, V. (2011) *Exploratory Social Network Analysis with Pajek*. Cambridge: Cambridge University Press.

Economic and Social Research Council (ESRC) (2012) *ESRC Secondary Data Analysis Initiative, phase 1 – 2012.* Available from www.esrc.ac.uk/research/skills-training-development/sdai/phase-one.aspx (accessed 10 Dec 2014).

Freese, J. (2007) 'Replication standards for quantitative social science: why not sociology?', *Sociological Methods and Research,* 36(2): 153–71.

Gelman, A. and Hill, J. (2007) *Data Analysis using Regression and Multilevel / Hierarchical Models.* Cambridge: Cambridge University Press.

Gelman, A. and Cortina, J. (eds) (2009) *A Quantitative Tour of the Social Sciences.* Cambridge: Cambridge University Press.

Gilbert, G.N. (2008) *Agent-Based Models.* Thousand Oaks, CA: Sage.

Greenacre, M. and Blasius, J. (1994) *Correspondence Analysis in the Social Sciences: Recent Developments and Applications.* London: Academic Press.

Greene, W.H. (2000) *Econometric Analysis, Fourth Edition.* New York: Prentice Hall.

Kohler, H.P. and Kreuter, F. (2012) *Data Analysis Using Stata,* 3rd edition. College Station, Texas: Stata Press.

Leckie, G. and Charlton, C.M.L. (2011) *Runmlwin: Stata Module for Fitting Multilevel Models in the MLwiN Software Package.* Bristol: Centre for Multilevel Modelling, University of Bristol.

Levesque, R. and SPSS Inc. (2010) *Programming and Data Management for IBM SPSS Statistics 18: A Guide for PASW Statistics and SAS users.* Chicago: SPSS Inc.

Long, J. S. (2009). *The Workflow of Data Analysis Using Stata.* Boca Raton, FL: CRC Press.

Lunn, D.J., Thomas, A., Best, N. and Spiegelhalter, D. (2000) 'WinBUGS – A Bayesian modelling framework: concepts, structure and extensibility', *Statistics and Computing,* 10: 325–37.

MacInnes, J. (2009) *Proposals to Support and Improve the Teaching of Quantitative Research Methods at Undergraduate Level in the UK.* Swindon: ESRC.

Michaelides, D.T., Yang, H., Browne, W.J., Charlton, C.M.J. and Parker, R.M.A. (2012) *eBook User Guide: For the eBook System Developed as Part of the Stat-JR Software package.* Bristol/Southampton: Centre for Multilevel Modelling, University of Bristol/ School of Electronics and Computer Science, University of Southampton.

Minitab 16 Statistical Software (2010) *[Computer Software].* State College, PA: Minitab Inc (www.minitab.com [accessed 14 Dec 2014]).

Mitchell, M.N. (2005) *Strategically using General Purpose Statistics Packages: A Look at Stata, SAS and SPSS.* Los Angeles: Statistical Consulting Group: UCLA Academic Technology Services (Technical Report Series, Report 1, Version Number 1). Available from http://citeseerx.ist.psu.edu/viewdoc/summary?doi=10.1.1.90.1292.

Payne, G. (2007) 'Social divisions, social mobilities and social research: methodological issues after 40 Years', *Sociology,* 41(5): 901–15.

R Core Team (2013) *R: A Language and Environment for Statistical Computing.* Vienna, Austria: R Foundation for Statistical Computing.

Rabe-Hesketh, S. and Skrondal, A. (2008) *Multilevel and Longitudinal Modelling Using Stata, Second Edition.* College Station, TX: Stata Press.

Rasbash, J., Browne, W.J., Healy, M., Cameron, B. and Charlton, C. (2011) *MLwiN, Version 2.24.* Bristol: Centre for Multilevel Modelling, University of Bristol.

Raudenbush, S.W., Bryk, A.S. and Congdon, R. (2011) *HLM 7 for Windows [Computer Software].* Lincolnwood, IL: Scientific Software International, Inc.

Röhwer, G. and Pötter, U. (1999) *TDA User's Manual.* Bochum: Faculty for Social Sciences, Ruhr University, Bochum.

SAS Institute Inc (2012) *SAS 9.3.* Cary, NC: SAS Institute Inc.

StataCorp (2013) *Stata Statistical Software, Release 13.* College Station, TX: StataCorp LP.

Steuer, M. (2003) *The Scientific Study of Society.* Boston: Kluwer Academic.

Treiman, D.J. (2009) *Quantitative Data Analysis: Doing Social Research to Test Ideas*. New York: Jossey Bass.

Turner, H. and Firth, D. (2007). *Generalized Nonlinear Models in R: An Overview of The GNM Package*. Southampton: ESRC National Centre for Research Methods, Paper 6/07 of the NCRM Working paper series.

UCLA Academic Technology Services (2014) *Statistical Computing Seminars / Workshops*. Available from www.ats.ucla.edu/stat/seminars (accessed 10 Dec 2014).

University of Essex and Institute for Social and Economic Research (2010) *British Household Panel Survey: Waves 1–18, 1991–2009 [computer file]*, 7th edition. Colchester, Essex: UK Data Archive [distributor], July 2010, SN: 5151.

University of Essex (2015) *Essex Summer School in Social Science Data Analysis*. Available from www.essex.ac.uk/summerschool (accessed 01 April 2015).

Uprichard, E., Burrows, R. and Byrne, D. (2008) 'SPSS as an "inscription device": from causality to description?', *Sociological Review*, 56(4): 606–22.

Vermunt, J.K. (1997) *lEM: A General Program for the Analysis of Categorical Data*. Tilburg, Netherlands: Tilburg University.

8

TEXT MINING AND SOCIAL MEDIA: WHEN QUANTITATIVE MEETS QUALITATIVE AND SOFTWARE MEETS PEOPLE

LAWRENCE AMPOFO, SIMON COLLISTER, BEN O'LOUGHLIN AND ANDREW CHADWICK

8.1 INTRODUCTION

'At no time in history has so much of the public's discussion... been so accessible to a wide audience and available for systematic analysis.' (Keeter, 2012)

The ongoing production of staggeringly huge volumes of digital data is a ubiquitous part of life in the early twenty-first century. A large proportion of this data is text. This development has serious implications for almost all scholarly endeavour. It is now possible for researchers from a wide range of disciplines to use text mining techniques and software tools in their daily practice. In our own field of political communication, the prospect of cheap access to what, how, and to whom very large numbers of citizens communicate in social media environments provides opportunities that are often too good to miss as we seek to understand how and why citizens think and feel the way they do about policies, political organizations, and political events. But what are the methods and tools on offer, how should they best be used and what sorts of ethical issues are raised by their use?

In this chapter we proceed as follows. First, we provide a basic definition of text mining. Second, we provide examples of how text mining has been used recently in a diverse range of analytical contexts, from business to media to politics. Third, we discuss the

>

challenges of conducting text mining in online social media environments, focusing on issues such as the problem of gaining access to social media data, research ethics, and the integrity of the data corpora that are available from social media companies. Fourth, we present a basic but comprehensive survey of the text mining tools that are currently available. Finally, we present two brief case studies of the application of text mining in the authors' field of political communication: a research project that analysed political discussion on the popular social media service Twitter during the British general election of 2010, and a study of the early-2010 'Bullygate' crisis in British politics.

We conclude with some observations about the proper place of text mining in social science research. Our overall argument is that text mining is at its most useful when it brings together quantitative and qualitative modes of enquiry. The technology can be powerful but it is often a blunt instrument. Human intervention is always necessary during the research process in order to refine the analysis. Indeed, rather than assuming that text mining software and big datasets will do the work, social science researchers would be wise to begin any project from the assumption that they will need to combine text mining tools with more traditional approaches to the study of social phenomena.

8.2 DEFINING TEXT MINING

Text mining is the term used to describe either a single process or a collection of processes in which software tools actively engage in 'the discovery of new, previously unknown information by automatically extracting information from different written [or text] sources' (Fan et al., 2006). Such text sources can be defined as information that has been indexed in specific ways, such as, for example, patient records, web pages, and information contained within an organization's customer relationship management software. Such data is usually termed 'structured data' and has been defined as 'any set of [text] values conforming to a common schema or type' (Arasu and Garcia-Molina, 2003: 337). Some textual information that is amenable to analysis by text mining software does not necessarily conform to common schemas or types. This typically resides on the Web and is generally not housed within specific databases or other data storage structures. This data may include documents, emails, tweets, blog posts, to name but a few, and is typically defined as 'unstructured data'. The central challenge of text mining is the accurate analysis of both structured and unstructured data in order to extract meaningful associations, trends and patterns in large corpora of text. The increasing volume and availability of digital data online in social media platforms like Twitter, Facebook, Flickr and collaborative online environments like Wikipedia provides new opportunities for researchers to investigate social, cultural, economic and political behaviour.

8.3 RECENT APPLICATIONS OF TEXT MINING IN THE SOCIAL SCIENCES

Text mining is emerging as an important tool for the natural sciences. One of its uses lies in deriving value from the unprecedented volume of scientific studies that are now generated every year by the global scientific community (Hey, Tansley and Tolle, 2009). Text mining allows for connections to be made between discrete scientific studies and research databases – connections that cannot be made manually due to the sheer scale of human effort that this would entail (Hearst, 1999). Text mining has also been used to reduce duplication in scientific research, to identify areas for potential collaboration across scientific fields and to evaluate the consistency of research data over time (Rzhetsky et al., 2008).

While these scientific applications of text mining are important, rapid growth in the production of personal information and public sharing afforded by the rise of Web 2.0 and social media, as well as the proliferation of tools and techniques for real-time data collection and automated analysis, are now expanding text mining's potential range of applications. In some respects, the emphasis is shifting away from the retrospective analysis of static datasets and toward real-time analysis and 'predictive intelligence', particularly in the commercial sector. While these changes are made possible through the emergence of new technologies, communication practices and research methods, they are also being shaped by many of the traditional concerns of longstanding disciplinary fields and research practices (Anstead and O'Loughlin, 2011a). Bollier (2009) has identified the currently most fertile contexts for text mining as politics, public health and business.

Measuring and managing public opinion through polling has long been a core component of liberal democracies. Both of these practices are now undergoing something of a transformation shaped by the availability of text mining and natural language processing (NLP) software. As Anstead and O'Loughlin have argued, '[i]t is not unrealistic … to imagine totally amalgamated real-time data' being used to inform political strategies in the very near future (Anstead and O'Loughlin, 2011a). Some recent U.S. studies have revealed a strong correlation between political opinions expressed via Twitter and official poll data, leading to the suggestion among some that real-time text mining might become 'a substitute and supplement for traditional polling' (O'Connor et al., 2010: 1). However, studies conducted during the 2010 UK general election found that social media environments may offer poor data with little predictive value, primarily because social media samples can be highly unrepresentative of the wider public. There are also problems with the basic analyses. Commercial text mining companies very rarely publish their methods, so the mechanisms of accountability in this sphere are much less developed than those for traditional public opinion polling (Chadwick, 2011a). In addition, the validity of text mining is impaired if automated text mining cannot detect irony and sarcasm, two linguistic techniques that feature prominently in online commentary of all kinds (Anstead and O'Loughlin, 2011b).

If the accurate prediction of public opinion remains elusive, text mining's usefulness for rapidly distilling the structures and meanings of large quantities of online political discourse is easier to grasp. For example, Wanner et al. (2009) successfully applied real-time text mining of news coverage to gauge sentiment around specific topics and candidates during the fast-moving 2008 US presidential campaign. These new forms of 'semantic polling' are coming to be seen by campaign managers in much the same vein as the focus groups that were first used by marketing companies in the post-war era to elicit more fine-grained interpretations of how consumers (and citizens) respond to particular aspects of a product or personality. In the field of politics, such intelligence is already evolving into a tool used by political actors seeking to strengthen their electoral strategies by adapting the content and delivery of their speeches and news announcements to public sentiment in real time (Anstead and O'Loughlin, 2010; Chadwick, 2011a; Chadwick, 2011b; Chadwick, 2013).

While such studies focus on text mining's application in broadly democratic contexts, scholars such as Leetaru (2011) have applied sentiment and geo-location analysis of broadcast, newspaper, and online sources to identify the precursors of unrest and to predict possible political uprisings or disruptive action by social movements. Adopting a similar technique, Papacharissi and de Fatima Oliveira (2011) have used text mining to explore the use of affective language and the geopolitical context in which it occurred to map the escalation and trajectory of revolutionary movements after the 25 January 2011 uprising in Egypt.

Business and economics scholars have also investigated text mining. Here, the emphasis has been on deriving commercial value from new types of market research and 'predictive sales intelligence'. In the entertainment industry, for example, sentiment and content analyses of social media data have been used to predict the likelihood of a film becoming a box-office hit (Asur, 2010; Mishne and Glance, 2006). Using a similar approach, Lee et al. (2008) and Pang and Lee (2008) analysed customers' online reviews in order to distil this public feedback for providers eager to improve their products or services. Archak et al. (2011) and Ghose et al. (2007) have taken the text mining of product reviews still further, with an econometric analysis that seeks an 'objective, quantifiable, and context-sensitive evaluation of opinions' (Ghose et al., 2007: 416. Italics in original) and a set of techniques that can predict how differences in product reviews may influence levels of sales. Real-time quantitative and qualitative analysis are also now routinely performed on data from television audiences who share their opinions via Facebook and Twitter while watching a show live as it is broadcast (Wakamiya et al., 2011a; Wakamiya et al., 2011b).

Text mining studies of social media have also been applied to commercially-sensitive environments, such as financial markets, to try to develop predictive models. A number of studies have found that the sentiment and the volume of online 'buzz' correlates with stock movements. Some argue that it may be possible to predict likely market movements in close to real-time (Bollen, 2011; Gilbert and Karahalios, 2010; Lidman, 2011). Others, however, are less bullish, and suggest that despite strong statistical correlations, the link between sentiment on social media and trading can be tenuous and difficult to predict (Antweiler and Frank, 2004).

In the area of public health, quantitative and qualitative text mining analyses of social media have been used to identify and track the spread of natural disasters and epidemics. Culotta (2010) mined Twitter conversations in order to validate the service's role as a means of alerting public health officials to influenza outbreaks in the US, while Chunara et al. (2012) were able to track the spread of disease during Haiti's 2011 cholera epidemic. Both studies point to the prospect of real-time predictive modelling in the field of epidemiology. Similarly, Chew and Eysenbach (2010) conducted content analysis of tweets relating to the 2009 H1N1 Swine Flu epidemic in order to assess the public's awareness of public health advice. Their conclusions revealed high levels of accurate knowledge among the public and they suggest that text mining of social media will offer a new way for health authorities to measure public awareness of their campaigns and respond to shifting concerns in real time. In a related field, public safety, the finding that there are strong correlations between discussions of earthquakes on Twitter and real earthquake events has revealed the potential of text mining as an addition to established early-warning systems (Sakaki et al. 2010; Doan, 2011). Indeed, Sakaki et al. claim that Twitter may often be a more efficient early warning system than traditional systems.

8.3.1 Computer Assisted Qualitative Data Analysis Software (CAQDAS)

Text mining software can be conceptualized as being within the wider group of technologies known as computer assisted qualitative data analysis software (CAQDAS). Indeed, the use of computers to assist with qualitative research 'are inextricably tied to the character of qualitative data...[as] Qualitative research often produces an "assemblage" of data' (Fielding and Lee, 1998). CAQDAS applications have been in use since the 1980s and many have included text mining functionality to deal with qualitative data in all forms, from fieldnotes to interviews to social media content.

CAQDAS was initially used by researchers for data management tasks, such as text retrieval and simple searching. Such features can now be found in common word processors. The second generation of software introduced facilities for coding, text, and manipulating, searching and reporting on the text to be used for analysis. Today, CAQDAS software developers emphasize tools to help with the analytic processes of qualitative research such as examining relationships within text and building theories and models.

8.3.2 Natural Language Processing

A prominent component of CAQDAS and text mining software is Natural Language Processing (NLP), a technology that allows researchers to conduct in-depth analyses of content and everyday linguistic expression. As such, this particular software is useful for the analysis of social media content.

The development of NLP from the 1960s onwards focused on the 'the need not only for an explicit, precise, and complete characterization of language, but for a well-founded or formal characterization and, even more importantly, the need for algorithms to apply this description' (Jones, 1994: 3). Further NLP research in the 1980s revealed the difficulties of developing reliable programs. During this period, work was characterized by a focus on developing computational grammar theory so that software could handle the refinements of linguistic expression, such as indications of time and expressions of mood. The 1980s was also marked by a focus on the lexicon, in the first attempts to exploit commercial dictionaries in machine-readable form.

Since the 1990s, NLP development has focused on statistical language data processing and machine learning: in other words, means by which software may use algorithms and probability calculations to undertake discrete analytical tasks, such as summarizing the meaning of very large texts, or connecting information on location, time, and behaviour.

8.3.3 Sentiment Analysis

Sentiment analysis has quickly evolved into one of the most popular applications of text mining, not least because it holds out the promise of automating the interpretation of the semantic tone of large corpora. Mejova has argued that sentiment analysis is the study of 'subjective elements' in language. These are 'usually single words, phrases or sentences' because 'it is generally agreed that sentiment resides in smaller linguistic units' (Mejova, 2009: 5; see also Eguchi and Lavrenko, 2006; Pang and Lee, 2008). Typically, sentiment analysis involves using software to run pre-compiled dictionaries of known positive and negative words against a corpus in order to identify the frequency with which these words appear and the contexts in which they are used. Leetaru (2011), for example, uses this approach in his analysis of a large historical news archive, including the entire 3.9 million-article database of the *Summary of World Broadcasts*, 5.9 million articles from the *New York Times* from 1945 to 2005 and data from a variety of online news crawls. Leetaru claims that increased negative sentiment in news articles is statistically related to major news events, such as political unrest and the outbreak of wars.

Sentiment analysis often has trouble dealing with the inherent complexity of even the most basic everyday communication (Hiroshi et al., 2004; Read et al., 2007; O'Connor et al., 2010). The linguistic idioms of online communication only add to these difficulties. Nevertheless, some interesting applications of sentiment analysis are now emerging. A good recent example is Twipolitico's analysis of Barack Obama's and Mitt Romney's tweets during the early stages of the 2012 US presidential campaign.[1] Twipolitico extracted tweets referring to each candidate from Twitter's public streaming application programming interface (API)[2] and calculated each tweet's sentiment using software provided by a company, AlchemyAPI. This tool uses natural language processing and machine learning algorithms to identify positive and negative sentiment.[3] Nevertheless, while Twipolitico's approach to text mining contains useful elements, it is not without weaknesses. For instance, it cannot identify whether a sentiment is being expressed in the grammatical first or third person. Human analysis of social media content is excluded in this approach, which relies wholly on computational analysis. Over-reliance on software tools and algorithmic analyses of text can overlook valuable insights that human coders are better equipped to detect, such as how the meanings of certain terms may differ according to the communicative contexts in which they are employed. Human coding effort is likely to remain an essential step in the application of text mining tools in the social sciences, not least as a means of providing a gold standard against which to train and validate the performance of the tools (Procter et al., 2013).

---

[1]Twipolitico: http://web.archive.org/web/20121210194043/http://cs.uc.edu/twipolitico

[2]Twitter's Public Streaming API is part of the collection of Twitter's Streaming APIs that provide developers with access to the company's stream of Tweet data. 2013, For further details, see 'The Streaming APIs': https://dev.twitter.com/docs/streaming-apis

[3]Machine learning Algorithms can be defined as artificial intelligence that allows computers to 'learn' when exposed to new data, without the need for additional programming.

8.4 CHALLENGES: PRACTICALITIES, ETHICS AND ACCESS

As socially useful as these applications of text mining are, as we have intimated, they are not without pitfalls. On the one hand, there are clear practical benefits to mining 'big data' generated through social media, and evangelists have argued that this should become the new standard for scientific inquiry (Anderson and Wolff, 2008; Bollier, 2009: 4–5). But a growing scepticism is also emerging. For example, boyd and Crawford (2011) ask whether data mining will 'narrow the palette of research options' (boyd and Crawford, 2011: 1). There is a risk that computational, technologically-determined, automated research practice may lead us to believe we can always identify and meaningfully know the complex reality in which we exist, solely by mapping patterns in purely digital data.

One potential way forward is to marry automated analysis with more adaptive, online ethnographic methods that use theoretical hunches and qualitative analysis of online text to explore the dynamics of socially produced online information flows. Studies such as those by Veinot (2007), Chadwick (2011a; 2011b), Awan et al. (2011), Al-Lami et al. (2012), Papacharissi and de Fatima Oliveira (2011) and Procter et al. (2013) have developed such approaches. Karpf (2012) puts the issue most starkly: since the internet keeps changing, the unit of analysis keeps changing; all we can aspire to in the field of internet research are short term, flexible and adaptive studies. A study of social media use over a 12 month period can lose validity if users start accessing those social media via different interfaces and devices and in different contexts and if the social media itself adapts. Long-term studies using 'our best methods will yield research that is systematically behind-the-times' (Karpf, 2012: 647).

Ultimately, we need to recognize that in the social sciences (and, indeed the natural sciences) theory and empirics are always symbiotic. Mining textual datasets, however large those datasets may be, must always be preceded by research questions that derive from the classical concerns of social research. There is no one-size-fits-all method or tool and compelling research questions cannot be generated entirely by the data itself. We maintain that as the field develops, social science approaches to mining social media text ought to be pluralistic, adaptive, and grounded in modes of enquiry and styles of presentation that are both intuitive and developed in dialogue with the norms and traditions of individual social science disciplines.

8.4.1 Practical Problems

On a practical level, users of text mining tools should be aware that these are not a panacea; they are inherently limited in what they can achieve. Sample bias and self-selecting samples are well-established risks with online studies. We should also be wary of conflating the expression of sentiment with actual behaviour. One of the main practical challenges of effective text mining is, ironically, linguistic. Despite the fact that English is still the Internet's most prevalent language, Chinese is now used almost as frequently, while other languages such as Spanish, Japanese, and Portuguese are also widely used (Internet World Stats, 2014). Moreover, the prevalence of non-Latin scripts in the top ten languages used online, such as Chinese, Japanese, Arabic, and Korean, only amplifies these problems. Some of these difficulties can be mitigated by the use of native-speaking human coders, and many commercial providers of text mining now claim that their products are 'language agnostic' (Crimson Hexagon, 2012a). However, social scientists must be alert to potential problems here. There is the obvious but important point that many concepts and meanings, not to mention devices such as humour and sarcasm, do not traverse linguistic divides.

These challenges are further compounded by the idioms and meta-languages that have developed over the last two decades, and in some cases much earlier, in computer-mediated settings. Text mining tools that are only equipped to process grammatically-correct English are acceptable for formal documents like legislation or applications in natural science research, where constructs like biological and chemical compounds remain stable. However, these tools will often struggle to effectively analyse online idioms such as 'LOLspeak'. Online, many individuals deliberately contract and alter grammatically-correct language to provide more responsive answers to others. Many examples of this can be seen in the use of instant message clients and microblogging platforms such as Identi.ca and Twitter, but these language forms are now widespread across all online settings. In addition, language use may be instantly detected by humans but difficult to code in software. Sarcasm, irony, and *double entendres* can only be understood with reference to extra contextual detail and, in social media environments like Twitter and Facebook, that detail may derive from very broad and often-fast-changing cultural references that are very difficult to integrate without human intervention to guide the automated analysis.

Interpreting potentially ambiguous online content is therefore a common problem for researchers operating in this new environment and manual analysis is often essential to account for the wider social context of online discourse. However, given the huge volumes of data available to researchers, manual coding may not always be practical. Compromises exist in the form of 'machine-learning' tools such as Crimson Hexagon and Netbase, which enable the researcher to identify and manually review ambiguous data that the technology cannot accurately code. The software can then be instructed to code the data according to the manual instructions. In this way, researcher and software work together to continuously identify and improve the quality and accuracy of the analysis, but this is a process far removed from the promise of fully-automated text mining.

8.4.2 Ethics

As Jirotka and Anderson (Chapter 12) explain, another set of challenges associated with text mining derives from the ethical questions raised by this form of social enquiry. Is it ethical to mine data that is generally comprised of conversations between subjects who did not consent to having their utterances used for research purposes? Do the usual ethical standards for gaining consent in human subject research fully apply in these contexts?

In online research more generally, since the 1990s a rough consensus has emerged that the effective study of computer-mediated communication may often require a number of modifications to the standard human subjects model of research ethics. In these fast-moving environments, where there is a general expectation of public exposure, gaining the consent of individuals would make much text mining research impossible (Sveningsson, 2004). In 1995 Sheizaf Rafaelli argued that researchers should treat 'public discourse on Computer Mediated Communication as just that: public.' He went on: 'Such study is more akin to the study of tombstone epitaphs, graffiti, or letters to the editor. Personal? Yes. Private? No...' (Sudweeks and Rafaeli, 1995: 121). This perspective may be convenient, but does it always work in today's social media environments, particularly Facebook, whose privacy settings constantly change and are notoriously difficult to understand for many users? Facebook is, of course, a commercial environment and is regulated indirectly via the agreement users read and digitally sign when they join the service. But if online communication is used in large-scale text mining studies of public opinion, does this require a new set of ethical guidelines? After all, traditionally-conducted public opinion polls always require the active consent of participants. Perhaps the same rule ought to apply to text mining. These are important questions that must be addressed as text mining becomes more embedded in political organizations and government.

8.4.3 Access

A related challenge is the absence of open and universal access to social media data. With the Web's transition from a broadly autonomous and fragmented network infrastructure to an increasingly centralized and controlled commercial space, the abundance of personal data produced through social media has a great deal of commercial – and political – value (World Economic Forum, 2012; Lohr, 2012). It is this transformation that has led Anderson and Wolff (2010) to declare that the Web is 'dead', at least in the context of its original conception as an open network. Although Anderson and Wolff's perspective is arguably an exaggeration (see Schonfeld, 2010), their assessment is useful in drawing attention to the spread of proprietary 'portals', 'walled gardens', and 'applications' which restrict the free flow of online information for commercial reasons (*The Economist*, 2010). User data is increasingly locked within proprietary platforms, out of the reach of scholarly researchers.

These developments have a number of implications for research. Consider Facebook, currently the largest global social networking platform. Given its extensive socio-cultural dominance and 1.1 billion global users by 2013, the quantity of personal data shared within its walled garden is vast. This information, however, remains locked within Facebook's proprietary platform, with full access available only to its own and approved researchers and commercial partners, for example, advertisers and developers (Bakshy et al., 2012; Deloitte, 2012). Facebook is arguably creating its own gigantic proprietary data repository. Social researchers can gain limited access to this data using Facebook's Graph API, which provides datasets of Facebook 'objects' – certain content, such as photos, Facebook Events and Pages, and the 'connections' between them, such as friend relationships, shared content and tagged photos (Facebook, 2015; Knguyen, 2010; Russell, 2011). But a great deal of Facebook users' content is off limits to researchers. And the range and volume of data available via Facebook's Graph API is now more tightly controlled than it was in the service's early days, when researchers were allowed greater scope (Golder et al. 2007; Gross and Acquisti, 2005; Lampe et al., 2006; Lewis et al., 2008; Mayer and Puller, 2008).

The same may be said of Twitter, which in the early 2010s moved to more tightly controlled access to its data in an attempt to enhance the company's profitability. At the time of writing, researchers have a variety of options to access Twitter data, ranging from Twitter's complete public data stream (the 'firehose') through to a 10 per cent or a 1 per cent sample of public tweets (the 'gardenhose' and 'spritzer' respectively) (boyd and Crawford, 2011; Gannes, 2010). This approach, however, favours commercial users over scholars. The cost of accessing Twitter's complete dataset prohibits what are often poorly-funded academic researchers. Although costs to access Twitter's firehose vary depending on the volume of tweets returned by search queries, Twitter's two official data resellers, Gnip and Datasift currently license access to a sample of tweets at prices that may exceed several thousand dollars per month.[4] Moreover, an update to Twitter's terms of service in 2011 further compounded researchers' ability to access data by expressly forbidding users from 'resyndicating' or 'sharing' Twitter content, even if the data is collected legitimately (Twitter, 2011, cited in Freelon, 2012). As a result, researchers, including the authors of this chapter, who previously benefited from access to datasets gathered by the research community in services like Twapperkeeper,[5] are prevented from conducting further studies because that data cannot be made public (Judd, 2011; Freelon, 2012; Shulman, 2011). More worryingly, there is some evidence that social media companies are increasingly keen to police research agendas. Citing a keynote talk by Twitter's internal researcher, Jimmy Lin, at the 2011 International Conference on Weblogs and Social Media, boyd and Crawford (2011) have argued that Lin 'discouraged researchers from pursuing lines of inquiry that internal Twitter researchers could do better given their preferential access to Twitter data' (boyd and Crawford, 2011: n4).

Twitter's restrictions on data access, however, are not without work-arounds. While Twitter prevents the sharing of individual tweet content or 'follow relationships', it does allow the distribution of 'derivative data, such as the number of Tweets with a positive sentiment' and 'Twitter object IDs, like a Tweet ID or a user ID' which 'can be turned back into Twitter content using the statuses/show and users/lookup API methods, respectively' (Twitter, cited in Freelon, 2012). But although this may offer some very useful and interesting possibilities for research,

---

[4]Both companies emphasize that pricing can be tailored to clients' needs. See https://gnip.com/products/pricing and http://datasift.com/pricing

[5]Twapperkeeper is now integrated with HootSuite. See http://twapperkeeper.com/index.html

these provisions prohibit independent large scale text mining, given the technological skills necessary to identify tweet content from object IDs or the likely timescales required to reverse engineer potentially very large datasets.[6]

Walled gardens pose a substantial challenge to the open flow of information across the web, but so, too, does another important recent trend: the growth of application-based platforms or 'apps'. The rise of apps is largely attributable to the late-2000s growth in smartphone and tablet computing and the platforms and protocols that govern how these devices operate. The challenge for researchers lies in the proprietary infrastructure of apps and mobile devices that 'use the Internet for transport but not the browser for display' (Hands and Parikka, 2011). As a result, data remain locked away and private companies become newly-important data 'gatekeepers'. Given the significant growth of smartphones and tablets and current industry predictions that tablet devices will outsell traditional personal computers by 2014 (Dediu, 2012), the value of this data needs to be taken seriously by researchers interested in large-scale text mining. In future, will academic text mining studies be able to compete with those carried out by commercial organizations? Will scholars have access to meaningful data when so much important discourse is taking place inside these closed environments?

8.5 TEXT MINING TOOLS: A BRIEF SURVEY

We turn now to a brief survey of the main text mining tools and services that are currently available and which have a focus on the analysis of online text. Before we do so, some caveats are necessary. First, given the rapidly evolving nature of this field, any overview is inevitably provisional. Free or open-source tools are continually developed and shared among user communities and established commercial technologies are often acquired and bolted on to other products. Second, while text mining may appear to be a cohesive field, as this chapter demonstrates there is a diversity of approaches and applications. There are no perfect technological solutions and this section makes no hard recommendations as to the suitability of specific tools. However, we do wish to highlight the tools that we believe offer good starting points. These are outlined immediately below and summarized in Table 8.1 in the chapter's Appendix, along with a selection of other tools and services.[7]

---

[6]Freelon suggests object ID datasets 'will be all but useless to anyone without at least a basic understanding of all of the following: APIs and how to retrieve data from them, a programming language like PHP or Python, and a relational database system such as MySQL.' Recreating a full dataset of tweets covering the Arab Spring political unrest using Twitter's permissible methods would take 'months of 24/7 automated querying given Twitter's API limits' (Freelon 2012).

[7]This overview of text mining tools is based on our personal experiences and invaluable consultation with colleagues. Particular thanks go to Peter Fontana and Carolin Gerlitz. Any errors or shortcomings are our own.

8.5.1 Sysomos MAP

Originally developed by researchers at the University of Toronto, Sysomos MAP is now arguably one of the better commercial text mining products for running basic analyses of social media content. MAP provides access to a database of 20 billion social media conversations, spanning platforms such as blogs, message boards, Twitter, and a sample of public Facebook pages. MAP's retrospective database consists of historical data from 2013 and claims to index eight million posts an hour in close to real time, which makes it useful for tracking live events. Sysomos has access to the full Twitter firehose, allowing researchers access to data from over 280 million Twitter users.

Sysomos MAP users can filter data geographically, potentially down to city level, provided the data is available, and demographically, according to the age, gender, and profession of individuals. Although MAP's automated sentiment analysis is useful, in practice the benefits can be limited. MAP provides a workaround by enabling researchers to override automated sentiment results and manually code more accurate sentiment scores for subsequent analysis. However, MAP's search algorithm does not automatically 'learn' from manual sentiment overrides. Search results are fully downloadable in a variety of formats, most usefully as CSV files. There are other services that compare favourably with MAP, such as Radian6 and Attensity, but Sysomos' strength lies in its relatively easy setup and relatively low cost.

8.5.2 NetBase

NetBase's 'Enterprise Social Intelligence Platform' takes the fundamental features found in commercial text mining tools such as Sysomos MAP or Radian6 and overlays a range of additional functionality. The service provides access to 100 million conversations from social media platforms and offers the ability to group common phrases and keywords in a dataset and automatically code these in the same way during future analyses. While NetBase does not permit access to the Twitter firehose, it claims that it indexes all of the public pages on Facebook. This gives NetBase an advantage over comparable tools that typically offer access to only a sample of public Facebook pages. A downside to NetBase is that some elements of basic functionality, for example, exporting data as CSV files, are not currently offered.

8.5.3 Crimson Hexagon Forsight

Crimson Hexagon Forsight offers functionality comparable with Sysomos MAP and NetBase, such as theme, sentiment, demographic, and influence analysis. Importantly, however, Forsight's analysis algorithm uses machine learning and is therefore 'trainable'. Researchers can manually code a data sample and instruct Forsight to 'learn' from this and apply it to future analyses. While not as accurate as data that is coded entirely by humans, this feature provides researchers with better options for gaining accurate results than many other tools. Crimson Hexagon's

Social Research Grant Programme, which offers 'in-kind access' for the academic and non-profit community (Crimson Hexagon 2012a), makes Forsight a relatively attractive tool for scholarly researchers.

8.5.4 COSMOS

The Collaborative Online Social Media Observatory (COSMOS) platform provides an integrated suite of tools for harvesting, archiving, analysing and visualizing social media data streams, together with the capability to link with other kinds of data, e.g., from the UK Office for National Statistics (ONS) via open APIs (Housley et al., 2014). COSMOS hosts a range of computational tools that include language detection, gender identification, location, sentiment, tension and topic discovery. The first version of the platform was made available for download in late 2014.

8.5.5 DiscoverText

DiscoverText is comparable with Crimson Hexagon's Forsight in that it offers a number of unique features likely to be of particular use to social scientists. It allows researchers to perform manual text coding collaboratively through the creation of cloud-based data 'buckets' which can be shared online among a dispersed researcher network. Validation tools enable lead researchers to test for coding validity at the micro-level of the coder as well as at the project level. DiscoverText incorporates the ability to automate the inter-coder reliability tests that are essential for team-based content analysis. A significant feature of DiscoverText is its 'ActiveLearning Customized Classifiers' functionality. Although still in beta phase, this allows researchers to customize coding classifications and 'train' the DiscoverText algorithms to detect sentiment and themes using machine learning. DiscoverText can also provide access to the Twitter firehose, though this incurs an additional cost.

8.5.6 Linguamatics I2E

I2E from Linguamatics provides text mining analysis using natural language processing. Originally used within the life sciences, I2E has recently been deployed for the analysis of social media content, as we discuss in more detail below.

8.6 APPLYING TEXT MINING I: SOCIAL MEDIA MONITORING DURING THE 2010 BRITISH GENERAL ELECTION

To illustrate the potential – and some of the pitfalls and work-arounds – of using digital methods for real-time analysis of political events, we now turn to a discussion of how I2E, developed by the Cambridge-based company Linguamatics, was used to analyse the opinions of Twitter users during and immediately after the live televised prime ministerial debates of the 2010 British general election. This was part of a larger collaborative project carried out in 2009 and 2010 to develop a real-time methodology for analysing public responses to emergent events.[8] The project consisted of several other experimental studies, including work on the autumn 2009 swine flu vaccination campaign in Britain, the December 2009 Copenhagen Climate Summit, the January 2010 Haiti earthquake, and the collapse of the Sony Playstation online network in March 2010.

The televised prime ministerial debates were the first events of their kind to have been held in the United Kingdom and there was great media interest. The allure of real-time results that could be delivered to the public at the end of each debate led a number of established polling companies to promise instant polls to broadcasters. For example, ComRes delivered a poll result within six seconds of the end of one debate by using a telephone panel survey in which a representative sample of voters were given keypads and told to press a button to indicate who they thought had 'won' (Anstead and O'Loughlin, 2012). But digital media also offered other sources of data. By spring of 2010 the 'two-screen' media event had become common in Britain. Many audience members now use laptops or mobile devices to offer their personal social media commentary on political or celebrity television broadcasts, in real time as they watch a show (Anstead and O'Loughlin, 2011b; Chadwick, 2011a; 2011b). In this context, the Linguamatics project aimed to see if there were patterned responses on Twitter to the party leaders' performances during each debate, with a particular focus on how each candidate was deemed to have performed in response to each question in the debates. The research team was also curious to see if the method could be used to predict the eventual 'winner' of the televised debates, though this proved entirely problematic, as we discuss below. Nevertheless, the project team was contacted by journalists who requested from them text-mining 'poll' results within hours of the end of each debate. This compelled the team to reflect on the ethics of how to present their research in meaningful ways.

The methodology and workflow for these studies depended upon a combination of human and automated analysis of social media content.

8.6.1 Setup Before the Event

- Human: decide key search terms and relevant queries based on expertise in the given field (for example, pharmaceuticals, climate change, financial markets, party politics).
- Technology: initial data search, aggregation, classification.
- Human: clean the data by refining search terms and vocabulary.

---

[8]'Monitoring of Complex Information Infrastructure by Mining External Signals', Technology Strategy Board, Award Reference TP: BK067C: David Milward (Linguamatics Ltd) and Ben O'Loughlin (Royal Holloway, University of London).

8.6.2 Real-Time Monitoring During the Event

- Human and Technology: continuous data stream from social media according to key search terms.
- Technology: process the data using I2E software.
- Human: interpret findings on an ongoing basis.

8.6.3 Integration and Presentation

- Human: integration of these results with other data, for example relationships between social media content and indicators such as share prices, sales of goods, or opinion surveys.
- Human and Technology: visualization tools to render key findings more quickly intelligibly.

The three live televised debates offered a chance to test this methodology and workflow. The debates were held on 15 April 2010 (ITV), April 22 (Sky News), and April 29 (BBC). Approximately 567,000 tweets from 130,000 Twitter users were analysed during the three debates. The framework of the study went beyond traditional keyword searches of important terms in the data corpus. For each debate, a sentiment analysis of the content referring to each of the political leaders was examined using the NLP technology in Linguamatics' I2E text mining tool. I2E examines the grammatical structure of each tweet and uses a conceptual vocabulary that enables inferences about the intention of a person posting a message. It should be noted that, as a business, Linguamatics keeps the precise nature of I2E a closely guarded commercial secret. Scholarly researchers need to balance this drawback against having access to the expertise provided by private sector providers. Some of the services we listed above may offer the appearance of analytical power but if the process of research is not transparent and replicable, peer-reviewed scholarly journals may be wary of publishing the research. However, Linguamatics were granted access to Twitter's streaming API. At the time of writing (June 2014), the API delivers one per cent of tweets at no cost to independent scholarly researchers.

Figure 8.1 below presents the volume of tweets about each leader, organized by the questions asked during the third televised debate. The research team were able to conduct fine-grained analysis of the television coverage to identify precisely which statements or audience reactions correlated with these spikes in online commentary (see also Anstead and O'Loughlin, 2011b). This chart also formed part of the coverage provided by the BBC's technology reporter Rory Cellan-Jones (2010).

In Figure 8.1 the Y-axis refers to the number of tweets per minute that contained positive commentary on a leader's response to a question or issue. For example, the tweet 'Clegg strong on the "the outrageous abuse of bankers' bonuses"' was coded as for Liberal Democrat party leader Nick Clegg on debate question 3 (Q3) at 21:00 hours. Tweets were coded in 60-second chunks. Twitter's streaming API only provided 10 per cent of all tweets, but still the numbers per minute seem relatively low (between zero and 50). However, Figure 8.1 excludes all tweets about leaders that were not connected to a particular issue or question. This relatively low number of tweets – 4,082 in total for the third debate – allowed for human coding in the hours after the debate to check the validity of how each tweet was coded by I2E. The project team also analysed each leader's popularity by issue, and found that Clegg and Brown shared the lead on immigration, Clegg was ahead on banking and tax, while Brown clearly won on the economy. However, patterns of response were often uneven. In the second leaders' debate, for example, a question about whether the Pope should visit Britain while the Catholic Church was confronting a sexual abuse scandal led to immediate responses on Twitter but also a later spike in interest, as Clegg briefly mentioned religion in response to another question. Discussion of issues and questions on Twitter did not map neatly onto the timelines.

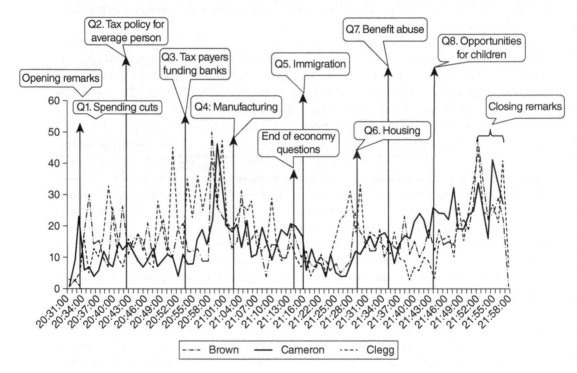

Figure 8.1 Volume of tweets about each leader's response to a question in the third debate
Source: The Technology Strategy Board

In terms of overall sentiment towards each of the leaders across the three debates, Figure 8.2 shows that Nick Clegg's share of positive sentiment dropped from 57 per cent in the first debate to 37 per cent by the end of the third and final debate. Gordon Brown's share stabilized at 32 per cent, while David Cameron's rose from 18 per cent to 31 per cent. Intriguingly, these trends eventually converged roughly with the final vote share on election day: Cameron's Conservative Party won with 36.1 per cent of the popular vote, Labour came second with 29 per cent, and Clegg's Liberal Democrats fell to a final 23 per cent.

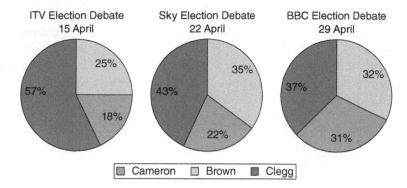

Figure 8.2 Share of positive sentiment for party leaders
Source: The Technology Strategy Board

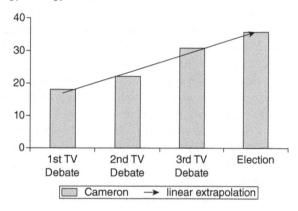

Figure 8.3 Trend in positive sentiment for Cameron
Source: The Technology Strategy Board

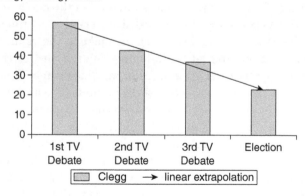

Figure 8.4 Trend in positive sentiment for Clegg
Source: The Technology Strategy Board

These trend lines make for striking visuals (Figures 8.3 and 8.4) that can be used to support simple media narratives about, for instance, the 'Lib Dem surge' that saw Clegg unexpectedly 'win' the first debate and then steadily lose support over the course of the general election campaign. However, using such analysis to predict election results is extremely problematic and should provoke instant caution. Twitter users are not representative of the whole electorate. A user's comments may not indicate how they will actually vote on election day, and of course events may occur between the final debate and election day that alter voting intentions. The same applies to any measurement of opinion around televised debates prior to elections, including telephone polls or devices such as 'the worm' that monitors and visualizes immediate audience responses to politicians as they speak. When the project team were contacted by journalists from national media organizations wishing for this social media analysis to be used in their reporting, it was not clear that journalists, the BBC's Rory Cellan-Jones aside, fully appreciated the differences between such analysis and traditional opinion polling (Anstead and O'Loughlin, 2012).

This raises important ethical questions about how text mining research is presented in the public domain. The Linguamatics team have tried to make clear that such research should be considered 'qualitative' insofar as it offers an understanding of how opinion forms and shifts. Due to the unrepresentative sample, the statistical patterns identified in Twitter data lack the validity and generalizability of traditional polling and have little predictive value for the whole population. However, social media analysis does allow researchers to delve into the data to ask different questions: whose comments are creating what response and why? Why did an issue suddenly re-occur in a debate? Who has power and influence in this environment? The spontaneity of much social media commentary allows researchers to analyse individuals' reasoning and their emotional responses to events, and on a large scale. Traditionally, this type of analysis has emerged only from research based on in-depth interviews or focus groups.

As we have argued, one of the challenges of mining text from real-time sources such as Twitter is establishing meanings through an awareness of linguistic idioms and broader cultural contexts. Consider Figure 8.5, which details the volume of positive sentiment tweets for each of the leaders during the third debate.

In Figure 8.5, the Y-axis shows tweets coded for positive sentiment towards each leader, measured in 60-second chunks. Notice the spike in the volume of commentary on David Cameron that occurred at 20:45 hours. The reasons for this were initially unclear. Twitter users often use irony and sarcasm, which can be frequently misinterpreted by text mining tools and even, of course, by humans. The increase in positive sentiment here was actually sparked by a well-known comedian and actor, Chris Addison, making a deeply sarcastic remark about David Cameron: '@mrchrisaddison: sky poll just in! David Cameron won the debate!...' At that stage Addison had approximately 24,000 followers on Twitter (as of October 2014 he had 294,000). But, more importantly, his comment was retweeted by many others. On the night, Sky had published a poll in the middle of the debate that put Cameron in the lead. Many Twitter users felt that Sky were promoting Cameron to the extent of publishing polls that were biased in his favour, since Sky TV is part of the Rupert Murdoch-owned News International group, whose outlets historically tend to favour right-of-centre parties. This example shows the necessity of combining automated natural language processing with human analysis. I2E or any other software is unlikely to possess an understanding of who Chris Addison is or contextual knowledge of public opinion regarding media ownership and a media mogul's support for a party. The spike in data could have been taken at face value, leading to an erroneous finding. However, I2E directed the researchers to this spike and this led to a more detailed examination of how and why Addison's joke was worth retweeting, why some found it shocking that an opinion poll might become a political tool, and hence a broader exploration about prevailing conceptions of authority, credibility, and trust among the British electorate (Anstead and O'Loughlin, 2011b).

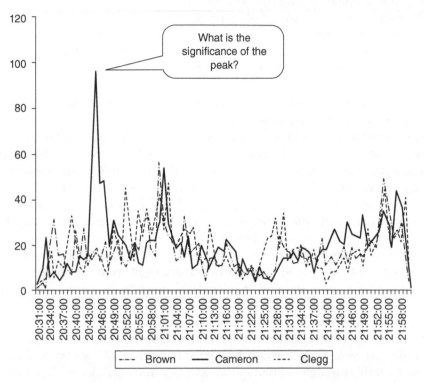

Figure 8.5 Volume of tweets expressing positive sentiment about party leaders in the third debate

Source: The Technology Strategy Board

This case study in 2010 was embryonic, and Linguamatics developers have been working on increasing the validity and reliability of their natural language processing, providing multi-lingual tools, and using social media analysis to segment and target social constituencies. Nevertheless, we contend that the most compelling research in this area will always involve an iterative workflow of human and automated analysis.

8.7 APPLYING TEXT MINING II: ANALYSING THE 'BULLYGATE' NEWS STORY OF 2010

Our second example of applying text mining to online content is Chadwick's (2011a) study of 'Bullygate', a political crisis involving the British prime minister Gordon

Brown during early 2010. Here we provide a summary of how some basic text mining and a great deal of manual work were used together in the qualitative analysis of a rapidly evolving political news story; one that revealed some important new aspects of news production.

Traditionally, the literature on news has been united by the fundamental assumption that the construction of political news is a tightly-controlled, even cosy game involving the interactions and interventions of a small number of elites: politicians, officials, communications staff, and journalists. While these elite-driven aspects of political communication are still much in evidence, the hybridization of older and newer media practices in political communication requires a rejuvenated understanding of the power relations now shaping news.

During a weekend in February 2010, just a few weeks before the most closely-fought British general election campaign in living memory, Gordon Brown, then prime minister, became the subject of an extraordinary media spectacle. The crisis was sparked by revelations in a book about the Labour government by Andrew Rawnsley, one of Britain's foremost political journalists. Extended extracts from the book were printed in the *Observer*, one of Britain's oldest and most respected newspapers, as part of its 'relaunch' edition. The *Observer*'s extracts centred on the prime minister's alleged psychological and physical mistreatment of colleagues working inside his office in Number 10, Downing Street. Bullygate, as it became known, was potentially the most damaging political development of the entire Brown premiership, not only due to its timing – on the verge of a general election – but also its shocking and personalized nature. These were potentially some of the most damaging allegations ever to be made concerning the personal conduct of a sitting British prime minister. The Bullygate affair became a national and international news phenomenon.

But during the course of that weekend and into the early part of the following week, Bullygate took several momentous twists and turns. New players entered the fray, most notably an organization known as the National Bullying Helpline, whose director claimed that her organization had received phone calls from staff inside Number 10, Downing Street. This information created a powerful frame during the middle of the crisis. As the story evolved, events were decisively shaped by mediated interactions among politicians, not-for-profit organization leaders, professional journalists, bloggers, and citizen activists organized on Twitter. Seemingly clear-cut revelations published in a national newspaper quickly became the subject of fierce contestation, involving competition, conflict, and partisanship, but also relations of interdependence, among a wide variety of actors operating in a wide variety of media settings. Over the course of a few days, following the introduction of largely citizen-discovered pieces of information, serious doubts about the veracity of the Bullygate revelations resulted in the story becoming discredited (Chadwick, 2011a).

Close, real-time, observation and logging, over a five-day period, of a wide range of press, broadcast, and online material, as the story broke, evolved, and faded, enabled a detailed narrative reconstruction of these interactions between politicians, broadcasters, newspaper journalists, and key online media actors. The aim of the analysis was to go beyond the accounts provided by traditional broadcast and newspaper media and to conduct a narrative reconstruction of the hybridized information flows surrounding the story. Chadwick was particularly interested in the roles played by non-elite actors, such as bloggers and influential Twitter users in the construction and contestation of the bullying allegations, and in how interactions between broadcast media and online media players came to shape the development of the story as part of what he termed a 'political information cycle.' Political information cycles, the study argued, are complex assemblages in which the personnel, practices, genres, technologies, and temporalities of online media are hybridized with those of broadcast and press media. This hybridization shapes power relations among actors and ultimately affects the flows and meanings of news.

8.7.1 Method and Setup

Studying political information cycles presents a significant challenge to researchers. Newspaper journalists now frequently post multiple updates to stories throughout the day and night and news sites have widely varying archive policies. The technological limitations of journalists' content management systems, as well as editorial policy, determine whether and how updates, additions, headline alterations, and picture replacements are signalled to readers. Most blogs and a minority of mainstream news outlets, such as the *Guardian* and the *Financial Times*, are transparent about an article's provenance. However, practices vary widely and it is common to see outdated time stamps, the incremental addition of paragraphs at the top or bottom of stories, and headline and URL changes to reflect new angles on developments as they emerge. Sometimes entire stories will simply be overwritten, even though the original hyperlink will be retained. All of these can occur without readers being explicitly notified.

Several 'forensic' strategies were used to overcome these problems. In addition to monitoring key political blogs and the main national news outlets' websites, the free and publicly-available Google Reader was used to monitor the RSS feeds and the timings of article releases from February 20 to February 25, 2010, for the following outlets: *BBC News* (Front Page feed), *Daily Express, Daily Mail, Daily Mirror, Daily Star, Daily Telegraph, Financial Times, Guardian, Independent, Independent on Sunday, Mail on Sunday, News of the World, Observer, Sun, Sunday Express, Sunday Mirror, Sunday Telegraph, Sunday Times* and the *Times*. Links were followed back to newspaper websites to check for article modifications, updates, and deletions. Google Reader consists of an effectively unlimited archive of every RSS feed dating back to when a single user first added it to Google's database. Evernote,[9] free and publicly available software, was used to store selected news articles.

The broadcast media archiving service, Box of Broadcasts, was used to store content from television, specifically Channel 4 News, BBC News at Ten, the BBC 24-Hour News Channel and ITV News. This enabled the qualitative analysis of pivotal moments during the flow of events on February 20, 21 and 22. This service is available to member

---

[9]www.evernote.com

institutions of the British Universities Film and Video Council.[10] Where they existed, links to public transcripts of television and radio shows were also provided.

The Twitter search function (at http://search.twitter.com) was monitored in real-time using a number of queries, such as 'national bullying helpline' and hashtags[11] such as #rawnsleyrot and #bullygate. In the period between the introduction of the Twitter search engine and the time of the fieldwork, Twitter only made public the results from approximately three weeks prior to running a query and, at the time of the fieldwork, no robust and publicly-available means of automatically extracting and archiving individual Twitter updates existed. To circumvent these limitations, screen outputs of selected Twitter searches were captured in real-time and stored in Evernote. In April 2010, after the initial fieldwork was conducted, Google launched its Google Replay Search (this later became Google Real-Time Search but was withdrawn in July 2011). This enabled searches of the Twitter archive going back to early February 2010 and it presented the results in a timeline format, though it cannot automatically account for changes to the names of individual Twitter accounts, which had to be followed up manually. Where possible, the Google Replay Search service was used to track and present publicly available links to key Twitter updates.

While this approach is obviously more time-intensive than using automated text mining, it offered several advantages for study of a political crisis that emerged and evolved very quickly 'in the wild' and which could not have been predicted in advance. While many text mining studies focus analysis on specific platforms like Twitter or Facebook, in this case it was essential to capture the Bullygate story as it emerged *across and between* media, in unforeseen locations and from the interventions of many previously unknown actors. Focusing on one medium alone would not have captured the story's spread and wider impact. As the episode developed, new information emerged, language use shifted and salient keywords evolved. Indeed, these shifts were part of the power relations in play. Twitter hashtags were particularly important here: they were created, adopted, and dropped with remarkable speed. New hashtags were added to the information flows as political parties, journalists, and citizen activists sought to exercise power by steering developments. Creating automated and inflexible search queries at the beginning of the crisis would not have captured the story's evolving narratives.

In short, this research combined almost constant and real-time human intervention with a number of tools used for the efficient storage and analysis of digital text and audio-visual content. The application of basic text mining in this case enabled a more nuanced and detailed understanding of the power relations in contemporary networked news systems. It was useful in generating a complex picture of the twists and turns of political news and the increasing centrality of actors such as grassroots activists and citizen journalists who are able to intervene in the news making process for brief but often decisive moments using social media like Twitter, often in real time.

---

[10]http://bobnational.net

[11]A hashtag is a tag embedded in a message posted on the Twitter microblogging service, consisting of a word within the message prefixed with a hash (#) sign. (See en.wiktionary.org/wiki/hashtag.)

8.8 CONCLUSION

Text mining technologies are likely to become increasingly relevant for social science research, whether we like it or not. Text mining of social media data has already enabled the identification, analysis, and potential prediction of patterns of behaviour and opinion. It is clear, however, that when opening the Pandora's box of big data, researchers will increasingly encounter ontological, ethical, technical, and legal issues. While technology is now essential for the large-scale analysis of big data, the inherent irreducibility and complexity of the social remains. It is extremely unwise, and in any case almost certainly impossible, to leave text mining to software automation.

We can distinguish discrete methods from methodology. We can use qualitative or quantitative methods, but the most appropriate response to big data for social scientists seeking to explain social, economic and political behaviour is to combine methods into a broader methodology, as in the two case studies we have presented in this chapter. Crawford (2013; see also Lewis et al., 2013) writes, 'new hybrid methods can ask questions about *why* people do things, beyond just tallying up *how often* something occurs. That means drawing on sociological analysis and deep ethnographic insight as well as information retrieval and machine learning'. Substitute hybrid methodologies for methods, and we agree.

These challenges also problematize some traditional distinctions between qualitative and quantitative research. Traditionally, qualitative research has used methods such as focus groups, interviews, and observation to elicit data that enable researchers to interpret sense-making among social actors. In many respects, being able to monitor and analyse huge swathes of naturally-occurring online conversations is akin to eavesdropping on large-scale versions of these traditional contexts of qualitative research. Now, however, the sheer quantity of freely-available digital data may often require that qualitative researchers use *quantitative* methods to get a basic grip on their data before qualitative analysis can sensibly begin. In another context, Nigel Thrift has argued that a new style of knowing that he terms 'roving empiricism' is emerging, 'which is more controlled *and* also more open-ended' (2005: 223, italics in original). John Law, meanwhile, has written of the emergence of what he terms 'qualculation': the statistical sorting and ranking of objects, for example, through databases, in order to arrive at qualitative judgements about the justice or significance of situations (Callon and Law, 2003: 3). In fields such as security, welfare, and public health, quantitative data are now being analysed on massive scales to help policy makers arrive at fine-grained decisions on whom to target – in these cases for interrogation, aid, or treatment. But such decisions will and should always depend on qualitative judgement and contextual understanding.

Text and data mining must be understood within the context of broader social and technological shifts that have been shaped by the emergence of computerization and data analysis since the mid-twentieth century. Contemporary programmes of 'e-Research' in the sciences, social sciences, and humanities constitute a 'vision' (Dutton, 2010: 33) that the integration of disciplinary knowledge, network infrastructures, tools, services and data will allow complex social problems to be addressed (Jeffreys, 2010: 51). Social media commentary, bank transactions and weather data, for example, all have different social meanings, and can be archived, analysed and visualized, often in real-time. But just because data can be gathered and stored does not make it valuable, though the current imperative appears to be to collect data now and hope that its usefulness may become clearer later (Wilks and den Besten, 2010). How commercial and scholarly researchers ought to treat this new mass of data will always be subject to debate. We hope that this chapter has illuminated this uncertain terrain and we invite readers to think imaginatively about how these methods can be combined with others to create compelling new forms of knowledge about the social world.

APPENDIX

Table 8.1 A summary of some of the more commonly used commercial and free text mining tools[12]

Text mining tool	Brief description
Attensity Analyze (Commercial) www.attensity.com	Specializes in social media and other unstructured data such as emails and text messages.
ClearForest OneCalais (Commercial) www.clearforest.com/	Analyses unstructured data through natural language processing.
Connotate (Commercial) www.connotate.com	Cloud-based solution monitors and analyses a wide variety of online content in real time.
COSMOS [Collaborative Online Social Media Observatory] (Free for academic users) www.cosmosproject.net	Integrated set of tools for harvesting and analysing social media.
Crimson Hexagon Forsight (Commercial) www.crimsonhexagon.com	Analyses and visualizes social media content, users, and basic audience demographics, as well as proprietary internal enterprise data.
Diction (Commercial) www.dictionsoftware.com/	Uses dictionaries (word lists) to search texts for attributes like complexity, activity, optimism, realism, and commonality.
DiscoverText (Commercial) https://discovertext.com	Enables collaborative manual and 'teachable' machine analyses of social media and other unstructured documents.
General Sentiment (Commercial) www.generalsentiment.com	Analyses social media content in real time to determine sentiment.
I2E (Commercial) www.linguamatics.com/welcome/software/I2E.html	Enterprise-level. Mines unstructured text documents. Allows for building and refining queries.
Language Computer Corporation (Commercial) www.languagecomputer.com/	Uses natural language processing technologies, including named entity recognition, information extraction, and question answering.

[12]All URLs in this section accessed 12 Dec 2014.

Text mining tool	Brief description
Lexalytics (Commercial) www.lexalytics.com/	Comprises multiple tools, including sentiment analysis, named entity extraction, entity and theme sentiment, and summarization.
Lextek (Commercial) www.lextek.com	Provides information retrieval and natural language processing technology.
Luxid (Commercial) www.temis.com/?id=201&selt=1	Searches and analyses information within structured databases.
MAXQDA (Commercial) www.maxqda.com/service	Content analysis and visualization, with a module for quantitative text analysis.
Meltwater Buzz (Commercial) www.meltwater.com/products/meltwater-buzz-social-media-marketing-software/	Monitoring dashboard for analysing content themes, influence, and sentiment.
Mindshare Text Analytics Suite (Commercial) www.mshare.net/solutions/mindshare-technologies-text-analytics.html	Analyses a range of online consumer conversations from social media.
Netbase (Commercial) www.netbase.com	Uses natural language processing to provide theme, sentiment, and influence analysis of social media content.
Netlytic (Commercial) https://netlytic.org/	Web-based. Allows users to automate analysis and identify social networks in online communication.
NVIVO (Commercial) www.qsrinternational.com/products_nvivo.aspx	Content analysis. Includes a web and social media module.
Radian6 (Commercial) www.radian6.com/	Real-time monitoring dashboard to track and analyse social media content, map demographic and gender data, and gauge sentiment.
Rosette Linguistics Platform (Commercial) www.basistech.com/products/	Allows for analysis of unstructured text in Asian, European, and Middle Eastern languages.
Sysomos MAP (Commercial) www.sysomos.com/products/overview/sysomos-map/	Analyses social media content, identifies influential participants, maps demographic and gender data, and gauges sentiment.
TextAnalyst (Commercial) www.megaputer.com/site/text analyst.php	Summarizes, analyses, and clusters unstructured text documents.
Text Stat (Free) http://neon.niederlandistik.fu-berlin.de/en/textstat/	Produces word frequency lists from multiple languages and file formats.
Visible Intelligence (Commercial) www.visibletechnologies.com/products/visible-intelligence/	For the analysis of unstructured social media data to conduct sentiment, theme, and influencer analysis.

8.9 BIBLIOGRAPHY

Al-Lami, M., Hoskins, A. and O'Loughlin, B. (2012) 'Mobilisation and violence in the new media ecology: the Dua Khalil Aswad and Camilia Shehata cases', *Critical Studies on Terrorism*, 5(2): 237–56.

Anderson, C. (2008) 'The end of theory: the data deluge makes the scientific method obsolete', *Wired*, 16 July. New York: Conde Nast.

Anderson, C. and Wolff, M. (2010) 'The Web is dead. Long live the Internet', *Wired*, 17 August. New York, Conde Nast. Available at www.wired.com/2010/08/ff_webrip/all (accessed 12 Dec 2014).

Anstead, N. and O'Loughlin, B. (2010) 'The emerging viewertariat: explaining Twitter responses to Nick Griffin's appearance on Question Time', UEA School of Political, Social and International Studies Working Paper Series. Norwich, University of East Anglia.

Anstead, N. and O'Loughlin, B. (2011a) 'Semantic polling and the 2010 UK general election'. Paper presented at the ECPR General Conference, Reykjavik. Available from www.lse. ac.uk/media@lse/documents/MPP/Policy-Brief-5-Semantic-Polling_The-Ethics-of-Online-Public-Opinion.pdf (accessed 12 Dec 2014).

Anstead, N. and O'Loughlin, B. (2011b) 'The emerging viewertariat and BBC question time: television debate and real-time commenting online', *The International Journal of Press/Politics*, 16(4): 440–62.

Anstead, N. and O'Loughlin, B. (2012) 'Semantic polling: the ethics of online public opinion', LSE Media Policy Brief 5. Available from www2.lse.ac.uk/media@lse/docu ments/MPP/Policy-Brief-5-Semantic-Polling_The-Ethics-of-Online-Public-Opinion.pdf (accessed 12 Dec 2014).

Antweiler, W. and Frank, M.Z. (2004) 'The market impact of corporate news stories', University of Minnesota Working Paper, 6 Dec 2004.

Arasu, A. and Garcia-Molina, H. (2003) 'Extracting structured data from web pages'. *Proceedings of the 2003 ACM SIGMOD International Conference on Management of Data*. New York: ACM: 337–48. Available from http://dl.acm.org/citation.cfm?doid=872757.872799 (accessed 12 Dec 2014).

Archak, N., Ghose, A. and Ipeirotis, P. G. (2011) 'Deriving the pricing power of product features'. *Management Science*, 57(8): 1485–1509.

Asur, S. and Huberman, B.A. (2010). 'Predicting the future with social media'. Paper presented at the International Conference on Web Intelligence and Intelligent Agent Technology, IEEE. Available from http://arxiv.org/pdf/1003.5699 (accessed 12 Dec 2014).

Awan, A.N., Hoskins, A. and O'Loughlin, B. (2011) *Radicalisation and Media: Terrorism and Connectivity in the New Media Ecology*. London: Routledge.

Bakshy, E., Rosenn, I., Marlow, C. and Adamic, L. (2012) 'The role of social networks in information diffusion'. Paper presented at ACM WWW, Lyon, France. Available from http://arxiv.org/abs/1201.4145 (accessed 12 Dec 2014).

Baym, N.K. (2009) 'A call for grounding in the face of blurred boundaries', *Journal of Computer-Mediated Communication* 14(3): 720–23.

Bollen, J. (2011) 'Computational economic and finance gauges: polls, search, and Twitter'. Paper presented at the Behavioral Economics Working Group, Behavioral Finance Meeting. Palo Alto, CA. Available from http://users.nber.org/~confer/2011/BEf11/Mao. pdf (accessed 12 Dec 2014).

Bollier, D. (2009) 'The promise and peril of big data'. Paper presented at Extreme Inference: Implications of Data Intensive Advanced Correlation Techniques'. The Eighteenth Annual

Aspen Institute Roundtable on Information Technology, Aspen, Colarado, The Aspen Institute. Available from http://bollier.org/sites/default/files/aspen_reports/InfoTech09_0.pdf (accessed 12 Dec 2014).

boyd, d. (2008) 'How can qualitative Internet researchers define the boundaries of their projects: a response to Christine Hine', in A. Markham and N. Baym (eds), *Internet Inquiry: Conversations About Method*. Los Angeles, Sage. pp. 26–32.

boyd, d. and Crawford, K. (2011) 'Six provocations for big data. A decade in Internet time'. Paper presented at the Symposium on the Dynamics of the Internet and Society. Oxford. Available from www.zephoria.org/thoughts/archives/2011/09/14/six-provocations-for-big-data.html (accessed 12 Dec 2014).

Callon, M. and Law, J. (2003) 'On qualculation, agency and otherness'. Centre for Science Studies, Lancaster University: Lancaster. Available from www.lancaster.ac.uk/fass/sociology/research/publications/papers/callon-law-qualculation-agency-otherness.pdf (accessed 12 Dec 2014).

Castells, M. (2009) *Communication Power*. Oxford, Oxford University Press.

Cellan-Jones, R. (2010) 'Online "sentiment" around the prime-ministerial debates'. BBC News, 30 April. Available from www.bbc.co.uk/blogs/thereporters/rorycellanjones/2010/04/online_sentiment_around_the_pr.html (accessed 12 Dec 2014).

Chadwick, A. (2011a) 'The political information cycle in a hybrid news system: the British Prime Minister and the "bullygate" affair', *The International Journal of Press / Politics*, 16(3): 3–29.

Chadwick, A. (2011b) 'Britain's first live televised party leaders' debate: from the news cycle to the political information cycle', *Parliamentary Affairs*, 64(1): 24–44.

Chadwick, A. (2013) *The Hybrid Media System: Politics and Power*. Oxford: Oxford University Press.

Chew, C. and Eysenbach, G. (2010) 'Pandemics in the age of Twitter: content analysis of tweets during the 2009 H1N1 Outbreak', *PLoS ONE* 5(11): e14118. DOI: 10.1371/journal.pone.0014118

Chunara, R., Andrews, J.R. and Brownstein, J.S. (2012) 'Social and news media enable estimation of epidemiological patterns early in the 2010 Haitian cholera outbreak', *American Journal of Tropical Medicine and Hygiene*, 86(1): 36–45.

Crawford, K. (2013) 'Think again: big data', *Foreign Policy*, 9 May. Available from www.foreignpolicy.com/articles/2013/05/09/think_again_big_data

Culotta, A. (2010) 'Towards detecting influenza epidemics by analyzing Twitter messages'. 1st Workshop on Social Media Analytics. Washington, DC, USA. Available from http://snap.stanford.edu/soma2010/papers/soma2010_16.pdf (accessed 14 Dec 2014).

Crimson Hexagon (2012a) 'Technical Specifications'. Available from www.crimsonhexagon.com/technical-specifications (accessed 14 Dec 2014).

Crimson Hexagon (2012b) 'Our quantitative analysis methods'. Available from www.crimsonhexagon.com/quantitative-analysis (accessed 14 Dec 2014).

Dahlberg, L. (2005) 'The corporate colonization of online attention and the marginalization of critical communication?' *Journal of Communication Inquiry* 29(2): 160–80.

Dediu, H. (2012) 'When will tablets outsell traditional PCs?' *Asymco*. Available from www.asymco.com/2012/03/02/when-will-the-tablet-market-be-larger-than-the-pc-market/ (accessed 12 Dec 2014).

Deloitte (2012) *Measuring Facebook's Economic Impact in Europe*. Available from www.facebook.com/notes/facebook-public-policy-europe/measuring-facebooks-economic-impact-in-europe/309416962438169 (accessed 12 Dec 2014).

Doan, S., Ho Vo, B.-K. and Collier, N. (2011) 'An analysis of Twitter messages in the 2011 Tohoku earthquake'. Paper presented at the 4th ICST International Conference on eHealth. Malaga, Spain. Available from http://arxiv.org/pdf/1109.1618 (accessed 12 Dec 2014).

Dredge, S. (2011) 'Smartphone and tablet stats: what's really going on in the mobile market?' *Guardian Apps Blog*. London, Guardian Media Group. Available from www.guardian.co.uk/technology/appsblog/2011/aug/01/smartphone-stats-2011 (accessed 12 Dec 2014).

Dutton, W.H. (2010) 'Reconfiguring access in research: information, expertise, and experience', in W.H. Dutton and P.W, Jeffreys (eds), *World Wide Research: Reshaping the Sciences and Humanities*. Cambridge, MA: MIT Press. pp. 21–39.

Eguchi, K. and Lavrenko, V. (2006) 'Sentiment retrieval using generative models' in EMNLP '06 Proceedings of the 2006 Conference on Empirical Methods in Natural Language Processing. pp. 345-354.

The Economist (2010) 'The Web's new walls: how the threats to the Internet's openness can be averted.' 2 September. Available from www.economist.com/node/16943579 (accessed 12 Dec 2014).

Facebook (2012) 'Graph API'. Available from https://developers.facebook.com/docs/reference/api

Fan, W., Wallace, L., Rich, S., and Zhang, Z. (2006) 'Tapping the power of text mining', *Communications of the ACM*, 49(9):76–82.

Fielding, N.G.G. and Lee, R. (1998) *Computer Analysis and Qualitative Research*. London: Sage.

Freelon, D. (2012) 'Arab Spring Twitter data now available (sort of)'. Available from http://dfreelon.org/2012/02/11/arab-spring-twitter-data-now-available-sort-of (accessed 12 Dec 2014).

Gannes, L. (2010) 'Twitter firehose too intense? Take a sip from the gardenhose or sample the spritzer'. *All Things D*. Available from https://allthingsd.com/20101110/twitter-firehose-too-intense-take-a-sip-from-the-garden-hose-or-sample-the-spritzer/ (accessed 12 Dec 2014).

Ghose, A., Ipeirotis, P.G. and Sundararajan, A. (2007) 'Opinion mining using econometrics: a case study on reputation systems'. Paper presented at the 45th Annual Meeting of the Association of Computational Linguistics, Prague, Czech Republic, Association for Computational Linguistics. Available from http://pages.stern.nyu.edu/~aghose/acl2007.pdf (accessed 12 Dec 2014).

Gibbs, G.R., Friese, S. and Mangabeira, W.C. (2002) 'The use of new technology in qualitative research. Introduction to Issue 3(2) of FQS', *Forum: Qualitative Social Research SozialForschung*, 3(2): Art. 8, May.

Gilbert, E. and Karahalios, K. (2010) 'Widespread worry and the Stock Market'. Paper presented at the Fourth International AAAI Conference on Weblogs and Social Media, Washington, DC, AAAI. Available from http://comp.social.gatech.edu/papers/icwsm10.worry.gilbert.pdf (accessed 12 Dec 2014).

Gluck, J. and C. Meador (no date) *Analyzing the Relationship Between Tweets, Box-Office Performance, and Stocks*. (Unpublished thesis) Swarthmore PA, Swathmore College. Available from www.sccs.swarthmore.edu/users/12/jgluck/resources/TwitterSentiment.pdf (accessed 12 Dec 2014).

Golder, S., Wilkinson, D. and Huberman, B. (2007) 'Rhythms of social interaction: messaging within a massive online network'. Paper presented at the Third International Conference on Communities and Technology, London. Available from www.hpl.hp.com/research/idl/papers/facebook/facebook.pdf (accessed 12 Dec 2014).

Gross, R. and Acquisti, A. (2005) 'Information revelation and privacy in online social networks (the Facebook case)'. Paper presented at WPES'05. 12th ACM Conference on Computer and Communications Security Alexandria, VA. Available from www.heinz.cmu.edu/~acquisti/papers/privacy-facebook-gross-acquisti.pdf (accessed 12 Dec 2014).

Hands, J. and Parikka, J. (2011) 'Platform politics'. Available from www.networkpolitics. org/content/platform-politics (accessed 12 Dec 2014).

Hearst, M. (1999) 'Untangling text mining'. Paper presented at the Proceedings of the ACL '99: the 37th Annual Meeting for the Association for Computational Linguistics. University of Maryland.

Hey, T., Tansley, S. and Tolle, K. (2009) *The Fourth Paradigm: Data-Intensive Scientific Discovery*. Redmond, WA: Microsoft Research.

Housley, W., Procter, R., Edwards, A., Burnap, P., Williams, M., Sloan, L., Voss, A. and Greenhill, A. (2014) 'Big and broad social data and the sociological imagination: a collaborative response', *Big Data and Society*, 1(2), DOI: 2053951714545135.

Internet World Stats (2014) 'Internet world users by language.' Available from www. internetworldstats.com/stats7.htm (accessed 12 Dec 2014).

Jeffreys, P.W. (2010) 'The developing conception of e-Research'. In W.H. Dutton and P.W. Jeffreys (eds), *World Wide Research: Reshaping the Sciences and Humanities*, Cambridge, MA: MIT Press. pp. 51–66.

Jones, K.S. (1994) 'Natural language processing: a historical review', in A. Zampoli, N. Calzolari, M. Palmer (eds), *Current Issues in Computational Linguistics: in Honour of Don Walker*, (Linguistica Computazionale, vol. 9–10). Pisa: Dodrect. pp. 3–16.

Judd, N. (2011) Who controls 'Twistory?' *TechPresident*. Available from http://techpresident.com/short-post/who-controls-twistory (accessed 12 Dec 2014).

Hiroshi, K., Tetsuya, N. and Hideo, W. (2004) 'Deeper sentiment analysis using machine translation technology', Proceedings of the 20th international conference on Computational Linguistics, Association for Computational Linguistics. p.494.

Karpf, D. (2012) 'Social science research in Internet time', *Information, Communication and Society*, 15(5): 639–61.

Keeter, S. (2012), 'Mining tweets for public opinion', *Wall Street Journal*. 10 February. Available from http://blogs.wsj.com/numbers/mining-tweets-for-public-opinion-1118/10 (accessed 15 Feb 2012).

Knguyen (2010) 'Facebook Crawler?' Available from http://stackoverflow.com/questions/2022929/facebook-crawler (accessed 12 Dec 2014).

Lampe, C., Ellison, N. and Steinfield, C. (2006) 'A Face(book) in the crowd: social searching vs. social browsing'. Paper presented at CSCW-2006, ACM, New York. Available from www.msu.edu/~nellison/lampe_et_al_2006.pdf (accessed 12 Dec 2014).

Lee, D., Ok-Ran, J. and Lee, S. (2008) 'Opinion mining of customer feedback data on the Web'. Paper presented at the 2nd International Conference on Ubiquitous Information Management and Communication. New York, USA. Available from http://ids.snu. ac.kr/w/images/7/7e/IC-2008-01.pdf (accessed 12 Dec 2014).

Leetaru, K.H. (2011) 'Culturomics 2.0: forecasting large – scale human behavior using global news media tone in time and space.' *First Monday* 16(9). Available from http:// firstmonday.org/htbin/cgiwrap/bin/ojs/index.php/fm/article/viewArticle/3663/3040 (accessed 12 Dec 2014).

Lefler, J. (2011) *I Can Has Thesis?: A Linguistic Analysis of Lolspeak*. Unpublished Masters Thesis. University of Louisiana at Lafayette, December 2011. Available from http://etd.lsu.edu/docs/available/etd-11112011-100404/unrestricted/Lefler_thesis.pdf (accessed 12 Dec 2014).

Lewis, K., Kaufman, J., Gonzalez, M., Wimmer, A., and Christakis, N. (2008) 'Tastes, ties, and time: a new social network dataset using Facebook.com', *Social networks*, 30(4): 330–42.

Lewis, S.C., Zamith, R. and Hermida, A. (2013) 'Content analysis in an era of big data: a Hybrid approach to computational and manual methods', *Journal of Broadcasting & Electronic Media*, 57(1): 34–52.

Lidman, M. (2011) 'Social media as a leading indicator of markets and predictor of voting patterns', Masters Thesis. Umea, Umea University, Department of Computing Science.. Available from www.christopia.net/data/school/2011/Fall/social-media-mining/project_proposal/sources/lidman-2011.pdf (accessed 12 Dec 2014).

Lindsay, R. (2008) 'Predicting polls with Lexicon', *Language Wrong*. Available from https://web.archive.org/web/20090805103621 http://languagewrong.tumblr.com/post/55722687/predicting-polls-with-lexicon?

Lohr, S. (2012) 'The age of big data'. *New York Times*, February 11. Available from www.nytimes.com/2012/02/12/sunday-review/big-datas-impact-in-the-world.html?pagewanted=all&_r=0 (accessed 12 Dec 2014).

Manning, C.D. and Schütze, H. (1999) *Foundations of Statistical Natural Language Processing.* Cambridge, MA: MIT Press.

Mayer, A. and Puller, S. L. (2008) 'The old boy (and girl) network: social network formation on university campuses', *Journal of Public Economics* 92(1): 329–47.

Mejova, Y. (2009) 'Sentiment analysis: an overview. Comprehensive exam paper'. Available from http://www.academia.edu/291678/Sentiment_Analysis_An_Overview (accessed 01 April 2015).

Mishne, G. and Glance, N. (2006) 'Predicting movie sales from blogger sentiment'. Paper presented at the Spring Symposium on Computational Approaches to Analysing Weblogs AAAI. Available from www.nielsen-online.com/downloads/us/buzz/wp_MovieSalesBlogSntmnt_Glance_2005.pdf (accessed 12 Dec 2014).

O'Connor, B., Balasubramanyan, R., Routledge, B.R. and Smith, N.A. (2010) 'From tweets to polls: linking text sentiment to public opinion time series'. Paper presented at the International AAAI Conference on Weblogs and Social Media, Washington, DC, May 2010. Available from www.cs.cmu.edu/~nasmith/papers/oconnor%2Bbalasubramanyan%2Broutledge%2Bsmith.icwsm10.pdf (accessed 12 Dec 2014).

Pang, B. and Lee L. (2008) 'Opinion mining and sentiment analysis', *Foundations and Trends in Information Retrieval,* 2(1–2): 1–135.

Papacharissi, Z. and de Fatima Oliveira, M. (2011) 'The rhythms of news storytelling on Twitter: coverage of the January 25th Egyptian uprising on Twitter'. Paper presented at the World Association for Public Opinion Research Conference. Amsterdam. Available from http://tigger.uic.edu/~zizi/Site/Research_files/RhythmsNewsStorytellingTwitterWAPORZPMO.pdf (accessed 12 Dec 2014).

Procter, R., Vis, F. and Voss, A. (2013) 'Reading the riots on Twitter: methodological innovation for the analysis of big data', *International Journal of Social Research Methodology*, 16(3): 197–214.

Read J., Hope D. and Carroll J. (2007) 'Annotating expressions of appraisal in English', Proceedings of the Linguistic Annotation Workshop, held in conjunction with the 45th Annual Meeting of the Association of Computational Linguistics, Prague.

Russell, M.A. (2011) *Mining the Social Web: Analyzing Data from Facebook, Twitter, LinkedIn, and Other Social Media Sites*. Sebastopol, CA: O'Reilly Media.

Rzhetsky, A., Seringhaus, M. and Gerstein, M. (2008) 'Seeking a new biology through text mining', *Cell*, 134(1): 9–13.

Sakaki, T., Okazaki, M. and Matsuo, Y. (2010) 'Earthquake shakes Twitter users: real-time event detection by social sensors'. Paper presented at WWW2010 – 19th International World Wide Web Conference, Raleigh, North Carolina. Available from http://ymatsuo.com/papers/www2010.pdf (accessed 12 Dec 2014).

Schonfeld, E. (2010) 'Wired declares the web is dead – don't pull out the coffin just yet'. *Techcrunch*. Available from http://techcrunch.com/2010/08/17/wired-web-dead (accessed 12 Dec 2014).

Shulman, S. (2011) 'Twitter asks discoverText to stop sharing tweet data'. Available from https://web.archive.org/web/20110812163324/http://blog.texifter.com/index.php/2011/05/04/twitter-cites-terms-of-service-violation (accessed 01 April 2015).

Sudweeks, F. and Rafaeli, S. (1995) 'How do you get a hundred strangers to agree? Computer-mediated communication and collaboration', in T.M. Harrison and T.D. Stephen, (eds) *Computer Networking and Scholarship in the 21st Century University*. New York: SUNY Press. pp. 115–36.

Sveningsson, M. (2003) 'Ethics in virtual ethnography', in E. Buchanan, *Readings in Virtual Research Ethics: Issues and Controversies*. Hershey: Idea Group.

Thrift, N. (2005) *Knowing Capitalism*. London: Sage.

Thrift, N. (2012) 'The insubstantial pageant: producing an untoward land'. *cultural geographies*, 19(2): 141–68.

Veinot, T. (2007) 'The eyes of the power company: workplace information practices of a vault inspector', *The Library Quarterly*, 77(2): 157–80.

Visible Technologies (2012) 'Visible technologies acquires cymfony to expand global product offering'. Available from www.marketwired.com/press-release/visible-technologies-acquires-cymfony-to-expand-global-product-offering-1641276.htm (accessed 01 April 2015).

Wakamiya, S., Lee, R. and Sumiya, K. (2011a) 'Towards better TV viewing rates: exploiting crowd's media life logs over Twitter for TV ratings'. Proceedings of the 5th International Conference on Ubiquitous Information Management and Communication, New York. Available from http://dl.acm.org/ft_gateway.cfm?id=1968661&type=pdf (accessed 12 Dec 2014).

Wakamiya, S., Lee, R. and Sumiya, K. (2011b) 'Crowd-powered TV viewing rates: measuring relevancy between Tweets and TV programs'. Paper presented at Proceedings of the 16th International Conference on Database Systems for Advanced Applications. Available from http://db-event.jpn.org/deim2011/proceedings/pdf/a1-4.pdf (accessed 12 Dec 2014).

Wanner, F., Rohrdantz, C., Mansmann, F., Oelke, D. and Keim, D.A. (2009) 'Visual sentiment analysis of RSS news feeds featuring the US Presidential Election in 2008'. Paper presented at Visual Interfaces to the Social and the Semantic Web. Sanibel Island, Florida, USA. Available from http://data.semanticweb.org/workshop/VISSW/2009/paper/main/6/html (accessed 12 Dec 2014).

Wilks, Y.A. and den Besten, M. (2010) 'Key digital technologies to deal with data', in W.H. Dutton and P.W. Jeffreys (eds.) *World Wide Research: Reshaping the Sciences and Humanities*, Cambridge, MA: MIT Press. pp.107–119.

World Economic Forum (2012) *Big Data, Big Impact: New Possibilities for International Development*. Geneva, World Economic Forum. Available from www.weforum.org/reports/big-data-big-impact-new-possibilities-international-development (accessed 12 Dec 2014).

9

DIGITAL RECORDS AND THE DIGITAL REPLAY SYSTEM

ANDY CRABTREE, PAUL TENNENT, PAT BRUNDELL AND DAWN KNIGHT

9.1 INTRODUCTION

Surfacing the usually hidden or opaque digital footprints recorded by computers as people go about their everyday lives can make a valuable contribution to the practice of empirical social science. This chapter describes the development of a software tool that makes the surfacing possible and enables a broad church of social researchers to exploit digital records. It focuses on the development of the Digital Replay System (DRS), a software system that enables researchers to combine the data contained in digital records with more traditional and established forms of social science data, such as audio-visual recordings and transcriptions. DRS also provides quantitative techniques for the analysis of the content of digital records. Digital records have the potential to make visible in fine-grained detail the wide range of interactions conducted within digital environments through the use of digital infrastructures, devices and services. In doing so, they open up for analysis of the broad range of human activities that animate the digital society and contemporary life. This chapter explicates the core notion of digital records, tools for creating and exploiting them, and methods that that these tools support. Further development of DRS is also considered, particularly its potential to support the crowdsourcing of digital data and mass participation in social science research in the twenty-first century.

Social scientists have a growing interest in digital records and the promise they hold to shape understandings of social media and social networks (Bohannon, 2006). Nonetheless, the initial impetus towards the development of DRS originated in the field of Human-Computer Interaction (HCI) circa 2004, in the effort to understand human interaction in emerging 'ubiquitous' computing environments. These complex socio-technical environments exploited new digital infrastructures (GPRS, GPS, WiFi, etc.), mobile devices and sensors (motion, acceleration, heart rate, etc.) and merged them with online services to create interactional settings in which 'users' were distributed both physically and digitally and interacted with one another via asymmetrical means (e.g., Benford et al., 2003; Brown et al., 2003; Rogers et al., 2004; Halloran et al., 2005). The distributed and asymmetrical nature of these environments made them difficult to study through traditional observational means – what one saw was fragments of interaction (Crabtree and Rodden, 2009) gleaned from individual standpoints within the broader nexus of activities. The idea emerged that researchers might be able to exploit digital records, or 'systems logs' to use the technological jargon, to develop a richer picture of human interaction within these settings (Equator IRC, 2013). This was not first time that system logs – digital records of computational events and states, including those created by human beings – had been made use of in HCI (e.g., Burrell and Gay, 2002) but early experiences of using them suggested it was a very labour intensive and time consuming process (Crabtree and Rouncefield, 2005) and that there was clear opportunity to develop computer support to assist analysis of human-computer interaction in this context (Crabtree et al., 2006a).

Other disciplines saw the potential of digital records for social research too, not only sociologists but also learning scientists and corpus linguists (ESRC, 2005). The UK e-Social Science programme (Halfpenny and Procter, 2009; Halfpenny and Procter, 2010) provided the opportunity to bring these analytic perspectives to bear on collaborative explorations of digital records in order to shape the development of software tools and promote their broader uptake and use. Research and development does not take place in a vacuum and the development of DRS was also shaped by contiguous research endeavours taking place at the UK universities of Glasgow, Bristol and King's College London (Morrison et al., 2006; Fraser et al., 2006) and through collaborations with participants in the US Cyberinfrastructure program (Adolphs et al., 2007). DRS was the outcome of these collaborative efforts (see SourceForge, 2007). It provides a suite of tools that enable researchers to visualize and inspect digital records, to synchronize them with audio-visual recordings and transcriptions and create rich multi-media documents, to replay synchronized datasets just as one can replay video, to code synchronized datasets, and to generate graphs and charts based on coded results. DRS also provides group support to facilitate collaborative research and meta-data management to support the organization of research activities.

DRS is a free to use software system that operates on Windows and Mac OS X operating systems. It has garnered broad interest in a wide variety of fields including HCI and ubiquitous computing, learning science, corpus linguistics, informatics, science and technology studies, performing arts studies, and qualitative research. Thus, the software has been used to conduct a range of substantive research, including studies of end-user programming (Starbird and Palen, 2011), the social use of spectator interfaces (Reeves, 2011) and multi-user touch surfaces (FitzGerald, 2012), novel amusement park rides (Schnädelbach et al., 2008), uses of domestic broadband and home networks (Rodden et al., 2009), crisis management (Palen et al., 2009), video conferencing (Allan and Thorns, 2008), new media performances (Giannachi and Benford, 2011), pervasive games (Foster et al., 2010), healthcare training (Weal et al., 2009), educational uses of virtual environments (Brundell et al., 2008) and multi-modal communication (Knight, 2011), and it has been drawn upon by social scientists to shape methodological debates around computing and visual methods (Zeitlyn, 2011; Spencer, 2010; Prosser, 2011). Despite the perceived salience of DRS to a wide variety of research endeavours it is, however, essentially a prototype not a production system. Its purpose has been to show the *possibilities* for social research of digital records, not to build commercial tools. In this respect, DRS has also inspired the development of new tools to support performance studies (Giannachi et al., 2011) and information visualization (Morrison et al., 2009), and driven burgeoning interest in the analytic purchase of new forms of data capture and use in the CAQDAS community, in particular (Silver and Lewins, 2010; Silver and Patashnick, 2011; Fielding, 2012). Below we elaborate the work that has driven broad interest in the potential of digital records to add value to social research and to further our understanding of life in the digital society.

9.2 WHAT IS A DIGITAL RECORD?

Twenty-first century life is increasingly conducted through the use of digital devices and services. We carry an expanding array of personal digital devices; computing networks are situated in our homes and workplaces; and we interact via a complex digital infrastructure in almost every environment we spend time in. Increasingly, our homes, our workplaces, and the public spaces we inhabit are populated by a digital infrastructure, which enables a plethora of devices to communicate with one other. Some of these devices are personal. They belong to us and are used by us; others are part of the organizations and institutions we rub up against and interact with in the course of our everyday lives. The underlying digital infrastructure is embedded in our environment, our streets, our buildings, our cars, our homes and our workspaces. This largely invisible infrastructure and the more tangible array of devices that hang off it are capable of creating records of *our activities*. Consider the following scenario, by way of example, which elaborates a mundane range of activities that generate digital records.

As part of Mary's morning routine she checks the weather forecast on the Internet in order to help her decide what to wear today. She has breakfast and sorts through her email while drinking her coffee before heading off to work. Mary drives to work, being careful not to go too fast through the average speed camera traps that line parts of the route. Today she is going to see a new client and she uses her smartphone to navigate to the client's address and to make a hands free call apprising him of her ETA in the face of heavy traffic. During her meeting with the client she uses her laptop to present and discuss various documents and emails notes to herself for future reference. Mary then goes to her own workplace to type up her notes and initiate next actions for the client. She enters the building by swiping a smartcard at the main door. She then logs on to a desktop computer and starts work. As she works she receives and responds to a text message from her boyfriend, Joe, arranging a place to meet after work for a drink. After Mary and Joe leave the pub they go and pick up a ready meal from the Sainsbury's supermarket near Mary's house, which she pays for with her credit card and collects reward points on her Nectar card. The CCTV on the streets makes Mary feel safer as the couple walk back to her flat. The couple eat their dinner while watching a programme on iPlayer before settling down for the night.

Not necessarily a typical day for you or me but there are a great many *familiar* features of this scenario that punctuate our everyday lives. Less familiar perhaps are the digital records that we produce as we go about our everyday business. At every twist and turn in Mary's day she leaves behind digital traces that elaborate where she has been, what she has been doing and even with whom. Her checking the weather forecast in the morning creates an entry in her web history log; sorting of email is recorded by the email server; speed cameras record her car registration and calculate her speed, her smartphone creates a GPS log of the route to the client and the phone call made; her laptop logs what documents she uses and the client's WiFi network logs traffic sent through it, Mary's entry into her own building is logged by the smartcard access system and the computing network as she logs on to the desktop computer, her smartphone creates a log of SMS messages, Sainsbury's, Nectar Card and her credit card company create various logs of her purchasing habits, the CCTV records her movements home, and her home network and internet browser log online activities as the couple eat their dinner. Digital records are being created throughout our day by the numerous devices and digital infrastructures that we interact with, whether we are cognizant of it or not. Any and most of the digital devices we use can – and do – record a whole range of our activities, our movements, our interactions and connections.

Digital records reflect the things we do with our devices in the environments we inhabit. They elaborate our communications, movements, purchases, and information-seeking behaviour. Our communications include email, SMS and IM, phone and video calls conducted across a variety of devices including smartphones, laptops, desktop PC, tablets and even landlines, and exploiting either commercial phone networks or our home network with a broadband connection. Our movements through buildings and along streets are recorded through the GPS satellite network accessed through smartphones and tablets. Our movements are also recorded via 3G, Bluetooth and WiFi networks, and CCTV is routinely used to track movements throughout spaces and across transport networks. Our movements in and out of buildings may be recorded through a variety of sensors and smartcard systems. The purchases that we make are recorded by vendors regardless of location, that is, whether we are in a shop or using the Internet. Purchases are also recorded by the financial organizations that support them, our credit card companies and banks. Our activities on the Internet are recorded locally on the device that we use to browse and search it, however, they are also recorded by the Internet service provider, by the particular service we are using, by third party services which reuse our online content, and even by government and security organizations. We call all of these digital records 'logs' or 'log files'. Logs are specific to the device that recorded them. For example, a smartphone GPS system may record spatial coordinates with an associated timestamp; a web browser might record the user, timestamp and URL of the site visited.

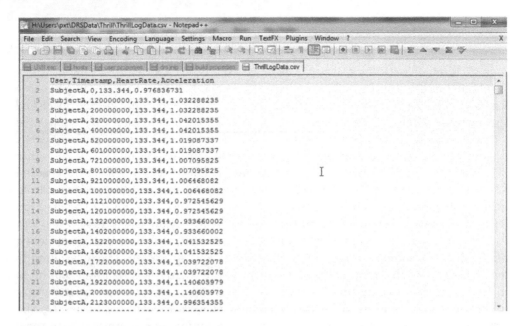

Figure 9.1   Example log file

As powerful a resource as they may be, log files are opaque. No doubt this will come as relief to many, the ethics of exploiting digital records are, of course, very important (see Chapter 12), but as one can see from the example (Figure 9.1), log files are quite unintelligible in their 'raw' state. The example displays the general character of a log file. It consists of several columns containing data that relate to one another – information – which is understandable to *whoever designed the recording system*. The initial challenge with logs, at least if we wish to exploit the rich seams of data they contain, is how to make them intelligible or accountable to *others* if they are to be of any value to social research? Of particular value is the potential to exploit them alongside traditional forms of social science research data, especially that routinely exploited by qualitative research. Logs preserve human and system interactions for subsequent analysis and provide the tangible possibility of augmenting traditional forms of data collection and analysis. They can be stored, archived, managed, manipulated, and replayed in much the same way that video data can be replayed to 'go back to' and 'go back over' what took place. Log files add value to the research endeavour by recording traces of the human interaction conducted through the increasingly pervasive use of computational systems and devices. Traditional forms of data capture only a partial record of such routine events and this underscores the potential of logs to add value to social research investigations.

Not only are raw logs unintelligible to anyone but a technical expert, they are also often very large – some log files generated in efforts to understand the use of home networks (Rodden et al., 2009), for example, contain over 20,000 records of unique web requests *per day*, that is separate records of URLs that devices on the network have connected to. While users of the network don't see this – they are only cognizant of the particular services they access (e.g., iPlayer, Facebook, Skype, etc.) web pages consist of many parts (images, adverts, banners, etc.) which might be actually downloaded from numerous web addresses, even though the final result looks like a single item. Also, many websites also regularly update themselves without user input, which results in further web requests being recorded. In addition to being unintelligible, raw logs are often very *'noisy'*. Depending on how the logging system was designed, and the purposes of the designer, there can be a great deal of information that is of limited value to social science researchers. For example, network records are often designed by system administrators for the purposes of comprehensively recording the performance of servers. Such logs may include huge amounts of information irrelevant to a social scientist. Logs may also be *fragmentary*. Recording may be interrupted and when looking at multiple logs from the same context, but recorded on different devices, there can be asynchronies and significant variations in the frequency of log entries.

There are then several problems that beset the use of systems logs (intelligibility, noise, size and fragmentation) and we need to be able to address these if we are to transform them into resources that are available for analysis. The initial approach in HCI towards resolving these issues was to 'clean' the logs by removing irrelevant log entries to reduce noise, to create bespoke 'log viewers' to visualize remaining content and make it intelligible, and to combine the resulting representations with time-based resources (audio and video recordings) generated by researchers in the field to help cover gaps and round out the picture of human interaction (Brown et al., 2003; Barkhuus et al., 2005; Benford et al., 2005). There are two key problems with using bespoke log viewers, however. Firstly, to make one requires significant programming skills and takes a considerable amount of time. Secondly, there may be limited access to the software, and even less to the people who designed it, and this inhibits our understanding of the technical details contained in a log, that is, what the log content actually refers to and means. This may seem trivial but understanding exactly what a time code, for example, represents when looking at a log from the past is not obvious – it's about time, yes, but the timing of what? Therefore, and ideally, we want general-purpose viewers that are open to a broad set of users. In the past, general-purpose tools for dealing with logs were typically limited to spreadsheets and statistical analysis packages. If we are to fully exploit the potential of logs there is a need to find some way to turn the streams of numbers and text they contain into something we can understand. In short, we need a new *method of representation* that will make logs accountable to social researchers and developing this solution was the driving force behind the design of DRS.

9.3 MAKING LOGS ACCOUNTABLE

The Digital Replay System (DRS) is a cross platform tool developed to handle system logs and built with a view to supporting qualitative analysis with an element of quantification. DRS supports the importation, viewing, synchronization, replaying, annotation, and coding of heterogeneous datasets. It functions through organizing and relating multi-modal records in a database. Importing logs into a database is a complex task because logs are rarely in a standard format. They can, however, generally be distinguished as being one of two basic types: *state* and *event*. State logs contain the type of data that can be used to reconstruct the internal workings of a system at any given time and are characterized by being representable within a single consistent database table. They essentially come in two forms *regular* and *irregular* because data is sampled either at regular or irregular intervals. State data is well-suited for display on certain types of graphs such as time series. The fact that state data can be stored in a single table makes handling it relatively simple for log viewers. Conversely, we have event type data. Event data typically describes irregular discrete occurrences. While in some cases it may be suitable to describe this data as irregular state data, the size of the table necessarily increases with the number and complexity of events. This method is more suitable for recording events that either happen or don't, user interface interactions for instance. A simple example is that of a thermometer application. It runs constantly, but the user must press a button to check the temperature. The temperature is regularly sampled and stored as state data, the user's checking of the values as event data. Assuming we sample every 30 seconds, we have a regular state value that can be plotted easily on a time series. We can similarly plot the user's interactions with the system on an event series. Selecting a user interaction event in the event series, we will be able to look up the last sampled state at that particular time.

This simple separation of logging types leads to an extensible, generalized architecture for storing logged data in a database. With that standardized system we can significantly reduce the complexity required for viewer components to be able to handle the data. This approach (encapsulated in DRS) is sufficiently flexible to handle virtually any type of system log. We call this system the 'log file workbench', which processes raw log files and turns them into usable database tables. The raw log file shown in Figure 9.1 consists of a digital record generated by riders on a fairground attraction collected as part of the Thrill project; a public understanding of science project conducted at the Science Museum in London in October 2006 (Walker, 2006). The project exploited a telemetry system consisting of accelerometers, heart rate monitors, and head mounted video cameras to explore and visualize to the public embodied characteristics of 'pleasure, frisson, and excitement' (Walker, 2006) in an engaging way. The log file contains a record of subject identity, time of the log entry, the subject's heart rate and acceleration at each timed entry. Importing the log file into a database allows it to be re-represented and its content to be visualized. Figure 9.2, for example, re-represents the heart rate in a line chart and plots it against the time series (running horizontally).

The representation in Figure 9.2 may seem prosaic. However, most chart generation systems, such as those provided by Microsoft Excel, create discrete charts that are not well connected to the related data. If they are linked to a selection of data, then they are not linked to any other charts. In DRS, charts are intrinsically *connected to each other*, and also allow for both *dynamic* and *interactive selection*. Figure 9.3, for example, shows a histogram of all heart rates of all subjects (bottom left), when any part of the histogram is selected acceleration is displayed for that data point (top right) and heart rate (bottom right). Two different time series are shown as acceleration and heart rate are represented through different sets of numbers (heart rate is typically around 100, acceleration is 0–1); consequently acceleration loses its clarity if it is represented on one chart with heart rate. The histogram shows the distribution of heart rate samples (not time), so picking one towards the right hand side of the histogram when the ride is still moving displays a relatively high heart rate as visualized in the bottom right display and acceleration at that point in the top right display.

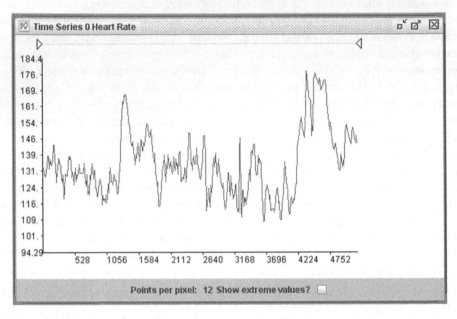

Figure 9.2　Re-representing logs: a line chart visualizing heart rate over time

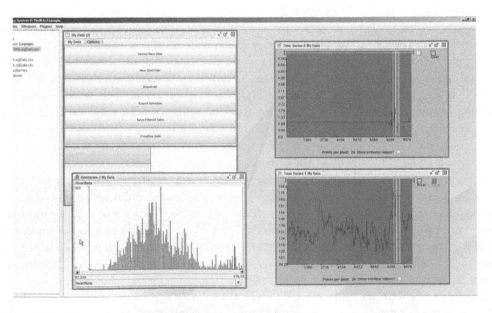

Figure 9.3　Connected and dynamic interactive charts

DRS enables much richer forms of representation and re-representation than existing tools. It allows researchers to visualize the content of system logs, to create multiple 'linked' representations of their content, and to interact with and interrogate multiple representations in fine-grained detail. Making system logs accountable to social research requires more than visualizing content, however. There is also a need to enable researchers to combine logs with more traditional datasets to support the production of 'thick' descriptions (Crabtree et al., 2006b). DRS supports thick description by enabling researchers to add contextual data and to synchronize it with log content.

9.3.1 Adding Context to Logs

DRS supports the widespread practice of *bricolage* (Denzin and Lincoln, 2005), where heterogeneous forms of data are combined into a cohesive corpus of analytic materials. Thus, social researchers can combine log file content with audio-visual materials and annotations (fieldnotes, transcriptions and codes). DRS provides an approach to data curation which allows researchers to combine related data sources into 'projects' and perform discrete 'analyses' upon all or subsets of those data (Figure 9.4). Data in DRS are synchronized primarily by *time* and so each analysis in a DRS project has its own abstract timeline. The timeline allows data to be replayed with a series of controls (such as play, pause, rewind, etc.), not dissimilar to a video recorder, through a tool called the 'track viewer'. Data sources are arranged on the timeline according to:

- Explicit temporal information contained in the data (e.g. start/end of videos).
- Direct links between resources (e.g. coding tracks associated with movies).
- User specified relationships between resources.

When viewing all these resources together, synchronization is important because it allows the researcher to cue any visualization component with any other. Thus,

- Moving the timeline in the track viewer synchronizes the playback point on *all* time-based data items associated with an analysis.
- Selecting an utterance in a transcription synchronizes *all* other time-based data items in the analysis to the time the utterance occurred.
- Making a selection on a graph synchronizes *all* time-based data items in an analysis to the first selected value and replicates the selection on other charts.

In short, having synchronized multiple data items together, whichever item the user selects and views, is coordinated with all other data items in an analysis: if one piece of video is selected, the others play along with it insofar as their timings correspond, as do the transcripts associated with the dataset and any log visualizations; alternatively, the user may scroll through a transcript and select utterances and this will take them to relevant sequences of video where the utterance occurred or which are related to the utterance; or the user may select a point in a line chart and all other media relevant to that point will be synchronized with it. DRS will also support synchronization and dynamic linking between multiple instances of data types. That means that multiple videos, transcriptions, and log viewers can be synchronized and replayed side-by-side, the only constraint being the processing power of the host machine and screen size.

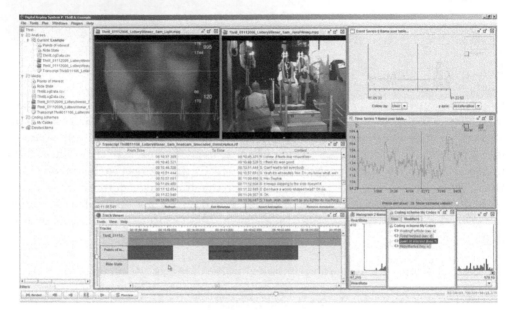

Figure 9.4 Synchronizing heterogeneous data

Annotations may also be added to the track viewer to thicken up the dataset and support analytic work and interpretation. Notes, codes and other textual 'mark ups' may be inserted by the researcher and be associated with particular events contained within a data item (e.g., a short sequence of video, an utterance in a transcript, or a photograph), which in turn is or may be synchronized with other data items as outlined above. Figure 9.4 shows a set of codes that have been applied to the dataset in the track viewer – in the box to the right of the track viewer, overlaying a histogram. Essentially, annotation involves anchoring 'subjects' (textual descriptions of interesting content) with 'regions' (stretches of time); Figure 9.5 provides a schematic of the arrangement. The 'interesting content' is the subject matter of the annotation – this can consist of either narrative descriptors or predetermined analytic codes – which is anchored to the region of time to which it applies within the data or 'media' item being annotated.

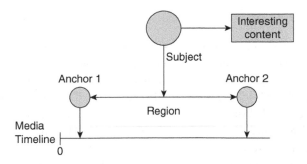

Figure 9.5   Annotation schema

Annotations are organized into annotation sets (Figure 9.5). An annotation set could be a transcription, a set of non-overlapping textual annotations arranged in temporal order, or a set of pre-determined codes signifying behaviours observed in the data (e.g., types of utterance, bodily movements, gestures, etc.). In the case of codes, the set of codes (the coding scheme) from which annotations are selected are constructed in advance of their application. Annotation sets are associated and viewed alongside other data through code tracks and the track viewer. In the example track viewer shown in Figure 9.6, the two upper tracks are transcription annotation sets, the two lower tracks are coding tracks, which show when certain behaviours are taking place (smiling, frowning, grimacing, etc.).

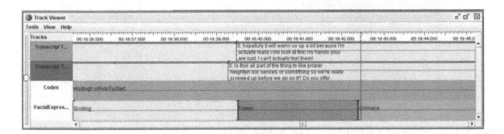

Figure 9.6   Annotation sets and coding tracks

Multiple coding tracks can be created to enable coding of concurrent actions and events. Codes can be applied while the video is playing through keyboard commands, or they can be applied by selecting stretches of time on the timeline and inserting them. The range and organization of codes is entirely controlled by the researcher who designs the coding scheme. There are a number of preselected code types (e.g., fixed length or variable length). These are aids to the researcher, but any type of code can be created and used. It is important to note that due to the design of the DRS database, annotations are treated in the same way as log file data and can similarly be *visualized*. This means that charts and graphs can be generated through coding to represent numerical frequencies and patterns within a dataset.

9.3.2 Thick Description

DRS supports thick description via the 'document viewer' (Figure 9.7), which can be used to create *live texts*. The document viewer allows social researchers to create rich multi-media documents whose content is connected to the underlying dataset and annotations. Thus, video, photos, and transcripts can be embedded in the document alongside textual descriptions and these are linked to the datasets they are drawn from, which means that they can be replayed and re-inspected to support the production of analytic and interpretive accounts. Codes can also be applied within the document viewer, enabling researchers to mark up transcriptions and narrative descriptions within the live text. This means that coded events can be indexed, that the document can be searched, and specific instances of coded events can be readily replayed and reviewed. Thus, the document viewer is both a resource for constructing texts and for conducting analytic work involved in their production.

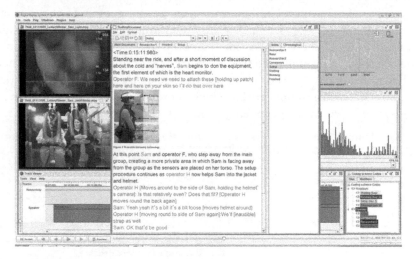

Figure 9.7   Thick description – creating live texts

To summarize, DRS elaborates potential ways in which digital records may be exploited through a suite of software tools that make system logs accountable to social research. These included tools for importing and visualizing system logs, synchronizing them with audio-visual resources and transcriptions, coding heterogeneous datasets, and creating thick descriptions. There is more to new forms of digital social research than this, however, and it is towards the elaboration of further possibilities that we turn below.

9.4 EXTENDING DRS – MOBILE AND LOCATION-BASED DATA

Social interaction is increasingly conducted through the use of mobile devices, particularly smartphones and pads. In addition to interactional content, these kinds of devices also log locational data. Widespread awareness of this was raised by a battery of scare stories about the 'hidden' tracking capabilities of smartphones (see Williams (2011), for example). The potential to track users certainly exists, and raises important ethical issues both for society and the developers of computing infrastructures and systems (Borenstein, 2008). A benign assessment would be that smartphones and tablets are designed to exploit location not in order to spy on people, but to deliver 'contextually relevant' services to them – i.e., services that are perceived as relevant to the user's current location (e.g., WiFi hotspots, maps, cafés and shops, etc.).[1] In principle, however, this logging capability means that it is possible, with user consent, to reconstruct people's movements around the world and inspect the services they access and use at various locations as they go about their everyday lives. It is also possible to log 'geo-tagged' content – i.e., photographs, videos, audio recordings, notes, and routes, etc. – to enable social researchers or participants in a study to explicitly generate data through the use of smartphones and tablets. Mobile and location-based data and data logging may, then, provide an effective means for social scientists to foster broader participation in research, and the location data generated by participants through the use of mobile devices can, in turn, provide a resource for organizing, querying, filtering, and interrogating the datasets they generate.

The potential of mobile and location-based data was explored in the context of DRS development by corpus linguists. Having already demonstrated the salience of multi-modal corpora (Adolphs and Carter, 2007; Knight, 2011), researchers sought to explore the purchase of mobile and locational data to understanding language-in-context. Seen from a linguistic perspective, mobile and location-based data provide a potential means of exploring patterns of language use across speakers, different modes of interaction, time, and place. In turn, this opens up the possibility of developing a better understanding of the importance of contextual features of discourse, marking a significant step-change in the potential for linguistic research. Developing understandings of language-in-context is a complex matter however, as the process of capturing, representing and defining context is difficult. Context is not a fixed or easily specifiable concept but dynamic and always changing (Goodwin, 2000). It combines not only extrinsic social, cultural and interactive factors but also intrinsic cognitive, affective and conative factors (Duranti and Goodwin, 1992; Kopytko, 2003; Fetzer, 2004). Context is therefore understood as everything *outside* of an utterance or expression itself that is necessary for its effective interpretation (Heylighen and Dewaele, 2003).

There is broad interest in linguistics, and in other disciplines too, to develop a 'multifaceted picture' of context that 'integrates' linguistic features of discourse (vocabulary, syntax, rhetorical structures, etc.) with salient features of the external discursive situation (the speakers, hearers, time and place of the exchange, etc.) and the sociocultural knowledge which the researcher draws upon to interpret language-in-context (Bazzanella, 2002). In exploring this challenge, linguists involved in the development of DRS set out to collect a corpus of materials that would enable them to inspect 'a day in the life' of a language user, gathering discourse across different spaces, places and

---

[1]It must also be acknowledged that this information is often to create location-specific advertisements; might be logged without the user's consent/knowledge, and sold so third parties. (For a discussion see, e.g., http://techcrunch.com/2014/04/18/facebook-location-advertising.)

modes of interaction (rather than just from fixed and static locations) as a means of elaborating core elements of discursive context. Data was initially gathered through a collection of recording devices (including a smartphone for recording location data, a camera for video and photographs, and an audio recorder) and assembled into a coherent dataset using DRS after the event. However, dissatisfaction with the synchronization challenges associated with collecting data streams from multiple devices, as well as the need to actually carry and coordinate the use of those devices, shaped the development of a smartphone application called 'fieldwork tracker' (Figure 9.8), a tool designed to do the work of several devices at once in a single, portable, device.

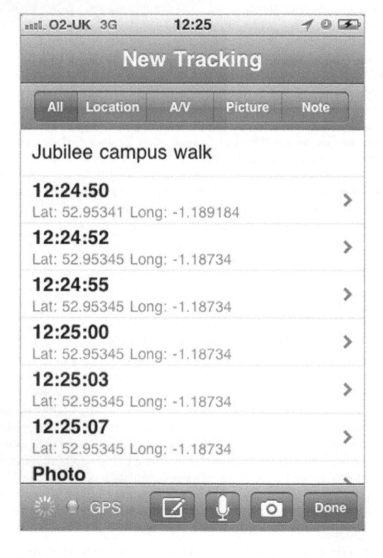

Figure 9.8   Fieldwork tracker

Fieldwork tracker is a smartphone application that creates detailed location-based logs. It was developed to enable researchers or participants in a study to collect data through a simple multi-function device which allows for the automated synchronization of data with DRS. Logs have unique names and record geo-tagged images, video, audio and textual notes. They also contain routes logged via GPS. Device time is automatically synched computationally, which means that data from multiple devices can be systematically synchronized. Captured logs – such as that shown in Figure 9.9 – can be uploaded either by email or through a Dropbox account and then be imported into DRS.

	A	B	C	D	E	F	G	H	I
1	User	Timestamp	Latitude	Longitude	HorizontalAccuracy	Altitude	VerticalAccuracy	MediaFilename	MediaTitle
2	F	0	52.965777	-1.168422	65	0	-1	null	null
3	F	0	52.96577	-1.168439	65	0	-1	null	null
4	F	2	52.965767	-1.168475	65	0	-1	null	null
5	F	3	52.965767	-1.168475	65	0	-1	null	null
6	F	17	52.965752	-1.168529	65	0	-1	null	null
7	F	31	52.965752	-1.168529	65	0	-1	null	null
8	F	44	52.965746	-1.168579	65	0	-1	null	null
9	F	58	52.965746	-1.168579	65	0	-1	null	null
10	F	72	52.965756	-1.168502	65	0	-1	null	null
11	F	81	52.965756	-1.168502	65	0	-1	2010-12-15 10:20:43	null
12	F	85	52.965785	-1.168402	65	0	-1	null	null
13	F	99	52.965785	-1.168402	65	0	-1	null	null
14	F	113	52.965857	-1.16842	78.409595	0	-1	null	null
15	F	126	52.965857	-1.16842	78.409595	0	-1	null	null
16	F	140	52.96578	-1.168451	65	0	-1	null	null
17	F	154	52.96578	-1.168451	65	0	-1	null	null
18	F	167	52.96578	-1.168451	65	0	-1	null	null
19	F	181	52.96578	-1.168451	65	0	-1	null	null
20	F	194	52.96577	-1.168444	65	0	-1	null	null
21	F	208	52.965858	-1.16828	65	0	-1	null	null
22	F	214	52.965858	-1.16828	65	0	-1	null	null
23	F	228	52.965858	-1.16828	65	0	-1	null	null
24	F	232	52.965858	-1.16828	65	0	-1	null	null
25	F	246	52.96578	-1.168398	65	0	-1	null	null

Figure 9.9 Fieldwork tracker log file (an example)

The example field tracker log file is from a study of visitor interaction at the 2010 British Art Show. The interactions of three pairs of gallery visitors were tracked and recorded resulting in over 10 hours of data being generated, including video and photographic data generated by the participants themselves. The data elaborated interactions involved in way-finding between the various galleries involved in the arts show, planning engagement with exhibits, viewing art works, coordinating viewing as a pair, and linguistic variations as the pairs made their way through various changing contexts and social encounters (e.g., as they moved from the home, through the streets and gallery and engaged with different parties including friends, acquaintances, and strangers).

Because fieldwork tracker and DRS were designed to function together, data does not have to be processed through the log file workbench as outlined previously. Instead, DRS supports 'one click' imports of fieldwork tracker logs. All geo-tagged data collected using the fieldwork tracker are uploaded into a DRS project and automatically represented at the associated point on a map to display the location where they were gathered. This process includes GPS routes generated by researchers or participants (Figure 9.10).

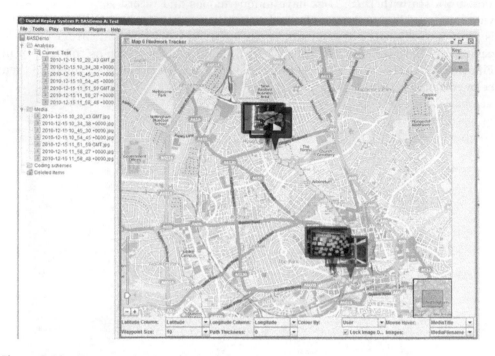

Figure 9.10   Representing geo-located data

Audio-visual data collected through other means (e.g., through a standard video camera or audio recorder) can also be synchronized with the map data. Then, as the video or audio is replayed, the relevant points on the map at which these extraneous recordings were made are highlighted, which helps tie the conversation to the location it took place. From a corpus linguistic perspective, with data in hand, the next step in such a study is to transcribe the audio. This can be done within DRS, which enables time-stamped annotations within a transcript (i.e., individual turns at talk) to be tied both to their specific temporal position in the audio track and to the geo-tagged locations within the map where they occurred.

9.4.1 Corpus Analyses of the Data

Corpus linguistics is a 'mixed methods' approach – i.e. a combination of qualitative and quantitative methods – utilized in the study of textual records, including transcriptions, of naturally occurring language. These records are called 'corpora'. They provide the means for investigating linguistic patterns and the semantic, grammatical and prosodic associations of lexical items across large bodies of language-in-use. Multi-modal corpora have extended the research focus beyond text to incorporate physical gestures (Adolphs and Carter, 2007), and these are themselves being extended to incorporate 'ubiquitous' mobile and location-based resources to further elaborate the real world character of language-in-context (Adolphs et al., 2011). The typical way into the analysis of corpus data primarily involves profiling the rate of use of linguistic terms and phrases. This basic approach can be used to identify particular patterns of usage of, for example, specific parts of speech by given speakers in given locations, or by a particular speaker over time, or to identify the rate at which lexemes are used by a population (i.e., across an entire corpus). DRS supports this profiling by enabling the construction of word frequency tables. These show the range of words within a corpus and the frequencies with which they occur (Figure 9.11).

Figure 9.11   Creating a frequency table of words

Concordancing Key Words In Context (KWIC) is also a standard approach used by corpus linguists. A concordance is an output derived from searching for a specific word or phrase in a corpus. It lists the incidence of words identified in frequency tables and situates them within the surrounding textual environment or utterances in which they occur. Concordance can be used to examine collocation in a corpus as well as colligation – i.e. the co-occurrence of grammatical choices in corpora. Concordancers are thus used to identify instances of a lexeme within a corpus, providing details of the immediate lexical co-text and wider context in which it is used. Figure 9.12 presents a concordance of the word 'yeah', listing the number of times it occurred in arts show corpus and showing the utterances in which it is embedded and used.

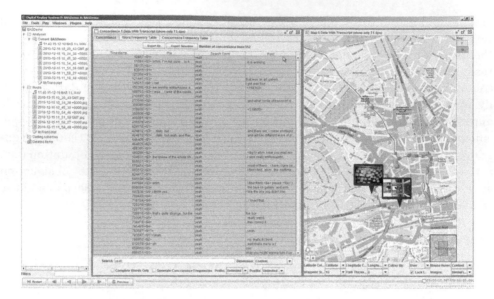

Figure 9.12 Simultaneous concordance

The synchronization, visualization, transcription, frequency tables and concordance tools provided by DRS enable interrogation of the location-based data captured by the field tracker during the arts show study. Thus, DRS supported linguistic investigation of some of the basic differences between the use of deictic markers within the art galleries in comparison to their use externally when participants were planning routes and walking between them. Deictic markers are grammatical function words, such as personal pronouns (e.g., 'you', 'it', 'them', 'I', 'we'), determiners (e.g., 'the', 'and', 'a') and demonstrative directive adverbs (e.g., 'this' and 'that'). Deictic markers are used to refer to speakers, objects, and incidents in discourse according to their specific spatial and temporal locations. In the arts show study, we worked on the premise that we would expect to see a general increase in the use of location-based deictic markers when participants were inside the museums (i.e. those with some form of spatial reference such as 'this', 'that' and 'here') and personal pronouns when participants are outside the museums negotiating their route between them due to the interactive and collaborative nature of the activity. Initial results suggest that this hypothesis was correct. Based on the GPS information, locations on the map could be browsed, highlighted and classified as 'inside' or 'outside' locations. Separate data log tables could be generated (subcorpora as it were), based on this classification and utilized as a way of filtering the data for corpus-based analyses. DRS supports the use of simultaneous concordancing facilities, which provides the means to search for key terms across multiple data logs instantly, thus enabling the researcher to compare and contrast the frequency, co-text and discursive context of deictic markers. Based on this process, we discovered that when counted together, the personal pronouns were used at a significantly lower rate inside the galleries, while demonstrative directive adverbs were used at a significantly higher rate outside the galleries. There was no significant difference seen in the use of determiners across the different contexts (Adolphs et al., 2011).

This location-based approach is novel to corpus-based research. The notion of locational context to date has been restricted to static descriptive categories, (e.g., 'home' and 'work'), rather than accurate GPS defined, geographically based definitions. Consequently, it has not been possible to account for what happens in the spaces between home and work, for example, and the exact points where one changes to another, given that the fluidity of context in the wild is difficult to capture manually and through fieldnotes alone. The additional layer of locational information that can now be made available provides the opportunity to carry out more detailed descriptions of language use according to flexible descriptors generated through the analysis of sub-corpora, which can be created and redefined as often as desired, and help the corpus linguist develop more accurate accounts of the real world character of discourse. Ultimately, tools and resources that enable corpus linguists to factor context into their analysis help to generate useful insights into the extent to which everyday language and communicative choices are determined by different spatial, temporal and social contexts (Adolphs et al., 2011).

9.5 FURTHER DEVELOPMENT OF DRS – CROWDSOURCING DATA

The potential of digital records to enhance social research may be further leveraged through the 'crowdsourcing' of data. Crowdsourcing is a distributed approach to problem-solving that increasingly exploits digital technologies as means of involving the public in research. The approach is increasingly being used in business (e.g., Mechanical Turk, Crowdflower, Microtask), science (e.g., DREAM, Galaxy Zoo, The Open Source Science Project), journalism and documentary film (e.g., Demotix, the *Guardian*'s investigation into the MP expense scandal in the UK, and Kevin MacDonald's acclaimed documentary Life in a Day), community engagement projects (e.g., Mapping for Change, Strandlines, Communities 2.0), culture and heritage (e.g., Tate Britain's Art Maps project, Victoria and Albert Museum's Help Improve Search the Collections project, and the British Museum's History of the World project) and the humanities (e.g., The World Archives project, The Great War Archive, and Transcribe Bentham). Crowdsourcing is of increasing interest to a broad range of agencies and actors across society, yet uptake in the social sciences has been less pronounced. As Harris puts it,

Huge potential exists to harness the power of crowdsourcing for the study of society and human behaviors … but it's just not happening as well as it could … it seems odd that social science researchers appear to have been comparatively slow to investigate the potential of crowdsourcing … social research could be enhanced by the involvement of the public – from helping to set research agendas, contributing to and helping to analyse data sets, to formalizing findings and conclusions. Social science issues are human issues, after all – they are about how we relate to each and organize our society and economy – so there seems to be a natural fit with crowdsourcing that's largely being overlooked. This raises some obvious and legitimate concerns – from representation to research ethics and integrity – but none of these seem insurmountable. Indeed, social scientists would surely benefit from greater public engagement with their work. The prize is surely quicker, cheaper and more imaginative research – the findings from which could benefit us all. (Harris, 2012)

Crowdsourcing provides the opportunity to engage the public in social research and provides access to rich and varied datasets, though they do tend to be rather less multi-modal in nature. By way of example, both of what crowdsourcing datasets may look like and how they may be purposed in DRS, consider a crowdsourced dataset generated during the Haiti earthquake disaster of 2009. The dataset was created using the Ushahidi crowdsourcing platform, a free to use Open Source online and mobile service available to anyone, anywhere.[2] The Haiti dataset consists of over 3,600 incident reports submitted to Ushahidi in the aftermath of the earthquake by civilians, news agencies and aid workers. Messages could be sent via SMS, email, Twitter or submitted online via the Ushahidi website. Each message was verified by an administrator and given location and timestamp if it did not already contain this information. These geo-referenced messages are then used to create a crisis map displaying the location of incidents. The collection of messages is stored in a comma-separated values or CSV file, which enables subsequent analysis. The CSV file contains the following data about each message submitted:

- Incident number
- Descriptive title
- Category (from one of eight main categories and 25 sub categories)
- Time and date
- Whether it has been verified or not
- A full description of the event
- The location (both numerical and descriptive).

As the data is CVS format it can be imported into DRS via the log file workbench (Tab Separated Value or TSV files may also be imported directly into DRS). Locational data not only enables the messages to be plotted on a map in DRS, just as with the Ushahidi platform, but also allows them to be *filtered* on the basis of the textual descriptions and categories assigned to messages. Coupled with the visualization capabilities of DRS this enhances the researcher's ability to dynamically *inspect* and *interrogate* the dataset.

By way of example, selecting an early period of time in the event series (lower half of Figure 9.13), makes it visible in the histogram (top half of Figure 9.13) that the vast majority of incidents in all categories were reported in the immediate aftermath of the earthquake; over the first month or so (N.B., the red column in the upper half of Figure 9.13 is an automatic pre-select that indicates that these columns can be clicked on and their details viewed). Looking at the reverse – selecting from the histogram (top half of Figure 9.14), which serves as an easy *cue* for selecting a category

---

[2]http://ushahidi.com

in complex arrays of data points, makes it visible in the event series (lower half of Figure 9.14) that 'vital lines' come in distinct groups; in the immediate aftermath of the earthquake people mostly needed food, water and medical supplies, however, after a few months the principal need becomes one for shelter.

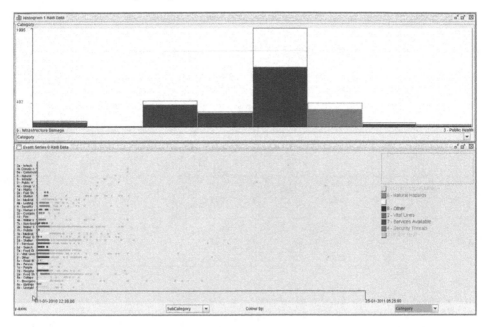

Figure 9.13   Visualizing crowdsourced data (an example)

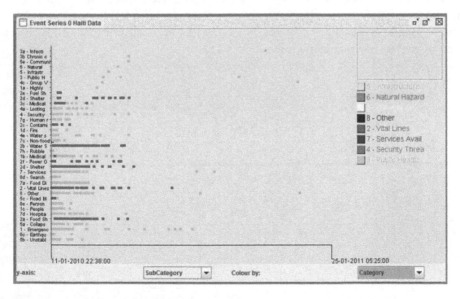

Figure 9.14   Histogram and event series showing dynamic selection and interrogation

Thus, in a few short clicks the researcher can begin to interrogate and elucidate the dataset. This may be further enhanced through the use of locational data, which enable visualizations of the spatial distribution of events (Figure 9.15).

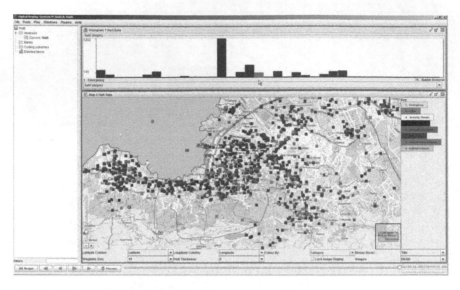

Figure 9.15   Spatial distribution of events

As Figure 9.15 makes clear, while it is possible to plot all data onto a map, there are so many points contained within a crowdsourced dataset that they tend to occlude one another. This problem can be handled by using the histogram, again as a selection tool, to display particular categories or subcategories of data. Figure 9.16, for example, displays messages relating to medical emergencies; Figure 9.17, the opening up of emergency medical clinics.

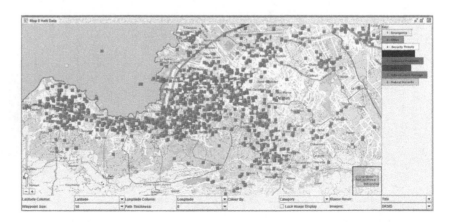

Figure 9.16   Medical emergencies

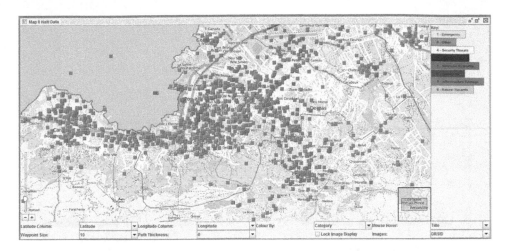

Figure 9.17   Emergency medical clinics

Comparing these maps reveals a visual correlation between the need for emergency medical care in specific locations and the emergency clinics subsequently operating in the area. The ability to quickly flick between maps enables the researcher to establish that visual correlation. While that data could easily be displayed together on the same map, there is a danger of one data set obscuring the other, especially in examples such as this where we might expect a spatial correlation.

In each of the above crowdsourcing examples, there are dropdown boxes at the bottom of the visualization. The reason for these is that all the visualizations in DRS are designed to handle lots of different dimensions and data types. They have not been created just to deal with the data represented in any single visualization, but rather to allow the researcher to 'plug in' any data column contained within a log file to any dimension of any visualization, assuming it makes sense to do so (e.g., a time series won't take a non-numeric value as a dimension because that doesn't make sense to plot). This, in turn, makes a small set of visualizations extremely flexible. Thus, while the set of categories that comes with the data is useful, the researcher may want to *define their own categories* to drill down into the data and develop their analysis. This can be achieved by adding new columns or dimensions to the data then filling these in by making and storing selections. Again by way of example, one might make a new dimension to show a separation between urban and rural incidents to see if there is a change in the distribution of incident types. To do this, the researcher needs first to add a new column to the data table, in this case one called 'location-type'. Next she uses the map to select subsets of the data that might be considered 'urban' and 'rural' (naturally the quality of the comparison depends of the granularity of selection; the more fine-grained the selection, the more accurate the results will be). She then has a new column in the dataset showing if incidents were urban or rural, which enables her to explore relationships between the two. Figure 9.18 shows that the incident count is dramatically higher in rural areas than in urban ones, but also that the general distribution of incident types is approximately equivalent.

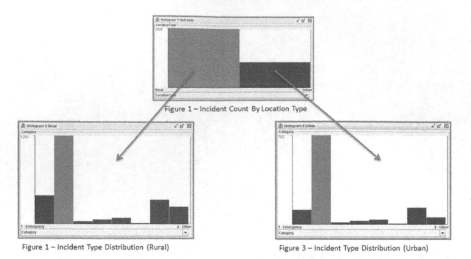

Figure 1 – Incident Count By Location Type

Figure 1 – Incident Type Distribution (Rural)

Figure 3 – Incident Type Distribution (Urban)

Figure 9.18   Creating and exploring new categories of data

Crowdsourcing provides new possibilities for social research. The kinds of facilities offered by tools like DRS provide the potential for social researchers to open up such datasets to inspection and analysis. Not only may they be filtered and interrogated through a rich array of visualizations exploiting charts, maps, event and time series, it is also possible to combine these visualizations with a broader range of data types (audio-visual and textual) and to annotate and code these heterogeneous datasets. As noted earlier in this chapter, DRS is nothing more than a prototype. It is not a robust production quality tool that will evolve over time. Rather, it is intended to demonstrate that such possibilities are achievable; that social science researchers *can* make use of digital records should they wish; that they *can* exploit the vast array of data that is 'born digital'; and that they *can* do so through an array of tools that integrate new forms of data together with traditional forms. Exploiting digital records in social research is not limited to the examples we have presented here; they are simply examples used to elaborate the possibilities. If data is recorded digitally then whatever it is it can be opened up to inspection and account. Our purpose in developing DRS has been to demonstrate ways in which software tools might support a mixture of research methods to enable a broad church of social researchers to exploit a primary source of data in contemporary life.

9.6 CONCLUSION

Everyday life in contemporary society is pervaded by computers and our interactions are increasingly mediated by them. No longer is computing restricted to the workplace; it now permeates just about every aspect of our personal and collective lives. As we go about our business on-line and on-the-streets, the burgeoning array of mobile devices the computers we use and come into contact, with generate digital footprints – i.e., records of where we have been, what we have been doing, and even with whom. These digital records may be seen as a threat to our liberty and privacy, and they may well be so if society does not control technology development. However, they also provide an unprecedented amount of data and data collection resources that can be made good and ethically responsible use of in social research. The surfacing of digital records, which makes our digital footprints visible, provides the possibility for social researchers to open up, inspect and analyse the host of digitally-mediated interactions that animate everyday life. If that possibility is to be realized it is necessary to make digital records *accountable* to a broad cohort of social researchers. Their intelligibility is currently restricted to those with technological expertise. Our purpose in this chapter has been to demonstrate that the restriction can be overcome. Our demonstration has involved elaborating the core functionality provided by the Digital Replay System (DRS), a research prototype developed to marry digital records with heterogeneous datasets and support the widespread practice of bricolage. DRS enables social researchers to combine qualitative datasets with quantitative representations of content contained within digital records, not as means of conducting statistical research (though quantitative results may be exported to SPSS for further analysis), but as a way of interrogating complex datasets (e.g., visualizing event series, frequencies, concordance, etc.). DRS is not a solution, however, but merely a demonstrator that manifests the possibility of opening up digital records for social research in the 21st century. DRS can be downloaded from the project website: http://thedrs.sourceforge.net.[3]

9.7 BIBLIOGRAPHY

Adolphs, S., Bertenthal, B., Boker, S., Carter, R., Greenhalgh, C., Herald, M., Kenny, S, Levow, G., Papke, M. and Pridmore, T. (2007) 'Integrating cyberinfrastructure into existing e-Social science research', *Proceedings of the 3rd International Conference on e-Social Science*. Ann Arbor, MI: NCeSS. Available from http://citeseerx.ist.psu.edu/viewdoc/download?doi=10.1.1.186.330&rep=rep1&type=pdf (accessed 12 Dec 2014).

Adolphs, S. and Carter, R. (2007) 'Beyond the word: new challenges in analysing corpora of spoken English', *European Journal of English Studies*, 11(2): 114–28.

Adolphs, S., Knight, D. and Carter, R. (2011) 'Capturing context for heterogeneous corpus analysis: some first steps', *International Journal of Corpus Linguistics*, 16(3): 305–24.

Allan, M. and Thorns, D. (2008) 'A methodological quest for studying interactions in advanced video conferencing environments', *Proceedings of the 4th International Conference on e-Social Science*, Manchester, NCeSS. Available from http://ir.canterbury.ac.nz/bitstream/10092/732/1/12608657_Allan%20and%20Thorns%20full%20paper%20%20final3.pdf (accessed 15 Dec 2014).

Bazzanella, C. (2002) 'The significance of context in comprehension', *Foundations of Science*, 7: 239–52.

---

[3]User support is provided by the CAQDAS Networking Project at the University of Surrey: www.surrey.ac.uk/sociology/research/researchcentres/caqdas/support/index.htm

Any party wishing to adapt and/or extend DRS can download the source code from Sourceforge: http://sourceforge.net/projects/thedrs

Barkhuus, L., Chalmers, M., Tennent, P., Hall, M., Bell, M., Sherwood, S. and Brown, B. (2005) 'Picking pockets on the lawn: the development of tactics and strategies in a mobile game', *Proceedings of the 7th International Conference on Ubiquitous Computing*. Tokyo: Springer. pp. 358–74

Benford, S., Anastasi, R., Flintham, M., Drozd, A., Crabtree, A., Greenhalgh, C., Tandavanitj, N., Adams, M. and Row-Farr, J. (2003) 'Coping with uncertainty in a location-based game', *IEEE Pervasive Computing*, 2(3): 34–41.

Benford, S., Rowland, D., Flintham, M., Drozd, A., Hull, R., Reid, J., Morrison, J. and Facer, K. (2005) 'Life on the edge: supporting collaboration in location-based experiences', *Proceedings of the SIGCHI Conference on Human Factors in Computing Systems*. Portland, OR: ACM. pp. 721–30.

Bohannon, J. (2006) 'Tracking people's electronic footprint', *Science*, 314: 914–6.

Borenstein, J. (2008) 'Privacy: a non-existent entity', *IEEE Technology and Society Magazine*, 27(4): 20–26.

Brown, B., MacColl, I., Chalmers, M., Galani, A., Randell, C. and Steed, A. (2003) 'Lessons from the lighthouse: collaboration in a shared mixed reality game', *Proceedings of the SIGCHI Conference on Human Factors in Computing Systems*. Fort Lauderdale, TX: ACM. pp. 577–85.

Brundell, P., Tennent, P., Greenhalgh, C., Knight, D., Crabtree, A., O'Malley, C., Ainsworth, S., Clarke, D., Carter, R. and Adolphs, S. (2008) 'Digital Replay System (DRS) – a tool for interaction analysis', *Proceedings of the 2008 International Conference on Learning Sciences*, Workshop 3. A Common Framework for CSCL Interaction Analysis, Utrecht, ICLS. Available from www.cs.nott.ac.uk/~axc/work/ICLS08.pdf (accessed 15 Dec 2014).

Burrell, J. and Gay, G. (2002) 'e-Graffiti: evaluating real-world use of a context-aware system', *Interacting with Computers*, 14: 301–12.

Carter, R. and Adolphs, S. (2008) 'Linking the verbal and the visual: new directions for corpus linguistics', *Language and Computers*, 64: 275–91.

Crabtree, A. and Rouncefield, M. (2005) 'Working with text logs', *Proceedings of the 1st International Conference on e-Social Science*, Manchester, NCeSS.

Crabtree, A., French, A., Greenhalgh, C. Benford, S., Chevherst, K., Fitton, D., Rouncefield, M. and Graham, C. (2006a) 'Developing digital records: early experiences of record and replay', *Computer Supported Cooperative Work: The Journal of Collaborative Computing*, 15(4): 281–319.

Crabtree, A., Benford, S., Greenhalgh, C., Tennent, P., Chalmers, M. and Brown, B. (2006b) 'Supporting ethnographic studies of ubiquitous computing in the wild', *Proceedings of the 6th Conference on Designing Interactive Systems*. University Park, PA ACM. pp. 60–9.

Crabtree, A. and Rodden, T. (2009) 'Understanding interaction in hybrid ubiquitous computing environments', *Proceedings of the 8th International Conference on Mobile and Ubiquitous Media*, Article No.1, Cambridge, ACM.

Denzin, N. and Lincoln, Y. (2005) 'Introduction: the discipline and practice of qualitative research', in .N. Denzin and Y. Lincoln (eds), *The Sage Handbook of Qualitative Research*, Thousand Oaks, CA: Sage. pp. 1–33.

Duranti, A. and Goodwin, C. (eds) (1992) *Rethinking Context: Language as an Interactive Phenomenon*, Cambridge: Cambridge University Press.

Equator IRC (2013) http://en.wikipedia.org/wiki/Equator_IRC (18 April 2015).

ESRC (2005) *Understanding New Forms of Digital Record for e-Social Science*. Available from www.esrc.ac.uk/my-esrc/grants/RES-149-25-0035/read (accessed 12 Dec 2014).

Fetzer, A. (2004) *Recontextualizing Context: Grammaticality Meets Appropriateness*, Amsterdam: Benjamins.

Fielding, N. (2012) 'The diverse worlds and research practices of qualitative software', *Forum Qualitative Sozialforschung*, 13(2), Article No. 12.

FitzGerald, E. (2012) 'Analysing video and audio data: existing approaches and new innovations', *Surface Learning Workshop*, Bristol, European Network of Excellence in TEL. Available from http://surfacelearning.org/uploads/46/FitzGerald-SurfaceLearning2012.pdf (accessed 12 Dec 2014).

Foster, J., Benford, S., Chamberlain, A., Rowland, D. and Giannachi, G. (2010) 'Riders have spoken: a practice-based approach to developing an information architecture for the archiving and replay of a mixed reality performance', *International Journal of Performance Arts & Digital Media*, 6(2): 209–23.

Fraser, M., Hindmarsh, J., Best, K., Heath, C., Biegel, G., Greenhalgh, C. and Reeves, S. (2006) 'Remote collaboration over video data: towards real-time e-Social science', *Computer Supported Cooperative Work: The Journal of Collaborative Computing*, 15(4): 257–79.

Giannachi, G. and Benford, S. (2011) *Performing Mixed Reality*. Cambridge, MA: MIT Press.

Giannachi, G., Lowood, H., Rowland, D., Benford, S. and Price, D. (2011) 'CloudPad – a cloud-based documentation and archiving tool for mixed reality artworks', *Digital Humanities 2011*, Stanford, ADHO. http://dh2011abstracts.stanford.edu/xtf/view?docId=tei/ab-154.xml;query=;brand=default (accessed 15 Dec 2014).

Goodwin, C. (2000) 'Action and embodiment within situated human interaction', *Journal of Pragmatics*, 32(10): 1489–522.

Halfpenny, P. and Procter, R. (eds) (2009) 'Special issue on e-social science', *Social Science Computer Review*, 27(4): 459–66.

Halfpenny, P. and Procter, R. (2010) 'The e-Social Science research agenda', *Philosophical Transactions of the Royal Society A: Mathematical, Physical and Engineering Sciences*, 368(1925): 3761–78.

Halloran, J., Hornecker, E., Fitzpatrick, G., Millard, D. and Weal, M. (2005) The Chawton House experience: augmenting the grounds of a historic manor house, *Proceedings of the International Workshop on Re-Thinking Technology in Museums*. Limerick, Ireland: Interaction Design Centre. pp. 54–65.

Harris, M. (2012) 'Oh man, the crowd is getting an F in social science', *Daily Crowdsource*, June. Available from http://dailycrowdsource.com/content/crowdsourcing/1158-oh-man-the-crowd-is-getting-an-f-in-social-science (accessed 15 Dec 2014).

Heylighen, F. and Dewaele, J.M. (2003) 'Variation in the contextuality of language: an empirical measure', *Foundations of* Science, 7: 293–340.

Knight, D. (2011) *Multi-modality and Active Listenership: A Corpus Approach*, London: Continuum Books.

Kopytko, R. (2003) 'What is wrong with modern accounts of context in linguistics?', *Vienna English Working* Papers, 12: 45–60.

Morrison, A., Tennent, P. and Chalmers, M. (2006) 'Coordinated visualisation of video and system log data', *Proceedings of the 4th International Conference on Coordinated and Multiple Views in Exploratory Visualization*. London: IEEE. pp. 91–102.

Morrison, A., Bell, M. and Chalmers, M. (2009) 'Visualisation of spectator activity at stadium events', *Proceeding of the 13th International Conference on Information Visualisation*. Barcelona: IEEE. pp. 219–26.

Palen, L., Vieweg, S., Liu, S. and Hughes, A. (2009) 'Crisis in a networked world', *Social Science Computer Review*, 27(4): 467–80.

Prosser, J. (2011) 'Visual methodology: towards a more seeing research', in N. Denzin and Y. Lincoln (eds) *Handbook of Qualitative Research Methods*. London: Sage. pp. 177–212.

Reeves, S. (2011) *Designing Interfaces in Public Settings*. Berlin: Springer.

Rodden, T., Tennent, P., Chalmers, M., Grinter, R., Edwards, K. and Crabtree, A. (2009) 'Homebase: developing a corpus of domestic network usage', *Proceedings of the SIGCHI Conference on Human Factors in Computing Systems*, Workshop on Home Behaviour Datasets to Advance HCI and Ubiquitous Computing Research, Boston, ACM. Available from www.cs.nott.ac.uk/~axc/work/CHI09w.pdf (accessed 15 Dec 2014).

Rogers, Y., Price, S., Fitzpatrick, G., Fleck, R., Harris, E., Smith, H., Randell, C., Muller, H., O'Malley, C., Stanton, D., Thompson, M. and Weal, M. (2004) 'Ambient wood: designing new forms of digital augmentation for learning outdoors', *Proceedings of the Conference on Interaction Design and Children*. New York: ACM. pp. 3–10.

Schnädelbach, H., Egglestone, S.R., Reeves, S., Benford, S., Walker, B. and Wright, M. (2008) 'Performing thrill', *Proceedings of the SIGCHI Conference on Human Factors in Computing Systems*. Florence: ACM. pp.1167–76.

Silver, C. and Lewins, A (2010) 'Computer assisted qualitative data analysis', in P. Peterson, E. Baker and B. McGaw, *International Encyclopedia of Education*, 3rd edition, Kidlington, Oxon: Elsevier. pp. 326–34.

Silver, C. and Patashnick, J. (2011) 'Finding fidelity: advancing audiovisual analysis using software', *Forum Qualitative Sozialforschung*, 12(1), Article No. 37.

Spencer. S. (2010) *Visual Research Methods in the Social Sciences*. Abingdon: Routledge.

Starbird, K. and Palen, L. (2011) 'More than the usual suspects: the physical self and other resources for learning to program using a 3D avatar environment', *Proceedings of iConference '11*. Seattle, ACM. pp. 614–21.

SourceForge (2007) Digital Replay System. Available from http://sourceforge.net/projects/thedrs (accessed 12 Dec 2014).

van Dijk, T.A. (ed.) (1977) *Text and Context: Explorations in the Semantics and Pragmatics of Discourse*, London: Longman.

Walker, B. (2006) 'Fairground: thrill laboratory'. Available from www.aerial.fm/docs/projects.php?id=18:0:0:0 (accessed 15 Dec 2014).

Weal, M., Michaelides, D., Page, K.,De Roure, D., Gobbi, M., Monger, E. and Martinez, F. (2009) 'Tracking and annotation in skills-based learning environments', *Proceedings of the 7th International Conference on Pervasive Computing and Communication*, Workshop on PervasivE Learning. Galveston, TX: IEEE Press. Available from http://eprints.soton.ac.uk/267020/ (accessed 15 Dec 2014).

Williams, C. (2011) 'Apple iPhone tracks users' location in hidden file', *The Telegraph*, 20th April. Available from www.telegraph.co.uk/technology/apple/8464122/Apple-iPhone-tracks-users-location-in-hidden-file.html# (accessed 15 Dec 2014).

Zeitlyn, D. (2011) 'You can't build a car with just one wheel', *First Monday*, 16(9). Available from http://firstmonday.org/htbin/cgiwrap/bin/ojs/index.php/fm/article/view/3332/3044 (accessed 15 Dec 2014).

10

SOCIAL NETWORK ANALYSIS

ROBERT ACKLAND AND JONATHAN J. H. ZHU

10.1 INTRODUCTION

The last decade has witnessed a surge in research into social networks using trace data collected from the Web. While sociologists have been studying social networks for decades, the interest in researching social networks from other disciplines (e.g., other parts of the social sciences, applied physics, computer science) has arguably been triggered by the availability of data on social interactions in social network sites such as Facebook and information sharing environments such as newsgroups, blogs, and micro-blogs (e.g., Twitter).

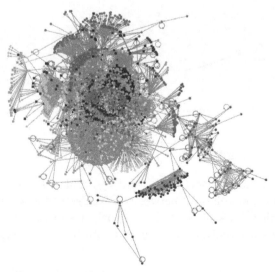

Figure 10.1   A semantic network of top hashtags from Twitter

(www.nodexlgraphgallery.org/Pages/Graph.aspx?graphID=31160)

This chapter begins with an introduction to social networks analysis (SNA), outlining the major concepts and how the 'network perspective' differs from other social scientific approaches to studying human behaviour. We then provide examples of network research using trace data, highlighting some of the methodological approaches and tools that are available for this type of research. We continue by discussing the challenges and opportunities for network research using trace data. We conclude with some recommendations for researchers who are thinking about using network analysis on how to make best use of the method.

10.2 NETWORKS AND THE RELATIONAL PERSPECTIVE FOR STUDYING BEHAVIOUR

This section provides a brief introduction to network terminology and concepts, and introduces the network or relational perspective for studying behaviour.

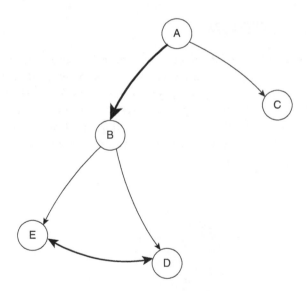

Figure 10.2   A directed and outdegree-weighted network

10.2.1 Network Terminology

A network is a set of nodes (vertices or entities) and a set of ties (edges or links) indicating connections or relations between the nodes.[1] In a social network, the network nodes are typically people and the network ties are relations between people. However, social network analysis is also used to study the behaviour of organizations

---

[1]For more on social network methods see Wasserman and Faust (2004) and Hanneman and Riddle (2005). For social network analysis in the context of social media data, see Hansen et al. (2010).

and groups. A visual representation of a social network is called a sociogram, often informally referred to as a network map (see Figure 10.2).

There are two types of attributes of nodes: graph-theoretic attributes are derived from the network (e.g., number of connections, or 'degree'), while non-graph-theoretic attributes are intrinsic to the node (e.g., gender, race, age). Discrete or categorical node attributes (e.g., race or gender) can be represented in sociograms by the colour or shape of the node, while numerical attributes (e.g., age, degree) can be represented by the size of the node.

Edges in a network can represent different connections (collaboration, kinship, friendship, citations, transactions, shared interests, etc.). There are two major types of edges. Directed edges have a clear origin and destination (e.g., person A nominates person B as an expert in a particular field, Twitter user A follows user B) and they may or may not be reciprocated. Directed edges are represented in sociograms as a line with an arrowhead indicating the direction of the tie. Undirected edges indicate a mutual relationship with no origin or destination (e.g., person A is a sibling of person B, person A is a Facebook friend of person B). By definition, undirected edges do not exist unless they are reciprocated. Edges can also have weights. An unweighted edge is where the edge either exists or not (e.g., a Facebook friendship either exists or doesn't), while a weighted edge has a value attached to it that indicates the strength of the relationship e.g., in a Twitter network a follower edge could be weighted by the number of re-tweets.

There are several types of social networks. An egocentric network (also known as an egonet, or personal network) consists of a focal node/person ('ego') and the people he or she is connected to ('alters'). A 1.0 degree egonet doesn't show connections between alters, while a 1.5 degree egonet does show connections between alters. A 2.0 degree egonet also includes people who are 2 degrees of separation from ego i.e. friends of the alters who are not also friends of the ego. In contrast, a complete network consists of a set of nodes where all possible ties between the nodes are indicated.

The type of network can also be distinguished on the basis of mode. A unimodal network contains only one type of node or vertex, while a multimodal network contains more than one type of node. A bimodal network contains exactly two types of vertices, and an example of a bimodal network is an affiliation network consisting of people and the wiki articles they have edited. In this bimodal network, people don't connect directly with people and wiki pages don't connect directly with wiki pages. However, a bimodal affiliation network can be transformed into two separate unimodal networks e.g., wiki editor-to-wiki editor and article-to-article.

Finally, multiplex networks have multiple types of edges. Indeed, most social networks are multiplex, that is, actors share more than one type of tie. For example, two people working in a firm may have a tie that describes their working relationship (e.g., person A reports to person B) but they might also be friends outside of work and hence have another type of tie that represents their affective friendship. With regards to online networks, there are also examples of multiplex networks. With Twitter we can have three types of directed edges: following relationships, 'reply to' relationships, and 'mention' relationships. Often multiplex ties are reduced to a simplex tie e.g., a tie is deemed to exist if any of the multiplex ties exists.

While sociograms are useful for providing an intuitive overview of a social network, social network researchers have developed a wide range of network metrics that are used to quantitatively describe a given social network and the actors within the network. We can distinguish between node-level and network-level metrics. Some of basic node-level metrics are:

- Indegree, Outdegree – number of inbound/outbound ties (only defined for directed networks).
- Degree – number of ties (only defined for undirected network).
- Reciprocity – indicator of the extent to which there are mutual ties between actors.
- Betweenness centrality – indicator of the extent to which an individual node plays a 'brokering' or 'bridging' role in a network and is calculated for a given node by summing up the proportion of all the shortest pathways between the other actors in the network that pass through the node.
- Closeness centrality – indicator of the extent to which a given node has short paths to all other nodes in the graph and it is thus a reasonable measure of the extent to which the node is in the 'middle' of a given network.

Some of the basic network-level metrics are:

- Network size – number of nodes in the network.
- Network density – number of network ties as proportion of the maximum possible number of network ties.
- Network inclusiveness – number of non-isolates as a proportion of the network size.
- Centralization – a network-level property that is calculated for a given node-level property and it broadly measures the distribution of importance, power or prominence among actors in a given network i.e. the extent to which the network 'revolves around' a single node or small number of nodes. The most highly centralized network is the star network, which comprises a single node (the 'hub') that connects to all other nodes, but these other nodes do not connect with one another (and hence are referred to as 'spokes').

10.2.2 Relational Social Science

Social network analysis (SNA) differs markedly from other social scientific approaches to studying human behaviour and outcomes. These differences are neatly captured in five fundamental and inter-related principles proposed by Wellman (1988), which together constitute the 'network perspective'.

First, the network perspective puts emphasis on the structure of relations, rather than the attributes of individual actors, in determining behaviour and outcomes. This can be seen clearly in the context of understanding the factors that contribute to labour market success, for example. The economic approach emphasizes human capital (e.g., experience, qualifications) as being important in determining whether a person gets a job. In contrast, the network perspective regards the person's social network as the main driver of labour market success, since networks can provide opportunities (and also impose constraints) that impact on behaviour and outcomes. In particular, Granovetter (1973) emphasizes the importance of 'weak ties' (connections with people with whom you do not share any or many friends) as potential sources of innovative and useful information in the context of labour market outcomes.

Second, the network perspective focuses on pairs of actors (known as dyads) as the unit of analysis, rather than the actors themselves. A hallmark empirical technique used in approaches that do not take a network perspective is ordinary least squares (OLS) regression. In the labour market example above, the human capital model is tested by regressing log wages on explanatory variables measuring the human capital of each individual, and in such an approach the unit of analysis is the individual. In contrast, a social networks approach to studying labour market outcomes might employ an empirical technique such as exponential random graph modelling (ERGM) where the unit of analysis is the dyad (see, e.g., Daraganova and Pattison, 2013).

While a detailed introduction to ERGMs is beyond the scope of this chapter, it is useful to think of the technique as a way of deconstructing a given network into its constituent network motifs or configurations, representing different social relations such as homophily – 'birds of a feather flock together', reciprocity – 'returning the hand of friendship', or triadic closure – 'a friend of my friend is also my friend'.[2] The technique then tests whether particular configurations occur more (or less) frequently than would be expected by chance alone. Similar to standard regression techniques, the model estimation produces parameter estimates and associated standard errors, and if a particular network configuration occurs at greater or less than chance levels, we can then infer that the associated social force has had a significant role in the development of the social network.

Third, while non-relational social science assumes that observations are independent (the error term in the labour market regression example above is assumed to be independently drawn from a normal distribution), the network perspective explicitly assumes the *interdependence* of observations. Say we have three people: Sally, Jen, Andrew. Assume that Sally and Jen are friends and Jen and Andrew are friends and we want to model the probability of a tie forming between Sally and Andrew. If we assume observations (dyads) are independent, then this would be equivalent to saying that the probability of Sally and Andrew forming a friendship is the same in this situation as it would be if Jen wasn't friends with either of them. This is clearly not plausible, since it overlooks a basic aspect of social behaviour, triadic closure.

Fourth, the network perspective recognizes that social networks can have both direct and indirect impacts on individual behaviour and outcomes. Simply put, the flow of information and resources between two people is not just dependent on their own relationship, but also on their relationships with everyone else. Smith

---

[2]See Robins et al. (2007) for an introduction to ERGM.

and Christakis (2008) review research into social networks and health and contrast the network perspective, which explicitly models the impact of indirect or supradyadic network effects on individual health, with the more standard social support approach. With the social support approach, social network effects are operationalized as individual-level measures of how helpful or supportive social contacts are in terms of financial resources, assistance with practical tasks, information, emotional contact, etc. (thus effectively involving an aggregation of the resources flowing through the dyadic ties that the individual participates in).

The principle that indirect social ties matter is also evident in Ronald Burt's work on structural holes – gaps or holes in the social structure of communication, which inhibit the flow of information between people (for a review, see Burt, 1992). Structural holes can present two types of strategic advantage, relating to brokerage and closure. With regards to the former, those people who bridge or span structural holes are more likely to gain opportunities for professional advancement because they are exposed to varying opinions, behaviours and sources of information, and may be able to combine this disparate knowledge in a way that provides productive advantage. Closure refers to the strategic advantage that is associated with not spanning a structural hole i.e. staying within a closed network where there is a high level of connectivity amongst actors (either directly or via a central person). Closed networks confer another important type of advantage to members: higher levels of trust and coordination (facilitated by high reputation costs for bad or unproductive behaviour, and increased probability that such behaviour can be detected), which can improve team effectiveness and efficiency by lowering labour and monitoring costs.

The fifth principle that underlies the network perspective is that people tend to belong to several overlapping social networks. That is, individuals tend to be members of several groups and the group boundaries are often fuzzy and hence hard to define.

10.3 EXAMPLES AND TOOLS

While almost all websites of user-generated content (UGC) are arguably online communities/networks of some sort, it is both informative and desirable for us to have a conceptual typology to delineate unique structural features for various online networks so that we can focus on 'networking' issues rather than content or functions of the websites. For that purpose, we employ a 2-by-2 scheme involving two dimensions of network ties – directionality and manifestation – to help organize the rich and fast growing body of studies on online networks.

Directionality of ties simply refers to the nature of the relations (i.e., *directed* versus *undirected*) between any pair of nodes. Manifestation of ties refers to the substantiality of the relations, with *explicit* ties formed by active acts (e.g., invitation, acceptance, reference, etc.) between the nodes whereas *implicit* ties created from inferences (e.g., co-occurrence or interactions). As shown in Table 10.1, the scheme results in four distinct types of online networks, including i) explicitly undirected ties, ii) explicitly directed ties, iii) implicitly undirected ties, and iv) implicitly directed ties.

Table 10.1 Online networks by direction and manifestation of ties

Manifestation of ties	Direction of ties	
	Undirected	**Directed**
Explicit	Friendship networks (e.g., Facebook, Google+, etc.)	Microblog networks (e.g., Twitter, Sina Weibo, etc.)
Implicit	Semantic networks (e.g., recommendation systems, social tagging systems etc.)	Newsgroups, blogs; WWW hyperlink networks

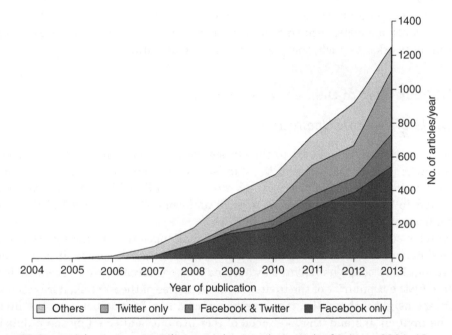

Figure 10.3 Articles on top 20 online social networks in Web of Science 2004–13

How much empirical research has each type of online network attracted? To gain a quick overview of the state of the art in online network research, we searched Web of Science (WoS) for studies that involve any of the 20 most popular social networking sites.[3] A total of 4,260 relevant articles are found between 2004 and 2013. Four discernible patterns emerge from the studies. First, an overwhelming majority (70 per cent) of the studies focused on two 'newcomers' of the top 20 list, i.e., Facebook and Twitter. Second, most (72 per cent) of the studies appeared in the last three years (2011–2013), with an increasingly accelerated growth rate (Figure 10.3). Third, more than 120 research areas (as defined by WoS) were involved, ranging from social sciences, business, and humanities to science, engineering and medicine,

---

[3]http://en.wikipedia.org/wiki/List_of_social_networking_websites.

suggesting that online social networks have become a truly multidisciplinary field of studies. Four, areas of science and technology led the studies, as shown in the top eight most active areas (each with a share of more than 5 per cent) including computer science (43 per cent), engineering (16 per cent), education (10 per cent), psychology (9 per cent), information and library science (8 per cent), business and economics (8 per cent), communication (7 per cent) and telecommunications (6 per cent). In comparison, only 2 per cent of the studies came from sociology (ranked the 13th), the traditional intellectual home of SNA.

A detailed review of the 4,200+ studies is obviously beyond the scope of the current chapter. We will instead highlight a few examples in the following sections. These studies are by no means 'typical' or 'representative' of the studies. On the contrary, they represent rather unconventional but rigorous efforts to conduct online social network analysis, resulting in new, insightful, or even disruptive, knowledge of social networks. As such, they deserve our close attention.

10.3.1 Four Types of Online Social Networks

Networks of Explicitly Undirected Ties

These networks are the closest to the classic notion of social networks, i.e., friendships that require mutual consent to establish, interactions often closed to members only, etc. As such, many of the previous studies on online friendship networks are motivated to extend existing theories, such as formation and effects of social networks, from offline settings to online settings.

Ugander et al. (2012) present a number of challenges to our existing knowledge of social network formation. For example, they report that the probability for a non-user to join Facebook, when invited by a friend who has already used Facebook, is not affected by the popularity of the inviter (i.e., the degree of the inviter), nor by the size of contact neighbourhood (i.e., the number of common friends between the inviter and the invited). Instead, the likelihood of recruitment is affected by the number of distinct components in the contact neighbourhood.[4] Most surprisingly, the impact of component diversity on recruitment is *negative* in that the more connected contacts on Facebook a non-user has, the *less* likely the person is to join Facebook. The findings sharply confront almost all existing relevant studies. However, given the huge size of the data (50 million users from Facebook), the rigorous design of the field experiment design, and the multiple statistical controls in the analysis, the findings certainly carry a lot of credibility.

Bond et al. (2012) carry out another experimental study using data from Facebook, which demonstrates the materialized effects of online social networks on real world behaviour. Based on a randomized online experiment design, over 60 million users

---

[4]A component is a set of nodes that are connected (either directly or indirectly) to one another. A strongly connected component (only defined for a directed network) is where each node is reachable by all other nodes.

were shown messages on their Facebook page with or without 'social information' showing how their friends voted in the 2012 U.S. Congressional Election. The results show that those users who are exposed to the social information have a turnout rate of 0.3 per cent higher than those who are not. Such a small difference would have been easily dismissed in any conventional experiment study. However, the big sample size of the current study, which amounts to a narrow sampling error of ±0.012 per cent, makes the observed difference to be highly significant not only in statistical sense ($z = 24$, $p < 0.001$) but also in practical sense (180,000 users who can easily change the outcome of many local or national elections).

Networks of Explicitly Directed Ties

The most visible examples in this type of networks are undoubtedly Twitter, Sina Weibo (a Chinese microblogging site with similar technical features as Twitter, but subject to political censorship) and other microblog sites. They differ from Facebook and other friendship networks primarily in their one-way, public mode of the relations among users. Most microblog sites were originally intended to be used as friendship networks similar to Facebook but unexpectedly, users 'reinvented' the media function of the sites and transformed them into the news sharing platforms that we know today. This unprecedented chapter of social network history is timely recognized and documented by Kwak et al. (2010) and Wu et al. (2011), among several other similar studies.

Kwak et al. (2010) start with a simple but unsettled question of Twitter at the time: Is it a social (i.e., friendship) network or a news medium? They focus on a key property of social network – the reciprocity between followers and followees – on Twitter. As it turns out, less than one quarter (22 per cent) of the user pairs reciprocally follow each other, whereas more than three quarters (78 per cent) have a one-way relationship. Coupled with other topological features of Twitter, such as a short effective diameter and a non-Power Law distribution of indegrees, it becomes clear that the microblog site is not a typical social friendship network but a news forwarding network.

Wu et al. (2011) move further to examine exactly how Twitter functions as a new medium – i.e., who says what to whom – by following the classic 5W model of mass communication (Lasswell, 1948). They first searched for the prevalence of four predetermined categories of news sources (or elite users), including celebrities, news media, institutions and professional bloggers, who account for only half a million (or 1.2 per cent) of the user population on Twitter. The most influential elite users (accounting for 0.05 per cent of the population) attract 50 per cent of the following links. The highly uneven distribution of attention illustrates the star-topology of microblog networks.

Networks of Implicitly Undirected Ties

Network of implicit ties are formed based on 'hidden' connections. Of implicit networks, those with undirected ties are the most 'invisible' because the links among the nodes are constructed or inferred by social network analysts post hoc, based on semantic similarity (e.g., co-usage or co-occurrence of keywords, tags, favourites, acts, etc.) between nodes of pairs. While the validity of such networks is sometimes questionable, they are often more informative about the substantive content of social interactions than what link-based social networks could reveal. Probably because of the latent nature of semantic similarity, it has not been frequently used in online social network research. However, a few existing studies demonstrate the unique value of such an approach.

For example, Capocci et al. (2010) evaluate the observed semantic similarity of photo tags between Flickr users against the corresponding friendship between the same users. The results show that semantic similarity does not result from social interactions among linked friends (i.e., peer influence hypothesis), but from existing similar background of users (i.e., social selection or homophily hypothesis).

Networks of Implicitly Directed Ties

Newsgroups (including various bulletin board systems (BBSs) and other online forums) are the most representative examples of implicitly directed ties. On the first glance, newsgroups do not look like a typical social network because nodes and edges are not directly observable. As such, researchers have to first 'explicate' nodes and edges of newsgroups before carrying out formal network analysis. Participants in BBS/forum discussions are often taken as nodes and their opinion exchanges as edges. Since online opinion exchanges usually involve a sequence of question-reply or post-comment, the derived networks are directed by nature. Occasionally, threads (i.e., topics) of exchanges are used as nodes whereas participants in the same threads are treated as edges between topical nodes, which necessarily result in undirected networks.

An example of research using newsgroup data is Welser et al. (2007), who investigate the use of network techniques for identifying 'answer people' – individuals who mainly respond to questions posed by other users instead of posing their own questions or getting involved in unproductive 'flame wars'. The authors argue that being able to identify answer people is important for developing better approaches for cultivating online communities of practice where such sharing of information is prevalent. They find that answer people tend to participate in threads initiated by others and typically only contribute one or two messages per thread. Second, the ego networks of answer people tend to contain alters who themselves answer few, if any, questions posed by others. Further, the 1.5-degree ego network of answer people tends to have small proportions of triads (i.e. their neighbours are not neighbours of each other) and they have few intense ties (i.e. they seldom send multiple messages to the same recipient).

While all social networks are built on hyperlinks, the term 'hyperlink networks' refers to a specific genre: graphs of web pages or websites that are tied together with hyperlinks. In a seminal study, Broder et al. (2000) examine the topological structure of the global WWW based on 200 million web pages collected by search engine AltaVista. They conclude that the Web was organized as a 'Bow Tie' consisting of four equally-sized components, with a strong connected component (SCC) in the centre, an IN component with one-way links to SCC, an OUT component with one-way links from SCC, and a component of Tendrils isolated from SCC. Later studies of hyperlinks at the national scope reveal a much more centralized graph, which looks like a 'Daisy' with SCC accounting for 80 per cent of the web pages in Italy, the UK, and five nations in Indo-China (Donato et al., 2005) or a 'Teapot' with 44 per cent of the web pages in China falling into SCC (Zhu et al., 2008). Parallel to these graph models of hyperlink networks by computer scientists, Halavais (2000) identifies the existence of national borders on the Web, based on the pattern that websites across a dozen nations were more likely to link domestic websites than foreign websites.

Hyperlink networks also prove to be insightful in examining the interplay between social movement actors. For example, Ackland and O'Neil (2011) study environmental activist hyperlink networks, extending Diani's (1992) network-theoretic approach to studying social movements to the online world. In keeping with our above classification of hyperlink networks as networks of implicitly directed ties, the authors do not contend that hyperlinks between environmental activist websites necessarily reflect the exchange of real-world resources. Instead, they emphasize the role of hyperlinks in the exchange of symbolic resources, thus helping to establish boundaries of inclusion/exclusion, and hence the formation of collective identity.

10.3.2 Tools for Collecting and Analysing Online Network data

This section presents a brief summary of tools for collecting and analysing online network data.

Tools for Collection of Online Network Data

Table 10.2 revisits the typology for online networks introduced above, presenting an example of a tool for collecting data from each type of network. It should be noted that the table only shows data collection tools that are publicly available, and only one example tool is shown for each type of network.

Table 10.2   Tools for collection of online network data[5]

| | Direction of ties | |
Manifestation of ties	Undirected	Directed
Explicit	Social Network Importer for Facebook networks (http:// socialnetimporter.codeplex.com)	Tweepy Python library for Twitter API (http://tweepy.github.io)
Implicit	Python Flickr API kit (http://stuvel.eu/flickrapi)	VOSON – hyperlink network collection and analysis (http://voson.anu.edu.au)

---

[5]All URLs in this table accessed 15 Dec 2014.

Social Network Importer is a plugin for NodeXL,[6] which is a free Excel 2007/2010 template for analysing networks in the familiar Excel spreadsheet environment. The predecessor of Social Network Importer was NameGen,[7] which was designed by Bernie Hogan at the Oxford Internet Institute (see, e.g., Hogan 2010). Social Network Importer queries the Facebook Application Programming Interface (API), allowing the extraction of ego network data for a given Facebook user. Depending on account privacy settings for ego and alters, the tool will also collect Facebook profile data and return the 1.5 degree ego network. According to the Facebook API terms and conditions, the data can only be collected for an ego who has provided his or her Facebook username and password, and hence Social Network Importer is currently mainly useful for researchers who want to collect their own ego network data or that of a small number of participants (who would need to use NodeXL on a machine that the researcher has access to). In contrast, NameGen was available as a Facebook application and it allowed the creators of NameGen to collect ego network data for people who consented to participate in the study (where consent was granted via the installation and use of the NameGen Facebook application).

While Social Network Importer conveniently hides the interactions with the Facebook API from the researcher, the *Tweepy Python library for Twitter API* is much more low-level in that its use requires the researcher to be able to program in Python. Typical use of Tweepy might involve the researcher querying the Twitter Search API to find all recent tweets that contain a particular hashtag. The Twitter User API could then be used to collect the directed follower network of the authors of those tweets.

The Collaborative Online Social Media Observatory[8] (COSMOS) platform provides an integrated suite of tools for harvesting, archiving, analysing and visualizing social media data streams, together with the capability to link with other kinds of data, e.g., from the UK Office for National Statistics (ONS) via open APIs (Housley et al. 2014). COSMOS hosts a range of computational tools that include language detection, gender identification, location, sentiment, tension and topic discovery. The first version of the platform became available for download in late 2014.

Similar to Tweepy, the *Python Flickr API kit* is designed for Python programmers who want to programmatically interact with the Flickr photo sharing website. A research use of the Python Flickr API kit may involve getting a list of meta data (e.g., descriptive tags) on photos uploaded by a particular Flickr member (or members) and then iterating over the list of meta data and constructing a semantic network where an undirected and weighted tie between two tags indicates the number of times they were jointly used to describe a particular photo.

Finally, the VOSON tool for hyperlink network collection and analysis (e.g., Ackland, 2010) is available as both a web application and a plugin to NodeXL.[9] Users can enter a list of seed URLs (typically, entry pages to websites) and the web crawler

---

[6]http://nodexl.codeplex.com

[7]See http://people.oii.ox.ac.uk/hogan/software

[8]www.cosmosproject.net

[9]The first-named author created the VOSON software and is involved in its commercialization.

will then crawl through each site and collect outbound hyperlinks and text content. Optionally, the crawler will also return inbound hyperlinks to each page in the site (this is currently achieved via the VOSON software accessing the Blekko web search engine API[10]). VOSON allows the user to construct networks of web pages or websites, and these can be visualized in the web application and it is possible to download networks for analysis in other network analysis tools.

Tools for Analysis and Visualization of Networks

Having collected online network data using, for example, one of the tools mentioned above, the researcher then needs to decide what software will be used for network analysis. The following is a brief and non-exhaustive list of freely-available software for network analysis.[11]

- NodeXL (http://nodexl.codeplex.com) was mentioned above in the context of data collection, but it also provides a menu-driven environment for network visualization and analysis.
- Pajek (http://pajek.imfm.si/doku.php) is a Windows-based menu-driven package, known for its ability to handle large networks.
- Statnet (http://statnet.csde.washington.edu) is a suite of R (open source statistical software) libraries for network handling and analysis, including ERGM.
- NetworkX (http://networkx.github.io) NetworkX is a Python language software package for network analysis.
- igraph (http://igraph.org) is a library for network analysis that runs in both R and Python.
- Gephi (https://gephi.org) runs on Windows, Linux and Mac OS and is a menu-driven network visualization tool.
- PNet (http://sna.unimelb.edu.au) is a menu-driven Windows package for ERGM.
- UCInet (https://sites.google.com/site/ucinetsoftware/home) is a menu-driven Windows package for social network analysis.

10.4 CHALLENGES AND OPPORTUNITIES

This section identifies challenges and opportunities for SNA researchers working with trace network data (network data that are collected unobtrusively from the Web).

10.4.1 Social Network or Information Sharing Network?

Is it always reasonable to conceive of an online network as exhibiting the hallmarks of social networks (e.g., interdependence, evolution, one-to-one ties, multiplex ties)?

---

[10]http://blekko.com

[11]All URLs in this list accessed 15 Dec 2014.

That is, having outlined the network perspective above, it is prudent to ask whether a given online network is likely to exhibit properties such that it can be viably studied under this perspective using SNA techniques.

Referring back to the typology of online networks introduced in Table 10.1, it was noted above that online networks involving explicitly undirected ties (e.g., Facebook) are more easily conceived of as social networks and Wimmer and Lewis (2010), for example, have used ERGM to provide new insights into friendship homophily using Facebook data.

In contrast, it is questionable as to whether modelling microblogs such as Twitter (networks of explicitly directed ties) as social networks is valid. The founders of Twitter have emphasized that it is an information sharing network, not a social network, and as noted above, research by Kwak et al. (2010) shows that Twitter resembles more closely an information network, compared to a social network.

The online network that is probably the hardest to conceive of as a social network is a semantic network (network of implicitly undirected ties). However, it is of interest to note that Capocci et al. (2010) made use of semantic networks in their study of role of social influence (people becoming more like their friends) versus social selection (similar people becoming friends) in determining the photo tagging behaviour of Flickr members, and their findings (discussed above) are largely consistent with what Lewis et al. (2012) find in their extensive analysis of Facebook data. In other words, networks inferred from semantic similarity provide an effective and efficient way to address some long-standing debates in social network research, such as the causal direction between social selection and peer influence, although Capocci et al. (2010) themselves do not acknowledge such implications.

Finally, while it is hard to conceive of all Web 1.0 hyperlink networks (networks of implicitly directed ties) as social networks, Lusher and Ackland (2011) have argued that the network perspective is valid for Web 1.0 hyperlink networks comprising particular types of actors. ERGM has been used by several authors to model NGO hyperlinking (e.g., Shumate and Dewitt, 2008; Gonzalez-Bailon, 2009; Ackland and O'Neil, 2011; Lusher and Ackland, 2011). In contrast, the hyperlinking behaviour of government agencies and academic research teams is possibly less likely to conform to the network perspective and consequently a lot of studies of these types of Web 1.0 actors have involved techniques that do not emphasize relational structure. In particular, webometric analysis of government visibility or centrality on the Web (Escher et al., 2006) and the academic authority of research teams in the biotech sector (Barjak and Thelwall, 2008) have eschewed the construction of complete network data and instead reduce network structure to being an attribute of the actors (indegree or outdegree) that, in the case of Barjak and Thelwall (2008), is then used as a dependent variable in regression analysis.

10.4.2 Construct Validity of Online Network Data

While researchers from some fields (e.g., new media and virtual ethnography) study online behaviour in its own right, other social scientists are often interested in online network data because they can potentially tell us something new about offline social processes, such as friendship formation, partnering behaviour, dynamics of teams and organizations, and social influence. The promise of online environments such as Facebook, Twitter and Second Life is that they can provide large quantities of precisely time stamped social behavioural data that would be impossible to collect using obtrusive methods, such as interviews or surveys.

However, many sociologists in the SNA tradition believe that the viability of online network data in this context is predicated on our being able to sufficiently demonstrate that there is a 'mapping' (Williams, 2010) between the online and offline world, or that online data have 'construct validity' (Burt, 2011) with regards to important offline behaviour. Burt (2011: 9) argues that '... the advantages of network data in virtual worlds are worthless without calibrating the analogy between real and inworld. If social networks in virtual worlds operate by unique processes unrelated to networks in the real world, then the scale and precision of data available on social networks in virtual worlds has no value for understanding relations in the real world.'

So, a major challenge for social scientists working with online network data is establishing that the data have construct validity for the purpose at hand. There are three ways in which construct validity might be demonstrated (Ackland, 2013).

First, the construct validity of web data may be demonstrated by showing that the online network displays structural signatures that are consistent with those displayed by real-world actors. For example: does Facebook friendship network data display homophily on the basis of race and ethnicity (Wimmer and Lewis, 2010)? Are divisions between different groups in the environmental social movement evident in hyperlink networks (Ackland and O'Neil, 2011)? To what extent is political affiliation reflected in political blog networks (Adamic and Glance, 2005)? If web networks display structural signatures that are significantly different from those shown in the real world, then the construct validity of the data in the real world is questionable.

Second, it may be possible to assess the construct validity of web data by testing whether variables constructed from web data are correlated with other accepted measures of the construct. For example, if counts of inbound hyperlinks to academic project websites are correlated with other characteristics of academic teams (e.g., publications, industry connections) that are used as proxies of academic authority/performance, then this is evidence of the construct validity of hyperlink data in the context of scientometrics, which is the science of measuring and analysing science (see, e.g., Barjak and Thelwall, 2008).

Finally, the construct validity of web data may be demonstrated if it can be shown that an actor's position in an online network influences his or her performance in a manner that accords with what is found in the real world. For example, Burt (2011) studies brokerage and closure in Second Life, making use of three types of relational data: one-to-one friendships (which operate in a manner similar to Facebook), group membership (again, similar to that in Facebook) and rights granted to friends. With regards to the last, Second Life allows a user to grant another user three levels of access (which imply increasing levels of trust): the right to know when you are online, the right to know your location in Second Life, and the right to directly modify your online inventory (thus impacting on the appearance and behaviour of your avatar).

Burt further constructs ego networks by defining and quantifying four types of directed tie: 'no tie' – users i and j are not friends; 'weak tie' – users i and j are friends but i either granted j no rights or only the right to know when j is online; 'average tie' – i and j are friends, and i granted j the right to know i's location inworld; 'strong tie' – i and j are friends, and i granted j the right to modify i's online inventory.

With regards to the closure hypothesis, there is no obvious Second Life analogue to team effectiveness and efficiency measures and so Burt focuses on the intermediate variable of trust and tests the hypothesis that closure is associated with higher levels of trust in relationships. Trust is measured by the three levels of rights that friends can grant each other and Burt finds support for the closure hypothesis, showing that the level of trust between two users is positively related to the level of network closure around the friendship, measured by the number of indirect connections between ego and the friend.

With regards to brokerage, the hypothesis is that occupying structural holes in Second Life is correlated with achievement, measured as the contribution of ego to the formation and maintenance of groups (one of the main types of infrastructure that attracts people to Second Life). It is found that people who have greater access to structural holes (measured by the number of non-redundant friends i.e. friends who are not connected to each other) maintain more groups and their groups are more likely to be successful in terms of membership and activity.

The above arguments draw on the conventional definition of construct validity. As online networks keep becoming increasingly ubiquitous, they may actually have started to evolve into a new 'world' that is fundamentally different from the real world. The scenario certainly challenges the requirement that the construct validity of online networks lies in the consistency between offline and online worlds.

10.4.3 Causality Versus Correlation

Identifying causality is one of the major bugbears of empirical social science. The problem arises because social scientists are often trying to identify the impact of a variable that the individual has some degree of choice over (e.g., the impact of years of schooling on wages, impact of peers on student performance). In the standard human capital model introduced above, for example, it has long been recognized that OLS estimates of the impact of an additional year of education on wages are biased upwards because years of schooling are likely to be correlated with unobservable variables such as ability (more able students are likely to get more years of schooling, on average).

The growth of interest over the past decade in the role of social networks in behaviour and outcomes has only served to highlight the methodological challenges associated with identifying causality. The problem for social scientists is that, unlike their counterparts in the natural sciences, social science data are typically observational rather than experimental, and it is therefore very difficult to control the variable of interest. However, the Web offers two major opportunities for overcoming methodological limitations relating to discerning the causal impact of social networks.

First, a major advantage of Web network research is the potential for collecting rich and precise time-stamped data. Burt (2011) noted that his results are based on a single snapshot of activity within Second Life; the fact that the sequence of friendship and group formation is not taken into account prevents any conclusions about causation. In particular, it may be that two people with high level of trust in their relationship subsequently acquire many mutual friends (hence building network closure). Similarly, a person who has established successful groups in Second Life may acquire friendships from diverse parts of the virtual world, with access to structural holes thus resulting from achievement, rather than the other way around. However, Burt notes that the availability of precisely time stamped network data from online environments such as Second Life may allow researchers to better understand the causal relationship between network position and outcomes. Although Burt does not explicitly explain how this will work, we believe that the time stamped data (usually on a daily or finer scale) allow social network analysts to test a variety of alternative models between pairs of reciprocal effects, something always difficult or impossible to do with offline data of crude timestamp (usually on a yearly or larger scale).

Second, the Web allows for field experimentation (experiments that are conducted outside of the laboratory but where the researcher still has control over the variable of interest) that would be very difficult to conduct in the real world and better equips researchers to discern the causal impact of social networks.

Centola (2010) uses an online field experiment to study the social transmission of health behaviour in an attempt to uncover the exact processes by which people are influenced by their social network. The 'strength of weak ties' literature (e.g., Granovetter, 1973) suggests that the diffusion of an innovation (e.g., information, behaviour) through a network is going to occur more efficiently where there is low redundancy of ties i.e. your neighbours do not tend to be connected to one another, and hence do not provide the same information. However, Centola and Macy (2007) suggest that while the 'weak ties' argument might hold for innovations such as information or disease, it may not hold up for transmission of behaviours where social affirmation from multiple sources is required for successful transmission (transmission will be aided by network structures that exhibit clustering, which increases the likelihood of contact from multiple sources). Centola and Macy (2007) term this 'complex contagion' and provide examples such as spread of high-risk social movements and avant garde fashions.

Centola (2010) explores the role of network structure in the promotion of social influence by creating an Internet-based health community containing 1,528 participants recruited from online health communities of interest. Participants were randomly assigned health 'buddies' from whom they could gain information about a new online health forum. The act of joining the health forum was the health behaviour under examination, and the study aimed to quantify the impact of number of sources of information on the probability of adopting the behaviour. Participants were randomly assigned to networks with differing levels of clustering, which meant there was variation in the number of network neighbours providing information about the new health behaviour. The author finds that the probability of adoption increased markedly when participants received social reinforcement from multiple network neighbours.

10.4.4 Natural Research Instrument

Online network data are being generated in what is effectively a huge natural research instrument, the Web. Wimmer and Lewis (2010) note that the fact that Facebook is a natural research instrument provides both opportunities and challenges for research into friendship formation.

The advantages are that there is no interviewer effect or recall error and there is no need to reduce the scope of the study (for cost reasons). This allows Wimmer and Lewis (2010) to collect complete network data for an entire cohort of undergraduate students in a residential college in the US, which would have been prohibitively expensive to do using traditional offline methods. The fact that Facebook users provide rich 'cultural preferences' data (e.g., favourite books, movies, music) also provides an opportunity for researchers. Such data would be difficult and expensive to collect using offline methods (friendship homophily research traditionally has involved only very basic demographic profile data such as age, gender and race). The availability of cultural preferences data allowed Wimmer and Lewis (2010) to provide new insights into how shared cultural tastes may influence friendship formation.

But Wimmer and Lewis (2010) also note that Facebook data provide challenges for friendship homophily researchers. In particular, what is the exact social meaning of a 'Facebook friend'? Further, the 'cultural preferences' data (e.g., books, movies, music) reflect both true preferences and strategic presentation of self, and this may pose problems (but of course, strategic self-presentation can affect other types of social research data, however generated).

Another important challenge relating to the Web as a natural research instrument is that we only get partial information about network participants. This challenge is particularly evident in research into social influence in social media. While an individual may be influenced via interactions in social media to change his or her behaviour (e.g., attitudes to politics or consumer preferences) we are not going to know this unless the behavioural change results in a digital trace that is picked up by the researcher. The study by Aral and Walker (2011) into social influence in an instant messaging network focuses on a measurable outcome (product adoption). But what about changes in a person's political identity or willingness to vote? Unless this change is somehow (easily) identifiable in the data, or else we conduct a survey or experiment to gauge how attitudes have changed, this will never be known by the researcher.

On Twitter, how do we know when someone has been influenced, that is, what is the appropriate measurable outcome? In research into social influence in Twitter, influence has often been conceptualized as attention, for example number of followers (e.g., Kwak et al., 2010; Cha et al., 2010). That is, what is really a dynamic process (e.g., A interacts with B and as a result of the interaction, A's behaviour changes) gets reduced to a static question of who is the most central or visible or important person in the social media network i.e. who is garnering the most attention? A current popular measure of influence in Twitter is the number of retweets (e.g., Kwak et al., 2010; Cha et al., 2010); while a retweet is a clear indication that someone has made a conscious decision to pass on information, a problem is that it is difficult to disentangle the influence of the content (some tweets are going to contain information that is innately 'viral') from the influence of the original tweeter (some tweeters might have greater authority that means people tend to retweet them, regardless of the tweet content). Harrigan et al. (2012) get around this problem by using conditional logistic regression, which allows the probability of retweeting to be estimated only for those people who follow the same tweeters (and hence the virality of tweets and the influence of their authors is controlled for).

10.4.5 Big Data and Network Sampling

Digital network datasets can be potentially huge. While the scale of online networks may not pose a problem in empirical techniques used by applied physicists and computer scientists, some established statistical SNA techniques (such as ERGM) currently do not scale well (there can be problems with model convergence with large and dense networks). An additional problem for social scientists is that the research often requires that more is known about the network participants than can be gathered via automatic data collection methods. This often means that only a subset of the available data are analysed, in order to make the human coding of the data feasible (Procter et al., 2013). For example, in their analysis of information flows on Twitter during the 2011 Egyptian and Tunisian revolutions, Lotan et al. (2011) only analyse the 10 per cent largest tweet flows, resulting in a subset of 963 users who either were first to post in a flow, or were retweeted or mentioned at least 15 times.

Social scientists are well versed in sampling approaches, with much empirical social science being based on representative samples of individuals or households drawn from a larger population. However, network sampling poses a different set of challenges: even if one is able to define the population of interest in an online network, random sampling is unlikely to be appropriate since the units of observation and hence error terms are not going to be independently and identically distributed, and the sampling approach should reflect this.

Sampling of online social networks involves in general four strategies: sampling of nodes, ego-networks, sub-networks, and full networks.[12] Of the four, it is the easiest to apply probability sampling to ego-networks because their alters (i.e., neighbours) are usually directly accessible from the chosen egos.

Probability sampling of nodes is possible, although costly, from the social networking sites with a known sampling frame (e.g., the URLs of all members are directly or indirectly known). For example, many social networking sites systematically assign a numeric ID to map the home page of their users, which provide necessary information

---

[12]Sampling of nodes is different from sampling of ego-, sub- or full networks as the former refers to studies that focus exclusively on characteristics of individual nodes without any concerns about characteristics of the networks in which the nodes embedded. Strictly speaking, such studies of nodes are not of social network analysis. However, given the popularity of this approach in the current literature and the inherent connection between nodes and networks, we include it here.

to construct a sampling frame for those sites. We have devised a random digit search (RDS) method, following random digit dialling (RDD) method used in offline telephone surveys, to detect the boundary and coverage rate of valid user IDs and then draw probability samples from the known range of URLs of a popular blog site in China (Zhu et al., 2011). It is necessary to note that the resulting samples, while providing unbiased and precise estimates of individual nodes, do not represent topological characteristics of the underlying networks from which the nodes are drawn.

Sampling of sub-networks involves the same methodological issues as those in sampling of full networks (as discussed next), plus the conceptual problem of generalizability of sub-networks. While popular among the previous studies, how universally applicable are the findings observed from student Facebook users at a single university or a few selected universities? Obviously, the issue goes beyond the scope of the current discussion.

Sampling of full networks is the ideal method for study of network characteristics. However, despite various efforts, no perfect solution has yet emerged. To begin with, as noted above, probability sampling is not only confined to certain sites, but is also incapable of capturing network topology. As such, most studies of network sampling employ various methods of snowballing. The most common, but also most problematic, method is breadth-first search (BFS), which samples every neighbour of chosen seeds and, if necessary, every neighbour of the chosen neighbours successively in the onward path until a desirable sample size is reached (Ahn et al., 2007). While highly efficient, BFS samples over-represent popular nodes, given the power-law distribution of edges on virtually all social networks (Kurant et al., 2010; Zhu et al., 2013).

To overcome the systematic bias of BFS, several schemes of random walk (RW) sampling have been proposed. Similar to BFS, RW schemes sample successfully neighbours of chosen seeds, by which they are also snowballing (i.e., non-probabilistic, despite the name of 'random walk'). Instead of including everyone along the path, RW sampling selects only one or a small number of nodes per step, based on different weighting strategies adopted by different RW schemes such as Respondent-Driven Sampling (RDS; Wejnert and Heckathorn, 2008), Re-Weighted Random Walk (RWRW; Gjoka et al., 2010), Metropolis-Hasting Random Walk (MHRW; Gjoka et al., 2010; Stutzbach et al., 2006), and Self-Adjustable Random Walk (SARW; Zhu et al., 2013). Each of the schemes presents some significant improvement over BFS. However, none of them can provide simultaneously unbiased estimates of multiple key parameters of network structure (e.g., mean degree, clustering coefficient, assortativity, etc.), when tested against large-scale, real social network data (Zhu et al., 2013). Sampling of online social networks remains one of the top challenges in the age of big data.

10.4.6 Proprietary Data

One of the advantages of researching Web 1.0 is that the data are generally available. The data may not necessarily be easy to collect (given the need for a web crawler and further pre-processing of the network data) but as long as the webmaster wants the site to be indexed by Google, then the researcher can also get the data via a web crawler. Furthermore, search companies such as Google and Yahoo also play a positive role in enabling network research by providing APIs that allow researchers to programmatically extract large quantities of hyperlink network data from search engine indexes (see, e.g., Thelwall, 2004).

With the advent of Web 2.0, the opportunities for social research using web data have expanded since more people are interacting online by, for example, blogging, using Facebook and Twitter. There are more social scientists who want to use web data for social network research, but these data are actually becoming harder to obtain. While there are tools for extracting egonets from Facebook (see, e.g., Hogan, 2010), research involving complete network Facebook data (e.g., that of Wimmer and Lewis, 2010) is generally going to require a data sharing agreement with Facebook, which are very hard to obtain. Similarly, Burt's (2011) research into Second Life involves use of a proprietary dataset. Twitter have been very open to research and there are several tools that can be used for extracting Twitter network data (e.g., Barash and Golder, 2010), but there are indications that the Twitter API will not always remain open for access by researchers.[13]

The challenge associated with proprietary data is that it might lead to proprietary researchers i.e. researchers working on topics that are most interesting to the data providers, and producing research that cannot easily be replicated or validated.

10.5 CONCLUDING REMARKS AND RECOMMENDATIONS

Big data of online networks have brought both opportunities and challenges to SNA researchers. We conclude with some recommendations for those SNA researchers who wish to benefit fully from the opportunities and meet the challenges:

- Engage in collaboration with scholars from sciences and engineering. SNA researchers should take the initiatives to reach out;
- Focus on identifying both similarities and differences in network structure and behaviour between the real and virtual worlds;
- Work out, preferably through interdisciplinary collaboration, scalable versions of the rich, existing models and algorithms of SNA to deal with large-scale online networks.

10.6 BIBLIOGRAPHY

Ackland, R. (2010) 'WWW hyperlink networks', Chapter 12 in D. Hansen, B. Shneiderman and M. Smith (eds), *Analyzing Social Media Networks with NodeXL: Insights from A Connected World*. Burlington, MA: Morgan-Kaufmann.

Ackland, R. (2013) *Web Social Science: Concepts, Data and Tools for Social Scientists in the Digital Age*. London: Sage.

---

[13]For example, in June 2013 Twitter 'whitelist accounts' (which provided substantially higher number of API calls per hour than the standard account) were turned off.

Ackland, R. and O'Neil, M. (2011) 'Online collective identity: the case of the environmental movement', *Social Networks*, 33: 177–90.

Adamic, L. and Glance, N. (2005) 'The political blogosphere and the 2004 U.S. election: divided they blog'. *LinkKDD '05* Proceedings of the 3rd International Workshop on Link Discovery. pp. 36–43.

Ahn, Y.Y., Han, S., Kwak, H., Moon, S. and Jeong, H. (2007) 'Analysis of topological characteristics of huge online social networking services', The 16th International Conference on World Wide Web (WWW2007), Alberta, Canada.

Aral, S. and Walker, D. (2011) 'Creating social contagion through viral product design: a randomized trial of peer influence in networks', *Management Science*, 57(9): 1623-39.

Barash, V. and Golder, S. (2010) 'Twitter: conversation, entertainment and information, All in one network!', in D. Hansen, B. Shneiderman and M. Smith (eds), *Analyzing Social Media Networks with NodeXL: Insights from A Connected World*. Burlington, MA: Morgan-Kaufmann. pp.143–64.

Barjak, F. and Thelwall, M. (2008) 'A statistical analysis of the Web presences of European life sciences research teams', *Journal of the American Society for Information Science and Technology*, 59(4): 628–43.

Bond, R.M., Fariss, C.J., Jones, J.J., Kramer, A.D.I., Marlow, C., Settle, J.E. and Fowler, J.H. (2012) 'A 61-million-person experiment in social influence and political mobilization', *Nature*, 489: 295–8.

Broder, A., Kumar, R., Maghoul, F., Raghavan, P., Rajagopalan, S., Stata, R., Tomkins, A. and Wiener, J. (2000) 'Graph structure in the web', *Computer Networks*, 33(1–6): 309–20.

Burt, R. (1992) *Structural Holes: The Social Structure of Competition*. Cambridge, MA: Harvard University Press.

Burt, R. (2011) 'Structural holes in virtual worlds', Booth School of Business (Univ. of Chicago) working paper.

Capocci, A., Baldassarri, A., Servedio, V.D.P., Loreto, V. and Gualino, V. (2010) 'Friendship, collaboration and semantics in Flickr: from social interaction to semantic similarity', *Proceedings of the International Workshop on Modeling Social Media*, Toronto, Canada. New York: ACM. Article Number 8.

Centola, D. (2010) 'The spread of behavior in an online social network experiment', *Science*, 329: 1194–97.

Centola, D. and Macy, M.W. (2007) 'Complex contagion and the weakness of long ties', *American Journal of Sociology*, 113(3): 702–34.

Cha, M., Haddadi, H., Benevenuto, F. and Gummad, K.P. (2010) 'Measuring user influence on twitter: the million follower fallacy', 4th International AAAI Conference on Weblogs and Social Media, Washington, DC. pp. 10–17.

Daraganova, G. and Pattison, P. (2013) 'Autologistic actor attribute model analysis of unemployment: dual importance of who you know and where you live', in D. Lusher, J. Koskinen and G. Robins (eds) *Exponential Random Graph Models for Social Networks*. New York: Cambridge University Press. pp. 237–47.

Diani, M. (1992) 'The concept of social movement', *Sociological Review*, 40(1): 1–25.

Donato, D., Leonardi, S., Millozzi, S. and Tsaparas, P. (2005) 'Mining the inner structure of the Web graph', The 8th International Workshop on the Web and Databases, Baltimore, USA.

Escher, T., Margetts, H., Petricek, V. and Cox, I. (2006) 'Governing from the centre? Comparing the nodality of digital governments'. Paper presented at the 2006 Annual Meeting of the American Political Science Association, Chicago, 31 August–4 September.

Gilad L., Graeff, E., Ananny, M., Gaffney, D., Pearce, I. and boyd, d. (2011) 'The revolutions were tweeted: information flows during the 2011 Tunisian and Egyptian revolutions',

International Journal of Communications, 5: 1375–1405. Available from http://ijoc.org/ojs/index.php/ijoc/article/view/1246/613 (accessed 15 Dec 2014).

Gjoka, M., Kurant, M., Butts, C.T. and Markopoulou, A. (2010) 'Walking in Facebook: unbiased sampling of OSNs', *Proceedings of IEEE INFOCOM*. San Diego, USA.

Gonzalez-Bailon, S. (2009) 'Opening the black box of link formation: social factors underlying the Structure of the web', *Social Networks*, 31: 271–80.

Granovetter, M. (1973) 'The strength of weak ties', *American Journal of Sociology*, 78(6): 1360–80.

Halavais, A. (2000) 'National borders on the World Wide Web', *New Media & Society*, 2(1): 7–28.

Hanneman, R.A. and Riddle, M. (2005) 'Introduction to social network methods', University of California, Riverside. Available from http://faculty.ucr.edu/~hanneman (accessed 15 Dec 2014).

Hansen, D.L., Shneiderman, B. and Smith, M.A. (2010) *Analyzing Social Media Networks with NodeXL: Insights from A Connected World*. Burlington, MA: Morgan-Kaufmann.

Harrigan, N., Achananuparp, P. and Lim, E-P. (2012) 'Influentials, novelty and social contagion: the viral power of average friends, close communities and old news', *Social Networks*, 34(4): 470–80.

Hogan, B. (2010) 'Visualizing and interpreting Facebook networks', in D.L. Hansen, B. Shneiderman and M.A. Smith (eds), *Analyzing Social Media Networks with NodeXL: Insights from A Connected World*. Burlington, MA: Morgan-Kaufmann. pp. 174–9.

Housley, W., Procter, R., Edwards, A., Burnap, P., Williams, M., Sloan, L., Voss, A. and Greenhill, A. (2014) 'Big and broad social data and the sociological imagination: a collaborative response', *Big Data & Society*, 1(2), 2053951714545135.

Kwak, H.W., Lee, C.H., Park, H.S. and Moon, S. (2010) 'What is Twitter, a social network or a news media?' Proceedings of the 19th International Conference on World Wide Web (WWW 2010). pp. 591–600.

Kurant, M., Markopoulou, A. and Thiran, P. (2010) 'On the bias of BFS (Breadth First Search)', The Annual conference of International Teletraffic Congress (ITC 22), Amsterdam, The Netherlands.

Lasswell, H.D. (1948) 'The structure and function of communication in society', in L. Bryston (ed.), *The Communication of Ideas*. New York: Harper and Row. pp.37–51.

Lewis, K., Gonzalez, M. and Kaufman, J. (2012) 'Social selection and peer influence in an online social network', *Proceedings of the National Academy of Sciences of the United States of America*, 109: 68–72.

Lotan, G., Graeff, E., Ananny, E., Gaffney, D., Pearce, I. and Boyd, D. (2011) 'The Revolutions Were Tweeted: Information Flows during the 2011 Tunisian and Egyptian Revolutions', *International Journal of Communication*, 5 (Feature): 1375–1405.

Lusher, D. and Ackland, R. (2011) 'A relational hyperlink analysis of an online social movement', *Journal of Social Structure*, 12(5). Available from www.cmu.edu/joss/content/articles/volume12/Lusher (accessed 15 Dec 2014).

Procter, R., Vis, F. and Voss, A. (2013) 'Reading the riots on Twitter: methodological innovation for the analysis of big data', *International Journal of Social Research Methodology*, 16(3): 197–214.

Robins, G., Pattison, P., Kalish, Y. and D. Lusher (2007) 'An introduction to exponential random graph (p*) models for social networks', *Social Networks*, 29(2): 173–91.

Shumate, M. and Dewitt, L. (2008) 'The north/south divide in NGO hyperlink networks', *Journal of Computer Mediated Communication*, 13: 405–28.

Smith, K. and Christakis, N.A. (2008) 'Social Networks and Health', *Annual Review of Sociology*, 34: 405–29.

Stutzbach, D., Rejaie, R., Duffield, N., Sen, S. and Willinger, W. (2006) 'On unbiased sampling for unstructured peer-to-peer networks', *Proceedings of Internet Measurement Conference (IMC 2006)*. Rio de Janeiro, Brazil.

Thelwall, M. (2004) *Link Analysis: An Information Science Approach*, Academic Press. Available from http://linkanalysis.wlv.ac.uk (accessed 15 Dec 2014).

Ugander, J., Backstrom, L., Marlow, C., and Kleinberg, J. (2012) 'Structural diversity in social contagion', *Proceedings of National Academy of Science*, 109(16): 5962–6.

Wasserman, S. and Faust, K. (2004) *Social Network Analysis*, Cambridge, UK: Cambridge University Press.

Wejnert, C. and Heckathorn, D.D. (2008) 'Web-based network sampling: efficiency and efficacy of respondent-driven sampling for online research', *Sociological Methods & Research*, 37(1): 105–34.

Wellman, B. (1988) 'Structural analysis: from method and metaphor to theory and substance', in B. Wellman and S. Berkowitz (eds), *Social Structures: A Network Approach*. Cambridge: Cambridge University Press. pp. 19–61.

Welser, H., Gleave, E., Fisher, D. and Smith, M. (2007) 'Visualizing the signatures of social roles in online discussion groups', *Journal of Social Structure*, 8(2). Available from www.cmu.edu/joss/content/articles/volume8/Welser (accessed 16 Dec 2014).

Williams, D. (2010) 'The mapping principle, and a research framework for virtual worlds', *Communication Theory*, 20(4): 451–70.

Wimmer, A. and Lewis, K. (2010) 'Beyond and below racial homophily: ERG models of a friendship network documented on Facebook', *American Journal of Sociology*, 116(2): 583–642.

Wu, S., Hofman, J., Mason, W.A. and Watts, D.J. (2011) 'Who says what to whom on Twitter', WWW 2011, 28 March–1 April, Hyderabad, India.

Zhu, J.J.H., Meng, T., Xie, Z.M., Li, G. and Li, X.M. (2008) 'A teapot graph and its hierarchical structure of the Chinese Web', *Proceedings of the 17th International Conference on World Wide Web (WWW'08)*. pp. 1133–4.

Zhu, J.J.H., Mo, Q., Wang, F. and Lu, H. (2011) 'A random digit search (RDS) method for sampling of blogs and other web content', *Social Science Computer Review*, 29(3): 327–339

Zhu, J.J.H., Xu, X.K., Zhang, L. and Peng, T.Q. (2013) 'A flexible sampling method for large-scale online social networks: self-adjustable random walk (SARW)', *The Annual Conference of International Network for Social Network Analysis (Sunbelt2013)*, Hamburg, Germany.

11

VISUALIZING SPATIAL AND SOCIAL MEDIA

MICHAEL BATTY, STEVEN GRAY, ANDREW HUDSON-SMITH, RICHARD MILTON, OLIVER O'BRIEN AND FLORA ROUMPANI

11.1 INTRODUCTION

In this chapter, we begin by surveying the development of computer graphics as it has influenced the development of the spatial representation of social and economic data, charting the history of computer cartography and geographic information systems (GIS) which have broadened into a wide array of forms for scientific visualization. With the advent of the World Wide Web and the widespread adoption of graphical user interfaces (GUIs) to most kinds of computer device, visualization has become central to most sciences and to the dissemination of many kinds of data and information. We divide our treatment of this domain according to three themes. First, we examine how the 2-dimensional map has become key to many kinds of spatial representation, showing how this software has moved from the desktop to the web as well as how 2D has moved to 3D in terms of the visualization of maps. Second, we explore how social data is being augmented by space-time series generated in real time and show how such real-time streaming of data presents problems and opportunities in which visualization is key. We illustrate these new data for basic feeds from cities but then move on to examine data from transit systems, social media, and data that is pulled from the crowd – crowdsourcing. Finally, we note the development of visual analytics showing how 2D and 3D spatial representations are essential to interpreting the outputs and the workings of more complex models and simulations. We conclude with the notion that much of what we develop in this chapter for the space-time domain is generic to the future representation of all kinds of social data.

11.2 DEFINING VISUALIZATION

Visualization as a distinct activity in computing emerged in the mid-1980s as computer memory became significantly cheaper. Personal computers acquired visual interfaces almost as soon as they emerged in the late 1970s and this gave a massive boost to computer graphics, which, hitherto, was largely generated 'offline', once computation had been done. To an extent, visualization was first associated with large-scale systems, which generated what at the time was 'big data' and which hitherto had rarely if ever been cast as imagery. In this sense, the initial excitement of visualization was that it provided opportunities for entirely new insights into scientific phenomena and it is no surprise that the first attempts in the early 1980s were labelled 'scientific visualization' and associated with massive physical systems, from galaxies to particles (Smarr, 1991).

Visualization is now defined much more widely for it pertains to the entire array of imagery that is associated with computation and this of course includes our access to computers which is now dominated by visual interfaces, often called GUIs (graphical user interfaces). In this chapter we will cast our net quite widely but visualization is now so dominant a force in digital media that we need to be clear about the limits to the range of ideas we will introduce. Our focus will be very much on the spatial – meaning geographical and architectural – representations of social and economic data, laced with physical representations of people and places, and drawing on the extensive interest in how people and places interact. In this context, our focus will be on networks as well as on ways in which we are able to make sense of social and spatial data using various kinds of visual analytics. This latter term we define as the application of analytical ideas from statistical analysis primarily to visual images and the patterns that they display. This will become clear as we introduce examples to show the reader what is possible.

Almost from the first digital computers, graphics was important to their usage. The original computer memories based on vacuum tubes could display a primitive kind of graphics (Dyson, 2012). These storage tube devices were slowly developed during the 1950s and 1960s – an example being the Chicago Area Transportation Study's display of trip data on the 'Cartographatron' (Plummer, 2003). To speed up these kinds of output, line printers were programmed to overprint characters to rapidly produce exploratory outputs. The Symbol/Synographic Mapping program (SYMAP) developed by Alan Schmidt in the late 1960s was widely used in landscape planning (Chrisman, 2006), while Mandelbrot reports similar usage at IBM for the production of fractal images of mountainscapes around the same time (Mandelbrot, 2012). However it was not until the development of machines with specific screen memories devoted to graphics that visualization really began to take off. As the graphics revolution intensified, the first major developments came in real-time animation, in virtual reality technologies, which initially enabled users to interact with graphic scenes either passively in Virtual Reality (VR) theatres or, more actively, in closed environments such as CAVES – Computer Assisted Virtual EnvironmentS. Much of this then moved into the domain of virtual worlds in which users interact with other users usually remotely across the internet but using software that was downloaded to the desktop. What is currently happening are forces driving software from the desktop to the web, and much of what we will say in this chapter relates to the fact that virtually everything we see on the desktop is, in principle, portable to the web. The evolution, for example, of geographic information systems (GIS) technologies has followed this path: mainframe, mini, workstation, PC – the last three essentially desktops – to the passive web (Web 1.0) and thence to the active/interactive web (Web 2.0) and then perhaps on to the semantic web (Web 3.0 and beyond).

In the last decade, various other visualizations of non-spatial data have emerged, the most notable being methods for displaying networks and various statistical graphs. These emerged almost prior to the revolution in scientific visualization, for example, from exploratory data analysis following Tukey's (1977) pioneering work and Tufte's (1992) popularization of information graphics. In fact, although there were rapid developments in graphics such as parallel plots, linked maps and charts, and in flow graphics, the real advances have come more recently in network analysis where there are now some impressive online packages. Web-based systems such as IBM's Many Eyes,[1] where the focus is on different and alternative visualizations such as treemaps, bubble diagrams, tag clouds, etc., dominate the field. We will show some of these, but the array of new graphics is now very large and although many developments centre on a tight set of techniques, there is considerable ingenuity currently being employed in extending this range (Lima, 2011).

To summarize these developments, the evolution of hardware has been one of providing devices for the display of data and other information, from raw to processed, and to interact with these using graphical (rather than text-based) interfaces; the development of software has become increasingly graphic-oriented in terms of how we display data and how we interact with the hardware; software has moved very quickly off-shore, so to speak – to servers where data is increasingly stored remotely and now no longer locally but globally in the Cloud;[2] and data itself in our field has suddenly jumped by orders of magnitude in size, largely because computers have reached the point where they are being embedded in cities to capture data that is streamed in real time. In short, it might be argued that, in the domain of the social sciences, there is a sea change occurring in the type, size, storage and mining of data from a world where data was cross-sectional, static, to one where time is of the essence. All these themes are resonant in the discussion that follows.

What is currently happening in spatial and social media is confusing because there are so many interacting trends and innovations that making sense of all this is difficult. The challenge we address in this chapter is primarily to look at social data

---

[1]www-01.ibm.com/software/analytics/manyeyes

[2]The cloud and cloud computing are 'metaphors for the internet' in that they represent constellations of services and storage that are remote from the user and whose location is of little consequence as long as access is fast. In short, the term is currently being used to define remote data storage and software users can define from any device that is connected to the net: www. dropbox.com is a typical routine example of a cloud service that many readers of this chapter will be familiar with. Also see: http://en.wikipedia.org/wiki/Cloud_computing

in the spatial domain and this does help bound our scope a little. But virtually every aspect of society that can now be represented digitally can be visualized in many different ways. To make sense of all this, we will divide our discussion into the following sections. First, we begin with traditional spatial data – with static maps drawn largely from sources, which may be digital but also hand-crafted rather than real-time data – and we show how the software for handling such data is moving from desktop GIS to the web. This is part of our focus on a 2-dimensional world and thence we move to three dimensions and broach visualization of the built environment.

Second, we move to real-time data – data that is streamed in real time but is usually visualized after the event. Such data is what we refer to as 'big data', one definition of which is data that will not fit into the current generation of an Excel spreadsheet, thus requiring very different mining, sorting and visualization methods than those used previously (Mayer-Schönberger and Cukier, 2013). We then shift to retrieving real-time data using digital techniques, introducing crowdsourcing, but still linked to maps. At this point, it will become clear that many techniques that enable us to visualize such data interact with one another. For example, our crowdsourcing merges with our online map work, while our online map work is used to visualize real-time data. Our third and last section deals with analytics – with modelling and simulation (see also Chapter 6), where we illustrate how traditional land use transportation models are utilizing online portals and open web-based software such as Google Earth. We then speculate on how big data and new visualization capabilities are changing the very systems that we are studying, thus reinforcing a central theme of this book: digital social media and the way we use and develop it is changing the very way we articulate the system of interest, thus illustrating the age old adage that 'more is different' (Anderson, 1972).

11.3 VISUALIZING MAP DATA: FROM 2D TO 3D, FROM THE DESKTOP TO THE WEB

11.3.1 The Rise of Geographic Information Systems and Science

Geographic information systems (GIS) emerged as a synthesis of computer cartography, usually plot or vector-line based with pixel or raster-based gridded spatial data, which, in turn, were underpinned by rudimentary spatial database technologies and spatial statistical analysis (now called spatial analysis). In parallel, mapping systems emerged as the web took hold and by the late 1990s, several online mapping systems emerged. But it was not until 2005 that Google Maps was released, which became the *de facto* online mapping system of choice. However, the move from purely passive, web-based applications, which the original map systems were focussed upon, to more interactive systems, which could be hacked to take additional layers and customized for various applications, also took place during the early 2000s. 'Map Mashups' took hold when Web 2.0 – web applications enabling user-generated content – began to take off (Batty et al., 2010). As these developments continued, GIS began to move onto the web with Internet map servers being common for large-scale professional applications, but with the real focus in this area on adding spatial analysis to such systems through plug-ins and various add-ons, which customize such systems for very large-scale applications.

Three other developments are significant; first the emergence of crowd-sourced maps, particularly Open Street Map (OSM)[3] which is now competing with many mapping agencies and provides a serious alternative to Google Maps and other online systems; second, the development of online and often free GIS systems such as Quantum GIS with many variants of these types of application at present; and third, the recent move of large-scale GIS systems to entire platforms that might be integrated with other web-based services such as the Cloud for remote storage, enterprise systems for large-scale corporate transactions processing, and real-time GIS for problems dominated by the online streaming of datasets.

11.3.2 Open Mapping and the Power of the Web

Desktop systems for GIS still tend to be more powerful than web-based systems but web-based systems enable much more integrated storage facilities. A good example of a web-based map analysis and storage system, which is, to an extent, a one stop shop for simple spatial analysis and map display is CASA's online resource MapTube[4]. MapTube is a portal, which provides access to software that enables any user to convert their own map to a form that can be layered across a non-proprietary map base such as OSM or Google Maps. The software lets the user convert their data file to the map layer and then provides them with a web page that displays their map on top of one of these map bases. As the user may not own the copyright of the map data in question, MapTube only stores the web page – the URL (Universal Resource Locator) – where the user locates the map they have produced using the free MapTube software and, in this way, using MapTube to access the map in question does not infringe any copyright. MapTube thus acts as an archive for maps as well and once the user creates the map, the user is asked to share the URL in the portal. If it is clear that copyright is not being broken, the map itself is stored on the MapTube web site. MapTube also contains a variety of simple spatial analytic tools. Obviously, building up map layers – that is, displaying different map layers on top of one another, thus searching for spatial patterns, which is key to GIS – is a major function of the software. This is akin to exploratory data analysis as has evolved from Tukey's (1977) work, but the software is also able to produce various simple indices and queries related to the map data and also to output certain quantitative data on various map attributes that define the various layers in question.

In MapTube, the most common representation is the choropleth map, where a boundary file is used with polygon areas coloured according to a value. Alternative

---

[3]OSM is at www.openstreetmap.org/ and http://en.wikipedia.org/wiki/OpenStreetMap

[4]www.maptube.org

representations of data might use lines e.g. to represent flows of traffic on roads, while point-based data offers great variation as both colour and size can be used to show the information, along with different icons or even pie-charts to show multivariate data at a point location. Finally, hybrid visualizations, like heat maps and gravitational interpolation, exist where point-based data is processed into a continuous space image. The aim in such contexts is to show how the data decays over distance from a source. Contour maps are closely related to heat maps and show lines of equal value or iso-surfaces as commonly seen in weather maps. Many of these features are invoked in MapTube but one must go to more comprehensive desktop GIS systems to enable the full range of such cartographic and display techniques to be invoked.

CASA's MapTube website provides geospatial data handling and visualization functions as a free service, so the process of having to source boundary files, join with your own data and then build a visualization from scratch is simplified. Using, for example, the UK 2001 Census, there are only a limited number of geometries that make sense when visualizing data and the spatial boundary files are generally an order of magnitude larger than the aspatial data. Due to the mismatch in sizes and re-use of boundary files, it makes sense to hold them on the server and so enable people to make maps by supplying only the aspatial attribute data. This is an approach that has been mirrored in Google's Fusion Tables[5] and is a form of geocoding with spatial join functionality. Taking this a step further, by defining a dataset as a URI[6] endpoint, maps can be built from raw data directly from the Internet, for example, from data in various public (open) datastores. Using MapTube's automatic map generation functionality, 145 variables can be mapped from the 2001 Census and now 2,558 variables from the latest 2011 Census.

As an example, population density maps from the 2001 and 2011 Census can be mapped using MapTube's CSV (Comma-Separated Value) upload functionality. The maps were built at 'Lower Super Output Area' level (LSOA) of which there are 34,753 in England and Wales. Raw data, for example, can be downloaded from the Census website as an Excel spreadsheet and a small amount of editing turns it into a table containing just a header row and rows of data values which can be uploaded to MapTube where the map column is automatically identified as one of the boundary datasets stored on the server, so the data can be plotted on the map immediately as we show in Figure 11.1 a) for the 2011 data.

Once data has been published on MapTube, visual comparisons between maps are possible by adding multiple layers and using transparency. In this way, maps can be compared even if they are not using the same geometry. Although the 2011 map in Figure 11.1 a) is almost identical to the 2001 map at the country level, by zooming

[5]Google Fusion Tables defined at http://tables.googlelabs.com

[6]URI is a uniform resource identifier, a 'string of characters used to identify a name of a web resource', see http://en.wikipedia.org/wiki/Uniform_resource_identifier, not to be confused with a URL, uniform resource locator or URN, a uniform resource name.

in towards the street level, significant differences can be detected, which is the main advantage of using a web-based map of this type. The scale doubles at each successive zoom level, so between zoom levels zero and 21, it is possible to represent detail that would be impossible on a paper map for an area this size. This is so obvious a point that it barely seems worth stressing but the real advantages of web-based systems (and desktop too) is that users can search for patterns at different levels as we show for population density in Figure 11.2.

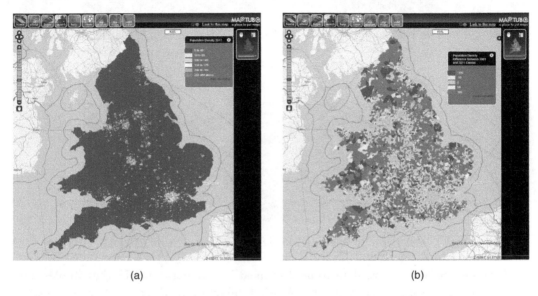

(a)   (b)

Figure 11.1 CASA's MapTube Website (www.maptube.org) showing a) population density in 2011 and b) changes in density 2001–2011

a) Plotted as 'Persons per Hectare' from the 2011 UK Census table QS102. The data picks out the population centres of London, Birmingham, Liverpool, Manchester, Leeds and Newcastle but in b) the differences plotted clearly distinguish declines in density in the large cities and increases in the rural and small town locations.

The two datasets used to make this example are simple CSV files and there are a whole host of open-source and free tools available that can be used to work with this type of data. With the right set of tools, it is possible to achieve considerably advanced analysis without much effort, so we can use any two such datasets to build our derived maps of change. Tools like Microsoft's Excel, Google Docs or OpenOffice can be used to edit CSV files, Google's Refine (formerly Freebase) can be used to clean data, and free databases like MySQL and PostgreSQL can be used for more complex analysis. Once the two tables have been joined and the result is available, the 'Export' function is used to save the data into another CSV file. In this way, population change per hectare which is plotted in Figure 11.1 b) is computed. One of the issues with data based on boundary files is that the boundaries change over time. In the case of the 2001 and 2011 data, this difference is very small, but there are a few white holes visible in Wales where the base map shows through. A good way round this is to grid the data, but this adds a layer of complex geospatial processing.

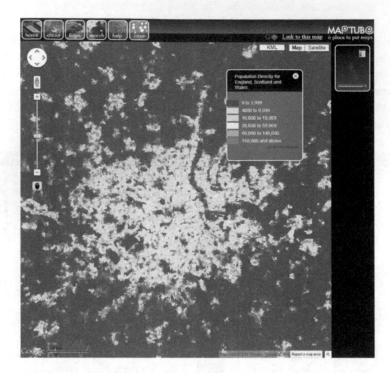

Figure 11.2 2011 Population density at the Metropolitan scale in Greater London

The system also allows data to be displayed in any desktop GIS that implements the Open Geospatial Consortium's WMS standard (e.g., Quantum GIS or ArcGIS). It is this blurring of the boundaries between the traditional GIS methods and the new methods in geospatial analysis now emerging on the web that can potentially offer new insights for social research. With today's web-based technologies, many components of a traditional GIS system can be implemented as web services, with the advantage of being able to handle much larger datasets more easily. Libraries like Geotools are starting to move into the Cloud and run on distributed systems like Hadoop, offering GIS services with the power and scalability of Microsoft's Azure, Amazon's EC2 and Google's AppEngine. This type of infrastructure can still be implemented by organizations internally, using their own hardware together with open-source software, but the flexibility now exists to push big problems onto Cloud systems when local computing power is inadequate. Through virtualization, computing power is now flexible enough that spare compute cycles can be harnessed to work on these big problems, perhaps running big geospatial analyses overnight on local computer systems and pushing really big analyses onto the Cloud as necessary. These considerations take our argument beyond the scope of this chapter and interested readers are referred to many of the excellent references that develop these ideas (e.g., Jurney, 2013)

In using computer mapping systems in general and GIS, in particular, it is worth noting that there are recurrent problems of ensuring that the map base – how the map is projected into the plane – is understood. Following the release of Google Maps, all contemporary Web mapping systems use the Universal Transverse Mercator projection, but with a spherical model of the Earth used for performance reasons. The benefits of using these systems are in the dissemination of research outputs to a wider audience via the Internet and the ease with which data can be placed into its spatial context. Base maps showing street layouts, cycle routes, satellite images or terrain maps are available using Google Maps, OSM or Bing Maps. The only requirement is the ability to draw the data over the base map in the correct location, which usually requires a coordinate re-projection. Most people are familiar with the WGS84 system of latitude and longitude expressed in degrees, which is a different coordinate system from the one used to make the base map. In the Google Maps API, points (as clickable pins), lines and polygons can be added as overlays using coordinates in WGS84, but only for a limited amount of data. The situation in OpenLayers is similar, but a conversion between the WGS84 data and Spherical Mercator map needs to be defined first. The main component of a web map is a web page containing a Javascript, Flash or Silverlight application to handle the drawing of the maps using image tiles or vector overlays, along with implementing the pan and zoom functions. There can be differing levels of complexity at this layer, with Google Maps API v3 targeting more lightweight applications that can run on smart phones, while OpenLayers is more of a Javascript client-side GIS containing functions to import data. It is also currently unique in its handling of different map projections and coordinate transformations, so it is correspondingly harder to use.

In order to make full use of web mapping systems for visualizing social data, we need a way of drawing the data onto the map tiles, that is onto the raster basis that the map is segmented into, and also an ability to compare maps from different sources of data. The base maps, which are required to give our data spatial context, are cartography, which is drawn using a set of rules for visualizing features like roads and rivers. In contrast to this, the visualizations shown in Figures 11.1 and 11.2 use a choropleth visualization technique where areas in a boundary file are coloured according to their data value. In this case, the boundary file is the Census Output Areas file, while the colour scale follows the 'person per hectare' field in the data. Here, we make a distinction between a tile renderer that can handle cartography and a specialized tile renderer for handling data. While tile renderers designed for drawing the base maps can usually draw choropleths using a similar set of rules, there are often more complex visualization techniques like heat maps and gravitational interpolation for visualizing density which require specialized systems.

11.3.3 From 2D to 3D: Populating the Built Environment with Social Data

The main way of displaying spatial data is the map, enshrined in the notion that the spatial variations of interest at all scales are best understood in the 2-dimensional thematic world of the point or choropleth map. This is based on the premise that the key feature of the spatial world is distance on the plane and that the third dimension contributes only a small fraction to the structuring and location of urban activity. In fact, there is variation of spatial attributes in this dimension but it is nothing like as rich as the plane and it is only during the last one hundred years that this has become significant due to our ability to build upwards. Nevertheless, the third dimension offers a much richer sense of understanding the built environment, in that non-experts identify more closely with pictures in this dimension than they do with maps. Simply in terms of communicating an understanding of some social variations in space, the third dimension is becoming more important. Moreover, there are now substantial variations in space within tall buildings and building complexes, which hitherto have almost gone uncharted. Here, we will briefly introduce these developments that we expect to gather pace over the next decade.

The first models of cities (which we will present in the last section of this chapter) were symbolic – representing social and economic relationships in two dimensional space and explaining how different activities locate and interact using various social physics and econometric methods for articulating causal effects. It was only when graphics really took off that the notion of modelling the city as a set of geometric objects became possible. In the last decade, geometric models of buildings have been extended city-wide, creating what have been called 'virtual city' models of which there are now many hundreds. Hard on the heels of Google Maps came Google Earth, which enabled the 3D geometry of buildings to be inserted into the software, thus providing a ready-made platform for building such models. CASA's development of a 3D block model for Greater London was operational by 2005 and was built using map parcel and street line data from the UK National Mapping Agency Ordnance Survey, supplemented by 3D height data from LIDAR surveys made by InfoTerra, all synthesized within ArcGIS, which provided the basic software for construction. Once models like this have been built, they can be exported into various other CAD (computer-aided design) software, which enables more elaborate graphics to be generated.

To an extent, our interest is in populating these geometric models with social data, that is, tagging key variables and attributes to buildings, noting, for example, things like working population, density and so on at the building or parcel level, while also linking these to more material attributes such as energy, information use, traffic generated, pollution and so on. There are not many examples of this so far, with most tagging smoothed map surfaces to 3D representations. In Figure 11.3 a), we show our typical block model of London for a portion of the centre – the model contains some 3 million building blocks out to the M25 orbital road or beltway– but we have only succeeding in tagging a fraction of these blocks to socio-economic attributes. We have, however, begun to merge these 3D geometries with 3D surfaces as we show in Figure 11.3 b), for example, for air pollution (Batty and Hudson-Smith, 2005). In Figure 11.3 c), we show how we can utilize 3D visualizations by building a crude geometry of the city using histograms. These are no longer buildings but levels of density or intensity – the 3D equivalent (with respect to floor-space this time) of the maps in Figures 11.1 and 11.2 rooted to a grid interpolated from geometric boundaries such as lower super output areas, a unit of geography used in the UK Census. We can fly around these maps and they do provide excellent ways not only to engage stakeholders and users of these datasets in policy issues but also to explore different possible patterns that come from looking at the city – at the data, that is – in 3D city form from different perspectives and angles. In Figure 11.3 d), we show how land use can be tagged to this kind of media at the more local scale, thus bringing alive the traditional land use map, which is coloured using the same shading as recommended in the UK 1947 Town and Country Planning Act.

(a)   (b)

(c)   (d)

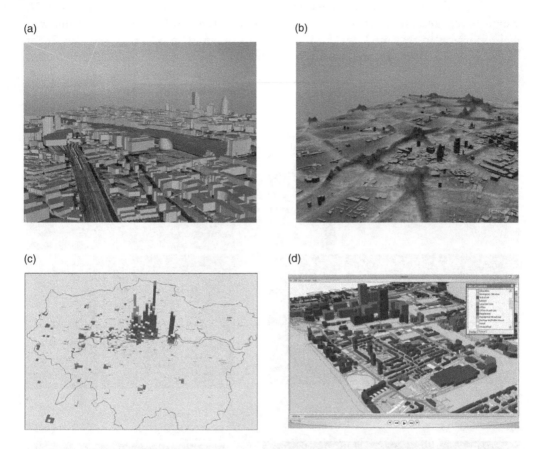

Figure 11.3   Moving to 3D visualization and navigating through the models

a) The virtual London model built from vector land parcel, streetline and 3D LIDAR data and visualized in ArcGIS. b) Layering a pollution surface (NO_2) across the model c) Office (blue) and retail (yellow) floorspace visualized as 3D histograms d) Land use mapping in Canary Wharf, London's second central business district.

There are many extensions of these kinds of 3D visualizations. First, we can embed these into virtual worlds, 3D environments in which users or stakeholders can appear as avatars and actually walk in the space in which the 3D city might be embedded. These worlds enable users to manipulate the scene. They are often considered as virtual exhibition spaces where users can engage in dialogue and debate, but they might also be considered as virtual design studios for design over the net where the designers are remotely logged onto the world as we show in Figure 11.4 a). Here, two avatars are positioning a high building from a menu of such buildings into the urban scene that is a portion of our Virtual London block model. These kinds of reality can be augmented on the spectrum from theatres where users engage passively in the scene to CAVES, which are more interactive and separate from the real world, all the way to internalized head set types of device that immerse the user completely in the scene. Many variants exist where there is a mix of immersion and external usage. For example, the notion of the 3D world being accessible as a fly-through but in a theatre-like context is one way of immersion in this medium. Flying through these 3D models we have built for London within the software is extremely slow still, with movies of such animations often made off-line.

(a) (b)

(c) (d)

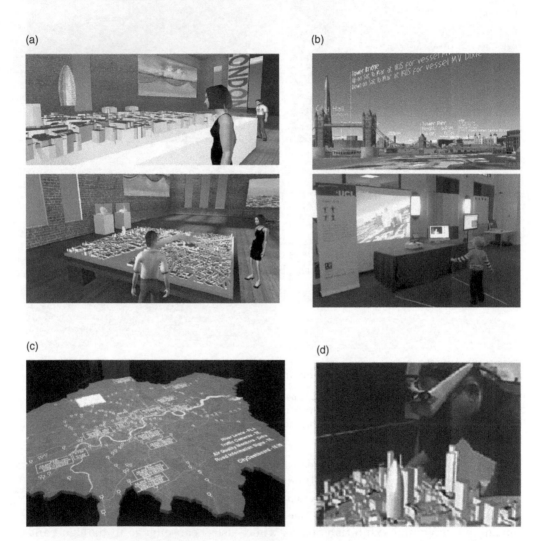

Figure 11.4 Augmenting 3D visualization merging the virtual with the real

a) Creating a virtual exhibition space/design studio where users can interact in a virtual world b) Easier navigation of a virtual model using gaming media c) The London Data Table: projecting digital media back onto a material surface d) A holographic like projection as seen through the headset of one of the users interacting with another

We have developed a fast method for such fly-through, which we call PigeonSim, illustrated in Figure 11.4 b), where a user is able to navigate through the model which is imported into Google Earth and then accessed using games technology, in this case through a Kinect motion sensing device that links an X-Box to a Windows application. Users can thus control their navigation in this way simply by standing in front of the box and controlling it with their body movements. We are also developing various other realizations of virtual media in more analogue-like contexts, where we consider that our digital media is best displayed in a more familiar way. Just as conventional material block models of the city are being augmented with digital inputs, we consider that augmenting our digital inputs with conventional material media is also a way forward to involve users and stakeholders. In Figure 11.4 c), we illustrate how we can gain real interaction between users and data by merging the virtual and the real by projecting our media for Greater London – animations of flows of traffic, GIS mapping and so on, onto the physical map that we call the London Data Table. Users can control the media from the computer but display it on the table. Last but not least, in Figure 11.4 d) we show how we can fashion a completely immersive environment where the virtual scene is projected directly into the headset with the users interacting with one another through the common scene.

11.3.4 Real-time Data: Sensing and Mining 'Big Data' in Space and Time

Much of the data that we work with is collected using traditional sources and then transcribed to digital media, with the best example being the population Census. Some of this data is being captured digitally in the first instance, while most of the secondary data that social scientists now use is already in digital form. However, as computers are increasingly embedded into the built environment and as ever larger proportions of the population are using hand-held devices, such as smart phones and tablets, an increasing amount of data is being directly streamed into archives or into applications that involve real-time actions. Here we will focus on data streams associated with transport and with social media: transport, which is associated with the use of smart cards (the Oyster card in London) and the location of vehicles used in public transit, and social media which is captured from micro-blogging (Twitter data).

Much of this real-time data clusters around weather, transit, road traffic, pollution, Twitter trends, stock market prices, utilities and local news, some of which are national rather than local data. Use of these feeds is fast becoming routine and we have organized some of these into what we call a City Dashboard.[7] This is available for several UK cities, our exemplar being London, which has more easily available data than any of the other cities (Birmingham, Brighton, Cardiff, Edinburgh, Glasgow, Leeds and Manchester) from which feeds are also taken. We show the dashboard for London in Figure 11.5. Each element can be placed on a different screen and this has been installed in the Greater London Authority on a wall of 12 iPads,

---

[7]http://citydashboard.org

which is shown alongside the dashboard in the figure. This visualization wall is built around the control room concept and displays citywide data gathered via the City Dashboard, updated on average every two seconds with feeds configurable from an array of options. The wall can also be controlled remotely via any computing device, allowing a user to not only change data but also enable a mode where a video can be shown across all 12 iPads simultaneously.

(a)

(b)

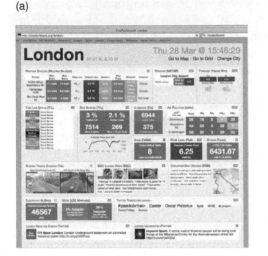

Figure 11.5   a) The Dashboard and b) its display in a visualization wall

11.3.5 Retrieving and Visualizing Real-time Transit Data

The simplest of such data is accessible using various applications programming interfaces (APIs). For example, we have adapted MapTube to archive, analyse and display data on times, locations and delays of vehicles on transit systems (in fact, only for Greater London so far) and this enables us to visualize the streaming data in near real time (with a latency of about three minutes from the time when the query is made on the server to when the data arrives on our computers). Positions of all tube trains in London can be plotted on a map of the network, along with buses and overground trains for the whole country. During the rush hour, there can be up to 450 tube trains running in London, 7,000 buses, 900 trains and 7,500 TfL Cycle Hire bikes, so we are capturing the daily cycle of people commuting to and from work, in terms of vehicles used not trips made, we should emphasize. Population density, unsurprisingly, follows transport links (or vice versa) as we show in Figure 11.6 a) below, but by putting all this data together we are able to gain insights into how the physical fabric of the city is linked to social segregation. Figure 11.6 b) shows in more detail the typical information available for the tube with respect to one of the trains on the Central Line.

This data is useful for computing delays but it needs to be matched to demand for transit if it is to be useful for journey planning by individuals. Many transit systems are now using smart cards for payment and all public transit in London is now covered in this way with about 80 per cent of all tube travellers, overground heavy rail and bus using the so-called Oyster card, as well as contactless payment cards. There are about 5–6 million tap in and tap outs on the London tube system each working (week) day, which is about 3 million travellers as recorded in July 2012. This data records origin station (tap in entrance) and destination station (tap out exit) for a unique identifier (passenger) and the time at which the record is stamped. We can construct the complete flow matrix from station to station in any interval of time using shortest routes algorithms, although the system is complicated and much work needs still to be done in piecing journeys together due to the fact that the underground has a complex geometry and many corridors linking tube stations. Moreover, the data is limited in parts due to the fact that there can be a mismatch between tap in and tap outs if barriers are open, because those with fixed season cards or free passes (over 60s and young children) do not get 'fined' (charged the maximum fare for all zones) if they fail to tap in or out. There can be a substantial mismatch between the data streams, although the data does enable one to identify these kinds of problem quite easily.

(a)   (b)

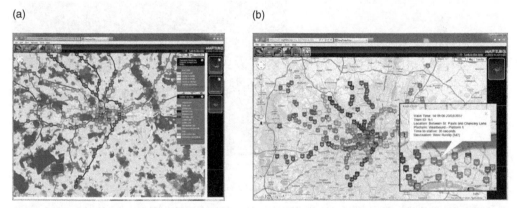

Figure 11.6   Real-time tube train locations

a) Population density from the 2001 Census overlaid on trains data on 11 March 2013 at 15:00 and b) tube delay data identified on 20 March 2012 at 14.39.

Within the dataset, we can easily explore routine behaviour over days and weeks and even months. It is straightforward to identify deviations that might be due to disruptions, school holidays, sporting events and so on from such data and, in principle, this provides important information for managing the system and ensuring that it is free-flowing. Moreover, like all interaction or flow data, we are able to construct not only flows but locational activity at hubs (stations) and in Figure 11.7 a), we show the actual tube network with its links between stations using contemporary graph visualization software and in b) the flow at the peak hour showing tap ins and tap outs at a typical morning peak. We have begun to use this dataset to explore questions of disruption caused by closing stations – a familiar enough occurrence at peak hours when some become overcrowded – and by closing segments of lines. We have done this for several key examples, such as closing main line rail stations where the tube is linked in with the network and where volumes are substantial at the peak hour. What we do is to reroute travellers onto other lines and re-compute the volumes that then enter or exit at all those stations unaffected by the disruption. In Figure 11.8, we show what happens when we close Liverpool Street, which is one the busiest main line stations with around 435,000 passengers moving through the tube stations that make up the complex each day. Figure 11.8 gives an indication of the increases in passenger volumes in the red bubbles, compared to decreases in the blue bubbles. Without going into considerably more detail, we can say that the impact of closing this station does not impact as much as might be anticipated. There are increases eastwards outside the Circle line but not much around it, for it seems that the redundancy of stations and lines in the centre of London is such as to mitigate such impacts. In one sense, as soon as we begin to broach these kinds of problems, then we invoke a new style of analysis, which is data-driven modelling. Visualization, of course, is essential to portray this kind of complexity.

(a)   (b)

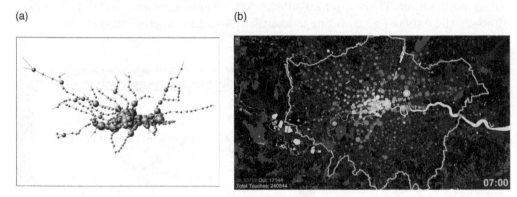

Figure 11.7   Geometry of the tube network and real-time volumes at stations

a) The network visualized with stations shown according to the number of lines that intersect (indegrees/outdegrees) and b) flow volumes at the morning peak where the maximum flow is shown at each station: green tap outs and red tap ins

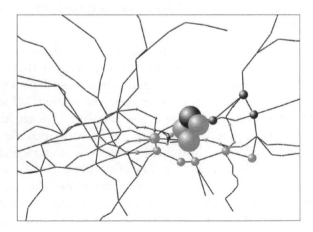

Figure 11.8   Impact of closing a mainline station (Liverpool Street) on flow of travellers passing through related stations

11.3.6 Visualizing Social Media

Other sets of data that show spatial and social behaviours in real time are based on Twitter and similar data. Again, we are able to record tweets in terms of the time they are sent, their location (if the GPS on the device is switched on), and their content using the Twitter API. At the time of writing, however, there are changes to the streaming of data that are likely to limit what can be obtained freely in the future. We are able to produce locational data quite easily and we have recorded the density of tweets by location for a dozen or so large cities around the world (Neuhaus, 2013). Developed around the populist name 'Tweet-o-Meter', we have developed a system to mine data within a 30 km range of urban areas, focusing on New York, London, Paris, Munich, Tokyo, Moscow, Sydney, Toronto, San Francisco, Barcelona and Oslo. In Figure 11.9 a) we show a map of the density of tweets in Greater London produced for a three week period during the months of February and March in 2011 and this is clearly highly correlated with population density, although it is possible by drilling into the map to associate tweets with particular activity locations, such as schools, parks and entertainment centres. Analysis of the content is much more problematic as content analysis of tweets is extremely difficult (Chew and Eysenbach, 2010). One useful picture is given by extracting the languages used by Twitter users. Using Google Translator software, Cheshire and Manley (2013) have produced a very detailed map of ten million tweets over three months for Greater London and this does excite interesting comparisons with ethnicity, multiple deprivation indices and related social area analyses. An earlier version of the map produced for the ten top Twitter languages is shown in Figure 11.9 b).

(a) (b)

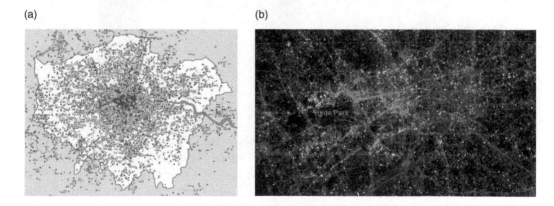

Figure 11.9   The spatial density of tweets in London

a) Recorded for three weeks in the months of February and March 2011 b) tweets by language where the grey foundation of the map is formed from the majority of tweets in English. Other nationalities, in order of most to least prolific, are Spanish (white), French (red), Turkish (blue), Arabic (green), Portuguese (purple), German (orange), Italian (yellow), Malay (cyan) and Russian (violet).

There are other social media such as Facebook, Google+, Foursquare and related sites that now enable their data to be mined and, in our context here, visualized in locational terms. Some of this data is particularly useful as it has much more substantive content than short text messages. A more focussed visualization and analysis of Twitter data, however, relates to particularly significant events and the way in which people react to these spatially. The London riots in August 2011 were a case in point. Most of the regular media channels were suggesting that social media was being used to direct the riots, which may well have been true initially using encrypted instant messaging (as on the Blackberry device), which we do not have access to. Towards the end of the four days of riots, we collected a snapshot from Twitter for all the UK to use for analysis, which we illustrate in Figure 11.10.

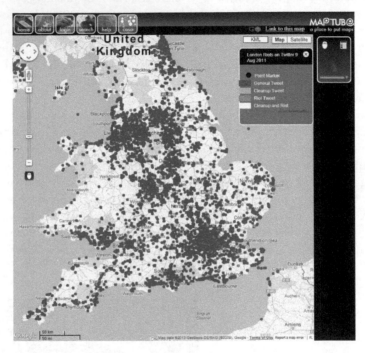

Figure 11.10   Geo-located tweets captured from Twitter between 15:00 and 22:00 BST on Tuesday 9th August 2011

Looking at the map of tweets, which we show in MapTube, the majority do <u>not</u> contain tags such as '#londonriots', '#ukriots', '#riots', '#riotcleanup' or '@riotcleanup'. However, by clicking on the individual points, we can explore the data and read the messages to find out what people are tweeting about. There are 34,314 points in this dataset and only 1,330 contained a riots hashtag (3.9 per cent). The problem here is that while comparatively few people are using a recognized hashtag that can be easily identified computationally, they are still talking about the riots. The missing link at the moment in terms of this type of analysis is that natural language processing (NLP) has not advanced to the point where our analysis can be any more meaningful than this. Moreover, tweets also have their own language rather like text-speak, so an NLP system trained on Standard English is going to perform poorly. We cannot be certain, but many of the messages appear to imply that these tweets are simply from persons who are saying they have left work early and got home safely, no more than that. Related analysis of Twitter data is explored in Chapters 2 (sections 2.2–2.4), 3 (sections 3.2.1–3.2.2), 8 and 10 (sections 10.2–10.4).

11.3.7 Retrieving and Visualizing Crowdsourced Data

Crowdsourcing is the term used for methods of data creation, where large groups of users not organized centrally, generate content that is shared (Howe, 2008). From direct public involvement via citizen science initiatives, such as the well-documented Galaxy Zoo, through to simply tapping into online data feeds, this is marking out a new era of volunteered information and knowledge creation. The data is captured in real time but the time scale may not be grounded in any routine process, largely because it depends on the 'crowd' responding. To gain substantial data, there needs to be some sort of broadcast medium to the crowd alerting them to the need to respond. The notion that there might be value in harvesting these kinds of response is based on the observation that, although a large number of individual estimates may be incorrect, imprecise, uncertain and ambiguous, their average can be a match for expert judgment (Surowiecki, 2004). Judiciously handled, randomly sampling the opinions or calculations of a large number of users might lead to data and information that are surprisingly accurate and that, in some cases, cannot be recorded in any other way. The potential of crowdsourcing methods applies across the sciences but it has had specific impact in spatial content through Volunteered Geographic Information (VGI) (Goodchild, 2007). Open Street Map (OSM), which we noted earlier, is perhaps the best-known VGI output, started in UCL in 2004 and it is based on over 400,000 volunteers creating a free editable vector map of the world. While many early volunteers were highly technically literate, they were not necessarily experts in geographical data collection. Yet, through crowd-based quality control and refined workflows aimed at members beyond the traditional community, OSM has become the map of choice for many users.

A series of toolkits and workflows – protocols and problem-solving processes which direct the way in which data is made computable – now exist to enable social scientists to collect and analyse data from the crowd as a means to include mass human input in spatial analysis. One such tool we have developed is a public website called SurveyMapper,[8] which allows 'anyone' (with access to a web site) to ask the crowd 'anything' and returns a live map of results on a number of geospatial levels from the globe to the street (SurveyMapper, whose backend is MapTube for visualization, has been used by the BBC (Radio 4, Look East, BBC North and BBC South) and the Greater London Authority as well as the wider academic community to carry out rapid data collection. Tens of thousands of inputs can be collected quickly, providing

---

[8]www.surveymapper.com

a near real-time view of research questions. Data can be exported later for more rigorous analysis or integration with existing datasets. In Figure 11.11, we show the example of a map of broadband speeds of TV viewers in the Eastern region of the UK who were asked to click on a link to measure the speed of their Internet connection and then key in a locational referent, such as a UK postcode. In this way, one can build up a dynamic map over the period when the survey took place and assuming the response is representative (a big assumption at present), this will converge to a picture of the data that is useful and whose bias is known. This data is streamed in real time and, in some circumstances, might be organized to actually reflect rapid response, although in the examples we have worked with, the crowd has been left to react over a matter of days or weeks.

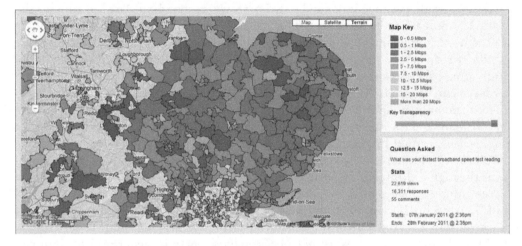

Figure 11.11   Spatial crowdsourcing: evolving data in real-time

All this kind of data raises enormous questions of privacy and security, as well as the degree to which it is representative. We are not able to explore these issues here but elsewhere in this book they are explored in some detail (see Chapter 12 which deals with ethics and confidentiality). These are important issues and are likely to become central to how we deal with the increasing deluge of digital social data.

11.4 PREDICTIVE ANALYTICS: INTERPRETING AND COMMUNICATING SPATIAL MEDIA

Finally, we move away from data and representation to ways in which we can understand the mechanisms used to model or simulate that data through digital visualization. There a strong momentum to abandon traditional ways of theory building and testing through empirical verification as the focus on data is generating many new ideas about how the world works that can be elicited through crowd-sourcing and the generation of big data (Anderson, 2008). Nevertheless, many traditional models are being extended and disaggregated through simulating every agent in a population rather than sampling a population or modelling them in aggregate (Heppenstall et al., 2012). This confronts big data head on in terms of inferring and deducing new theories from that data, but the fact that the data volumes are large and the models often compute intensive means that visualization is of the essence.

Visualization is needed for small data as well as big and models built on the basis of theory validation against traditional small datasets using extensive visualization are as new as those for big data. Moreover, the workings of the model can now be exposed in ways that are highly amenable to visualization, while the idea that observations and predictions can be exhaustively compared across many, many combinations of model calibrations elevates the problem of model visualization to that akin to visualizing real-time data. Linking model processes to outcomes generates novel ways of visualizing the relationships between processes and spatial outcomes. There are many such models that are now being visualized in these new ways and all we can provide here is a snapshot of our own experiences. Although we have worked with generative and agent-based models that tend to require visualization because aggregate statistics do not give real meaning to their outcomes, we will show two examples here of essentially aggregate models that generate locational activities to small areas such as census tracts.

11.4.1 Visualizing Empirically Calibrated Land Use Transport Models

The first model is an aggregative land use transport model that simulates the movement of people between work and home, work and shopping, home and shopping and other flows such as journeys to school and health care. These various sectors are simulated using spatial interaction (gravitational) models and are coupled together reflecting a sequence of competition between these activities, but brought to equilibrium through iteration around the sequence of simulations. These types of model have a long heritage (Batty, 2009); they are aggregate and also static in that they simulate urban structure at a cross-section in time. They tend to be parsimonious with respect to their parameters – essentially the parameters control the effect of gravity and potential and the coupling, so current models tend to have numbers of parameters in the tens rather than hundreds. Only recently have such models become statistically manageable in terms of the validation, as often the process of estimating parameters is through trial and error. The model we show here is for Greater London and its wider metropolitan region divided into some 1,767 zones (wards in UK Census terms). At every stage of the simulation, the model's outputs can be visualized in 2D map terms but it is easy to extend this to 3D using non-proprietary software which can be linked to the model outputs on the desktop and the web in the same manner we showed in Figure 11.3c) where we examined floorspace as histograms arrayed across the space of Greater London.

(a)

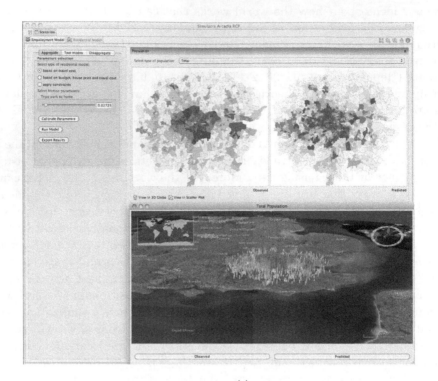

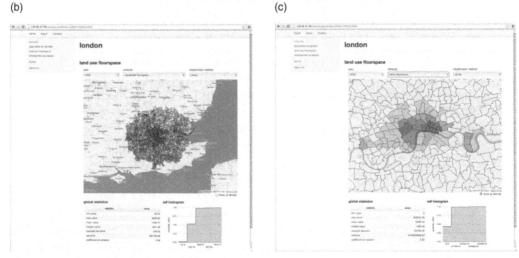

(b)   (c)

Figure 11.12 Visualizing model outputs a) in 2D and 3D with b) data at the metro-region level and c) at the local level

In Figure 11.12 a), we show outputs from the model region and their visualization in 3D using the NASA World Wind software, and different levels of zoom in the model portal windows in 11.12 b) and c). This enables visualization of outcomes from the model as the simulation runs and data can be piped directly to the 3D software, while non-model data can also be compared against model outputs. These models tend to work at the level of thematic map layers and thus more geometric and raster data, which is not required in the model simulation, can be compared with model outputs. We are now generalizing these kinds of model outputs into web-based portals, where the model type can be applied to many different examples. We show the model data used in London at two levels of zoom with some simple spatial analytics/statistics relating to the data in the portal window shown in Figure 11.12 b) and c). The ideas behind these kinds of visualization are explained in detail elsewhere (Batty, 2013).

11.4.2 Visualizing Theoretically Inspired Location Models

Our second model implements the basic theory of location first proposed by von Thünen in 1826 (Hall, 1966) within a 3D geometric CAD model framework. We have already seen how 3D geometric models of cities, which are essentially representations of urban activities tagged to the blocks associated with land parcels at the street level, can be tagged to urban activities data. Such models can be tagged to data that is from model outcomes or predictions, where they simulate the structure of activities in cities at the parcel/block level. ArcGIS has been extended to include methods of procedural modelling based on City Engine originally developed at ETH in Zürich. Such modelling is rule-based and enables users to create and render very large scenes by formulating rules that can be applied systematically to extensive areas of the block geometry. It can be used for a variety of purposes, from rendering the texture of large scenes to populating geometric models with blocks that conform to certain rules of urban structure, such as those developed using basic models of location, through to models that reflect spatial interaction based on gravitation.

Von Thünen's model essentially simulates the competition for land uses around a market centre. The model determines how different land uses occupy different concentric rings around the centre according to their ability to compete for land in terms of the payment of rent, which, in essence, depends on the importance of transport costs in the production process. Activities where transport cost is more important are likely to outbid activities where it is less important in such a way the land use in question locates nearer the centre and is able to pay more rent.

This bid rent model has been generalized by Wilson and Birkin (1987) and it can be extended to multiple market centres. What we are able to show using the procedural rules of City Engine is how a more complex dynamic than von Thünen's original model can be used to simulate complex radial structures of land use as we illustrate in Figure 11.13 a). The sliders in the interface in Figures 11.13 a) to c) indicate how we can change the structure of land uses in the city and visualize the outcomes, in much the same manner Steadman introduced for the same model using much simpler 2D software for small examples (Batty, Steadman and Xie, 2006). We also show in Figure 11.13 d) a generalization of the model to retail gravitation, where we introduce multiple centres and examine the intensity of spending around each centre. The application required a combination of Python and CGA rules (a scripting language used by the CityEngine interface) and the manual development of an information system where these two platforms automatically exchange information. This was a key feature, as it allowed the applications to perform the necessary calculations while maintaining an interactive capacity. The result is the real-time visualization of dynamic models, which can be directly affected by the user. These examples demonstrate real-time visualization of urban model structures and produce a 3D real-time interactive animation of how an urban structure might evolve. The user can participate in the simulation process by controlling or altering different attributes while the simulation is running and experiment with different scenarios. The outcome is both visual and analytical, as there is the option of providing 3D diagrams and matrices of different statistics.

(a)   (b)

(c)   (d)

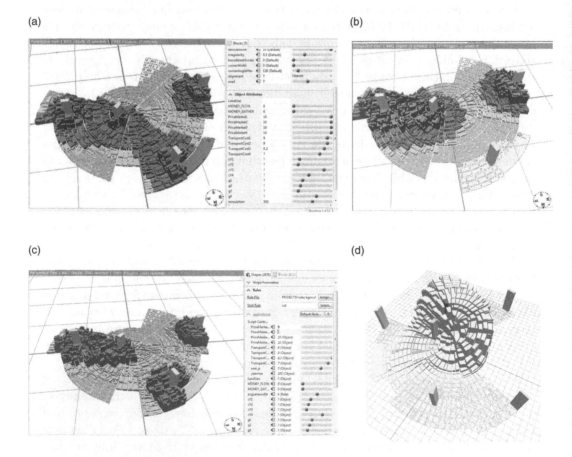

Figure 11.13 Using procedural modelling in City Engine to visualize radially structured land use activity patterns

Reflecting density, transport cost and rent a) user selects a location for a new city centre b) model calculates land uses in real time c) user can use the generated sliders on the right hand side to change the parameters of the model d) multiple centres and their impact on residential activity in a model of retail gravitation.

11.5 THE FUTURE OF DIGITAL VISUALIZATION

There are many developments in the visualization of spatial and social data that we have not been able to catalogue here. In particular, the whole field of infographics, which is essentially a development of exploratory data analysis, is giving rise to new kinds of representation more abstract than the illustrations we have included here. New methods of representing networks, bipartite graphs and flow structures, which present various kinds of correlations and interactions, are being rapidly developed. Many of these new varieties of graphic are augmented by animations that we have not been able to show here, although these are implicit in the construction of the pictures that illustrate these ideas.

The data we have mainly shown tend to be relatively large-scale in terms of capacity, largely due to the fact that spatial and temporal extent can massively increase the size of the dataset, but we have also noted that relatively small datasets, which still dominate the social world, are being radically improved through new methods of visualization. Software for such visualization is increasingly free, a good example being the IBM site Many Eyes and the sites that offer network software such as Pajek[9] and NodeXL.[10]

Much social data, which is often intrinsically non-spatial or where the spatial dimension is unimportant to the analysis, is likely to make use of this more abstract software. Our focus here on 2D and 3D and on temporal streaming represent new ways of thinking of social data in the spatial domain, but we believe that the use of these new dimensions is more generic than space or time itself. All spatial data implies sequences, which, of course, represent the organizing principles of space and time – adjacency in space and continuity and irreversibility in time. There are some who proclaim that big data and the web are heralding the end of theory but we have seen how theory building can also benefit. New ideas about how social systems interact that break with the simple principles of sequence that have marked all the examples here are on the horizon. These are evolving to understand social systems through the lens of globalization, which is destroying spatial and temporal simplicity as the world becomes more complex. These are the trends that are driving social and spatial science and in the next decades, we are likely to see radically new kinds of visualization driven as much by new ways of articulating the way social systems function as by the appearance of new forms of data and analytics.

11.6 BIBLIOGRAPHY

Anderson, C. (2008) 'The end of theory: the data deluge makes the scientific method obsolete', *Wired*, June 23rd. Available from www.wired.com/science/discoveries/magazine/16-07/pb_theory (accessed 15 Dec 2014).

Anderson. P.W. (1972) 'More is different', *Science*, 177(4047): 393–6.

---

[9]http://vlado.fmf.uni-lj.si/pub/networks/pajek

[10]http://nodexl.codeplex.com

Batty, M. (2009) 'Urban Modelling', in R. Kitchin and N. Thrift (eds), *International Encyclopedia of Human Geography*, Volume 12. Oxford: Elsevier. pp. 51–58.

Batty, M. (2013) 'Visually-driven urban simulation: exploring fast and slow change in residential location', *Environment and Planning A*, 45: 532–52.

Batty, M. and Hudson-Smith, A. (2005) 'Urban simulacra: from real to virtual cities, back and beyond', *Architectural Design*, *75* (6): 42–7.

Batty, M., Hudson-Smith, A., Milton, R. and Crooks, A. (2010) 'Map mashups, Web 2.0 and the GIS revolution', *Annals of GIS*, *16*(1): 1–13.

Batty, M., Steadman, P. and Xie, Y. (2006) 'Visualization in spatial modeling', in J. Portugali (ed.), *Complex Artificial Environments*. Berlin: Springer. pp. 49–70.

Cheshire, J. and Manley, E. (2013) 'The Twitter Map of London', *Guardian Newspaper*, Tuesday 26–03–13, 28–29; Available from http://spatialanalysis.co.uk/2012/10/londons-twitter-languages (accessed 16 Dec 2014).

Chew, C. and Eysenbach, G. (2010) 'Pandemics in the age of Twitter: content analysis of Tweets during the 2009 H1N1 outbreak', *PLoS One*, 5(11): e14118. DOI:10.1371/journal.pone.0014118

Chrisman, N. (2006) *Charting the Unknown: How Computer Mapping at Harvard Became GIS*. Redlands, CA: ESRI Press.

Dyson, G. (2012) *Turing's Cathedral: The Origins of the Digital Universe*. New York: Pantheon Books.

Goodchild, M.F. (2007) 'Citizens as sensors: the world of volunteered geography', *GeoJournal*, *69*: 211–21.

Hall, P. (ed.) (1966) *Von Thünen's Isolated State: An English Edition of Der Isolierte Staat by Johann Heinrich Von Thünen*. Oxford: Pergamon Press.

Heppenstall, A.J., Crooks, A.T., See, L.M. and Batty, M. (eds) (2012) *Agent-Based Models of Geographical Systems*. Berlin and New York: Springer.

Howe, J. (2008) *Crowdsourcing: Why the Power of the Crowd Is Driving the Future of Business*. New York: Crown Business.

Jurney, R. (2013) *Agile Data Science: Building Data Analytics Applications with Hadoop*. Sebastopol, CA: O'Reilly Media.

Lima, M. (2011) *Visual Complexity: Mapping Patterns of Information*. Princeton, NJ: Princeton Architectural Press.

Mandelbrot, B.B. (2012) *The Fractalist: Memoir of a Scientific Maverick*. New York: Pantheon Books.

Mayer-Schönberger, V. and Cukier, K. (2013) *Big Data: A Revolution that Will Transform How We Live, Work and Think*. New York: Houghton Mifflin.

Neuhaus, F. (2013) *Urban Rhythms: Habitus and Emergent Spatio-Temporal Dimensions of the City*, unpublished PhD thesis, CASA, University College London.

Plummer, A.V. (2003) *The Chicago Area Transportation Study: Creating The First Plan (1955–1962): A Narrative*. Available from www.surveyarchive.org/Chicago/cats_1954-62.pdf (accessed 15 Dec 2014).

Smarr, L.L. (1991) 'Visualization captures the imagination of physicists', *Computers in Physics*, 5(Nov/Dec): 564–7.

Surowiecki, J. (2004) *The Wisdom of Crowds: Why the Many Are Smarter Than the Few and How Collective Wisdom Shapes Business, Economies, Societies and Nations*. New York: Little, Brown and Company.

Tufte, E.R. (1992) *The Visual Display of Quantitative Information*. Cheshire, CT: Graphics Press.

Tukey, J.W. (1977) *Exploratory Data Analysis*. Reading, MA: Addison-Wesley.

Wilson, A.G., and Birkin, M. (1987) 'Dynamic models of agricultural location in a spatial interaction framework', *Geographical Analysis*, *19*: 31–56.

12

ETHICAL PRAXIS IN DIGITAL SOCIAL RESEARCH

R.J. ANDERSON AND MARINA JIROTKA

12.1 INTRODUCTION

When talking with colleagues about the ethical challenges which the rapid development of information technologies pose to the Natural and Social Sciences and especially those that are computationally intensive, we are often met with the following. 'I do (hardware, systems, algorithms, databases, infrastructure...). Ethics has got nothing to do with my research.' And to be fair, this is a very understandable (though we think misguided) response. Beyond the hinterlands of moral philosophy, ethics is usually perceived as a kind of Sunday sermonizing about such solemn topics as virtue, equality, justice and goodness and how they ought to guide our treatment of others. 'If my research does not involve people, how can ethics be relevant to me?' This question (which is actually a conclusion) is often tied to another. 'After all,' they say, 'it is not the technology which is ethical (or unethical, for that matter). It is what is done with it. And how can I control that?'

As we say, this is very understandable. In large measure, it is a consequence of how those who are interested in ethics[1] talk about their concerns. What they want to establish are strong arguments for the positions they advocate; that is, clearly followable courses of reasoning from self evident truths to irresistibly deduced conclusions which force a preference for doing right not wrong, good not evil, being virtuous not vicious. The arguments they have constructed are codified as sets of programmatic injunctions, principles, motivations or methods. The abstracted and often obscure nature of these codifications seems a long, long way removed from the practical considerations of doing actual research.

---

[1]They are often called 'ethicists', though this is a most unlovely term.

For Aristotle, whose work laid the groundwork for all discussion of ethics, the overriding objective was to answer the apparently simple question 'How should we live?' (Aristotle, 1955); a question, moreover, he saw applying to every part of human life. So, while he did indeed spend a lot of time considering the so-called moral virtues of goodness, generosity, bravery and the like, he also offered thoughts about the intellectual virtue of practical wisdom in science and art and how this might be engendered. While he uses arguments to explain and justify his views, he does not see ethics as simply a matter of the rational acceptance of such arguments. Rather, to put it in a modern idiom, in art and science as elsewhere he sees it as a matter of personal and community growth.[2]

This very early view of ethics is one that is much more aligned with the contemporary concerns of researchers than the codifications of later philosophers. Scientists know that science is a way of life, a set of practices carried out within a community and subject to the norms of that community. Even the recalcitrant colleagues mentioned above prize honesty in claiming and reporting results; applaud the generosity in the offer of and recognition for support; scrupulousness in the detailing of sources and references, and so on. All are part of the ethical praxis of any research. And, of course, once we start to think about science and ethics in this way, we can see that the development of ethics is an essential part of the development of research expertise, to be put alongside other such essentials as an understanding of method, the acquisition of research skills and preparation of research reports. Moreover, just as these latter skills are learned and developed in a community, so too are research ethics.

Two important things follow from this. First, on this view, the suggestion that ethics is bivalent (either something is ethical or it is not) ceases to be useful. Instead, as we do with other elements of research practice, we start to think about ethics in terms of a continuum or spectrum with novices struggling to acquire basic skills whilst experts are able to operate with insouciance and confidence. Second, just as research practice adapts and develops in the face of new problems, techniques, resources and data, so too do the ethical issues raised by the responses to them within that practice. As it adapts, the scientific community grapples with and solves its new problems within the context of the solutions it is already using for the old ones. Ethics in science evolves in much the same way that method, theory and bench craft do.

There is a further gain to be made from adopting this point of view. We believe that acceptance of ethics as a form of expertise in the praxis of research and the idea that such expertise evolves as we strive to adapt to changes of contexts within and outside science, mitigates against one of the most common complaints about research ethics, namely that it is 'a box ticking exercise'. Aristotle uses the term *enkrateia* (ἐγκράτεια) to describe this attitude. Although often translated at 'self control' or 'continence', in Aristotle's use it has more the sense of 'going through the motions' of being ethical or virtuous rather than being committed to that practice. For Aristotle, *enkrateia* is not

---

[2]Julia Annas (2011) provides a very readable introduction to this way of thinking. She also ties it back to Aristotle's discussion.

unethical, merely ethically under-developed. Striving to improve our research practice means striving to acquire greater facility and capability in all its facets.

In this chapter, we will review some of the challenges that are now emerging for the Social Sciences as they become more computationally intense. These challenges derive from a number of sources. There has been a growth in the range of contributions to the disciplinary cluster that uses information and communication technologies (ICT) to understand social issues and an increasing desire on the part of public funding bodies for demonstrations of the 'impact' of research investment. ICT research has extended further and further up what is called 'the value chain' towards the direct application of technology in services and products. With this extension has come a whole raft of issues associated with the likely consequences of deploying ICT enabled products and services in real world settings. The ability to gather and integrate data in large, centralized data warehouses has led to concerns over data confidentiality, security and possible misuse. The ability to 'e-enable' just about any kind of device (but especially video cameras in public settings), thereby making such devices sensors or monitors which can communicate information, has led to concerns about privacy, intrusiveness and protection of identity. Finally, concern has been expressed that the technologies themselves might be being designed and deployed (either deliberately or inadvertently) so as to promote certain kinds of interests and values. If this should be the case, then it is argued the technologies have become intrinsically ethical rather than simply having the potential for uses, which promote different values.

Of course, developments in science and technology have always run ahead of our ability to think through their consequences. What appears to be different today, especially in the domain of ICT, is the rate of acceleration of change. The Internet as a globally deployed, generally available and widely used infrastructure that dates from the early 1990s. The World Wide Web as a universal public service running on that infrastructure has been in place for less time. The take up of Internet shopping and banking has increased at an exponential rate since 2005. Facebook, YouTube, Twitter and other social networking sites that have become global phenomena, since 2007. The lesson we have to draw from this trajectory is that although researchers are predicting that we will approach the limits of the forms of technology we currently use, this is not going to happen in the very near future. As a consequence, we should expect to see ICT become even more pervasive, even more ubiquitous and, as a consequence, our environments becoming even more 'smart' (that is, incorporating more 'computational intelligence') than they currently are.

Although increasing concern has been expressed about the consequences of the widespread availability and use of the products of ICT, the scientific research process itself had been largely unaffected. At least, that was the case until the products and services of ICT research began to be used in support of scientific research itself, including ICT (see, for example, preceding chapters in this volume). At first, such thinking was restricted to using Internet infrastructure to share resources such as experimental set-ups, to pool computing to create distributed supercomputing, to form geographically distributed research teams and the like.. However, the tools and resources also began to be used in pursuit of broader agendas and applied to problems faced by other disciplines where ethical concerns were important, such as the medical and biological sciences and then the Social Sciences. With this shift, the ethics of using ICT in the research process became a significant issue.

12.2 E-SOCIAL SCIENCE: A CONSTRAINED ENVIRONMENT

To get a sense of the types and scale of the issues that are being raised in relation to e-Social Science, we will turn briefly to one specific research domain which has become known as our 'digital footprint' (Weaver and Gahegan, 2007; Sellen et al., 2009). As we mentioned earlier, sensors are now ubiquitous in the modern environment. As a consequence, our activities can be and are being captured as we go about our ordinary lives. Data from point of sale (PoS) devices record what we purchase. Cameras record our journeys up and down the motorways and our wanderings through town and city centres. Search engines record all our searches. In the near future, smart electricity meters will record when we shower, when we cook, when we watch television, when we go to bed. By themselves, each of these data streams is only of marginal interest. It is when they are integrated to provide profiles of us as individual users of services and products that they become *valuable information*.[3] Distributed storage capacity and other so-called 'cloud services' are making the ability to gather and integrate such information available to organizations and commercial companies for use in promoting their products and services. The same developments are happening within the Social Sciences with the same sensor infrastructure and data collection potential being used to gather data on social research problems at a scale that is quite unprecedented. The results of this research will undoubtedly change the way we think about social issues and problems, the policy lines to be developed on the basis of our research and the solutions that will be deployed. This collection of more and yet more data is justified by the assumption that the more data we have the more likely we are to understand the fundamental questions that challenge us. And yet, even as we see the first results of the use of this data deluge, questions are being raised as to whether this assumption is actually correct and what its potential consequences might be. The familiar issue of privacy has re-emerged in a new guise as a concern with where data is being stored, who can access it and how it is being authenticated. What happens when this data 'lives in the cloud' and thus is subject to the (very different) regulatory structures of multiple countries? And the profiles built up on the data? What are the quality assessment procedures to ensure goodness of fit between an individual and the profile projected for them? The scale and scope of the data being collected and the technical possibilities now being made available for

---

[3]James Goulding of Nottingham University has dubbed these profiles 'neodemographics'. www.cs.nott.ac.uk/~jog/neodemographics.html

its analysis, all change the nature of the relationship between researchers and their research participants and the 'social contract' that exists between them.[4]

As a result of these developments, concerns have been expressed about the multiple, potentially conflicting and certainly constraining professional and regulatory requirements now in place to manage the environment of e-Social Science research. Whilst every university has similar ethical approvals processes, these often differ from the processes of professional bodies,[5] agencies and major partner institutions such as the health service providers. In many cases, these processes not only differ, but even impose conflicting requirements on the researcher (Carusi and Jirotka, 2009). The net result is that ensuring appropriate approval from all relevant bodies can, and frequently does, take an inordinate amount of time and sometimes delays and possibly restricts research. Researchers are challenged to work their way through quite complex processes whilst under pressure to undertake the research in a defined time frame.

A key related issue is the complexity and confusion surrounding informed consent in e-Social Science.[6] Everybody signs up to the notion of the informed consent of participants as an aspiration.[7] However, this is becoming increasingly problematic in practice. Use of data from sources such as Twitter may become extremely difficult, if not impossible, should it be necessary to obtain participants' consent. In addition, in an environment where it is not at all clear how information about individuals may be stored and re-used, nor for what purposes it will be re-used, and where researchers themselves may not have control over such matters, informed consent becomes increasingly challenging. All this is unfolding in a technological environment that is fast changing and fast moving – which includes the virtualization of infrastructure – so that it becomes hard to know where data may actually be stored and hence under whose jurisdiction it falls. What seemed unlikely 10 years ago is now standard practice.

---

[4]The old social contract had two critical elements. First, the research process and its associated technology assumed that the identification of individuals other than by the researchers themselves was a practical impossibility. Furthermore, it operated on a human scale. Thus, the means by which data was collected and the data itself was scaled at a level as to be handled by one or a small number of people and the findings anonymized when they were generalized to groups and populations. As we will see, new analytic techniques enabling researchers to 'drill down' into shared databases threatens this assumption. Second, the information gathered was necessarily limited to the answers to the questions asked, the field notes gathered, the census and other public data available. Modern e-Social Science operates on a regional, national or even global scale and the data collected are, or could be, almost unrestricted.

[5]The code of conduct of the BCS can be found at www.bcs.org/upload/pdf/conduct.pdf, that of the ACM at www.acm.org/constitution/code, and proposals from the Association of Internet Researchers are at http://aoir.org/reports/ethics2.pdfacmconstitution/codewww.acm.org/constn/code

[6]Even in the biosciences where the concept was first developed, the current notion of 'informed consent' has been subjected to extensive and vigorous criticism. See Manson and O'Neil (2007).

[7]In brief, informed consent means obtaining agreement to the use of materials and resources collected from research participants.

Privacy, ownership and control of data have become a matter of particular concern. Researchers are increasingly able to use mobile technologies to gather location-based data on individuals. This data combined with other data that the device may be able to give (e.g., web feeds or web searches) enables a profile of an individual to be built that could be of value to researchers but equally could well violate the individual's privacy. The right to privacy might therefore be inadvertently contravened as a consequence of research activities. Looking to statute or case law for guidance here is likely not to be of much help since it is widely accepted that the legal concept of personal data is poorly defined (Marshall 2013). As a consequence, there is a pressing need for greater legal clarity to underpin the development of good practices in e-Social Science. The result of all these confusions and weaknesses is that, unknowingly and with the best of intentions, researchers might be at risk of infringing the law or, given the evolving interpretation of the law, should a case be brought they might be retrospectively found to have done so.

In the next section, we will look at three examples that illustrate this complex skein of issues. Each deals with a somewhat different set of concerns but all illustrate how even the most careful planning, with the best of intentions and adherence to apparent good practice, may not be sufficient to guarantee that ethical requirements are satisfied.

12.3 THE EDIAMOND PROJECT

12.3.1 Aims of the Project

In Chapter 1, the background to the development of grid computing was explained. eDiaMoND was a flagship UK project designed to provide a proof of concept demonstration of the value of this innovation.[8] The problem it sought to address was the national shortage of trained radiologists skilled in the analysis of mammograms taken as part of the investigation and diagnosis of breast cancer. UK government policy had determined that a greater age range of women should be screened for breast cancer and that such screening should take place every two years instead at the previous three yearly interval. These policy changes would not only add to the workload of radiologists in the National Health Service but also exacerbate the disparities in provision across the UK. To be useful for diagnosis, mammograms have to be extremely detailed and hence data intensive. In addition, the mammograms themselves may only be informative when used in the context of other, relevant patient data. Existing infrastructure could not handle this level of data intensity and so it was not possible for Health Authorities across the UK to share radiological diagnostic services. eDiaMoND was to demonstrate how grid computing would solve this problem.

12.3.2 The Project

The project was launched in 2002 and was planned to be completed in 2004. The team was a consortium of 14 partners comprising universities, screening centres and

---

[8]Details on the eDiaMoND Project can be found in Brady et al. (2002) and Jirotka et al. (2005).

industry, and was funded by a mix of public and private grants. The intention was to build four applications on a shared database of images and related patient data to demonstrate how the Grid would offer advantages. These applications would support:

* collaborative screening and diagnosis;
* distributed training;
* larger scale epidemiological studies;
* academic research on image management and analysis.

When planning the project, it was intended to pool real mammograms from the four partner screening centres, but to associate them with 'dummy' patient data. This would be enough to demonstrate the capacity of the system to deliver the level of service sought. However, a short while into the project, the project team came to the conclusion that the scientific basis of the demonstrator would be so much more powerful if it could be shown to be working 'live and for real'. And to do that required mammograms to be associated with actual patient data. As a consequence, the team re-designed the project deliverables in order to achieve that new objective.

12.3.3 The Ethical Challenges

Since data that would allow the identification of individual patients was now to be used, the project had to seek appropriate levels of ethical approval. Prior to the project re-design, this had been felt to be unnecessary because individual patients were not identifiable. Because eDiaMoND was developing an entirely new form of collaborative relationship among the screening centres, one where they would be sharing patient data when previously they had not, ethical approval was required from all four contributing centres. In addition, because the data would be shared between the screening centres, further national approval was required.[9]

To gain the necessary approvals, the team submitted applications to the relevant review bodies. The proposal was initially led by an academic and the application reflected this. Very quickly it became clear that eDiaMoND was a challenge to accepted practice and due process for health service-related ethical approval. A number of concerns were raised about how the data might be handled and whether existing informed consent by patients could be extended to the project. A further concern was raised as the project involved a major technology partner and the data was going to be used, not to run a clinical trial or evaluation, but to develop technology solutions that would provide benefit to clinicians potentially in the future. Thus, the procedure was not like a normal ethics clearance where the benefit to patients was more immediate. It was this disjoint between patient gain and the long-term benefits of providing the data that did not fit with normal ethical clearance processes. As a consequence, approval was refused. Until approval was gained, whilst the digitizing of images could proceed, data acquisition could not begin for the patient data components of the applications.

---

[9]At that point, university approval was not required. If eDiaMoND were to be repeated today, it would be.

Without such data, the applications would not demonstrate the functionality proposed. These work packages were, therefore, delayed. The team began a series of delicate and complex negotiations with the Local Research Ethics Committees and with the Medical Research and Ethics Committee to seek a way through the impasse and thereby overcome the delay. The following application was led by a medic who not only had sound experience of and connections to ethical committees but was also able to shape the proposal with respect to the issues the committees were likely to find contentious. Eventually, by agreeing to major changes in the way the data would be handled and to having a clinician lead the submission, ethical approval was obtained. This was 18 months into a 24 month project. In the event, the project was allowed a 1 year no cost extension to complete its deliverables, which it did successfully.

12.3.4 Conclusions

The eDiaMoND project did achieve its objectives and did demonstrate the value that e-Science could bring to pushing the boundaries of research and collaborative medical science. In doing so, it brought to light many issues that have since been discussed and debated, though they have not all been resolved. However, perhaps the most obvious lesson to draw from the project is less about personal information and the preservation of privacy *per se* than it is for practical management of ethical issues in a complex project. What appear to be small decisions taken for very laudable reasons can have large implications. Project teams need to think them right through before agreeing to them. Even if a change in plan seems to be obviously the right thing to do, it may not always turn out that way.

eDiaMoND highlights a number of important points with regard to the general issues of Social Science research ethics and research practice. Large-scale, multi-sector projects are always likely to be more than usually difficult to manage. When the issues addressed include different cultures and procedures surrounding ethical approval and the due diligence and process they require, these difficulties may become almost overwhelming. It is important, therefore, for the project team to have a clear and full understanding of both the obligations these processes may place on them *and* the conventions adhered to when they are followed.

In addition, if the collaboration involves multi-professional teams, the different practices in place within each profession must be understood and taken into account. With eDiaMoND such an understanding would have brought out two things that later became problematic. First, within epidemiology the research practice is for each team to collect and use their own data and to seek ethical approval for each new study they carry out. Approval, data and study seem to go hand in hand. Broad brush or open-ended approvals are not the norm. eDiaMoND was collecting data for studies that were as yet unplanned and which could only be designed and planned once its research was completed. e-Science was set up in order to create such possibilities. The value of curiosity-driven, open-ended scientific development came head to head with the value of tight control on confidentiality and informed consent. At the time, ethical approval was 'project shaped' – in that it catered for research designed to answer a single question. New paradigms of translational medicine and e-Science that aimed to keep, repurpose and combine data across projects challenged the conventional framework for making ethics decisions, stretching fundamental concepts such as what informed consent might mean. Ethical approval processes have been subject to processes of learning and change over the intervening period. 'Open ended' research streams based upon data corpora nowadays supplement individual consent with a strong commitment to public engagement activities (e.g. see the Generation Scotland website, http://www.generationscotland.co.uk). One can see this as part of the changing nature of the 'social contract' between participant and research born from the evolving emerging demands of ICT enabled research practices.

Second, the practices of sharing data differed markedly from one professional environment to another. Within radiological and medical practice, the sharing of data and collaboration on cases is oriented to and limited by what is in the best interests of particular patients. Better diagnostic outcomes or treatment might outweigh strict adherence to informed consent norms. But such loosening of norms is organizationally and locationally constrained. Staff may share with staff they know and trust (Jirotka et al., 2005). Moreover, this sharing is on the basis of professional judgment and is on a case-by-case basis. This is directly in contrast to the motivation to impersonal, resource efficient sharing that that lay behind eDiaMoND, even if that form of sharing might, in the end, be in the best interests of all patients. The possibility that such ethical expectations might be out of joint is one of the issues project teams must address in project planning. Unless the potential conflicts are addressed in advance, they will undoubtedly surface in the project and might, if the team is unlucky or not fleet of foot enough, derail it.

The legacy of the eDiaMoND project is twofold. First, it did build a successful demonstrator of grid computing. In addition, it raised a number of new and important problems, particularly with regard to large multi-disciplinary teams. The steps that have been taken since to ensure explicit planning of the management of ethical issues at the start of projects have gone some way to ameliorate the frustrations which the eDiaMoND team felt. However, as such projects become even more complex and draw upon broader and broader multi-professional teams, the issues ramify. As a consequence, the management of ethics in a multi-site, multi-professional project remains a long way from being 'a solved problem'.

12.4 THE TASTES, TIES AND TIME (T3) PROJECT

12.4.1 Aims of T3

Social relationships and the networks they fall into have long been a central concern for Social Science.[10] However, our understanding of their dynamics has been somewhat limited. These limitations arise either because we have been heavily reliant on self-reported data, which is subject to personal bias, or because we have not been able

---

[10]For a full exposition of the T3 project and its aftermath, see Zimmer (2010). This account draws heavily on Zimmer's discussion.

to study any one network for long enough to understand how it might develop and change. With the advent and rapid growth of social networking sites on the Internet, particularly as the data on individuals' profiles are permanently stored by the host site, this situation changed. Given access to these profiles over a long enough period, it should be possible to reveal the way these kinds of networks evolve. In order to take advantage of this opportunity, a project team from Harvard University and University of California Los Angeles undertook a study of Facebook. With the permission of Facebook and the students involved, the team gathered the profiles of the whole intake of Harvard University students for 2006. The updated profiles were re-collected in 2007, 2008 and 2009. The data included demographic, regional, relational and cultural information relating to likes and dislikes of fashion, music, etc., for each subject. In addition, the team also acquired data on the courses that the students followed and their living and accommodation arrangements. Its size and detail made this data set unique. The project reported its initial findings in Lewis et al. (2008).

The project was funded by the US National Science Foundation (NSF) and two crucial steps had to be taken for it to proceed. The project had to ensure that it satisfied the lead university's (i.e., Harvard's) internal ethical approvals process (which it did). The project also had to agree to make its data available to other researchers. This latter requirement is now quite normal for most funding bodies. To comply with the NSF requirement, the project team planned to release data from each phase of the project as they became available. Having 'taken a number of precautionary steps... to ensure the identity and privacy of the students in the study remain protected' (Lewis, 2008: 29), including the anonymization of the university at which the students studied, the first tranche of data and the associated code book were released (Lewis, 2008). Researchers wishing to use the data set had to apply to the project team for permission and to agree to a formally binding set of terms and conditions. The aim was both to control the uses to which the data could be put and to ensure that no individual student could be identified.

12.4.2 The Unravelling of T3

Initial Concerns

Once the data was released, discussion began on the possibility of identifying individuals. Fairly quickly it was realized that each individual's profile represented a unique social graph that is potentially identifiable. Furthermore, since some of the demographic data had such small numbers (even singletons for some nationalities) and as the distinctive list of courses might make the university concerned identifiable, then particular individuals could, at least in theory, be identified.

Partial Re-identification

Stimulated by these comments and his own concerns over the strength of privacy protection on Facebook, Michael Zimmer of the University of Wisconsin began to examine the T3 case. Using only the released code book (i.e. *not the data itself*) and publicly available information, Zimmer quickly narrowed down the university where the project was located to one of seven in North-East USA. A comparison of the course offerings of these seven universities with those of the data set as summarized in the code book allowed Zimmer to identify the university as Harvard. This identification was confirmed when, in a video on the project by the Principal Investigator Jason Kaufman, off the cuff remarks about the living arrangements of the students came to light. These arrangements are identical with those of Harvard and are quite unusual. In response to the identification of the university and hence the partial re-identification of the subjects as a particular cohort of students (the Harvard class of 2009), the data set was withdrawn. However, this only happened after the project had become a *cause célèbre* in the blogosphere and among privacy researchers.

12.4.3 Reflections on T3

At no point has anyone suggested that the T3 team were negligent in their management of the project or of the data they collected. Indeed, they took a number of steps to ensure the anonymity of the participants. The main provisions made were:

1. The research assistants (RAs) who collected and coded the data were only able to collect data to which they had default access. If a student wished part of the profile to be shielded from peers at Harvard, this data remained so. No student was contacted for further information.
2. All identifying information was either encoded or deleted immediately it had been downloaded.
3. Release of the 'cultural labels' for each student (i.e. the potentially unique elements of the social graph) was to be delayed until after students had left the university.
4. A stringent set of terms and conditions were put in place to ensure the anonymity and privacy of participants.
5. All of the arrangements were subject to and approved by Harvard's ethical approvals process.

Unfortunately, despite what might reasonably be thought to be the best efforts of the T3 team, as Zimmer (2010) points out, these defences proved insufficiently robust or reassuring.

Who Had Access to What?

The T3 team used RAs from the Harvard undergraduate and graduate population to code the data. They accessed only the data to which they had default access. Given the level of Facebook membership among the student body (97 per cent), the RAs would almost certainly have had differential access to profiles depending on the privacy settings of the individual participants. To take an example, if a participant wished to reserve some information as 'private to Harvard users only' and the rest of the information was to be open to the general public, the Harvard RAs would inadvertently be able to download both the private data *and* the public data. Publication of the data set would make that data publicly available. The same would hold if an RA had a particular 'friendship status' with an individual participant. Data reserved for that friendship status group would be downloaded and released.

How Anonymous is Anonymous?

Removing the obvious personal identifiers from data does not mean that individuals are no longer identifiable. Cross-referencing of general tags (for example, gender, race, home state and nationality) might result in clusters with very small or even unique memberships. Given the national position of Harvard, the achievement of an individual's success in gaining entry to Harvard might well have been featured in local media, school and college yearbooks and so on.

When is a Delay not a Delay?

The team recognized the importance of delaying the 'cultural tastes' data until after the individuals had left the university. However, the strength of this moratorium was undermined by the suggestion that, should other researchers wish to access this data before the general release and providing they could give a convincing enough case to the research team, then the data would be made available. Thus, the general principal was subject to exceptions. However, no guidance was given on what would be sufficiently strong grounds for such an exception to be given.

Whom Can you Trust?

Two formal steps were included in the arrangements: the agreement to a set of terms and conditions and the submission to the Harvard ethics process. The strength of the first relies upon the willingness of researchers to identify when their proposed use of the data might run counter to the ethos that the team had enshrined in the terms and conditions and, recognizing this conflict, not proceed with the agreement. That is, the team required other researchers to be wholly trustworthy. Second, the team also required them to be wholly conscientious and to read through the complete terms and conditions before they indicated their agreement. Both assumptions seem somewhat Panglossian.

The failure of the Harvard ethics process to identify the potential pitfalls of the T3 project tells us more about the current state of ethics scrutiny than it does about Harvard's own process. The model generally adopted has largely been taken over from the medical and biosciences and has not kept pace with the changing character of 'privacy' and 'confidentiality' as these concepts have evolved in the online world. Certainly, prior to the T3 project and the furore it caused, very few ethics committees involved people with experience of privacy issues in relation to the Internet. As a consequence, the trust that the T3 team put in their local process to surface and highlight any weaknesses which they themselves had overlooked, was misplaced.

12.4.4 Conclusion

The T3 project and its aftermath brought to light the difficulties of ensuring the privacy and confidentiality of data collected from sites such as Facebook. Despite what they undoubtedly felt were their best efforts, subsequent analysis demonstrated that such privacy and confidentiality might well be breached simply by correlating anonymized data with other publicly available data. Personal identifiers are not the only way to perform personal identifications. Further, the T3 project demonstrates how important it is to consider privacy and confidentiality from the participants' perspective and the settings they might have used rather than opting for defaults. It also highlights the need to ensure that any scrutiny and approval of the ethics of such research should be carried out by those familiar with the technological context. Finally, the T3 project raises questions about any funding bodies' requirement for centralized and shared data. Whilst this arrangement may well appear to be more cost effective and efficient, when the data are about human subjects, concerns over privacy and confidentiality might outweigh such managerial values. The sharing of data is motivated by an ethical principle itself in the value of common resources. This may well conflict with the ethical value of a participant's privacy and confidentiality.

12.5 THE ACTION PROJECT

12.5.1 Introduction

One of the key challenges currently facing modern societies is the aging of the population. The proportion of the population living beyond 70 years of age is increasing rapidly. This has meant a correlated increase in the number of infirm or frail elderly people who are unable or unwilling to cope entirely by themselves. It is generally accepted that there are good social, ethical and economic reasons for us to want to try to enable such people to remain in their homes and to maintain as much personal independence as possible. However, the burden of taking up the 'caring slack' of such individuals cared for in the community usually falls upon the immediate family supported by whatever provision is offered by the state. Despite their willingness to shoulder this burden, families often lack the knowledge and skills to provide optimal care for their loved one. In addition, the state has limited resources, which have, therefore, to be rationed (either explicitly or implicitly).

The ACTION Project (Hanson et al., 2002; Magnusson et al., 2002; Magnusson and Hanson, 2003) was a pilot R&D project to determine if a relatively simple technological intervention on behalf of the caring families could (at least in part) address this situation and provide significant benefits. The technological 'solution' consisted in providing a broadband link between the homes of the elderly person and the caring family together with cameras at each end, and a computer and Internet connection in the family's home. The cameras were attached to the television in both homes.[11] The Internet connection provided the caring family with access to a number of multimedia programs designed for their situation, together with the increasing level of resources being offered across the Internet. The pilot was deployed with families in Sweden, Northern Ireland, the Republic of Ireland, England and Portugal.

The multi-disciplinary team undertaking the project were very aware of the ethical dimensions of the intervention they were proposing. From the outset they adopted a user-centred design philosophy based around a number of widely accepted principles promoting autonomy, maximizing benefits and avoiding harms, valuing independence and improving quality of life. However, despite this explicit and careful framing of ethical guidelines, at every stage in the project the ACTION team faced ethical challenges and dilemmas.

12.5.2 Ethical Issues

In their post-project reflection on the study (Magnusson and Hanson, 2003), the project team identified a number ways in which the principles they had enunciated might have been compromised.

Autonomy

The principle of autonomy prioritizes control over decision making, with informed consent being one of the mechanisms by which this is assured. However, families were selected for inclusion in the study by their professional carers rather than as volunteers. That is, the carers chose the families and then promoted the project to them. Whilst the families still had a clear choice over becoming involved, it is not clear that the person who was being cared for necessarily had the same level of choice. Informed consent was given by the family on that person's behalf.

There is a second aspect to this limitation on the effectiveness of informed consent. The families were chosen because they had little or no experience of ICT and did not have a computer and Internet connectivity. Participation in the project meant that they would acquire both. This could well have swayed a number of families to participate either to acquire this resource or because of the prestige (at that time) of having this technology. Certainly there were cases where families, unaware of the possibilities and limitations of the technology, joined the project only to be disappointed. Because of their lack of knowledge and familiarity with ICT, the intervention offered them few rewards.

A second mechanism assuring autonomy is the right to withdraw. The participants should always have the right to terminate their participation. Again, though, this seems to have turned out to be somewhat constrained. As with informed consent, it is not clear that the person being cared for knew about or felt in control of

---

[11]This project was competed in the early 2000s when domestic access to broadband technology, the Internet and related services was still relatively limited.

the possibility of withdrawal. The implementation of that decision lay with the family that was providing the care. Second, because of what we might call the project's traction or momentum, families felt it was difficult to limit their engagement or to refuse to engage in project-related activities such as answering follow up questionnaires. In addition, and this is perhaps an under-examined element of the ethical nature of all projects, participants built up relationships with the project team and so felt themselves to have obligations towards the team which made them reluctant to deny the project requests. Respect for the ordinary social norms of social life meant that they were unwilling to disappoint the team or cause offence to them.

Independence

The principle of independence was interpreted as enhancing the families' capacity to choose the care arrangements to be put in place. It was certainly the case that families were able to obtain more information and support. However, over the course of the project, the families became more, not less, dependent on the project for information, guidance and support arrangements. This, in turn, created a problem in the latter stages of the project and once the project was completed when the array of services were no longer being supported. Because of the cost and lack of appropriate skills, the professional care teams could not replace the project team. Given the ways that they had adapted their caring to the technology, it could be argued that, post-project, the families were actually less independent than they had been before.

One aspect of independence, which is often emphasized in ethical discussions, is confidentiality. Interestingly, although concerns were raised at the beginning of the study over the possibly intrusive nature of the technology, these fears were unrealized (at least for the families).

Justice

The principle of justice was interpreted as meaning equal access to services for everyone. It was for this reason that families with no experience of ICT were chosen. The intervention sought to rectify what has recently been termed 'digital exclusion'. However, when the project finished, although they kept the technology, many families once again became 'excluded' since they lacked the finances to pay for the line rental, the skills to manage the software and so on. The issue that is posed, then, is whether, in the long run, temporarily compensating for social or digital exclusion (or both) really is a benefit.

Related to this issue is the problem of creating unrealizable expectations. This is similar to, but not the same as, the problem of post-project withdrawal of services. Whilst they have access to the technology, and especially to the information resources, families learned about care systems and care programmes which neither the project nor the professional care service could provide. Awareness of these services but being unable to access them, led to a feeling of frustration and relative deprivation on the part of many families. It was considered to be particularly 'unfair' if the service or support was actually being offered elsewhere in the country.

Other Ethical Concerns

At several points in the summary above, we have noted that what might have been of benefit or value to the family would not necessarily be of benefit or value to the person being cared for; or might not be on the same level or scale. This raises the issue of value prioritization and how the project team should determine such prioritization. At first, it might seem obvious that if the family wants one thing and the person being cared for disagrees or wants another then the wishes of the person being cared for should take precedence.[12] However, cases are rarely so clear-cut. More often than not, it is a question of where the balance of effort should be placed rather than whether something should or should not be done. What mechanism should the project team use to determine where that balance should lie? The point about the principles that the team adopted is that they are binary rather than partitionable. The rights to autonomy, independence, justice and so on are either secured or they are not. Although we might say that an intervention tended to promote autonomy, sought to optimize independence and so on, without a clear way of fixing where the balance should be placed, the arrangements lack the ethical force that the principle supposedly provides. It might be argued that this is a meta-ethical matter about the principles being appealed to, and so it is. But this does not mean it is not ethical (i.e. one of the rightness or goodness of the arrangements for making such decisions).

A second meta-ethical consideration is the process for resolving conflicts between principles. We have seen that promotion of independence could, under certain circumstances, run up against the commitment to justice. Equally, the principle of autonomy right runs up against more general social values of the kind we illustrated. How should the project team proceed in those circumstances? What is clear is that despite their careful planning issues such as this and those touched on above were not considered.

12.5.3 Conclusion

The ACTION project team were motivated by high ideals and sought to offer help to families dealing with the difficult problem of caring for elderly or frail relatives. It is also clear than in planning the project, extensive and careful thought was given to delineating the ethical principles that should guide the research. The intervention was made and the project carried out with the team doing their best to follow their principles.

However, at each stage in the project, issues arose that which seemed to undercut the principles or posed dilemmas for the management of the project. Ethical decision-making turned out to be a permanent part of managing the project rather than a clearly circumscribed process which, once agreed upon, could be closed off. Moreover, post-project review identified that, despite their best intentions, not all aspects of the project had managed to satisfy the principles set out. Of course, it might be said that the team *optimized* rather than satisfied the principles. But to justify this claim,

---

[12]This is on the assumption that the individual concerned is capable of making decisions of this kind. Of course, *that* judgement might itself be contested.

resort would need to be made to some procedure for measuring benefits and harms, etc. The problem here is that there is absolutely no agreement on which principles to use, or on whether any of them would do the job required.

What the ACTION project brings out is that whilst good intentions, careful planning and sensitive project management are virtues to be sought, they are not always enough.

12.6 THE TEMPTATIONS OF BIG DATA

Since Thomas Kuhn (1962), no-one views the history of science as one of continuous, steady progression. Rather, we all accept that scientific research practice develops in fits and starts, with periods of relative stasis intermixed with frenzied action. During such frenzied action, all sorts of claims and counter claims are bandied about regarding the revolutionary breakthroughs on hand and the future of the disciplines concerned. The kinds of studies we have described in the previous section and the research promise of our 'digital footprint' have been taken as evidence by some that we are now in the midst of just such an upheaval. Luminaries such as Savage and Burrows (2007; 2009) have foretold the death of the discipline with the emergence of big data and the associated data analytics being developed by commercial companies and government departments. Such organizations will know so much more about so many more members of society that the Social Sciences will be defunct. Similarly, Pentland (2012) has announced that the availability of big data has made conventional Social Science theory from Adam Smith to Karl Marx and beyond if not redundant, then definitely less secure than heretofore. In big data, such people see the possibility of a wholly new Social Science and a wholly new form of society for it to study.

No doubt many will be more than a little jaundiced about such claims (after all, Social Science has a history of large promises resulting in small outcomes). Nonetheless, it is worth taking them seriously because they do point to a number of ethical challenges that the use of big data in social research will face. In the clamour surrounding the reckless pursuit of the trending, such concerns might well be drowned out. In this section, we will draw on many of the threads of the discussion earlier in this chapter to summarizing the ethical issues raised by the debate over big data. Broadly, these fall into two categories. What can you properly say on the basis of big data? This is, in effect, a return to Aristotle's concern over the practical wisdom in the arts and sciences. Second, assuming there is something you can say, given how it has been obtained, should you say it? This is, of course, no more than Aristotle's question concerning the virtue of moral responsibility.

So, what then is 'big data'? In essence, it is a colloquial term used to describe the integration of different sorts of information about individuals. There are four broad categories of such information:

1. Data held by government and other public agencies that is now being made available online. This covers data from the census, for example, or submissions, complaints or other interactions with planning agencies, land registry entries, the voting register and the like.

2. Data held by private companies and traded by them. This might be records of purchases, credit card records, service records, call data, security camera images and so on.
3. Online content uploaded by individuals and available at various levels of granularity either for free or for payment. Examples include Facebook entries, Twitter posts, and so on.
4. So-called 'digital traces' held by Internet providers and service companies such as geolocation data, web search histories, text message and email usage etc.

Developments in data mining, data analytics and data repurposing have made such information a new asset class which has considerable value for some business domains and for the development of social policy. It also represents a much broader spectrum of data than the Social Sciences have ever been able to access before. Companies such as Twitter, Google and Facebook and many of the supermarkets and credit card companies have made some or all of the data they hold available to researchers as part of their business development strategies and as an earnest sign of their good intentions or for a fee.

The attractions of access to large integrated data sets are very obvious. Who could deny the value of being able to comb the whole national archive of patients receiving a particular therapy to uncover patterns of responses and side effects? Who would not want to examine government datasets to evaluate the combinatorial consequences of rafts of national policy initiatives aimed at particular categories of deprivation? And, of course, companies would love to be able to target their sales and marketing efforts on precisely those niches of potential customers likely to buy their products. This would be so much more efficient than the more usual scattergun approach. Surely these are gains worth the having?

Of course, everyone who gathers, acquires and uses this data is aware of the privacy concerns that surround it. Steps are taken to 'anonymize' entries by either stripping obvious personal identifiers (name, address, date of birth, reference number) from them or by aggregating the data into various broader categories. Until recently this has seemed satisfactory. However, as a number of commentators such as Paul Ohm (2010) have made very clear, once multiple auxiliary sets of data are re-combined, the overlap between categorical descriptors can make it very easy to re-identify individuals. This is often referred to as 'the jigsaw effect' (O'Hara et al., 2011. Machanavajjhala and Reiter (2012) summarize one of the central cases as follows:

> Arguably the most sensational privacy breach occurred in 2006 when AOL released 20 million search queries posed by users over a three-month period in order to facilitate research on information retrieval. They knew the information in Web searches contained potentially identifying and sensitive information (including social security and credit card numbers) and hence attempted to anonymize the data by replacing user identifiers with random numbers. Within a couple of hours of releasing the anonymized data, two reporters from the New York Times uncovered the identity of user No. 4417749 based on just her search history: 'landscapers in Lilburn, GA,' several people with last name Arnold,

and 'numb fingers.' This breach had far reaching consequences. Not only were several high-ranking officials at AOL fired, search companies are now reluctant to release search logs and other personal information. Even researchers are wary of using the now publicly available AOL data. Similar re-identification is possible from social network data, location traces, and power usage patterns (Machanavajjhala and Reiter, 2012: 20–21).

Ohm describes the AOL case and several others. One involved medical data released by a US Government agency, the Group Insurance Commission. Pains had been taken to strip the data of personal identifications, however, as Sweeney, a researcher at the University of Massachusetts demonstrated (1997), using readily available auxiliary data it was very easy to identify particular individuals in the data, including the Governor of Massachusetts! Another related to the release by Netflix, an online video rental site, of the ratings given to movies by its subscribers. Two researchers from the University of Texas (Narayanan and Shmatikov; 2008) showed just how easy it was to work back from the released data and other available information to the identification of the ratings (and thus the movies viewed) by individuals. The kinds of consequences that can follow from such re-identification have been starkly summarized in a story re-told by Brendon Lynch, Microsoft's Chief Privacy Officer.

> I am using my phone in a grocery store to find out more about the items on the shelves and it is mashing up that with my private data to personalize my experience. So here I downloaded a recipe and customized it for my dietary needs. If it's a trusted system, that's a great experience. On the other hand, consider the US company, Target, which recently generated a lot of press about its pregnancy prediction score. This was based on what people were purchasing in Target stores, they are able to indicate a shopper that appeared to be pregnant. The concern about how Target can figure out such details about customers shopping in its stores, who are not explicitly sharing that information, is the concern. And what does it do with those insights? In this particular case, they sent some mailers to the individual involved – it was a teenage girl and her father was very offended that they were wrongly marketing to her, but it eventually did come out that she was in fact pregnant. Target knew a lot more than her father knew. (Lynch, 2012: 3)

The above cases are obvious causes for concern, and undoubtedly public pressure on the companies that hold such data (as it has with Facebook and Google) and the introduction of 'privacy by design' (ICO, 2008) may lead to better designed and robust mechanisms for ensuring that privacy can be maintained. In their recent book, Elliott and his colleagues (Duncan et al., 2011) have described some of the statistical and other techniques that can be used to 'perturb' or otherwise strengthen the resilience of the data to privacy incursion. Whether such mechanisms can *assure* privacy is, however, uncertain. Given enough anonymized but correlated data, identification is always possible in principle. And yet, these may not be the only nor even the most important ethical issues we should worry about in relation to big data. Privacy will in the end resolve itself to some way or other and the remit of the regulatory bodies will gradually be extended to encompass the Wild West frontier of big data. (Of course, by then, the technology and associated furore will have moved elsewhere.) The issues that should most concern us are more normal and familiar ones associated with the professional character of Social Science disciplines. In a word, on many counts the use (rather than the collection and analysis) of big data in Social Science research runs the risk of being seriously unprofessional.

First of all, anyone who spends time analysing data knows only too well that *volume cannot compensate for quality*. The age old dictum 'garbage in; garbage out' applies as much to data and its use as to anything else. Big data consists of data that has been acquired, collected or gleaned largely in an uncontrolled manner. There have been no rubrics applied to ensure consistency in the 'responses'. There have been no controls on the composition of the data sets. The Law of Large Numbers only saves you if you are certain that your sample is a fair representation of the total population. But there are no such certainties regarding the sample populations of Twitter users, Facebook users, drivers of cars on urban highways and everyone else whose data is aggregated. Many of the research instruments that we customarily use (be they ethnographic fieldwork, structured questionnaires, large scale question-naires, official records, controlled experiments or whatever) are explicitly designed to ensure that the lenses we apply in collecting data correct for any potential distortions that might *per accidents* be present in the data. In addition, an important facet of the research setting is that the meaning of the research encounter is contexted. The research and the respondent/subject can come to a common understanding of what is going on, what is being asked for, how it will be used and so on. Those who glean 'friendship patterns' from Facebook pages have no idea what precisely 'friendship' in this context might mean to the individuals concerned nor how they distinguish online 'friends' from off-line ones or from correlated relationships such as 'colleague' or 'acquaintance'. Not knowing how these differ matters for the meaning we might attribute and the inferences we might draw.

Second, much big data is not collected by trained and competent social scientists but *harvested for specific organizational or policy purposes* by Government or other public bodies as well as commercial organizations. Those purposes drive the way the variables and their parameters are defined. For a long time, we have known about the dangers of an overly blithe social scientific use of official statistics and organiza-tional records (see, for example, Kitsuse and Cicourel, 1963; Garfinkel, 1967) and we know only too well that all organizations collect and keep only that data that serves their needs. The fact that we have lots of such data magnifies rather than reduces the problems therein.

The point about the interpretation of data (and the meaning of data is always in the eye of the beholder) alerts us to another important issue. There is a major difference between *information that is given and information that is given-off* (to use Goffman's (1959) phrase). Information that is given, be it to a Governmental or commercial organization, is provided in a context by a subject/respondent and has some meaning for them. They are, to be blindingly obvious, answering the questions they have been asked. This is a well understood social activity. When your image is captured in a garage forecourt as you fill up, or as you drive down the motorway, or when you walk around the centre of a town; when you pay for your purchases in the supermarket; when you turn on the kettle, lights and shower in your home, you are not answering questions set by the security companies, the police, credit card companies, or the power companies. In doing these things you might well be doing all sorts of social things, but the data being collected is given off, not given. The same holds for the traces we leave behind in our web searches. Patterns that might be discerned in these data are not patterns we have put there; they have no meaning for us. As a consequence, they provide no basis for inferring the reasons behind what we are doing. They have no more meaning than any other such ethological behavioural patterns. Analysing patterns behaviour and attributing meaning to them is more or less akin to taking a Rorschach test. Whatever you find there has more to do with your interests in looking at the data than the data itself. Whilst it is possible to map discerned data patterns onto to one another, such correlations are very likely to be spurious and certainly have no causal meaning at the level of lived social life of the individuals who contributed the data.

In using big data, then, social scientists have a number of ethical considerations to bear in mind. These questions do not have easy or straightforward answers and certainly none of a yes/no kind. They require the reflective ethical praxis that is part of a fully developed and mature research practice. From our discussion in this chapter, we would like to highlight the following (and these are by no means exhaustive).

1. If the data is of the form that is given-off rather than given, do the subjects have a right to the same kind of civil disattention that applies when we are otherwise in public places? When we walk through city streets or drive down highways, we do not expect to have our actions actively and continuously monitored by those around us nor do we monitor those of others except in so far as might be necessary to manage traffic flow. Should the norm of civil disattention apply to data that could be collected from us in such settings and what would this look like? If it should, do we violate the privacy of those with such a right when we use information derived from such data?

2. If information about personal preferences, personal histories or personal opinions are shared with others through social media, is that sharing the same as broadcasting the same information? Even though we might doubt that Facebook friends or Twitter followers stand in the same relationship to us as personal friends and acquaintances do, nonetheless they do have some relationship to us. We have chosen (wisely or not) to share the information and our choices are made in a context of expectations about trust (again, sensible or not). Such sharing is not the same as placing an ad in a paper, going on TV or the radio and expressing our views or listing personal facts about ourselves. We do have some sense of with whom we are sharing. When information is broadcast, we have to accept that it is loose in the world for others to find and use pretty much as they will (modulo the libel, slander, copyright and other laws). This is the social norm that governs broadcasting. If we are using measures derived from shared data garnered from social media sites, are we violating the expectations about trust

that those who shared the data have? The claim that those who were trusted violated that trust first (in re-tweeting or blogging) cannot justify or excuse us doing the same.

3. If, for whatever reason, information is put into the public domain, does that necessarily mean that it has been publicized? Have those who have contributed or cooperated in the collection of the data *agreed* to its being used as if it had been publicized? Moreover, if they have agreed to the data being put in the public domain, does that mean they have agreed for it to be used in any way we like. Is any principle of informed consent (a) in play here and (b) being respected?

4. How far is there an obligation on researchers to act as role models in the accessing and use of data (and, if so, role models for whom?) by demonstrating they adhere to the highest standards in relation to the data they have acquired? Even though it may be possible to use the data, and even though the use of that data might well be valuable or even vital, should they use it if in so doing they violate the privacy or other expectations of those about whom the data has been collected?[13]

These questions raise both the central issues of moral responsibility and practical wisdom which Aristotle first addressed in the *Ethics* and which have been at the heart of ethical and moral discussions ever since. That, in the twenty-first century and in the midst of massive change within society and science both are still relevant, is a clear signal that they are deep and important. e-Social Science will ignore them at its peril and to its detriment.

12.7 CONCLUSIONS

The issues we have identified in the cases set out above and the tendencies we summarized at the beginning of this chapter all seem to point to a number of important implications for the conduct of e-Social Science and especially for how we should think about ethics in relation to that research. These implications fall into three groups: implications for the research process; implications for research management; implications for the topics of research. We will take each of these in turn.

12.7.1 The Research Process

For some areas of Social Science, the introduction of techniques and methods facilitated by new technologies on the Internet or otherwise makes very little difference to the character of the research. Counts of types of website visited by age, gender,

---

[13]This is but a particular instance of a favourite moral dilemma widely discussed in Ethical Theory.

ethnic and other demographic variables, the coding of online questionnaires, and the collection of excerpts from virtual documents and media are not all that different from their counterparts in the offline world. Statistical summaries are provided and analysed, colligations of types are presented. Where e-Social Science does seem to be taking a distinctive new turn is in research areas where the participation of the researcher on the scene being studied had been a requirement for the research to be undertaken. These are mostly observational and qualitative forms of research. These changes come at a time where this kind of *interpretive Social Science* is gaining ground as a potential research contributor in just the kind of large scale multidisciplinary teams that e-Research was set up to encourage. What e-Social Science presents us in some areas, then, are mostly old problems (standardization and completeness of data, consistency in adherence to coding protocols, data cleansing, securing anonymity and so on) in new guises. In other areas, entirely new problems are being thrown up. With qualitative Social Science, what secured the validity and ethical acceptability of the research was the personal relationship that researchers entered into with their research subjects. This relationship might include explicit acknowledgement of the fact that the research was being carried out or it might not. But either way, for the research to be possible, the investigator had to be accepted into and become part of the scene being studied.

In qualitative Social Sciences the researcher established a relationship with their participants and that was the nexus of the ethical relationship. With e-Social Science, distancing is possible. Researchers can join and leave networking sites or online communities at will; observe interactions in public places and settings without being present; gather profiles of interests, tastes, habits and activities by drawing upon online data stores. The social norms that surrounded participation in the social world of the research participants are no longer in force. The social contract between researcher and researched has changed.

Very much related to this are the changes that are taking place in our view of the materials, resources and data we gather. Increasingly, these are not being defined as personal research property but rather as common goods, to be shared with and placed at the disposal of others. This sharing and the consequent re-use and re-purposing makes any 'informed consent' which participants might have given, meaningless. And it is not just the fact that the construction of research data warehouses will allow 'drilling down' by other researchers and so potentially undermine anonymity. These warehouses now contain video and audio data, diaries, memorabilia and much, much else. As we will see below, this has the consequence of making the ethics of research in a particular case one of the research topics for that case. Another aspect to this should be noted as well. The notion of what might or might not be personal or private data is far from clear both legally and normatively. With this lack of clarity over what information the participant has control over together with the multitude of ways in which such data might be used, re-used and used for differing purposes, many researchers are coming to the conclusion that the notion of informed consent is more of a misconception than a reassurance.

12.7.2 Research Management

The cases we examined all underscore one important point: The resolution of ethical challenges in research cannot be treated simply as a part of project planning. Ethical issues appear and re-appear throughout the research process. Certainly, it is a cardinal error to work on the assumption that completing detailed analysis of potential ethical issues in advance is enough to arm the project against ethical challenges. Detailed and careful planning is necessary; but it is not sufficient. This injunction applies to the ethical approvals process as well. The challenges posed by the requirements of different ethical approvals process are such that, when considered from the point of view of timely project management, many project leaders are shying away from large multi-institutional, multi-professional projects, even though these are commonly viewed as being best fitted to the complexities of the problems being addressed. Ethical approvals processes for simple, tight knit and small projects are just easier to manage!

Related to this is the second lesson we can draw from the cases. No single approach will fit all instances. We will have to shape our approach to ethics to respond in the context of research in which we find ourselves. This is particularly important where our project intervenes in the lives of others. Although we may have clear goals and strong principles, we need constantly to re-assure ourselves that the way the project is unfolding actually is in conformity with our initial aspirations. And if it is not, then we will have to be brave enough to take the appropriate action, even if this means early termination of the project and disappointment all round.

12.7.3 Research Topics

In our view, the engagement with ethical considerations has had two major consequences for the topics we develop when we are planning research. First, increasingly we are seeing that determining the most appropriate approach to the ethics of the research process is treated as a research output in its own right. It has to be discovered in and through the research. The ethics of *this* research in *this* context is becoming a defined topic for each project.

Second, and this is a clear response to increasing awareness of the practical character of ethics, the ethical practices deployed in any setting are themselves becoming of research importance. Where information, materials, resources, decisions which bear upon the ways that others lead their lives are used, deployed, managed or controlled within a setting, then matters will be subjected to ethical practice by those in the setting. This practical ethical action is an important feature of the moral order of the setting being investigated and must be reflected in the ethical approach of research in that domain.

The ethics of research is both a spur and a challenge. This has always been so for the social sciences. However, with the advent of e-Social Science and the impact that it is having on our research lives, the spur has got noticeably sharper and the challenge noticeably more demanding.

12.8 BIBLIOGRAPHY

Annas, J. (2011) *Intelligent Virtue*. Oxford: Oxford University Press.

Aristotle (1955) *Ethics*. Harmondsworth: Penguin Books.

Brady, M., Gavaghan, D., Simpson, A., Parada, M. and Highnam, R. (2002) F. Berman, G. Fox and T. Hey (eds), in *Grid Computing – Making the Global Infrastructure a Reality*. London: Wiley.

Carusi, A. and Jirotka, M. (2009) 'From data archive to ethical labyrinth', *Qualitative Research,* 9(3): 285–98.

Duncan, G., Elliott, M. and Salazar-Gonzalez, J-J. (2011) *Statistical Confidentiality: Principles and Practice*. London: Springer.

Garfinkel, H. (1967) 'Good organisational reasons for "bad" clinic records', in H. Garfinkel *Studies in Ethnomethodology*. Englewood Cliffs, NJ: Prentice Hall. pp. 186–207.

Goffman, E. (1959) *The Presentation of Self in Everyday Life*. London: Allen Lane.

Goulding, J., Smith, G. and Barrack, D. (2012) 'Neo-demographics: distributions in the digital shadow', in Proceedings of Digital Futures 2012, October 22–25, Aberdeen, UK.

Hanson E., Magnusson L., Oscarsson T. and Nolan M. (2002) 'Benefits of IT for older people and their carers', *British Journal of Nursing*, 13: 867–74.

ICO (2008) 'Privacy by Design', UK Information Commissioner's Office, Wilmslow. Available from https://ico.org.uk/for-organisations/guide-to-data-protection/privacy-by-design (accessed 13 Jan 2015).

Jirotka, M., Procter, R., Hartswood, M., Slack, R., Simpson, A., Coopmans, C., Hinds, C., and Voss, A. (2005) 'Collaboration and trust in healthcare innovation: the eDiaMoND case study', *International Journal of Computer Supported Cooperative Work*, 14: 369–98.

Kuhn, T. (1962). *The Structure of Scientific Revolution*. Chicago: University of Chicago Press.

Kitsuse, J. and Cicourel, V. (1963) 'A Note on the Uses of Official Statistics', *Social Problems*, 11(2): 131–9.

Lewis, K., Kaufman, J., Gonzalez, M., Wimmer, A. and Christakis, N. (2008) 'Tastes, Ties, and time: a new social network dataset using Facebook.com', *Social Networks,* 30(4): 330–42.

Lynch, B. (2012) Transcript of Keynote Speech. IAPP European Data Protection Congress.

Machanavajjhala, M. and Reiter, J. (2012) 'Big privacy: protecting confidentiality in big data', *XRDS*, 1 9(1): 20–3.

Magnusson L., Hanson E., Brito L., Berthold H., Chambers M. and Daly T. (2002) 'Supporting family carers through the use of information Technology – the EU project ACTION', *International Journal of Nursing Science*, 39 (4): 369–81.

Magnusson, L. and Hanson, E. (2003) 'Ethical issues arising from a research, technology and development project to support frail older people and their family carers at home', *Health and Social Care in the Community*, 11(5): 431–9.

Manson, N. and O'Neill, O. (2007) *Rethinking Informed Consent in Bioethics*. Cambridge: Cambridge University Press.

Marshall, J. (2013) *Human Rights Law and Personal Identity*. London: Routledge.

Narayanan, A. and Shmatikov, V. (2008) 'Robust de-anonymisation of large sparse datasets', in *Proceedings of the 2008 IEEE Symposium on Security and Privacy*. pp. 111–25.

Ohm, P. (2010) 'Broken promises of privacy: responding to the surprising failure of Anonymisation', *UCLA Law Review*, 57: 1701–77.

O'Hara, K., Whiteley, E. and Whittall, P. (2011) Avoiding the Jigsaw effect: experiences with Ministry of Justice Reoffending data. Available from http://eprints.soton.ac.uk/273072/8/AVOIDING%20THE%20JIGSAW%20EFFECT (accessed 13 Jan 2015).

Pentland, A. (2012) 'Reinventing society in the wake of big data', *Edge*. Available from www.edge.org/conversation/reinventing-society-in-the-wake-of-big-data (accessed 15 Dec 2014).

Savage, M. and Burrows, R. (2007) 'The coming crisis of empirical sociology', *Sociology*, 41(5): 885–99.

Savage, M. and Burrows, R. (2009) 'Some further reflections on the coming crisis of empirical sociology', *Sociology,* 43(4): 762–72.

Sellen, A., Rogers, Y., Harper, R. and Rodden, T. (2009) 'Reflecting human values in the digital age', *Communications of the ACM*, 52(3): 58–66.

Sweeney, L. (1997) 'Weaving technology and policy together to maintain confidentiality', *The Journal of Law, Medicine & Ethics*, 25(2–3): 98–110.

Weaver, S.D. and Gahegan, M. (2007) 'Constructing, visualising and analysing a digital footprint', *The Geographical Review,* 97(3): 324–50.

Yang, M., Sassone, V. and O'Hara, K. (2012) Transparent government, not transparent citizens: a report on privacy and transparency for the Cabinet Office. Available from www.cabinetoffice.gov.uk/resource-library/independent-transparency-and privacy-review (accessed 11 Jan 2013).

Zimmer, M. (2010) '"But the data is already public": on the ethics of research in Facebook', *Ethics of Information Technology*, 12: 313–325.

13

SOCIOLOGY AND THE DIGITAL CHALLENGE

MIKE SAVAGE

13.1 INTRODUCTION

In 2007, with my colleague Roger Burrows, I published a paper 'On the Coming Crisis of Empirical Sociology' in the journal *Sociology*, the official journal of the British Sociological Association (Savage and Burrows, 2007). In all honesty, this was not a deeply researched piece of work, or a carefully crafted scholarly paper, but a set of provocative reflections on how the proliferation of digital data might affect the future jurisdiction of social scientific research. Noting the relative methodological conservatism of sociologists, who often preferred to remain loyal to their 'tried and trusted' methods of the interview and the survey which were now well over 50 years old, we speculated that the explosion of digital data offered fundamental – but also untried – resources for social science. Yet at the same time, this potential was challenging for sociologists, especially given the scale and complexity of digital data sets. We pondered whether sociologists had the conceptual or methodological expertize to address them. We provocatively wondered whether digital data would make empirical sociological research redundant as new generations of computer scientists, physicists, biologists and other natural scientists took the opportunity of modelling and simulating social relations on the basis of these vast new data sources.

Our paper was deliberately designed to be provocative. And so it proved from the outset. The reviewers of the paper had fundamentally different views of paper's quality. One referee noted that it was 'badly written, extremely weak, rambling and ill-informed piece of work.... totally misguided'; another that it was 'a really well written piece, provocative and thought provoking in a way that raises critical and controversial issues for the future of sociology'. Regardless of its quality, on its publication it generated extensive debate, leading to several critical comments in the pages of the journal (Crompton, 2008; Webber, 2008; Savage and Burrows 2009; McKie and Ryan, 2012). We were invited to parade its arguments in front of numerous methods specialists, including market researchers. It is easily the most widely cited paper that the journal *Sociology* has published in recent years.[1] It played into increasing concerns about 'big data', which have been taken up extensively by research funders (e.g., ESRC, 2009).

I do not wish to defend the quality of the paper here. It is sufficient to note that that its reception clearly reveals that the digital remains unsettling for sociology. My chapter here offers some further thoughts on the digital challenge to sociology written some seven years later than our original piece. The succeeding years have in some respects caused further perturbations to the social sciences. We have seen the proliferation of mobile devices associated with the smartphone, the development of the social network and social media technologies (e.g., Murthy, 2012), accelerating concerns with open data and the semantic web (Halford et al., 2013), and considerable initiatives linking digital records together (e.g., Ruppert, Law and Savage 2013). Interests in 'digital sociology' have matured (see e.g., Orton-Johnson and Prior, 2013) and some university departments are investing specifically in this area. The launch of the results of the BBC's Great British Class Survey in April 2013 (Savage et al., 2013), with data collected by digital web survey (buttressed by a face to face national survey) showed the potential of new modes of data generation to generate unprecedented public interest – and controversy!

My starting point, however, is to contest the view that 'digital sociology' is a straightforward project which can be defined around specific defined technical parameters. In fact, it raises fundamental questions about the nature of the 'sociological imagination'. It is enshrined in a familiar though also problematic legacy of technical boosterism, which can be traced back to the industrial revolution, in which new technical forms are assumed to betoken new kinds of social relationships. Thus, just like the steam engine, electric switch or internal combustion engine, the digital has been identified – in and of itself – as the marker of revolutionary transformation (see notably Castells, 2000a; 2000b; 2004). This claim is problematic to sociologists given the extensive reflections within science studies which insist on the need to place technical devices within a wider network of relationships (see e.g., Yearley, 2005; Latour, 2005; Ruppert et al., 2013). Accordingly, my argument in this chapter is that to truly understand the digital challenge, we need to avoid seeing it as some kind of bearer of epochal change, and instead place it more subtly within proximate historical processes which pre-date and contextualize it. Only through placing the digital in the context of previous ways of doing social science, can we properly appreciate the more specific challenges which the digital poses, so that we can better understand the potential for digital social research in the future.

Accordingly, the first part of this chapter places the digital in the context of three historical repertoires for apprehending social life: narrative, accounting, and the

---

[1]In January 2015 it was noted to be the ninth most cited article ever published by *Sociology*. The most recent article placed higher than this had been published in 1995.

glance. I argue that these three modes have existed for centuries, but that the twentieth century saw the striking emergence of a distinctively social scientific rendering of the relationships between them. In this, the glance is relegated in importance and the accounting model becomes dominant in a way that enrols the popular narrative within it through forms of sampling. It is against this prior context that the digital needs to be placed. I argue that the digital mimetically enhances all three of these conventional repertoires, at the same time that it emphasizes the exchange, or switch, as having distinctive ontological priority over narratives. In my conclusion I reflect on the forthcoming prospects for digital sociology itself with some observations about how the Great British Class Survey is an indication of the complex stakes involved.

13.2 NARRATIVE, ACCOUNTING, AND THE GLANCE

It is commonplace to reflect on the way that different media permit differing 'ways of knowing' on the basis of their very organization and character. In the famous words of Marshall McLuhan (e.g. 1949), 'the medium is the message'. However, these frameworks characteristically focus on the properties of textual media, notably printing (as in the case of McLuhan himself) or of visual reproduction (as famously by Walter Benjamin). It is much less common to place social scientific knowledge within this purview. The brief comments below attempt to rectify this (though see also, Savage, 2010).

In order to understand the significance of the digital challenge to social research, we might usefully draw on Kittler's (1990) interest in how 'discourse networks' allow the input, storing, transmission and utilization of information. This leads me to suggest, simplistically, a contestation between three previously dominant institutional discourses of social life: narrative, accounting and the glance. I thereby insist that we should not see knowledge of the social as somehow intrinsically 'modern', but that we need to place the striking later twentieth century development of the 'social science apparatus' (as I call it in Savage, 2010) in this wider historical context. Throughout human history, these three modes of organizing social meaning have competed with each other, each mobilizing different kinds of device and discourse networks in order to do their work. It is important to place social knowledge in this long term context in order to challenge the erroneous view that social science is largely a modern phenomenon

Narrative is perhaps the most familiar mode of organizing social knowledge. It is common to relate the rise of epic poetry as fundamental to the emergence of human society itself. Walter Benjamin (1973) emphasizes how the emergence of narrative from spoken and remembered forms, to stories inscribed in writing, changes the character of human understanding, invoking a class of expert tellers – notably in religious fields – as well of audiences of various kinds. We can trace the role of narrative in the development of historical consciousness back to Herodotus' *History* written in the fifth century BC as the first self-conscious narrative that seeks to explicate the origins of Greek society. But narrative should not just be construed as fundamentally old, as its association with printing and mass reproduction proved a highly dynamic form in its elaboration as fiction and its role in constructing modern national narratives (Moretti, 2007), and in thus instantiating concerns with interior consciousness, and with the ordinary and mundane as significant through their implication in a wider plot which reveals hidden or obscure aspects of their functioning.

Accounting has an equally long history, and can be construed as a form of listing, akin to the mode of classification, which Pickstone (2000) sees as an aspect of natural historical modes of knowing. Rather than the sequential focus of the narrative, such listing elaborates a stable account of the assets or attributes of individuals, corporations, nations, and other kinds of entities, through modes of classification and enumeration. Accounting typically uses forms of writing, but also champions the deployment of numerical expertise, which in a digital era can be differentiated from writing. It too, has its momentous forbears – from the Egyptian hieroglyphics onwards, the landmarks of accounting history are well known: in the British case, the Domesday book carried out in the late eleventh century; the development of vital statistics (of birth, marriage and death); the emergence of dual entry book keeping from the fifteenth century, and the development of censuses and surveys from the seventeenth century. Its role in delineating concepts of the 'economy', and of social groups such as castes has been unravelled by writers such as Mitchell (2002) and Dirks (2005).

The *glance* is actually the oldest device for apprehending the social, but arguably the least appreciated. I use the term 'glance' rather than 'gaze', as popularized by Foucault, deliberately, in order to evoke the way that the visual cues from material objects – buildings, artefacts, relics, clothes and so forth – are deployed to organize understandings of power, deference, servility and social relationships. These are the modes of understanding famously characterized by Benjamin (1973) as 'auratic', as conveying meaning through their unique location in time and space and hence their place within a constellation of linked objects. Whereas narrative and accounting could proliferate – especially with the emergence of mechanized modes of production associated with printing – objects subject to the glance were more fleeting and difficult to render. The emergence of photography during the nineteenth century changed this, yet only partially since meanings were more commonly apprehended through glimpses and glances.

These three modes[2] of apprehending social life remain, but were placed into a fundamentally new configuration with the expansion of the academic social sciences in the twentieth century. For it can be argued that the second half of the twentieth century, parallel but separate from the emergence of digital information, saw the remarkable rise of social scientific 'discourse networks' which marked a distinctive crystallization of these three modes of apprehension in new and (for a certain period of time) compelling ways.

---

[2]I am not claiming here that these are the only modes of social knowledge. Pickstone (2002) valuably highlights the role of analytical and experimental modes in the natural sciences – however, as I discuss shortly, these methods have not been widely deployed hitherto to address social knowledge.

Firstly, the most obvious impact of the emergent social sciences was to criticize the traditional deployment of narrative devices as means of knowing the social through the reliance on historical and literary accounts linked to a sequential unfolding of events. These modes of knowing, which we now associate with the humanities disciplines, are now not normally seen as conveying social knowledge, yet until the recent past they were in fact fundamental to such concerns. This can be seen most evidently in considering the rise of nationalist discourse. Whereas earlier currents had relied strongly on history and literature to provide accounts of national identity and formation, social scientific interventions sought instead to champion new forms of accounting mechanisms which offered alternative measures of 'the state of the nation'. These included the inflation rate, unemployment, the balance of trade, gross national product and the like. These measures had the effect of detracting from more narrative based idioms of the 'national character' which has previously been more significant and which drew on literary and historical motifs (see notably Mandler, 2005). Undoubtedly the most fascinating example of these developments is revealed by the changing role of national legend. The Arthurian stories, which had long sought to define a form of primeval Englishness fed into a series of literary constructions of Englishness throughout the twentieth century, as enacted in the writings of John Cowper Powys or Antony Powell. These stories, following in a well-worn groove, established Englishness through an appeal to myth, enshrined in tensions between the Celtic mystical tradition threatened by the rationalist Anglo Saxon culture. Yet from the 1950s, a fascinating development, marked most obviously by the huge interest in Tolkien's *Lord of the Rings,* saw mythical idioms redefined as 'other worldly', no longer pertaining directly to the nation, but instead evoking an alternative reality. The rise of science fiction saw a similar process in which the popularity of narrative form was increasingly defined through its 'escapist' appeal, as a mode not of apprehending social relationships but of offering an alternative to them. What we see, then, is the social sciences wresting claims over society away from narrative fiction, and history, through an insistence on its capacity to define properly social indicators.

Secondly, we can also see the social sciences championing a new motif of popular narrative, the idea that 'everyone has their story to tell'. For much of the historical record, it was only thought that the powerful had stories to tell, and indeed the capacity to tell stories was a marker of such power – or, in the famous words of Walter Benjamin (1973), 'there is no marker of civilisation that is not also the marker of barbarism'. The limitation of literacy to small numbers of people until the twentieth century was a material underpinning of this limited deployment of narrative. We can trace challenges to this use of narrative from the romantic movement in the nineteenth century, with its concern to recover folk songs and folk tales as part of developing a more popular and inclusive vision of the nation, yet its full potential is only elaborated with the use of the qualitative interview method as a means of eliciting 'ordinary narratives' which proliferated from the 1950s.

I have told the remarkable story of the rise of the interview as a means of securing 'scientific narratives' elsewhere (Savage, 2008; Savage, 2010) and here only provide a précis. Interviews have a long history, and in their usual form, such as in the confessional or in the practice of social work, they allowed a mechanism for individuals to stake a claim (such as for welfare, employment, or even salvation) to a figure of authority. From the middle of the twentieth century, the interview became ostensibly democratized, where, influenced by the use of the 'free interview' in psychotherapy, anthropologists, sociologists and oral historians became interested in using these conversations to get previously marginalized social groups to provide narratives, of their lives, relationships and identities. Such interview methods also proliferated in the broadcast and print media, and were instantiated in routine institutional practices such as the job interview, appraisal, and assessment in what increasingly became identified as the 'confessional society' (Beer, 2008). The social sciences thus played a key role in allowing the narrative to be extended into mundane features of social relationships.

Thirdly, accounting methods proliferated, notably through the deployment of census and 'vital statistics' but increasingly through the deployment of sampling procedures. Until the later nineteenth century, the idea of 'partial' accounting had little purchase. Effective accounting needed to list all relevant items, with the result that the census enumerated the entire population. Even the 'pioneering' poverty studies of Rowntree and Booth in the late nineteenth century mapped all the households in York and London respectively (see for instance, Kent, 1981). This insistence on comprehensive accounting should not be seen as arcane: indeed within business practice it would be incomprehensible not to have complete records on all transactions, but drawing on insights from agricultural production, the social sciences became interested in the way that one could generate a comprehensive social understanding on the basis of sampled material – often indeed on the basis of a very small sample. The development of probability theory played a decisive role, and from the early twentieth century the systematic sample survey was pioneered as a means of providing accounts on the basis of a small number of relevant cases. Institutionalized in the opinion poll and the Government Social Survey, it now became possible to generate an account of the 'social' without a comprehensive accounting of an entire population. As I discuss elsewhere (Savage 2010) the resulting proliferation of sample surveys in the latter decades of the twentieth century has been profoundly significant in guiding government policy, corporate strategy, and social scientific understanding of social relationships.

Fourthly this new social scientific reworking of narrative and accounting methods took place at the expense of concerns with the visual which had historically been highly significant modes for apprehending social relationships. Even within the social sciences, visual and figurative devices which had been important during the later nineteenth and early twentieth century were 'retired' and visualization became far less important for presenting social scientific arguments with the development of methods for survey analysis during the later twentieth century. Here the contrast with the natural sciences which deployed ever more sophisticated visual 'inscription devices' (Latour, 1986) is striking. The visual became confined to specific academic disciplines (such as art history) and was not seen to offer a rigorous way of understanding social relations.

13.3 THE DIGITAL CHALLENGE IN THE CONTEXT OF SOCIAL SCIENTIFIC EXPERTISE

I have argued above that it is important not to place the digital challenge into some kind of epochal frame where it is deemed to have intrinsic powers to remake social science in and of itself. Rather, the more particular challenges and affordances it offers to modes of knowing need to be discerned by placing them in the context of prior modes of expertise. In my previous section, I (inevitably schematically) laid out the particular configuration of social science research as it was defined in the later twentieth century. I now seek to highlight how the digital affects it.

At the outset it is worth reminding ourselves that until the early 2000s there was a remarkable lack of dialogue between expertise in computer science associated with digitalization and the academic social sciences (leaving aside a few specialist areas such as computer supported co-operative work with its ties into ethnomethodology and conversation analysis). The development of interview methods and survey analysis took place until the 1960s with little direct input from digital experts, with the exception of the storage of large data sets on mainframe computers. The emergence of user friendly software packages such as SPSS (Uprichard et al., 2008) increasingly allowed social scientists to analyse survey data rapidly, but the collection of such data took place using traditional face to face methods and paper questionnaires well into the 1990s, at which point computer supported interviewing methods became more common. It was not until the early 2000s that there were serious interests, supported by e-Social Science initiatives (see the opening chapter for examples) to rectify this, to explore how social scientists could take advantage of the increasing amounts of 'byproduct' transactional and administrative data which were accumulating.

Let me draw out the implications of this issue. Social scientists have historically intervened in social life in order to do their research. They have conducted ethnographies, interviews or surveys in order to produce data which otherwise would be lacking and from these interventions they have elaborated their research 'findings'. They have thus generated data that can be 'scientifically' mobilized, and which as social scientists they can claim expertise to analyse properly. The digital challenges these presuppositions of how social research should be done. It is now data on the traces of transactions, which are created and which have the potential for social scientific analysis. Given that most social scientists have not staked their expertise on 'naturally occurring' data of this kind, fundamental issues arise as to the remit of their intellectual authority.

This point is significant in forcing us to reconsider the expertise of social scientists themselves. Whereas previously their empirical research skills have been based on their capacity to conduct skilled interventions – for instance to gather appropriate samples, to design effective questionnaires, to conduct skilled interviews or ethnographies – the nature of their skill base is cast into question when data proliferates without their conscious intervention. The potential for crowdsourcing and for the mobilization of numerous individuals in the collection of digital data is already evident across several domains (for an example of the use of crowdsourcing in the British MPs' expenses scandal, see Ruppert and Savage, 2012), leaving the role of the academic social scientist uncertain. One response, possibly the easiest, is to denigrate the quality of digital data deposits and to insist on the value of more specifically designed social scientific instruments – but this then leads us back to the challenge with which I started this chapter.

In my view, a more effective and mature response is to maintain sociological claims to our existing research expertise in survey and interview methods, but also to reflect seriously on the potential for drawing additionally on digital data sources. Accordingly, in the remainder of this chapter, I draw out different, sometimes contradictory ways, that digitalization affects social scientific research methods, and allow the potential reconfiguration of narratives, accounting and the glance with which I began this chapter.

Firstly, we need to recognize the remarkable capacity of digitalization to allow *mimesis.* As Kittler presciently noted, whether with respect to text, sound or vision, the digital allows the ready copying, storing and processing of material that had previously been kept in analogue form and which was generally more recalcitrant to easy access or use. So, in this respect, going back to the early years of the computer mainframe, generations of social scientists saw digitalization as (sometimes massively) enhancing their potential through allowing them to work more quickly and efficiently. This applies to all forms of social scientific research, both qualitative and quantitative. It is this capacity for the digital to strip down complex phenomena into binary form so that they can be manipulated more easily which explains the enthusiasm which social scientists – as all other kinds of users – frequently exhibit when their data becomes digitized and when they use computerized modes of analysis.

My point here is that this initial capacity of digitalization is accompanied by a sense of empowerment, leading to a sense that what are actually traditional forms of data collection, storage and manipulation are enhanced. As a result, it is easy to adopt the view that rather than the digital being a challenge, it has in fact been absorbed into the social scientific mainstream. But in fact, this would be a rather complacent response.

This leads onto my second point, regarding *the scope for large scale research.* As I have explained above, one of the most fundamental differences between social scientists and natural scientists is that the former remain much more comfortable working with small, sampled, datasets. It is, of course, conventional to contrast qualitative methods, applied to a few cases – possibly only one – with quantitative datasets with many more cases. However, such quantitative datasets, often derived from surveys, generally remain small. The largest UK sample survey, *Understanding Society* has 40,000 respondents. Although the Census is a (mostly) comprehensive rendering of the entire population, it contains only a few questions and its raw data is not available for social scientists to use (until 100 years after each Census). Much recent innovation in the social sciences concerns more sophisticated analysis of small data sets (such as Abbott's (1995) use of sequencing methods, or Ragin's (2000) interests in Qualitative Comparative Analysis and fuzzy sets). Typically, however, in business applications as well as in the natural sciences, huge digital datasets of many millions of records are routinely processed. The challenge here is to know how to conduct appropriate 'large N' analyses in ways which are meaningful. This leads onto my next point....

Thirdly, we can reflect on the potential of digital data to see *the expansion of accounting methods*, rather than those based on narrative. Here, I return to my point that social scientists pioneered the a particular use of narrative as fundamental to their expertise: partly through the collection of extensive narratives (in the form of interviews), and partly through championing 'causal accounts' in which different elements could be linked together into a comprehensive 'model'

Traditionally, as I have discussed above, social scientists preferred to provide narrative analyses of their findings, often in the name of developing causal models in which different variables could be linked together. Digitalization, however, strips out narrative and accentuates listing and classification. Email archives can be searched rapidly on the basis of key terms to reveal the specific email required, rather than being placed in a narrative thread (in which one might recall the date it is received or what kind of response it is). Digital software to analyse qualitative interviews allow common codes to be linked across interviews or cases, so massively enhancing the potential 'descriptive assemblages' (Savage, 2009b). We might see this as allowing accounting models to supplant narrative models of social analysis, in the form of new kinds of descriptive repertoires.

Fourthly, and relatedly, we see a new interest in a descriptive concern with outliers and exceptions. The predominant focus of social science was historically in developing causal accounts linked to 'main effects' quantitative models, focusing on general, typical, and representative processes. The statistical methods typically used treated outliers and variants as aspects of sampling or other error and sought to minimize their role, as 'noise' that could largely be discounted. By contrast, the deployment of large scale data sets of whole populations permits interests in exceptions and outliers to be elaborated. Social scientists are sometimes rightly suspicious of this approach insofar as it can be allied with concerns to highlight 'pathological' or 'deviant' cases (as for instance, it is used in e-Borders research, as Amoore, 2009 demonstrates). However, theoretical interests in complexity and chaos theory have shown the value in recognizing the role of distinctive cases. A particularly interesting application here has been in the development of 'field theory' (Martin, 2011), which places considerable emphasis on specifying relationships between all elements within a field. Social network analysis emphasizes a similar concern to articulate the relationships between elements within an entire population.

Fifthly, we see potential for the reworking of temporal and spatial parameters of social research. Conventional social scientific methods abstracted from both time and space through conducting located and temporally specific interventions, and then introduced linear measures of time and space into the resulting data (for instance by conducting quasi cohort analysis on survey data, or by using textual accounts to impart narrative to an interview). Even where more dynamic methods are used, as in longitudinal analysis, these deploy linear benchmarks, which distinguish distinctive temporal clumps. As several chapters in this book demonstrate, digital data has the potential to handle events in 'real time' and 'real space' for instance as people move around the city during the course of the day. The potential for these more fluid approaches to time and space are manifold as they allow theoretical currents, which insist on the 'emergent' properties to be more fully registered.

Sixthly, and again, relatedly, this concern with the aggregate patterning of whole populations leads to a new concern with visualizations. Standardized textual accounts find it difficult to render specific cases other than as additional pieces of text, whilst quantitative tabular presentations focus on the 'main effects'. Visualizations, however, permit the isolation of outliers within an overall pattern of relationships and so dramatically enhance the analytical role of visualization and the 'glance', which had previously been denigrated within orthodox social science. Digital data thus sees the proliferation of innovative kinds of visualizations such as 'word clouds' and sociograms, which permit fundamental new capacities for social research. Such perspectives seek thus seek to reveal the ordering of the social not by causal statistics of textual hermeneutics but through a mode of visual aesthetics. This sensibility is not one which sociologists have historically been expert in.

Finally, we see a challenge to the typical social scientific focus on *the individual case* which was the centrepiece of interviews and survey methods. This recognition of the role of the individual was generally associated with cognitivist assumptions about the hermeneutic and/or strategic capacity of thinking individuals to make decisions and hence engage in specific forms of behaviour. Digital data, by contrast, records switches or transactions – as particular purchases are made, or as journeys or modes of communication are enacted – and typically has little or no information on the individual privy to such switches. For some social scientists this is a serious limitation as it makes it more difficult to enact causal accounts, which (in Weber's terms) are 'adequate at the level of meaning'. However, for those drawing on various kinds of post-humanist social theory, in which the individual agent has little role, this is not a disabling feature, and may indeed allow novel modes of analysis to focus on flows, patterns and rhythms.

13.4 CONCLUSIONS: TOWARDS A DIGITAL SOCIOLOGY?

Let me now conclude my arguments by returning to the themes of the 'coming crisis of empirical sociology' paper to offer some final reflections on the digital challenge to social research. I have endeavoured here to resist any simple teleology in which the nature of digital social research is known in advance, so to speak. For these reasons, to proclaim that information is necessarily flat and uncritical (Lash, 2002), or that it indicates the move towards a network sociality (Castells, 2000a; 2000b; 2004) is unconvincing.

Rather, the future is up for contestation and debate. It is this that makes this area so exciting. But how is sociology seeking to define its interest in digital sociology? It is striking that there is now a rapidly burgeoning literature, with books such as Orton-Johnson and Prior 2013 or Beer 2013, and a clutch of journal articles (e.g., Halford et al., 2013; Murthy, 2012; Ruppert et al., 2013). There is also a study group of the British Sociological Association. Currently, however, digital sociology has taken a particular form. Much of the concern is with the digital as a distinctive and emerging social object (e.g., Murthy, 2012 on 'Twitter'; Burrows, 2012 on metrics) but the sociological analysis remains reliant on more conventional social scientific approaches to apprehend these objects. There is a related interest in how social media platforms might allow sociological research to be circulated more rapidly, for instance through a growing use of blogs.[3] This approach is nonetheless a contrast, for instance, with Batty et al.'s chapter in this volume, which shows how some geographers and modellers actively deploy digital data in their analysis (Chapter 11). On the whole, sociologists have few equivalents of this kind of practical orientation to such data (though for an exploratory exception see Beer and Taylor 2012). This is not necessarily a problem or deficiency – given the problems that such data might be seen to have – but it is the sign of a certain ambivalent sensibility.

These issues are intriguingly revealed by the reaction to the BBC's Great British Class Survey (Savage et al., 2013; 2015a; 2015b). This analysis of class was based on the unusual deployment of a large web questionnaire hosted on the BBC's LabUK website examining respondents' cultural, economic and social capital, which had 161,400 respondents. This data was hybrid rather than fully digital, in that it was buttressed by a conventional nationally representative sample survey. The detailed information from the web survey sources did allow the seven classes identified to be 'drilled' down to much greater levels of detail (for instance through mapping the classes to geographical locations, through specifying particular universities which members of classes attended) than was usual using conventional sociological data. The circulation of the story was highly unusual in being fuelled by the social media, as respondents sought to assess their own 'class position' through responding to a few questions on the BBC's 'class calculator' which was easily transmitted digitally. These interventions were also deployed with innovative graphical journalism to mock up the seven proposed classes. This led to an astonishing take-up amongst the public, with the story becoming one of the most prominent of the year, and also generated extensive critical reaction, especially on blog sites. The fact that much of this reaction was on digital platforms (through blogs, comments on the social media etc.) was itself testimony to the significance of digital modes communication for contemporary sociology.

What does the massive, yet also ambivalent, response to the project tell us about the prospects for digital sociology? The ambivalence is in part due to the way that the project is hybrid rather than digital character. The study was neither a conventional survey based analysis, nor one which uses mash up visualizations of existing digital data sources (such as tweets, as with Batty et al., above), and hence could attract ire from conventional survey researchers (for not being 'rigorous' enough in standard sociological terms because it relied on a self-selected sample to a web survey and only a small national sample survey). From other perspectives, it might also be seen to be insufficiently innovative in relying on self-completion questionnaires rather than transactions. This reaction is indicative of a broader lack of sociological confidence in

---

[3]Though sociologists are probably behind political scientists in their extensive use of such platforms.

innovating and improvising within fully digital platforms (for an interesting exception, see Halford et al., 2013). Sociologists find it easier to treat the digital as an object of study, rather than construing the digital as itself central to their research.

This sensibility, I have suggested, needs to be contextualized in terms of the residual power of the infrastructure associated with the social science apparatus which become powerful in the latter decades of the twentieth century through hosting devices which conducted social research through expert interventions (predominantly) using surveys, ethnographies and interviews. Over recent decades social scientific expertise has been powerfully institutionalized, not only in academic departments but also in research institutes, and public and private sector organizations. In ways that Roger Burrows and I did not draw out in our 2007 paper, these institutional strengths will not suddenly be eclipsed, and will continue to have significant strengths in the foreseeable future. However, as new kinds of research infrastructure emerge which offer different perspectives using digital data, there is a danger that sociologists look poorly equipped to compete. A key issue here for the social sciences is therefore how to relate to the growing numbers of computer and natural scientists who have the capacity to make the world their laboratory through working on digital data traces.

In asking this question, I have also argued that digital data should be seen to have significant affordances, which speak to current theoretical concerns in the social sciences. Currently, it is paradoxical that whilst post-humanist theory enjoys a considerable vogue, most social research continues to focus on textual disclosures by human subjects. Digital data, by contrast, allows remarkable potential for examining switches, flows, and rhythms, in real time and space and the potential for cross fertilization with complexity theory, field analysis, network analysis is great (see the discussion in Roseneil and Frosh, 2012).

My final point, however, is to return to the empowerment of the visual which the digital allows. I have argued that 'the glance', which has historically been a central means of conducting social research, has been steadily subordinated to narrative and accounting methods of social research, and that the social science research apparatus had very little role for visualizations. This eradication of the visual is now being fundamentally challenged. Partly because visualizations can be readily derived digitally, but also because they become a prime means of making sense of the patterns of large number complex datasets. The challenge of this new development is manifold. It allows the potential for a new aesthetically oriented inter-disciplinary approach to social research, which might have wide appeal. It might suggest new alliances between innovative forms of quantitative and qualitative methods. But, as I have argued in this chapter, the future for digital sociology is not a given, but for the making.

13.5 BIBLIOGRAPHY

Abbott, A. (1995) 'Sequence analysis: new methods for old ideas', *Annual Review of Sociology*, 21: 93–115.

Amoore, L. (2009) 'Algorithmic war: everyday geographies of the war on terror', *Antipode*, 41(1): 49–69.

Beer, D. (2008) 'Researching a confessional society', *International Journal of Market Research,* 50(5): 619–29.

Beer, D. (2013) *Popular Culture and New Media: The Politics of Circulation.* Basingstoke: Palgrave Macmillan.

Beer, D. and Taylor, M. (2013) 'The hidden dimensions of the musical field and the potential of the new social data', *Sociological Research Online,* 18(2). Available from www.socresonline.org.uk/18/2/14.html (accessed 15 Dec 2014).

Benjamin, W. (1973) *Illuminations.* London: Fontana.

Burrows, R. (2012), Living with the h-index? Metric assemblages in the contemporary academy, *Sociological Review,* 60, 2, 355–372.

Castells, M. (2000a) *The Rise of the Network Society, The Information Age: Economy, Society and Culture, Vol. I,* 2nd edition, Oxford: Blackwell.

Castells, M. (2000b) *End of Millennium, The Information Age: Economy, Society and Culture Vol. III,* 2nd edition, Oxford: Blackwell.

Castells, M. (2004) *The Power of Identity, The Information Age: Economy, Society and Culture Vol. II.* 2nd edition, Oxford: Blackwell.

Crompton, R. (2008) 'Forty years of sociology: some comments'. *Sociology,* 42(6): 1218–27.

Dirks, N. (2001) *Castes of Mind: Colonialism and the Making of Modern India.* Princeton NJ: Princeton University Press.

ESRC (2009) *Strategic Plan 2009–2014. Delivering Impact through Social Science.* Swindon: ESRC.

Halford, S. Pope, C. and Weal, M. (2013) 'Digital futures: sociological challenges and opportunities in the emergent semantic web', *Sociology,* 47(1): 173–89.

Kent, R.M. (1981), *A History of British Empirical Sociology,* London, Gower.

Kittler, F.A. (1990) *Discourse Networks 1800/1900.* Stanford, CA: Stanford University Press.

Kittler, F.A. (2006) 'Number and numeral', *Theory, Culture & Society,* 23(7–8): 51–61.

Lash, S. (2002) *Critique of Information.* London: Sage.

Latour, B., (1986) 'Visualisation and cognition: drawing things together', in H. Kuklick (ed.), *Knowledge and Society Studies in the Sociology of Culture Past and Present,* vol. 6. Greenwich, CT: Jai Press. pp. 1–40.

Latour, B. (2005) *Reassembling the Social: an introduction to actor-network theory.* Oxford: Oxford University Press.

Mackenzie, A. (2005) 'The performativity of code: software and cultures of circulation', *Theory, Culture & Society,* 22(1): 71–92.

Mandler, P. (2005) *The English National Character: the History of an Idea from Burke to Blair.* New Haven, CT: Yale University Press.

Martin, J-L. (2011) *The Explanation of Social Life.* Chicago: Chicago University Press.

McKie, L. and Ryan, D. (2012) 'Exploring trends and challenges in sociological research', *Sociology, e-special.* Available from http://soc.sagepub.com/content/46/6/1 (accessed 15 Dec 2014).

McLuhan, M. (1949) *Gutenberg Galaxy.* Toronto: University of Toronto Press.

Mitchell, T. (2002) *Rule of Experts: Egypt, Technopolitics, Modernity.* Berkeley, CA: University of California Press.

Moretti, F., (ed.) (2007) *The Novel,* (vols 1 and 2). Princeton, NJ: Princeton University Press.

Murthy, D., (2012), *Twitter: Social Communication in the Twitter Age.* Cambridge: Polity.

Orton-Johnson, K. and Prior, N. (eds) (2013) *Digital Sociology: Critical Perspectives.* Basingstoke: Palgrave.

Pickstone, J. (2002) *Ways of Knowing.* Manchester: Manchester University Press.

Ragin, C. (2000) *Fuzzy Set Social Science.* Chicago: University of Chicago Press.

Roseneil, S. and Frosh, S. (2012) *Social Research after the Cultural Turn*. Basingstoke: Macmillan.

Ruppert, E. (2011) 'Population objects: interpassive subjects', *Sociology*, 45(2): 218–33.

Ruppert, E. and Savage, M. (2012) 'Transactional politics', in L. Adkins and C. Lury (eds), *Measure and Value*. Sociological Review Monograph Series. Oxford: Wiley-Blackwell, pp. 73–92.

Ruppert, E., Law, J. and Savage, M. (2013) 'Reassembling social science methods: the challenge of digital devices', *Theory, Culture and Society*, 30(4): 22–46.

Savage, M. (2008) 'Elizabeth Bott and the formation of modern British sociology', *Sociological Review*, 56(4): 579–605.

Savage, M. (2009a) 'Against epochalism: conceptions of change in British sociology', *Cultural Sociology*, 3(2): 217–38.

Savage, M. (2009b) 'Contemporary sociology and the challenge of descriptive assemblage', *European Journal of Social Theory*, 12(1): 155–74.

Savage, M. (2010) *Identities and Social Change in Britain since 1940: the Politics of Method*. Oxford: Oxford University Press.

Savage, M., Devine, F., Cunningham, N., Friedman, S., Laurison, D., Miles, A., Snee, H. and Taylor, M. (2015a). 'On Social Class, Anno 2014.' Sociology: 0038038514536635. (online first).

M., Devine, F., Cunningham, N., Friedman, S., Laurison, D., Lisa Mckenzie, Miles, A., Snee, H. and Wakeling, P. (2015b) *Social Class in the 21st century*. London: Penguin.

Savage, M. and Burrows, R. (2007) 'The coming crisis of empirical sociology', *Sociology*, 41(5): 885–99.

Savage, M, and Burrows, R. (2009) 'Some further reflections on the coming crisis of empirical sociology', *Sociology*, 43(4): 762–72.

Savage, M., Devine, F., Cunningham, N., Taylor, M., Li, Y., Hjellbrekke, J., Le Roux, B., Friedman, S. and Miles, A. (2013) 'A new model of social class? Findings from the BBC's Great British Class Survey experiment', *Sociology*, 47(2): 219–50.

Uprichard, E., Burrows, R. and Byrne, D. (2008) 'SPSS as an "inscription device": from causality to description?', *The Sociological Review*, 56(4): 606–22.

Webber, R. (2009) 'Response to "The coming crisis of empirical sociology": An outline of the research potential of administrative and transactional data', *Sociology*, 43(1): 169–78.

Yearley, S. (2005) *Making Sense of Science: Understanding the Social Study of Science*. London: Sage.

INDEX

Note: Figures and Tables are indicated by page numbers in bold print

access to data
  attenuating data 112
  big data 25–6, 32–3, 60, 287–8
  commercial sources 35
  Facebook 169–70, 288
  and freedom of information 34
  Labour Force Survey 38
  mandatory for social science 78
  new data types 77–8
  and open data 33, 52, 77
  personal data 112
  restrictions 112
  social media 51
  social surveys 38, **111**, 112
  for text mining 169–71
  Twitter 170–1
  see also privacy
accounting 300, 301, 302
  expansion 305
ACTION project 283–7
  ethical issues 284–6
Addison, Chris 178–9
Address-Based Sampling 87
administrative data 89–90
Administrative Data Liaison Service (ADLS) 32, 41
age of data 25–6
ageing population 283
agile ethics 50
Amazon 40
Anderson, C. and Wolff, M. 169
Annual Population Survey 38
anonymity 76, 282, 288
  breaches 288–9
  see also privacy
Anselin, Luc 133
Anstead, N. and O'Loughlin, B. 163
AOL 288, 289
Aral, S. and Walke, D. 238
archives 110
  creation 65, 78
Aristotle 272–3, 287, 292
Arthurian legends 301
AstroGrid project 132
Attensity Analyze 184
audio recordings 88
avatars 94
  see also Second Life

Barjak, F. and Thelwall, M. 234
Bayesian extension 146

Beattie, G. 70, 71
Beer, D. and Burrows, R. 76
Behavioural Insight initiative 47
Bender, S. and Heining, J. 112
Benjamin, Walter 299, 300, 301
Berners-Lee, T. and Shadbolt, N. 25
Bhutta, C.B. 91
big data 18, 26–7, 60, 85–6, 131, 287–92
  access 25–6, 32–3, 60, 287–8
  categories 287–8
  collection by non-Scientists 290
  ethical issues 291–2
  given and given off 290–1
  and new Social Science 287
  and privacy 288–90
  quality 290
biofeedback 89
blogging 44–5
Bond, R.M. et al 228
Booth, Charles 25, 124, 302
Boraston, Z. and Blakemore, S.J. 70
Boston, Lincolnshire 66
Bowman-Grieve, L. and Conway, M. 36
Box of Broadcasts 181
boyd, d. and Crawford, K. 167, 170
breadth-first search (BFS) 240
bricolage 201
British Art Show: linguistic research **207**, 210
British Cohort Study (BCS) 31, 42
British Crime Survey 31
British Household Panel Survey (BHPS) 43–4, 106
British Library 78
British Social Attitudes Survey 31, 43
British Sociological Association (BSA) 69, 306
Broder, A. et al 230
Brown, Gordon 176, 177, 179–82
Bucicovschi, O. et al 46
built environment: visualization 253–7
Burt, Ronald 226, 235, 236, 237

Cameron, David 176, 177, 178
Capocci, A. et al 230, 234
carbon footprint labelling 71
CASA
  3D model of London 254
  mapping 133
  MapTube 133, 249–**51**
causality 236–7
Cellan-Jones, Rory 178
Census 37–8, 250, 257, 304

Census Longitudinal Studies 31, 112
Census of Population and Households 131
Centola, D. 237
Centola, D. and Macy, M.W. 237
Centre for Multilevel Modelling 145
CESSDA (Council of European Social Data Archives) 115
Chadwick, A. 179, 181
charts 199–201, **200**
Cheshire, J. and Manley, E. 261
Chew, C. and Eysenbach, G. 164
Chicago School 123
child development 70–1
Chunara, R. et al 164
cities: modelling 254
citizen social science 67, 70
Citizens Advice Bureau (CAB) 38
City Dashboard 257, **258**
City Engine 267
civil unrest in UK (research) 63–5
ClearForestOneCalais 184
Clegg, Nick 175–6, 177
Cloud 247, 247n2, 249, 252
cloud computing 97–8
coding 202, **203**, 204
cohort studies 42
collaboration 19, 241
Cologne University Statistical Resources 145
commercial sources of data 35, 38
computations skills 78
computer-assisted interviewing (CAI) 85, 87
Comres 174
Connotate 184
consequential data 28
consumer behaviour, data on 39–40
context of language 205–6
COSMOS 78–9, 173, 184, 232
Couper, Mick 87
covert methods, ethics of 69
Crimson 168
Crimson Hexagon Forsight 172–3, 184
crowdsourcing 30, 36, 97, 211–16, 303–4
    and informed consent 50
    maps 249
    spatial distribution **214, 215**
    uses 211
    visualization **213–16**, 263–4

DAMES (Data Management through e-Social
    Scientce) project 114, 115, 116, 117
data
    abuse 51, 76–7
    nature of 27–8
    primary/secondary distinction 48
    quality 48–9, 60
    and reporting 52
    research areas
        consumer behaviour 39–40
        economic circumstances 37–9
        education, training and employment 42–3
        health and well-being 40–2
        public attitudes 43–5
        social behaviour 45–7
    from social media 29, 35–7, 51
    structured and unstructured 162
    types 27, 28–9, 53
    use of digital data 27
    see also access to data; big data

data abuse 51, 76–7
data arrays 53, 74
data collection
    by diverse groups/individuals 59
    and ethical issues 274–5
    subjectivity 30–1
    Twitter data 65
data environment 27
Data For Development, Orange 77
Data Fusion Tool 117
data generation 1–2, 26, 30, 36–7
data management 110–18
    GESDE (Grid Enabled and Specialist
        Environments) 116–18
    online resources 114–16
    research projects: examples **115**
    software use 113–14
    storage 110–**11**, 112, 115
    transformation of variables 112–13
Data Protection Act (1998) 76
Data Service Secure Access facility 112, 118
data sharing 277, 279
data storage 4, 110–**11**, 274, 275
    personal data 112, 275
data streams 53, 74
data traces 29
data-driven research 74
data/subject boundaries 47–8, 54
datasets 304, 305
    see also big data
Davies, A. and Ghahramani, Z. 94
Decision Support Systems (DSS) 133
deductive and inductive processes 74–5
Diction 184
digital archives 30
digital footprint 274, 287
digital records 193–5
    and log files 196–8
digital replay system (DRS) 193–217
    annotations 202, **203**
    charts 199–201, **200**
    coding 202, **203**, 204
    combining data 201
    and context of language 205–6
    crowdsourcing data 211–16
    importing logs 198–200
    in linguistics 205–10
    mobile devices 204–5
    synchronized data 201–**2**
    thick description **204**
    timelines 201
    uses 194–5
digital traces 288
discourse networks 299, 300
DiscoverText 65, 173, 184
dissemination 51
Domesday Book 300
Dropbox 19
Duan, S. et al 97
Dunnhumby 40
dyads 225

e-Infrastructure 2–7, 195
    academic reward system and sustainability 6
    see also digital records
e-Research 2
e-Science programme 3, 6, 20

e-Social Science 4–5, 194, 293
and ethical issues 274–5
Economic and Social Research Council (ESRC) 3, 69, 148
eDiaMoND project 276–9
ethical approval 277–8
education and training: sources of data 42–3
Egyptians 300
Elliot, M. 47
Elliot, M. et al 27, 75, 76, 78
embodied conversational units (ECAs) 94
employment, sources of data 43
English Longitudinal Study of Ageing (ELSA) 31, 40–1
Englishness 301
environmental awareness and attitude change 72
ethics 271–94
access to data 281–2
anonymity 282, 288
big data 291–2
case studies
ACTION project 283–7
eDiaMoND project 276–9
Tastes, Ties and Time (T3) project 279–83
codes of ethics 69, 275
covert methods 69
data abuse 51, 76–7
data sharing 279
ethical approval 275, 277, 278–9
and handling of data 277–8
independence 285
informed consent 50, 98, 168, 169, 275, 277, 293
and autonomy 284–5
justice 285
multi-professional teams 278
multi-sector projects 278
and new types of data 60, 76, 274–5
privacy 76, 169, 274, 276, 280–3, 288
randomized controlled trials (RCTs) 71–2
relevance to research 271–2
and research management 294
shared information 291–2
surveillance 291
surveys 98–9
and technological change 273
European Social Survey 44
event logs 199
Everyday Sexism Project 36
exceptions 305
experimentation 237
Expert Systems (ES) 133
exponential random graph modelling (ERGM) 225, 234
eye tracking techniques 70–1, 89
Eysenbach, G. 92

Facebook
access to data 169–70, 279–83, 288
availability of data 241
and development of Internet 273
direction and manifestation of ties **227**
effects on real world behaviour 228–9
fake and multiple accounts 45
friendship patterns 290
Graph API 169–70
language 168
opportunities for research 238
privacy 169
probability of non-users joining 228

Facebook *cont.*
provision of data 288
sharing information 291–2
source of data 29
T3 project 279–83
usage 90
use for surveys 90–1
validity for social network analysis 235
see also Twitter
Facebook Application Programming Interface 232
Family Resources Survey (FRS) 39
field theory 305
fieldwork trackers **206**–8, **207**
Flickr 162, 230, 234
forums 230
Foucault, Michel 300
found data 29
freedom of information 27, 34, 78
friendship formation 238, 290
functional form 109, 109n5
Furberg, R. 96

Galaxy Zoo 263
Gallup Organization 49
gaze 300
General Election 2010 60–3, 173–9
General Sentiment 184
generalizability 49
Genesis 133
genomic data 41
geo-located data 205, **208**
GEODA 133
geographic information systems (GIS) 248–9, 252
geometric models 254
Geographical Analysis Machine 131
Geotools 252
GeoVUE 133
Gephi 233
GESDE (Grid Enabled and Specialist Environments) 116–18
glance 300, 306
Goodwin, C. et al 72
Google 40, 240–1
Analytics 40
Earth 248, 254
Fusion Tables 250
Maps 248, 253
provision of data 288
Reader 181
Replay Search 182
Translator 261
Trends 30, 40
government data 287
Government Social Survey 302
Granovetter, M. 225
Graph API 91
graphics, development 246–7
Great British Class Survey 299, 307
grid computing 3, 4
Gross, A. 76
Group Insurance Commission 289
Groves, R.M. 85

Hadoop 252
Haiti earthquake 212–16
happiness and well-being survey 29–30
hard-to-reach populations 91

Harrigan, N. et al 239
Harris, M. 211–12
Haydock 130
health forums 41–2
Health Survey of England (HSE) 40
health and well-being
    sources of data 40–2
    using genetic data 73–4
Herodotus 299
Hexagon 168
HLM 145
HMRC data lab 32
Holbrook, A.L. et al 86
human rights 36
Human-Computer Interaction (HCI) 193
hyperlink networks 230–1, 232, 234
hypothesis testing 75
hypothesis-driven research 74

ICT, global development of 273–4
Identi.ca 168
identities 45, 47
    revelation of 288–9
igraph 233
immersion 26, 256
individual cases 306
Information Commissioner 76
'information explosion' 26, 29
informed consent 50, 98, 168, 169, 275, 277, 293
    and autonomy 284–5
infoveillance 92
Integrated Household Survey 29, 29n7
International Passenger Survey (IPS) 66
Internet
    number of users 49
interpretive Social Science 293
interviews
    development of methods 303
    falsification of responses 89
    length 89
    and narrative 301–2

Jenkins, S.P. et al 90
Jivraj, S. et al 65
Johnston, R. et al 60–1
justice 285

Keating, M.D. 95
Keeter, S. 161
Key Words In Context (KWIC) 209
Khawaldah, K. et al 130
Kittler 299, 304
Kuhn, Thomas 287
Kwak, H. et al 229, 234

Labour Force Survey (LFS) 31, 37, 38
Language Computer Corporation 184
languages on the Internet 167–8
Law, John 183
Leech, John 62
Leeds: housing and regeneration 132
Leetaru, K.H. 164, 166
Lewis, K. et al 63, 234, 280
Lexalytics 185
Lextek 185
life logging 30
Limdep 145
Lin, Jimmy 170

Linguamatics I2E 173, 175, 184
linguistics
    concordance 209, **210**
    corpus linguistics 205, 208–9
    deictic markers 210
    language and context 205
    and locational data 205
    word frequency tables **209**
linking data 33, 110, 112
LIS project 112
locational data 204–5, 211, 212
log file workbench 199
logs 196–8, **197**
    of fieldwork trackers **207**
    re-representing 199–201, **200**
    types 199
    see also digital replay system (DRS)
Longitudinal Study of Young People in England 42
longitudinal surveys 31, 43
Lotan et al 239
Lusher, D. and Ackland, R. 234
Luxid 185
Lynch, Brendon 289

McLuhan, Marshall 299
Mancini, C. 76
Many Eyes 269
'Map Mashups' 248
Marres, N. 59–60
Martin, J.-L. 48
Mass Observation movement 68
MAXQDA 185
Mayer-Schönberger, W. and Cukier, K. 28
media, and ways of knowing 299
Mejova, Y. 166
Meltwater Buzz 185
'messy' data 109–10
metadata 87, 108, 114
MethodBox project 115, 117
microsimulation 125
Microsoft Excel 199, 251
Microsoft Social Media Research Lab 77
migration and mobility in England (research) 65–7
Millennium Cohort Study (MCS) 41, 42
mimesis 304
Mindshare Text Analytics Suite 185
Minitab 145
missing data 32, 33, 35, 109, 112
Mitchell, C. et al 73
mixed methods 75
MLwiN 145, 149, 151
mobile application data 46
mobile computing 95–7
mobile phones 95–6
    call tracking 46, 205
    texting 96
modelling 123–39
    3D visualization **255**
    behaviour and movement patterns 138
    calibration 131–2
    collaboration 133–4
    data-driven 131
    embodying theory 126
    emergence 128
    Geographical Information Systems (GIS) 130, 133
    gravity models 130
    impact of e-research 129–34

modelling *cont.*
  model disaggregation 130–1
  multilevel 145
  MyGrid Bioinformatics workbench 134
  NeISS (National e-Infrastructure for Social
      Simulation) project 115, 134–**5**, 136
  new data sources 131
  research lifecycle 134, **135**
  support systems 133
  types 125–9
    agent-based model (ABM) 127–8
    behavioural models 127–8
    entropy-maximising models (EMM) 126–7
    microsimulation models (MSM) 125–6, 128
    models of population of actors 125–6
    spacial interaction models (SIMs) 126–7
    statistical models 128–9
  visualization 132–3
  visualizing model outputs 265–7, **266**
  workflow architecture for social simulation **136**
modes of apprehending social life 299–300
multi-professional teams 278
multi-sector projects 278
Mumsnet 39, 41
Murphy, J. et al 89, 90, 99

NameGen 232
narrative 299–300, 301, 305
  and interviews 301–2
national borders on Web 231
National Child Development Study (NCDS) 42
nationalist discourse 301
Nationwide Survey of High School Physics Teachers 94
Natural Language Processing (NLP) 165
Nesstar 31
NESSTAR tool **111**
Netbase 168, 172, 185
Netflix 289
Netlytic 185
NetworkX 233
new types of data 26, 60, 76, 274–5
newsgroups 230
Nicholaas, G. 88
nodes 222, 239, 239n12
NodeXL 233, 269
NVIVO 185

Obama, Barack 166
observation 69
Observer, The 180
Office of National Statistics (ONS) 27–8
Ohm, Paul 288, 289
online discussion groups 39
ONS Neighbourhood Statistics 38
Open Data 33, 52, 77
Open Grid Software Initiative (OGSI) 134
Open Science 20
Open Street Map (OSM) 38, 249, 263
OpenLayers 253
Orcutt, Guy 124
origins of data, typology 28–9
orthodox intentional data 28
outliers 305
ownership of data 28, 49–50, 76, 138, 240–1, 276

Pajek 233, 269
Papacharissi, Z. and de Fatima Oliveira, M. 164

paradata 85, 87–9
  categories 88
participative intentional data 28
patterns of behaviour 291
Pentland, A. 287
personal data 28, 35, 112
Personal Data Stores 78
Pew Research Center 90
photography 300
Pickstone, J. 300, 300n2
Planning Support Systems (PSS) 133
PNet 233
Polgreen, P.M. et al 92
PolicyGrid 115
population density maps 250, **252**
Preis, T. et al 30
privacy 76, 169, 274, 276, 280–3, 288, 289–90
private companies: data 288
probability theory 302
Procter, R. 113
Procter, R. et al 63
public attitudes: sources of data 43–5
Public Opinion Quarterly 85
Purdam, K. 67
'pure' and 'applied' research 6
Python Flickr API kit 232

qualitative and quantitative research 183
Quantified Self 30
quantitative revolution 129
Quantum GIS 249

R freeware 145, 151, 158
R Journal 152
Radian6 185
Rafaelli, Sheizaf 169
randomized controlled trials (RCTs) 71–2
Randomized Response Technique (RRT) 95
Ravenstein, E.: 'Laws of Migration' 123
Rawnsley, Andrew 180
real space 305
real time 305
real time consumption data 40
real-time data 248, 257–60
    Internet connection speeds in Eastern England **264**
    London tube: impact of closing mainline station **260**
    London tube network volumes at stations **260**
    London tube train locations **259**
    transit data 258–60, **259**
    types 257
recognition of facial expressions 70
record linkage 89
Refine 251
reliability 48, 60
representativeness 49, 100, 177–8, 290
Research Councils UK 2
research methods case studies
    attitudes, behaviour and eye tracking data 70–1
      use of technology for research 71
    civil unrest in UK 63–5
      data visualization **64**
      Rumour Spreading Graphic **64**
      sampling 65
      tools for collecting tweets 65
      use of tweets in Twitter 63
    elections, communication and campaigning 60–3
      email communications 61–2

research methods case studies *cont.*
  sampling 61
  websites 61, **62**, 63
  health and well-being using genetic data 73–4
    probability of post-natal depression **73**–4
  migration and mobility in England 65–7
    Geographical Distribution of Pupil Immigrants **67**
    use of School Census data 66
  social policy interventions 71–2
    environmental awareness and attitude change 72
    randomized controlled trials (RCTs) 71–2
  street begging 67–70
    ethics of covert methods 69
    findings 69
    observation sheet **68**
    recording observations 69–70
    volunteer observers 68
research process 292–3
research questions 65
researchers
  as participants 293
  relationship with participants 293
  researcher/subject boundaries 47–8, 59–60
  as role models in use of data 292
  'social contract' with participants 275, 275n4
Rhodes, B.B. and Marks, E.L. 91
Richards, A.K. and Dean, E.F. 95
Romney, Mitt 166
Rosette Linguistics Platform 185
Rowntree, S. 25, 302
rumours 64

sampling
  Address-Based 87
  bias 65, 167
  online social network analysis (SNA) 239–40
  representativeness 49, 177–8, 290
  sample size 32, 49, 290, 302
Satellite Sentinel Project 36–7
Savage, M. and Burrows, R. 7, 51, 287, 297
  'On the Coming Crisis of Empirical Sociology'
    297–8, 308
Saving for Education, Entrepreneurship, and
  Downpayment for Oklahoma Kids 91
Sayer, Andrew 132
Schelling, Thomas 128
scholarly communications 20
School Census 42, 65, 66
science fiction 301
science, progression in 287
Second Life 94–5, 235–6, 237
  usage 94
secure data 32
Secure Data Service 32, 39
self-published data 29
sentiment analysis 92
service delivery 7
sexism 36
Sina Weibo 229
smartphones 96–7
  and apps 171
  tracking 205
  usage 49
SmartSteps 138
SMS texting 96
social behaviour
  self-reporting 45–6
  sources of data 45–7

social class survey 67–8
Social Complexity of Diversity 37
social media
  change of data 65
  fake accounts 45
  identities 45
  sources of data 35–7
  as sources of data 86
  sources of data 29
  visualization 261–3
  see also Facebook; social network analysis (SNA);
    Twitter
social network analysis (SNA) 221–41
  closure 226, 236
  differences from other social scientific approaches
    224–6
  directed and outdegree network **222**
  focus on pairs (dyads) 225
  interdependence of observations 225
  network terminology 222–4
    edges 223
    egocentric networks 223, 236
    multiplex networks 223
    network-level metrics 224
    node-level metrics 224
    nodes 222
    sociograms (network maps) 223
    unimodal/bimodal networks 223
  online networks 226–30
    directionality of ties 226, **227**
    manifestation of ties 226, **227**
    networks of explicitly directed ties 229
    networks of explicitly undirected ties 228–9
    networks of implicitly directed ties 230–1
    networks of implicitly undirected ties 229–30, 234
  online research
    advantages of Web research 238
    breadth-first search (BFS) 240
    causality vs. correlation 236–7
    challenges 238, 239
    construct validity of data 234–6
    experimentation 237
    friendship formation 238
    health community study (Centola) 237
    incomplete information about participants 238, 239
    proprietary data 240–1
    recommendations 241
    sampling 239–40
      full and sub-networks 240
      random walk (RW) sampling 240
    social influence in social media 238–9
    tools for analysis and visualization of networks 233
    tools for collection of data **231**–3
    viability for study with SNA techniques 234
  overlapping networks 226
  structural holes 226
Social Network Importer 232
social policy interventions 71–2
social science data 26n4
social science expertise 303–4
social scientists: new skills 78–9
social surveys 38, **111**, 112
Sociology (journal) 297, 298
software (CAQDAS) 108, 113–14, 165
  data collection 65
  modelling 133
  Natural Language Processing (NLP) 165
  statistical software 143–58, 303

software (CAQDAS) *cont.*
  1EM 151
  'Balkanisation' 147
  elements 143
  interoperability 148–9, 155
  learning to use 151–2
  linear regression 151
  Minitab 145
  proliferation 146
  R freeware 145, 151, 158
  scripting **150**, 151
  specialist packages 145
  SPSS 108, 113, **144**–5, 149, 303
  Stat-JR 153–**4**
    DEEP eBook 155–7, **156**
  Stata 108, 113, 145, **150**, 151, 157
  templates 153
  textual commands 151–2
  transparency 149–50
  for visualization 269
  see also digital replay system (DRS)
software co-production 6
software development 6
software engineering 78
Spatial Decision Support Systems (SDSS) 133
Speizer, H. et al 88
SPSS 108, 113, **144**–5, 149, 303
  to perform correspondence analysis **144**
Stat-JR 153–**4**
  DEEP eBook 155–7, **156**
Stata Journal 152
state logs 199
Statistics and Registration Service Act (2007) 28
Statnet 233
Steadman, P. 267
street begging 67–70
Sturgis, P. et al 41
surveillance 69, 274, 291
SurveyMapper 263–4
surveys 85–100, 105–19
  administrative data 89–90
  advantages in use of social media 86
  challenges of using new technology 86–7
  cloud computing 97–8
  coding 109
  crowdsourcing 97, 137
  data analysis 303
  data management 110–18
  diaries 93
  and digital data 75
  ethics 98–9, 112
  evaluation of new methods 98, 99
  Facebook 90–1
  falsification of responses 89
  features of social survey data 105–10
  Google 92
  international 31
  large scale 105, 106
  limitations 31–2
  longitudinal 31, 43
  'messy' data 109–10
  mobile computing 95–7
  numerical and textual data 108–9
  opinion mining 93–4
  paradata 87–9
  Randomized Response Technique (RRT) 95
  reliability of answers 32
  representativeness 100

surveys *cont.*
  response rates 86, 88, 106
    and calling strategies 88–9
  sampling 87
  selection of cases and variables 107
  sentiment analysis 94
  SMS texting 96
  software 108
  telephone coverage 86–7
  text mining 94
  Twitter 91–3
  uses by geographers 131
  variable-by-case matrices 106, **107**, 108, 109
  virtual worlds 94–5
sustainability 6
Sweeney, L. 289
synchronized data 201–**2**
syntax programming (scripting) 114
synthetic data 29, 37
Sysomos MAP 172, 185
systems logs *see* digital records

tablets 96, 171, 205
  see also smartphones
TALISMAN 133
Tastes, Ties and Time (T3) project 279–83
TDA 145
telephone surveys 86–7
Tesfaye, C.L. 94
text mining 161–85
  access to data 169–71
  applications 162–6
  in business 164
  case study: 'Bullygate' story 2010 179–82
    method and setup 181–2
  case study: General Election 2010 173–9
    integration and presentation 175
    positive sentiment for leaders **177**
    positive tweets 178–**9**
    prime ministerial debates 174
    real-time monitoring 175
    setup before the event 174
    volume of tweets 175–**6**
  consent 169
  definition 162
  ethics 168–9
  in health 164–5
  and idiomatic language 168
  limitations 167
  for natural sciences 162–3
  and online languages 167–8
  in politics 163–4
  and prediction of public opinion 163–4
  sentiment analysis 166
  software 163, 165, 166, 168
    limitations 166
  tools 171–3, **184**–5
Text Stat 185
TextAnalyst 185
theory, importance of 54
threeD visualizations 254, 255–**7**, **256**
Thrift, Nigel 183
Thünen, J.H. von 267
Tolkien, J.R.R.: *Lord of the Rings* 301
Torgerson, D.J. and Torgerson, C. 71, 72
tracking movement 205
Treiman, D.J. 116
Tukey, J.W. 249

Twapperkeeper 170
Tweepy Python library for Twitter API 232
Twipolitico 166
Twitter
  access to data 170–1, 241
  attitude data 44
  'Bullygate' story 180, 181, 182
  in civil unrest research 63–5
  data collection 65
  and development of Internet 273
  diaries 93
  direction and manifestation of ties **227**
  Egyptian and Tunisian revolutions 239
  fake and multiple accounts 45
  function as social network 229, 234
  general election debates 174, 175–**6**, 178
  information sharing 234
  and informed consent 275
  language forms 168
  languages used for tweets 261
  motivations 48
  number of users 49
  opinions and poll data 163
  ownership of tweets 50
  privacy 76
  provision of data 288
  reliability of data 49, 178
  sharing information 291–2
  social influence in social media 238–9
  source of data 35, 36
  spatial density of tweets **261**
  in surveys 91–3
  and text mining 165
  top hashtags **221**
  tweets during 2011 riots **262**
  US presidential campaign 2012 166
  usage 29
  see also Facebook
Twitter Search API 232

UCInet 233
Ugander, J. et al 228
UK Biobank 41
UK Data Service 31
UN Global Pulse 78
Understanding Society survey 105, 304
United Nations 36
Universal Transverse Mercator projection 253
Uprichard et al 145
USA
  Cyberinfrastructure program 194
  Decennial Census Post Enumeration Survey (PES) 89

USA *cont.*
  Energy Information Administration 97–8
  Fragile Families and Child Well-being Study 73
  National Science Foundation (NSF) 279
  National Survey on Drug Use and Health
    (NSDUH) 88, 89
Ushahidi 212

validity 48, 60
van Imhoff, E. and Post, W. 125
Virtanen, V. et al 96
Virtual Reality 246–7
virtual research environment (VRE) 19
virtual worlds 94–5
Visible Intelligence 185
visual devices 302
visualization 248–69, 306
  built environment 253–7
  calibrated land use transport models 265–7, **266**
  crowdsourced data 263–4
  definitions 246
  geographic information systems (GIS) 248–9
  location models 267–8
  London riots (2011) **64**, **262**
  mapping systems 248
  of non-spatial data 247
  predictive analytics 264–8
  real-time data 257–8
  social media 261–3
  web-based mapping 249–53
Volunteered Geographic Information (VGI) 263
VOSON 232–3

Wang, K. et al 88
Wanner, F. et al 163
Web 2.0 4, 19, 163, 241
Web Observatories 78
Web Science Trust 51, 78
Wellman, B. 224
Welser, H. et al 230
Wikipedia 162
Wilson, A.G. and Birkin, M. 267
Wimmer, A. and Lewis, K. 234, 238
Winkler, W.E. 89
World Values Survey 31, 44
World Wide Web 273
Wu, S. et al 229

Yahoo 240–1
YouGov 44
YouTube 35, 273

Zimmer, Michael 280–1